Divorce
& New
Beginnings

Divorce  &New Beginnings

SECOND EDITION

A Complete Guide to Recovery, Solo Parenting, Co-Parenting, and Stepfamilies

Genevieve Clapp, Ph.D.

John Wiley & Sons, Inc.

New York • Chichester • Weinheim • Brisbane • Singapore • Toronto

This publication is designed to provide accurate and authoritative information in regard to the subject matter covered. It is sold with the understanding that the pub-
lisher is not engaged in rendering professional services. If legal, accounting, medical,
psychological or any other expert assistance is required, the services of a competent
professional person should be sought.

Library of Congress Cataloging-in-Publication Data:

Clapp, Genevieve.
    Divorce and new beginnings : a complete guide to recovery, solo parenting,
  co-parenting and stepfamilies / Genevieve Clapp.—2nd ed.
    p.   cm.
  Includes bibliographical references and index.
  ISBN 0-471-32648-8 (pbk. : alk. paper)
    1. Divorce—United States. 2. Divorced people—United States—Psychology.
  3. Children of divorced parents—United States. 4. Single parents—United States.
  5. Stepfamilies—United States. I. Title.

HQ834.C58 2000
306.89—dc21   00-25516

Printed in the United States of America.

10 9

To Jerry,
This is almost as much your book as it is mine.

I withdrew to a higher vantage
to start anew ...
The anger has passed,
now only remains a calm.
Confusion replaced with conviction
that transitions are made
... pain with memories
... fear with understanding
... loneliness with vision
old joys with new beginnings.

Anonymous

Preface

This is the second edition of *Divorce and New Beginnings*. The first edition, published in 1992, has been widely read by men and women who are divorcing, who have ended committed unmarried relationships, who are parenting in one-parent homes, and who are living in a stepfamily.

This book has three goals: one, to provide you with a road map of what lies ahead, drawn from the experience of thousands who have weathered the rupture of their relationships and have started over again; two, to provide you with a repertoire of good coping skills so you can avoid many of the problems faced by so many others; and three, to guide your way in building successful new beginnings, both for yourself and your children, if you have children.

This second edition has a new richness. It is enriched both by the new insights arrived at by researchers during the past eight years and by the insights I have gleaned from my own work during these years with more than 2,000 families who are going through divorce and its extended aftermath, many of which have already formed stepfamilies, whether through marriage or living together. There are seven new chapters in this edition. As for the existing chapters, each has been updated and enriched, and many new sections added.

As did the first edition, this book capitalizes on the flood of research findings reported across the country and the collective insights of hundreds of experts studying divorce, one-parent homes, and stepfamilies. In addition to the 400 resources drawn upon in the first edition, more than 175 new sources have enriched this second edition. Be assured that this is by no means an academic report. *It is a one-hundred-percent practical guide geared directly to your needs!*

The good news reported in the first edition continues. Combined research findings reveal paths you can take to emerge from your ruptured relationship unscathed and build a rewarding new life. They guide your way in creating an environment that will enable your children to weather the storm and then go on to thrive. And they guide your way to healthy new committed relationships and successful stepfamilies, should you choose that path.

This is a true self-help book that will take you each step of the way, both now and in the years to come. To help you handle your daily problems and long-term concerns, it contains hundreds of practical suggestions and effective coping strategies based on the findings and collective insights of hundreds of experts. Throughout the book, case studies illustrate points made or coping tools discussed. Some have had identifying characteristics altered to ensure anonymity, some are composites of several people, and some have been cited from other sources.

Your goal, and my goal, is new beginnings and a fulfilling new life.

Acknowledgments

My sincere thanks to the hundreds of researchers and mental health professionals throughout the country whose work forms the basis of this book. I sincerely apologize for not including each and every source that made a contribution to these pages, but space limitations preclude this.

This book would have been a very different product had it not been for some very special people. Foremost is my husband, Jerry, who spent long hours discussing ideas and reading and rereading every page of both editions of the manuscripts. His critiques and suggestions were invaluable. So was his bottomless reserve of support and humor, which has kept me afloat more than a few times over the years. Had it not been for his fervent belief in the first edition and strong encouragement, this second edition would not have been undertaken. I especially thank my many colleagues at Family Court Services who have provided invaluable input and insights over the years, which heavily contributed to the shaping of evolving ideas. Thanks to Dr. Barbara Jean Shea, who was always ready to assist, with her keen clinical mind. A special thanks to my editor, Jennifer Simon, for her enthusiasm, encouragement, and feedback. The unfailing support and encouragement from my children, Gary and Karen, my sister, Dr. Marion Potts, and many close friends has been greatly appreciated. And thanks to the more than two thousand families with whom I have worked over the past eight years, who have shared their pain, problems, and triumphs. You have been my most practical teachers.

Genevieve Clapp

San Diego, California
July 2000

Contents

I

Laying the Foundation:
Coping Successfully with Divorce

1

The Aftermath of Marriage

Barbara, an attractive 40-year-old brunette, sat mesmerized at a divorce workshop. It was the first time she had heard about the feelings and problems that people encounter as they go through divorce. "My God," she blurted out, "you're describing my life for the past five months. I didn't know everyone felt like that." There was an immediate restlessness in the room—some nervous laughter, some mumbled comments, one or two heads nodding. "God," Barbara's voice seemed to boom, "what a relief, it's not just me!"

Over the past two decades, there has been an explosion of studies on divorce and its aftermath, providing us access to the experience of thousands who have weathered the rupture of their marriages and families. Thanks to those who have gone before you, the course of divorce is no longer unmapped, and you can be prepared for what lies ahead. If you understand the psychological process of divorce and know what to expect, the upcoming months and years will be considerably less stressful.

This book is more than a road map of the coming years. It is a survival guide, replete with the information and coping tools you need to successfully navigate the years ahead and to successfully guide your children through them. Armed with a road map and a repertoire of good coping skills, you can more easily clear the hurdles of divorce and avoid many of the difficulties that complicate the lives of so many divorcing couples and their children. Your divorce will likely remain a significant event in your life, but it does not have to remain the dominant one.

THE IMPACT OF SEPARATION AND DIVORCE

In the 1970s, two northern California researchers, Judith Wallerstein and Joan Kelly, began an intensive year-long study of divorcing couples and their children. The researchers wished to learn how families are affected by divorce and how they resolve the disruptions to their lives. Wallerstein and Kelly had fully expected families to have recovered by the end of the study, since parents would have been separated 18 months by that time. But the researchers had been mistaken: The majority of adults and children had not yet resolved their divorce-generated difficulties. Wallerstein and Kelly were stunned to find that most families were still in crisis and had not gotten their lives back together yet. More disturbing, a large number of children were doing worse rather than better.

Were the findings of this groundbreaking study a fluke? Since that time, many other studies have been published that confirm that adjustment to divorce is neither quick nor easy. On the average, people need two years before they regain their equilibrium. They usually need additional time to become emotionally detached from an ex-spouse and to establish a stable and satisfying new lifestyle.

You are probably wondering why divorce adjustment should take so long. After all, divorce is the solution to so many problems, isn't it? It may be easy to see why divorce is difficult for someone who had fought against it or for someone whose partner suddenly walked out. But is divorce also difficult for the person who leaves? Is it also difficult for couples who bitterly argue for years and finally call it quits? Usually, yes. It appears that relatively few people escape the effects of divorce easily. In general, divorce is difficult for both the "leaver" and the "left," for men and for women, for those who have bickered and fought and for those who have lived in indifferent silence, for those married 25 years and for those married 5 years (although breakups of short-lived marriages tend to be less distressing). Of course, divorce is more difficult for some people than for others. For some the adjustment period is shorter, for some longer. Two years is only an average.

Once you learn more about divorce, you will see why it has such an impact on each member of the family and why such a long adjustment period is commonly needed. Undoubtedly, the best way to understand the nature of divorce is to look at the experiences that most people encounter.

Loss and Turbulent Emotions

Divorcing men and women are often astounded by the extent of their losses. The marriage that had been an important part of life at one time is now gone. So is a lifestyle, future plans, a chunk of one's identity, and perhaps a home, financial security, free access to children, and shared friendships. The list goes on. For many, the massive losses create a feeling of rootlessness—a need to feel connected. For many, the feelings of loss and unconnectedness are entangled with a gnawing sense of failure and dwindling feelings of self-worth.

Lives are further complicated by turbulent and conflicting emotions. Men and women who are filled with bitterness, resentment, and anger may suddenly feel stunned by surges of love and yearning for their former partners. Their predominant feelings of self-pity, sadness, and depression are suddenly displaced by intoxicating feelings of euphoria, well-being, and freedom. Then, as suddenly as it appeared, the euphoria is snatched away. The pendulum swings back and forth, leading people to feel as if they were on a tiny raft being tossed around in stormy seas or as if they were on an emotional roller coaster.

The Upheavals

We tend to think of divorce as a single event in people's lives. Nothing could be further from the truth. Separation and divorce set in motion a chain of events that spans an extended period of time. Each link in the chain represents upheaval and change, and each change must be dealt with—changes in routine, finances, personal and social lives, family life, identity, and expectations and life goals. Studies suggest that divorce requires more readjustment and reorganization than any other stressful life event in our society, except for the death of a spouse.

Few divorcing men and women are prepared for the extent to which their lives are disrupted. Of course, most know there will be major changes, but they usually underestimate them. They also do not anticipate how unsettling and disorienting the changes in daily routines and comfortably entrenched habits will be.

For some, the changes are staggering. Consider the upheavals for a parent who moves out of the family home, sets up a new household, loses daily contact with family life, and becomes a weekend visitor to his or her children. Or the changes for a former stay-at-home parent who must now find and tackle a full-time job and sort out a confusing array of day care options, all while shouldering the major responsibility for distraught children. Consider the disruptions to the life of a "corporate wife," whose life has revolved around her husband's career, or the changes faced by a family whose finances were already spread thin and who now must pay for two substandard residences.

Besides the upheavals, most divorcing men and women encounter a host of practical problems that would tax anyone's resources, even under the best circumstances.

The Practical Hurdles

With divorce come time-consuming paperwork, the necessity of dealing with an unfamiliar legal system, new loneliness, difficulties concentrating, countless questions from relatives and friends, and the endless list of decisions (new living arrangements, how every material possession will be divided, where the children will live, how parenting will be shared, how to handle holidays, and on and on).

Divorcing women must suddenly assume the household tasks that may have been formerly in their husbands' domain. Home and car maintenance and repairs, tax returns, and financial planning often top their list of practical problems. Women with primary physical custody of children have a particularly difficult time. Their problems multiply exponentially with the responsibility for dealing with hurt, baffled children who may develop any number of transient problems in response to their family's rupture (See Chapter 6). Typically, divorcing mothers' lives and homes are in a state of disorganization. Financial worries, caused by their inevitably reduced resources, are a major source of stress. Mothers who had stayed at home or worked part-time often must return to full-time employment, turning an overloaded schedule into an exhausting one. Many report having to stay up past midnight just to get the bare essentials done. Yet those who remain at home often complain of being locked in a child's world. Many mothers report that their stress is overwhelming. (See Chapter 14 for help.)

Divorcing men have their own set of problems. Many wind up in small or furnished apartments, bitter that they have lost so much of what they had spent years building. A surprising number are lost when it comes to the mechanics of cooking, shopping for food, cleaning, and doing laundry. Fathers without custody report feeling rootless, shut out, guilty, and anxious. The great majority miss daily contact with their children, some desperately so. One 25-year-old man, divorced for a year and a half, complained, "Their mother claims she has no time to herself and tells me about all my freedom. Freedom? No! It has another name; it's called loneliness." [1]

Many men are astonished at the intensity with which they miss being involved in their children's daily lives and say they never would have predicted it. Even men who have not been involved fathers miss their children, becoming aware for the first time of all the things they never did when they had the opportunity. Nor do most fathers predict the practical problems involved in becoming a part-time parent. Where do you go in your time together? What do you do? How do you relate to your own children in these strange new circumstances? (See Chapter 15 for solutions.)

Reflecting their stress, fathers tend to sleep less, eat erratically, develop physical symptoms, and bury themselves in work during the first year after separation. It is also common for them to engage in a frenzied social life, not because it is satisfying or pleasurable but because it helps ward off feelings of being shut out and rootless.

The Uncoupling Hurdle

In their study of almost a thousand divorced men and women, Morton and Bernice Hunt discovered that few people realized before they were separated how totally bound they were to their former partners because of the years spent together, shared experiences, entrenched habits developed to accommodate one another, children, shared friends and relatives, emotional commitments, mutual obligations, and jointly acquired possessions. Essentially the strands of spouses' lives are woven together into a single fabric. The task of disentangling the threads of their lives is an enormous one that may extend over a period of years.

Disentangling yourself from your spouse could be the most difficult struggle you have after divorce. It includes becoming *emotionally* detached, which is difficult enough. But you may also find that a large chunk of your identity is entangled with your former partner's and with your role as a husband or wife. Divorcing men and women commonly talk of an "identity crisis," and the question they ask over and over again is, "Who *am* I?"

So along with everything else you must do after divorce, you need to forge a new identity for yourself and establish a new lifestyle that is satisfying to you. You will no longer be tied to the life goals you formulated with your spouse, to the kind of person your spouse accepted or expected you to be, or to the lifestyle you developed together. You can now determine what things you enjoy, what kind of lifestyle you wish to have, what kind of person you want to be, and what you want to do with the rest of your life. Chapter 10 will help you with becoming emotionally detached and Chapter 11 with forging your new identity.

Some people find the prospect of developing a new identity exhilarating, as did 31-year-old Ted:

> I felt such exuberant freedom. I had a second chance at life. I no longer had to make the "sensible" and "responsible" choices as Phyllis always insisted. I decided I would leave my dead-end job and take a chance at starting my own business. I didn't care if I had to work sixteen-hour days, seven days a week to make it work.

Others find the prospect terrifying, as did Helen, a 48-year-old Michigan mother of a 17-year-old son:

> I would sit by the window in a trance for long hours watching the world go by, feeling my life was over. I would keep coming back to the same question, "What will I do with the rest of my life?" Sometimes I would become so afraid I'd go into a panic. My heart would race, my hands would sweat, I'd shake all over. At first I was afraid I was cracking up. Then I began to wish that I would so Ralph would feel some guilt about what he had done to me.

By now there may be no skeptics among you. Adjusting to divorce *is* hard work. It requires learning how to cope with extensive loss, pervasive change, endless practical problems, and intense emotions that may play havoc with your life. It motivates reappraisal, soul-searching, and self-exploration. It necessitates breaking with the past, reorganizing your life, and restructuring family relationships. It is no wonder that people so often take a number of years to adjust.

Progression through divorce can be divided into three broad stages: *preseparation, transition-restructuring,* and *recovery-rebuilding.* Learning about these three stages can provide you with a road map of what may lie ahead. The road map is only a rough one, sketching the types of experiences and feelings common in each of these stages. You will probably have many of the same feelings and experiences discussed in this book, but you may not experience them all, and you may not experience them as intensely as many others have.

PRESEPARATION

People's experiences are most varied *before* they make the decision to separate and file for divorce. For some, the long months, and perhaps years, before the decisive separation are a volatile period of acrimony and anger. For some this period is marked by mutual indifference and alienation. For others it is a period of sinking disillusionment and hopelessness. Some engage in endless discussions and negotiations in an attempt to save their marriages. Some try marriage counseling. Others are taken by complete surprise when a spouse leaves. In one Pennsylvania study, 29 percent of the people who had been left by a spouse reported surprise at their spouse's decision, as was Jenny:

> To this day I still don't understand it. Some sort of midlife crisis, I suppose. We were considered the ideal family in the community—the ones everyone assumed would be together forever. He kept up the charade of the loving husband right up till the end. Oh, he was having more than his share of troubled moods, but he always passed them off as trouble at work. I never suspected a thing. We went out to dinner for his birthday—a celebration, I thought. That's the moment he chose to drop the bomb. I guess it symbolized his independence day or something. No discussion, no nothing. He just wanted out. He had already rented himself a condo.

Women often experience the preseparation stage as more stressful than do men. Women are more likely to report having been depressed, pessimistic, and lonely during this period. Between two-thirds and three-quarters of divorces are initiated by women, so their greater preseparation distress may reflect their turmoil while wrestling with their decision to divorce or not. For some, the preseparation period is the most traumatic period of their divorce. This was certainly true for Jean:

> The year before Jean first left Michael was like a progressive, downhill spiral. She was so depressed that there were days she never made it out of bed. And when she did, she was virtually immobilized. She cried uncontrollably and suffered from migraine headaches for days at a time. A friend helped her make the decision to leave and, using connections, got her a job. Although life still was not easy, Jean found she liked working, and co-workers liked and respected her. Eventually, she formed several good friendships, got a promotion, and began to feel good about herself. Then Michael talked her into coming back to him, promising he would change. He tried for a short while but then drifted back to his

old destructive patterns. Finally accepting the futility of the marriage and realizing she was well on her way to establishing an independent and satisfying life for herself, Jean left him for the second and final time.

TRANSITION-RESTRUCTURING

The stage of transition-restructuring begins with the separation and lasts, *on the average,* two years. It is during this period that the majority of divorcing men and women seem to encounter the most similar experiences and feelings—sometimes referred to as the "divorce experience"—although with differing intensity.

During this stage, divorcing partners usually experience far more trauma and disorientation than they had anticipated. Sure, the continuous battles have ended. So have the constant criticism and uncomfortable indecision. But this is the time of turbulent and conflicting emotions, when people are literally assaulted with loss, change, and practical problems. It is a time when the familiar past is traded for the unknown future.

People express their anxiety and distress in different ways. Some withdraw into the sanctuary of their homes; others engage in a frenzy of activity to escape. Some sleep the days away; others feel fortunate to sleep a few uninterrupted hours each night. Some bury themselves in work; others can't concentrate. Some barely eat enough for sustenance; others find food to be one of their greatest comforts. Some are apathetic, others irritable. Some cry uncontrollably; others stoically hold in everything. Some turn to friends; others turn to alcohol, tranquilizers, violence, religion, or counseling.

Transition Phase

In the first half of the transition-restructuring stage, the decision to divorce can become a waking nightmare. Many men and women become tense, listless, painfully lonely, and overwhelmed with feelings of failure, inadequacy, poor self-esteem, and "not belonging" anywhere. Too often, they feel out of control, victims of intense emotions previously unknown to them. Self-pity and depression leave many wondering if they will ever feel like their old selves again. Bitterness, anger, and resentment fuel fantasies of revenge. Guilt, fear, and panic cause some to question their sanity.

Barbara, a high-level manager in a profitable company, was baffled by her reactions.

Why am I acting like this? I'm a competent professional, in charge of million-dollar contracts and 75 people, and here I am, feeling like a frightened, helpless little girl! I thought I wanted this divorce. What's wrong with me?

But it is the intensity of their anger that frightens many people the most. Twenty-five-year-old Wendy, married for five years, entered divorce counseling because she was so alarmed at the intensity of her rage.

At first I was okay. I had no anger at all. It had always disgusted me to see divorcing people acting so vindictively toward one another. I was sure it would never happen to me. Then, just when I was patting myself on the back for being so rational, a dam broke. Right now, I'm so angry, I'm out for revenge. I find myself plotting my next moves! I've never thought of myself as a vindictive person. I don't know what's happening to me.

For a minority, rage is so intense that it incites disturbed and sometimes bizarre behavior toward a former spouse. A New Orleans man shredded his ex-wife's favorite clothes. A New York man held his former wife hostage and shot up her living room. In San Diego, a man left bloody hunting knives in his ex's mailbox. A Dallas woman dumped her estranged husband's $500 suits out a second-story window into a muddy backyard. A southern California woman rammed her car into her ex-husband's house while he and their children were inside. Breaking down doors, obscene phone calls, physical violence, and hysterical rages are not uncommon. In a northern California study, about one-fourth of the men and women displayed such behavior.

Most people swing back and forth between periods of sadness, anxiety, and anger and exhilarating periods of bliss. In their euphoric moods, people insist the divorce was the best thing that ever happened to them. They talk of feeling intoxicated by their newfound freedom and independence, and they report feeling more alive than ever. They see life as an adventure and feel as if they can attain any goal they want. For some, euphoric periods last for several months; for others it may be only days until the pendulum swings back again.

During the transition phase, divorcing men and women usually become obsessed with thoughts about their former spouse and broken marriage. The history of the marriage is relived time and time again—

the fights, the accusations, the significant events, the trivial occurrences that may have contributed to the breakup. When did the trouble start? Who is to blame? Was it inevitable? For some, the obsessive thoughts become maddening.

Although a minority of couples report they get along better once they no longer have daily contact, the majority report having primarily explosive and conflictual interactions after separation. Yet despite the conflict, the majority of divorcing men and women are haunted by memories of the good times, and many fall victim to impulses to call, initiate dates, seek out information about their ex's new life, or just drive past their ex's home or office. The majority of divorced people studied have questioned, at some time, whether they made the right decision to end the relationship. People vacillate between feelings of love and hate, longing and anger.

During this first half of the transition-restructuring stage, many people report feeling "split," "on the edge," or "not themselves" anymore. Many report their major goal is making it through till tomorrow without cracking up. People who are asked to recall this period of their divorce frequently offer comments such as "I couldn't believe how awful I felt" and "I felt I couldn't go on." When interviewed on *Saturday Night with Connie Chung*, Jane Fonda remarked about her own divorce, "All I can say is that I experienced pain unlike anything I've ever felt in my life."

Not everyone encounters the divorce experience. A minority of divorcing men and women feel primarily relief, hope, and even positive feelings at the end of their marriages. They may talk of being released from prison or bondage, of new beginnings, of a chance for a better life. Sometimes there are celebrations and self-indulgences like massages, facials, new wardrobes, and new cars. They function fairly well and quickly begin to rebuild their lives. Many immerse themselves in dating and the singles scene immediately, sometimes at a hectic pace, as if making up for lost time. Morton and Bernice Hunt found that 20 percent of their very large study group fit into this category.

Although this initial positive outlook and functioning may continue, it sometimes proves to be fragile. Many a divorcing person is stunned to find his or her initial enthusiasm and aplomb shattered after a few months, often when the first personal failure is encountered. It is almost as if a bubble bursts: spirits, once high, take a nosedive and the divorce experience, heretofore unknown, becomes their new reality.

Though it is tempting to assume that the leavers are the ones who breeze through separation and divorce and that their reluctant partners are the ones who suffer, reality is not so black and white. Those who are left usually *do* have more to overcome immediately after separation and frequently do have more problems at this time. They are more likely to feel helpless, vulnerable, and pessimistic. They are more likely to have difficulty accepting the breakup. Their self-esteem may plummet. Many report intense feelings of despair, outrage, and anger.

But the picture is not a rosy one for leavers either. Although they are more likely to feel relief, leavers still have high levels of stress, which is the natural consequence of a major life change. It appears that leavers are more likely than those who are left to experience high levels of stress *before* separation and feelings of guilt *after* separation. In their large study group of almost one thousand, the Hunts found that approximately one-third of the leavers felt bad "all or almost all of the time" after separation, complaining of general depression, sleeplessness, and loss of appetite. They didn't want to go back, but they didn't expect to feel as bad as they did. A University of Tennessee study reported that leavers, as a group, felt similar levels of emotional trauma to those who were left, but the *timing* of their peak stress levels was different.

Contrary to conventional wisdom, whether one leaves or is left may not affect how rapidly he or she recovers from divorce. Although reluctant partners have more problems immediately after separation, studies report that these differences diminish. Some leavers have surprisingly slow recoveries, whereas some who were left are found to recover surprisingly quickly, even when the separation had been unexpected. Some people who had been adamantly opposed to the divorce admit later that it was the best thing that could have happened to them.

Incidentally, in the great majority of cases, divorce is not mutually desired. It appears that one spouse wants the divorce far more than the other in 75 to 90 percent of divorces.

Restructuring

Usually, sometime during the first postseparation year most people begin to achieve a more even keel emotionally. As less energy is needed for survival, more can be devoted to the task of restructuring life and attending more closely to the needs of children. Nothing will mark the onset of this time for you, and your progress is not likely to be smooth. For a long time, you will likely have one foot in each world. You will probably experience a lot of peaks and valleys, starts and stops in which your productive periods of restructuring will be followed by setbacks, periods of discouragement, and apathy.

The uneven course that progress usually takes was clearly illustrated in a well-known study conducted at the University of Virginia by E. Mavis Hetherington and her colleagues. Within the first year following their legal divorces, people in this study group, as a whole, were immersed in a flurry of self-improvement activities, such as changes in physical appearance, physical fitness programs, new social activities, and classes. Yet at the end of that year, the majority felt they were at an all-time *low*. Perhaps they were merely discouraged that their lifestyles were not yet satisfactory, but a significant majority of the study group reported that they were functioning poorly, that the divorce had been a mistake, and that they should have worked harder to save their marriages. Other study groups confirm that things usually get worse before they get better.

In the process of restructuring, most people at some time enter a phase of experimentation and do things they have always wanted to do by trying out new activities, interests, and relationships. Journalist Abigail Trafford, author of *Crazy Time,* humorously refers to this as the hummingbird phase, because of the tendency to flit from plan to plan, interest to interest, and relationship to relationship. The frenetic pace that is often evident in this phase is easily detected in this man's plans:

> My plan right now is to enroll in graduate school, which will be a big switch. And I think I've got to learn to play tennis, because I need exercise bad. And I have bought a ten-speed bike, and I am going to start doing the bicycle trails. And I really want to get back into sailing. I used to play golf, too, and I want to get back.... I plan to go to Europe ... and I could take my oldest son with me.[2]

People enter the experimentation phase at widely varying times, some dashing into it rapidly, others waiting until they gain some semblance of equilibrium in both their own and their children's lives. It is only a phase. Gradually the frenetic pace slows, and people become more selective in their activities and plans.

When Judith Wallerstein and Joan Kelly reinterviewed their study group 18 months after separation, they found that most people were still grappling with restructuring their lives and coming to terms with their divorce. However, three-fifths of the men and slightly more than half the women were pleased with the direction their lives were taking.

RECOVERY-REBUILDING

The recovery and rebuilding stage is sometimes humorously referred to as the "phoenix stage"—when people rise from the ashes of divorce. Whereas the stage of transition-restructuring was a time of reacting to divorce and surviving it, this is a period of personal growth. The former may have been a time of frenetic experimentation; this is one of self-discovery and carving a new identity. *On the average,* people enter the recovery-rebuilding stage roughly two years after separation, and it lasts two to three years. However, some people get stalled here for many years.

Those who successfully complete this stage have learned to accept the end of their marriages and the role they played in the breakup. They have disentangled their lives from those of their former spouses and created separate identities. They have achieved detachment from their former partners, so there is no longer a need for either hostility or dependence. And they have clarified their priorities, set realistic goals, and found a satisfying lifestyle.

As in the transition-restructuring stage, progress during this period does not follow a smooth course but has starts and stops. You may find that success in this stage is unrelated to the ease or difficulty you had with the earlier stages. A devastating postseparation period does not predict a poor recovery, just as early feelings of relief, hope, and optimism do not necessarily predict a good recovery. Carl is an example:

> Carl and Elizabeth had been married 12 years and had three children. Carl's life was his home and kids, but Elizabeth fell in love with Ted, a co-worker with eclectic interests that excited her. The two kept the affair secret for a year before Elizabeth made the difficult decision to leave Carl and marry Ted. Carl was devastated, went into a deep depression, and became suicidal. Eventually his rage surfaced, and he ranted about Elizabeth's "betrayal" to any captive audience, especially the children. Carl and Elizabeth shared custody of the children, none of whom fared well after the breakup. Two of the children were referred for counseling. Fortunately, Carl remained a sensitive and caring father and was able to see, with the therapist's help, how he was exacerbating his children's problems. He then sought help himself.
>
> As of this writing, three years later, Carl has picked up the pieces of his life. He has his children much of the time, and they've discovered bicycling, hiking, and camping together. He's developed a passion for cooking and photography, and he reports he is "involved with a

wonderful and caring woman." He says he is happy, feels whole again, and is finding life to be surprisingly good. Meanwhile, Elizabeth's second marriage is in trouble. A few years ago, Carl confides, he would have taken great satisfaction in this, but at this point he feels a tinge of compassion for her.

As Carl's story shows, a successful recovery from your divorce will depend not so much on the amount of stress you encounter but on how well you cope with that stress, how thoroughly you put the past behind you, and how successfully you rebuild your life. Chapters 3 through 5, 10, and 11 will guide you each step of the way so you can emerge from divorce a stronger person.

IS DIVORCE WORTH IT? THE VERDICT IS...

Although the specific figures differ from study to study and from poll to poll, the majority of divorced men and women maintain that yes, the divorce was worth the trauma and subsequent difficult years. For example, in the northern California study reported by Judith Wallerstein and Joan Kelly, about two-thirds of the men and slightly more than half the women reported five years after their decisive separation that the divorce had been beneficial and had improved the quality of their lives. Slightly less than 20 percent considered the divorce to be an unqualified failure, while the remainder had mixed feelings. A University of Virginia study reported that only two years after the divorce was final, 75 percent of the women felt they were happier in their new lives than they had been during the final year of their marriages. Common themes among these satisfied women were their newly found independence, self-fulfillment, and competence developed as a result of the challenges of divorce and single parenting. Studying a divorced sample of almost one thousand, Morton and Bernice Hunt reported that the majority claimed to be both happier and more successful human beings because of the divorce that occurred earlier in their lives. In a national survey reported in *Parents Magazine,* 72 percent of the divorced respondents said they were happier now than they had been before their divorces. And in a Gallup poll, 82 percent of the divorced respondents believed the decision to divorce had been a good one.

Speaking retrospectively about their divorces, many people conclude that their marriages and divorces have played an integral part in their growth as human beings. They are not necessarily people who initiated the divorce or who sailed through it relatively smoothly. Many were considerably traumatized at the time and experienced a great deal of pain in the aftermath of their marriages. Thirty-two-year-old Louisa is an example. Looking back on a difficult divorce, she concluded:

> It was a hard lesson to learn but I'm so glad I learned it. I'm a competent, well-liked, talented human being in my own right. I can survive alone and will never fear it again. . . . Looking back now I'm almost glad it all happened. I'm a far better person, more understanding of myself and others—and isn't that what living is all about?[3]

2

Legal Fundamentals:
What Everyone Should Know

Divorce law and procedures are the subjects of entire books written by attorneys and are beyond the scope of this book. This chapter will look at some very basic ABCs of current legal trends and the psychological implications of some of your alternatives.

Each state has its own divorce laws, and frequently each county within a state follows somewhat different procedures. For this reason, you would do well to get some straight legal information from an attorney who specializes in family law about how your state laws and county procedures may affect you personally. The visit will not obligate you to hire the attorney if you do not choose to.

A PRIMER ON CURRENT DIVORCE TRENDS

In January 1970, California became the first state in the nation to put into effect a "no-fault" divorce law. The concept of no-fault removed the traditional notion that one party is guilty and the other innocent in divorce. Either spouse could obtain a divorce without the consent of the other and without having to prove marital wrongdoing. Irreconcilable differences became satisfactory grounds in the eyes of the law. Since that time, virtually every state has passed some form of no-fault laws.

In general, continuing alimony (called spousal support or maintenance in many states) is also a thing of the past. Spousal support, when awarded, is usually temporary and designed to give a spouse time and opportunity to become self-supporting. Exceptions may be made in long-term marriages or when a spouse has poor employment prospects due to age or health. Each state has its own guidelines.

All states now have child support guidelines, which usually consider at least the parents' incomes and *necessary* expenses. In most states, judges have discretion to consider other issues and modify the guidelines. States are now required by the federal government to take steps to enforce child support orders, and they are becoming increasingly aggressive in doing so. Wage attachments and parent-locator services are widespread. Some states withhold drivers' licenses and professional licenses for failure to pay. Some states are prosecuting deadbeat parents. Although enforcement is improving, state laws are effective to varying degrees. The federal government is also getting into the enforcement business, now attaching income tax refunds.

How marital property is divided varies, once again, from state to state. Some states have community property laws, but the great majority have equitable distribution laws. Generally, in community property states each spouse is entitled to an equal share of the marriage assets, although in some states the court has discretion to consider other factors, such as marital wrongdoing, when dividing assets. Equitable distribution laws, at least theoretically, emphasize fairness rather than equality. Although these laws vary from state to state, common factors technically considered include the duration of the marriage, respective contributions to it, support awards, likely financial circumstances in the future, minor children, health, and age. In some states, marital misdeeds are also considered. Judges in equitable distribution states have a great deal of discretion, and there is wide agreement that the lower-wage earner generally receives far less than 50 percent of the marital assets in these states.

In most states, marital property includes assets acquired during the marriage up until the date of separation, regardless of who has legal title to the property. However, there are some state-to-state exceptions and variations in what is considered marital property; inheritances are an example.

You can find additional help on legal matters in Appendix D.

SELECTING AN ATTORNEY

Before selecting an attorney, do some research! Start by getting referrals from others, and specifically ask what they liked about the attorney. Talk with several recommended attorneys before making your decision; the initial consultation is usually free or inexpensive.

Law is a highly specialized profession, and one attorney is *not* necessarily as good as another. Even if you restrict yourself to an attorney who specializes in family law, attorneys have different amounts of experience in complicated negotiations and in litigation. They differ in the time they have practiced in your jurisdiction and in their awareness of individual judges' previous rulings. They differ in cost. They differ in how thoroughly they prepare cases and in how responsive they are to your phone calls and needs. Some will handle your case themselves, while others will turn it over to an associate—perhaps an inexperienced one. Some will agree to act as a coach if you decide to represent yourself, providing information and advice and reviewing agreements you have reached with your spouse.

Attorneys also differ philosophically, both in the way they deal with clients and in the way they approach cases. In a study of attorneys, social psychologist Kenneth Kressel found that they seem to fall primarily within two broad groups, which he labeled the "advocates" and the "counselors." Advocates, he reported, enjoy the legal challenge of divorce cases, endorse the adversarial approach, emphasize "winning," and do not feel responsible for their clients' emotional welfare. Studies on conflict indicate that some of the tactical maneuvers advocates commonly use generally escalate conflict between divorcing couples. Examples are instructing clients to cease communication with former spouses, advising them to take extreme positions so there will be greater negotiating room, and encouraging them to level exaggerated allegations against a spouse to get the upper hand.

In contrast, the second group of attorneys, labeled the counselors by Kressel, are concerned with the emotional climate of divorce. They provide clients with support and practical advice, watch out for the welfare of children, emphasize finding a cooperative solution that will be fair to all, and take steps to de-escalate conflict. Connecticut Superior Court Judge Joseph Steinberg refers to these two approaches as the "Rambo" and the "Mother Theresa" approaches.

If you decide to be represented by an attorney, think carefully about these differences and determine what kind of attorney you want. Make out a list of questions to use while interviewing attorneys that will give you the information you need to make a wise choice. In a University of Southern California study, 50 percent of the study group were unhappy with their attorneys, complaining of exorbitant costs and of the divorce being worse than it needed to be. Realize that *your attorney works for you* and should take action *only* with your explicit approval or direction.

Choose an attorney who is competent and whose approach you like. However, if you are in a vengeful state of mind, be careful. Be sure to read about the pitfalls of litigation in this chapter, and if you have children, be sure to read Chapter 8 prior to making a decision.

West Virginia Supreme Court of Appeals Judge Richard Neely, author of *The Divorce Decision,* advises that the best attorney is one who has a good deal of experience in contested divorces and who is well versed in the "tricky procedural rules." He warns against the attorney who *never* goes to court because his reputation is known by other attorneys who may demand higher terms in exchange for an out-of-court settlement. He also warns against the "mindless litigator" who does not encourage good-faith negotiations.

MARITAL SETTLEMENT AGREEMENTS

Usually, before your divorce is granted, the issues of custody, visitation, support, and property distribution will have to be settled in some manner and set down in legal language in a *marital settlement agreement.* The settlement may also include other provisions, such as for life and health insurance, payment of legal fees, and the use of a jointly owned home. (In some states, an attorney can get some of these issues set aside for future decision to expedite the divorce.)

Many couples arrive at a settlement through their respective attorneys. Others reach an agreement on these issues themselves. However, domestic law can be very complicated. Justice Neely compares "do-it-yourself lawyering" to "do-it-yourself brain surgery." If you reach your own agreement and have children, assets, or obligations, have your agreement reviewed and written by an attorney. It can be far more costly in the long run if the agreement is written incorrectly or if you have not considered a myriad of tax implications or other issues with which professionals are familiar. A word of caution: Beware of relying on your spouse's personal attorney, since attorneys must represent their clients' interests, which may be at odds with yours. Increasing numbers of couples are now reaching their own agreements with the help of a divorce mediator. Mediation will be discussed shortly.

If a settlement is reached, the divorce is considered uncontested, and the court basically rubber-stamps the agreed-upon terms. Child support usually can be modified at a future date. Custody can also be modified, although in practice, the longer children are in the custody of one parent, the less likely judges are to remove them from their home because of their need for stability. Whether spousal support is modifiable depends on the wording of the marital settlement agreement. The terms of a property settlement are unlikely to be changed unless fraud can be shown.

LITIGATION

If no agreement can be reached, the divorce remains a contested one and is settled in court. The number of divorces that go to litigation is relatively small. Attorneys traditionally estimate 10 percent, but studies suggest it may be higher.

Litigation has a number of serious financial and emotional pitfalls. Legal fees may escalate out of proportion to your assets. When you take your case to court, your life is scrutinized in public and your future is turned over to a judge who neither knows your family nor has the time to tailor a decision to your unique case. His or her ruling is determined by some combination of formulas, the opinions of experts if called in on your case, and the judge's own leanings. Justice Neely warns that litigation is chancy and courts unpredictable. He points out that every trial lawyer has had the experience of turning down settlement offers because they were too low, only to obtain far lower settlements in court.

Divorcing partners who go the adversarial route are more likely to feel helpless, pessimistic, depressed, and detached, reported Florence Kaslow, director of the Florida Couples and Family Institute, and Penn State psychologist Lita Schwartz in their book *The Dynamics of Divorce*. Not every case that goes to court gets nasty, but many do. And for the many divorcing men and women who fall into the pattern of deception and game playing, point out Kaslow and Schwartz, the usual consequence is a plummet in their own self-esteem as well as an escalation in ex-spouses' anger, resistance to settlement, and vindictiveness in the future. As an example, studies suggest that when disputes have been bitter, court-ordered support payments are less likely to be complied with, and the parties are more likely to be back in court in the future. More legal costs!

If there are children involved, they are the greatest losers. Please read Chapter 8 about the devastating repercussions to children of prolonged parental conflict and custody battles.

Avoid litigation if you can!

DIVORCE MEDIATION:
AN ALTERNATIVE TO AN ADVERSARIAL DIVORCE

Mediation is an alternative to the traditional two-attorney adversarial path to divorce and is being used by increasing numbers of people. In mediation, an impartial professional helps divorcing spouses hammer out agreements that are fair, informed, workable, and acceptable to *both* spouses. In mediation, there is no winner and loser, as there so often is in an adversarial divorce. Mediators take a win-win approach. Some couples use mediation to negotiate all issues: parenting arrangements, support issues, and property division. Some use it only for decisions related to the children, while their attorneys handle their financial issues.

Don't confuse mediation with arbitration. In arbitration, parties accept the decision of the arbitrator. In mediation, a settlement is completely voluntary. Mediators neither make decisions nor force a decision. If the parties do not reach a decision on one or more issues in mediation, they are free to resolve them through their attorneys or the courts. Don't confuse mediation with counseling or therapy, either. Mediators do not help you decide whether to get divorced or help you work through your emotions and losses, as therapists do.

Mediation can be used at any time. Some couples use it before one moves out of the home, others after they have met with an attorney. Some try it as a last attempt to avoid litigation, although by this time conflict has often escalated out of control. Some couples seek family mediation *after* divorces are final to settle new disputes that have arisen over children. Some use it after remarriage to work out a detailed parenting agreement in which everyone's roles and responsibilities are spelled out when one or more stepparents are involved.

How Mediation Works

In mediation, the mediator helps the parties clarify issues, individual needs, and priorities; develop and evaluate a variety of options; and hammer out agreements that are acceptable to both parties. Parties are also helped to compile information needed to make informed decisions, such as financial records, their separate living expenses, pension valuations, and property and business appraisals.

How do mediators guide emotional and angry spouses to reach decisions? They break down issues into small, manageable pieces and help parties tackle them one at a time. They keep parties focused—on the issues, on solving problems, and on the present and future. Angry and hurtful comments are reframed in neutral language. Information is drawn out from each party so each can see the other's perspective. Mediators look for ways to narrow the gap between parties—searching for trade-offs, concessions, and areas of compromise. If one party rigidly clings to unrealistic demands, mediators challenge faulty assumptions so the person becomes more in tune with reality. Mediators control the parties' conflict. They also strive to correct power imbalances between the parties so they will be on an equal footing; since the parties make their own decisions, it is important for them to be on an equal playing field.

There are ground rules in mediation to which parties must agree. For example, couples who are mediating property settlements must agree to fully disclose all assets and liabilities, provide supporting documentation, and make no changes to the status of their assets except by mutual consent.

After mediation has been completed, the mediator drafts a "memorandum of understanding," detailing the agreements reached. Usually the memorandum is reviewed by the spouses' attorneys to ensure that the rights of each were protected, that tax consequences were considered, and so forth. Typically, an attorney adds the legal language to the memorandum, and it is incorporated into the marital settlement agreement. If any issues were not resolved in mediation, they can be resolved in whatever way the couple and their respective attorneys see fit.

Why Mediation?

"The adversarial legal system can do for families in divorce what the hand grenade does for interior design," stated a 1999 *Chicago Tribune* article, calling for "a kinder, gentler divorce."[1] Mediation is a path to that kinder, gentler divorce. In fact, the majority of states now have mandated mediation for couples with disputes about their children. In one such state, California, only 9 percent of an 1,100-person study group were unable to *completely* resolve parenting arrangements themselves, and only 2 percent required a full custody trial.

If divorce will be the end of the relationship, the hand grenade approach may not be so catastrophic. But in cases involving underage children, divorce is not the end of the parents' relationship, but a milestone. Mediation gets spouses communicating in a constructive way. It demonstrates that cooperation can be more to their advantage than confrontation. It models communication and negotiation skills that can be used in the future. This is quite a contrast to the escalating bitterness and conflict that are so often by-products of adversarial divorces and that inevitably color future interactions.

Couples in mediation typically report feeling empowered to shape their own futures rather than victimized by a callous system. Mediation is less time-consuming, less costly, and less stressful than is the adversarial path to divorce, and people generally report more satisfaction with mediation and mediated agreements than they do with adversarial procedures and their resultant settlements. Studies report that people are also more willing to adhere to their mediated agreements and less likely to drag one another back to court.

The Drawbacks of Mediation

Mediation is not a panacea. It is a poor choice if either party is fixated on revenge or "winning," or if either is determined to hide assets despite agreements for full disclosure. It is not a good alternative if one party's functioning is seriously impaired due to very low intelligence or severe psychopathology. If a spouse cannot let go of the marriage, he or she may not be willing to resolve all issues because to do so would mean the end of the marriage. And if one spouse has clearly dominated the relationship or if there has been ongoing domestic violence, it takes a very highly skilled and astute mediator to guide the couple to a fair agreement.

Selecting a Mediator

As of this writing, there are no set educational or experience requirements for mediators, so select a mediator carefully. You can obtain a list of qualified mediators in your area from the Academy of Family Mediators, the primary professional organization for family and divorce mediators (address: 5 Militia Drive, Lexington, MA 02173; phone: 781–674–2663; web site: www.igc.apc.orglafm). Some skilled mediators do not appear on the Academy's referral list, so you might also check the database of the Mediation Information and Resource Center (www.mediate.com).

Before choosing a mediator, ask candidates about their training in mediation, how many divorce cases they have mediated, how they use

outside financial experts such as tax experts and professional apprais-
ers, their position on consulting an attorney while you are in mediation, and their own professional background. Most are either mental
health professionals or attorneys. When attorneys act as mediators, they
cannot give you legal advice, although they can provide legal information.

Successful mediation may mean you can avoid years of bitterness,
hard feelings, court battles, and relitigations. It is a process far better
suited to families than is the adversarial process, particularly for issues
concerning children. If all issues are not resolved in mediation, you can
always fall back on adversarial means to resolve them. Mediation is an
option well worth considering at any time during the divorce process.

3

Stress and the Emotional Roller Coaster: Tools to Cope

Amy and Kyle had mutually decided to separate because, as they put it, they couldn't be in the same room for more than an hour without being at each other's throats. Amy had the children with her most of the time and had been able to change her part-time receptionist job at a large medical clinic to a full-time position. Three months later, she reported that her life was a shambles and that she was barely able to keep her head above water. Eleven-year-old Jake was angry about the pending divorce. He was sullen, surly, explosive, and rebellious. Four-year-old Max had become whiny and clinging, was wetting his bed again, and had been sick four times in the past three months. Some mornings he clung to her so tightly when she tried to leave him at day care that she arrived at work wrinkled and disheveled.

As hectic as her job at the clinic got, often it was the best part of her days. Each night she returned home with a sinking feeling in her stomach, feeling as if she were going into battle. Besides the kids to deal with, the house was always a mess, and she always seemed to be behind in laundry, grocery shopping, and bill paying. They seemed to live on sandwiches because she had so little energy left over after work to cook. There just weren't enough hours in the day.

She was always worried. How would they make it financially? There wasn't enough money to go around now that they needed two places, full-time day care, another car, and additional furniture for Kyle's apartment. She was lonely living alone and her future looked bleak. She had no idea what lay ahead. Would her life ever get any better? Sometimes she was overwhelmed with anxiety or even panic. At other times she was "just plain angry," as she put it—at Kyle for being so difficult to live with, at herself for failing to make her marriage work, at the kids for making it so hard, at fate for being so cruel. When they'd gotten married, they'd had such hopeful plans for the future together.

COPING WITH STRESS

Divorce has an inevitable fallout. It causes profound disruption—both internally and externally in almost all areas of life. With divorce come pervasive losses, an overload of major and minor life changes, a seemingly endless array of unfamiliar practical problems, and intense and wildly fluctuating emotions. Divorce demands the restructuring of relationships with former partners, with friends, and even with children, as a single parent. It necessitates the forging of a new identity and the building of a new lifestyle, and it motivates self-exploration and reappraisal. Divorce is synonymous with disruption, change, readjustment, and reorganization—and consequently with stress.

Stress is generally worse for spouses who are left, particularly if they are unprepared for separation. Believing they have lost control over their lives, they often feel as if they are pawns at the mercy of their former partners. However, divorce is inevitably stressful for both spouses. With the exception of the death of a spouse, divorce has been identified as the most broadly disruptive and stressful event that people face in our society.

There is convincing evidence that the stress caused by separation and divorce can have a number of negative repercussions for you. Researcher Bernard Bloom and his colleagues conducted a very thorough and now well-known examination of the large number of existing studies on the topic of stress and divorce. They reported the following disconcerting findings:

- Separated people have an increased susceptibility to viruses and other illnesses.
- Automobile accident rates *double* for people during the six months before and after separation.
- The divorced are more frequent users of mental health services, most commonly for problems such as anxiety, depression, anger, and feelings of rejection.
- The separated and divorced have higher rates of alcoholism, suicide, and involvement in homicides.

I tell you this not to scare you but to emphasize the importance of learning some effective methods to deal with your stress. Effective coping will minimize the negative repercussions of this stressful time for you.

Ineffective coping will complicate your life even further. In fact, *how* you cope with your stress may be more important to your morale and functioning than the severity of your stress.

To many people, coping with stress means taking tranquilizers, drinking, smoking, or abusing other drugs. However, these methods will create further stress on your body. Fortunately, other stress-reducing methods have been found that will not further complicate your life and are more effective, too.

You will find that the strategies to cope with and reduce stress discussed in the following sections differ from the coping tools discussed throughout the remainder of the book. This is because stress causes physiological changes in your body. Therefore, some of the most effective strategies to combat it are physiological in nature. Don't minimize their importance or underestimate what they can do for you. They are well worth learning and incorporating into your life. Not only will they be helpful now; they will help you through *any* stressful period in the future.

If you have trouble motivating yourself to begin using the coping tools discussed here or in the remainder of the book or if you find yourself reverting to old patterns, turn to Appendix A. It contains a five-step method to help you get started with and stick to self-change programs. The method is not difficult, and it *is* effective.

Deep Relaxation

Learning a deep relaxation technique is a highly effective way to combat the physiological and psychological effects of stress. Deep relaxation is a method of creating beneficial physiological changes in your body. With deep relaxation, you can decrease your muscle tension, heart rate, and blood lactate level (blood lactate is a substance associated with anxiety). With deep relaxation, you feel calm, relaxed, and refreshed. It is difficult to feel tense when your entire body feels relaxed!

Learning a deep relaxation technique is not difficult, and once you have learned the technique, you will be able to relax with little effort, even in situations that are stressful, anxiety-arousing, or anger-provoking. Think of the tool you will have if you can relax, at will, during times of high tension!

You can learn the steps to an easy and effective deep relaxation method in Appendix B. Don't put off learning it because you "don't have the time." You will be trading 20 minutes a day for a less stressful life. It will likely prove to be the most productive 20 minutes in your day.

Autogenic Breathing

Here's a stress-reducing method taught to many emergency response workers to use on their way to emergencies. It's very simple but effective. Breathe in *very deeply* for four full seconds, and hold it for two seconds. Then slowly release the breath for four seconds, and hold for two additional seconds. Then repeat. When you breathe in, you should be able to feel it in your abdomen. You can do this anytime, any place, while doing anything. The longer you continue the better. Try for 20 minutes. Notice how relaxed and calm you feel, both physically and mentally.

Physical Exercise

One of the best antidotes for stress is exercise. Before you groan, read on. A regular program of aerobic exercise counteracts both the physiological and psychological toll of stress. Exercise relaxes your tensed muscles and increases your energy level. It clears your mind and helps you sort out problems. It has been found to improve self-esteem and promote feelings of psychological well-being. It's been found to decrease depression. It's even been found to improve your immune system.

Aerobic exercise is any activity that will increase your heart rate for a continuous period of 20 minutes or longer, such as jogging, fast walking, bicycling, swimming, aerobics classes, or rowing. If you make an exercise program a regular part of your routine, you will find that you miss it if you skip it.

Limiting the Amount of Change in Your Life

The more change you are bombarded with at once, the more stress you are likely to experience. Most people adjust better to separation if they can maintain a sense of continuity in other aspects of their lives. Be sensitive to the number of changes you introduce into your life, and try to keep them at a tolerable level. There is more about this in Chapter 10.

Taking Good Physical Care of Yourself

It is now generally accepted that stress negatively affects the immune system and makes people more susceptible to illness. Stress places extra demands on your body, which increase your need for both good nutrition and sleep. Believe it or not, good nutrition and sleep are so important during times of stress that scientists now consider them to be good coping strategies to combat some of the negative effects that stress can have. Paying attention to your diet and sleep will not only reduce the likelihood of your falling prey to viruses but also help you feel better physically and mentally. Watch your diet and sleep needs for at least the two-year period following separation. If you have children, watch theirs, too!

We'll turn now to the array of confusing feelings and emotions people experience after separation and divorce and ways to cope with them. These feelings and emotions are often called the "emotional roller coaster" because they so often come in turbulent waves of ups and downs. Noticeably missing from the discussion in this chapter are depression and anger, two important components of the emotional roller coaster. They are the subjects of Chapters 4 and 5 respectively.

If you adopt some of the coping tools discussed, you will feel more in control of your life, and the period after separation and divorce will be considerably less turbulent. These are all coping tools you can use on your own. You may wish to consider some counseling sessions as well. It is invaluable at this time to have at least one objective person to shore up your strength, provide you support, act as a sounding board, provide perspective, help you sort out your feelings and future options, and guide you along the way. Check your health insurance; some sessions may be covered. If not, and money is tight, some mental health professionals will adjust their fees to your ability to pay. You may also find a divorce support group an enormous help and source of support. These groups are becoming more common and are often offered through community or family service organizations.

DEALING WITH ANXIETY

There were times that I was so overwhelmed, I thought I'd go crazy. My whole world had collapsed. I had spent five years putting Tony through school and we spent another five building. I thought we had finally made it to the point where I could comfortably quit my job and raise a family. Then wham. Everything was gone—Tony, the house, our life, the bright future, and especially the chance to have kids.

I didn't know what to do or where to turn. What would I do with the rest of my life? I wasn't even sure who I was now that I was no longer

Mrs. Tony Simpson. I was a single person living in a rented condo who had a job I never did care about. But inside I screamed, "Is this really me?" I would flit wildly from one idea to another. Should I go back to college? Maybe I could find a more satisfying job. I could adopt an older child and become a single parent. What about marrying again? But did I ever want to take the chance of getting hurt this much again? I was so scared.

There were periods when I would keep a frenetic pace—doing anything to keep myself busy so I wouldn't have to think or spend time alone. I would go to bed well after midnight, drained and exhausted, but then a few hours later I would wake up in sheer terror, shaking and sweating. I just couldn't escape, no matter what I did.—*Pauline*

Anxiety, such as Pauline describes, is a familiar companion to most people after separation, and not surprisingly. Anxiety is almost inevitable at a time of such major disruption, when the familiar past is replaced with an unknown future, emotions are turbulent, decisions are pressing, and new day-to-day problems demand solutions. At times, anxiety may become so overwhelming that a person reaches a point of sheer panic, accompanied by a racing pulse, a tightened chest, shortness of breath, and sweaty hands.

As you make progress in sorting out your jumbled emotions, addressing your new problems, dealing with your children's pain, and planning for your future, your anxiety will gradually subside. However, there is a catch. You can't tackle problems constructively if you are too overwhelmed to function. You need to reduce your anxiety to a manageable level now. Here are some coping tools that will help you handle those anxiety attacks:

- Identify a small number of problems that are critical *at this point in time*. Focus on solving these, and table the rest for a later time. Once you've dealt with these immediate, high-priority concerns, you can choose a few more. Continue to prioritize your problems in this way, focusing on the few that are *most* important at the time.
- If you can't control your worrying about low-priority problems, ask yourself what's the worst thing that could happen. If it is something drastic, you may want to reorder your priorities. If not, it will help put these problems in perspective.

- Keep in mind that *all* your decisions right now do not have to be permanent ones. Making some stopgap decisions will help you feel calmer and more in control of your life.
- As soon as you feel yourself getting anxious, begin some autogenic breathing or deep relaxation.
- If you find worry and anxiety preventing you from functioning when you need to, set aside a designated time slot each day (one-half to one hour) for the sole purpose of worrying about your problems and trying to solve them. If you use this time consistently every day, worries are less likely to invade the remainder of your day.
- Part of your anxiety may stem from your attempts to bury overwhelming and confusing feelings rather than deal with them. Try to sort out your jumbled emotions. If you don't, you are likely to have residual emotion tied to your marriage and former spouse that may interfere with your ability to completely close the door on them. The remainder of this chapter and the next will help you identify and cope with these feelings.
- It may help to write in a journal during the time period you set aside. Writing in a journal helps you sort out your thoughts, feelings, and options. It allows you to keep track of your progress. It also gets your thoughts on paper rather than having them locked in your head where they are more likely to intrude during the day.
- If worry and anxiety continue to intrude during the day despite setting time aside to deal with them, try controlling them with *distraction*. You might have some fun or interesting things ready to think about when your anxiety begins to rise. Some people carry a small, challenging puzzle with them for these moments. Others play some type of game in their head. Another technique some people find effective is *thought stoppage:* Wear a wide rubber band around your wrist and snap it every time you begin to worry outside your scheduled time.
- At times a *new* concern or solution to a problem may pop into your head when you least expect it. Write it down immediately and set it aside until your designated time. This will get it off your mind and free you to go on to something else. (If you carry a small notebook with you to jot down your thoughts, they will all be in one place.)

CHECKLIST FOR DEALING WITH YOUR ANXIETY

✓ Prioritize problems, focusing on a few at a time.

✓ If low-priority problems worry you, ask yourself, "What's the worst thing that could happen?"

✓ Make stopgap decisions.

✓ Use autogenic breathing or deep relaxation as soon as you feel yourself getting anxious.

✓ Schedule a "worry- and problem-solving time" each day.

✓ Work on sorting out your jumbled emotions.

✓ Use a journal to sort out thoughts, feelings, and options.

✓ Use distraction or thought stoppage when worries intrude outside your designated time to deal with them.

✓ If solutions pop into your head during the day, write them down and set them aside for your designated time.

✓ If anxiety continues to be a problem, set smaller goals for worry-free periods.

✓ Shift your focus from the threats to the challenges.

✓ Use a deep relaxation technique every day.

✓ Follow a regular exercise program.

✓ Initiate counseling or seek medical help.

- Do you see threats assaulting you at every turn? Every crisis is like a two-sided coin, with threats on one side and challenges on the other. Try to do a tune-up on your thinking so you focus more on the challenging side of the coin. Focusing on the threats will encourage you to feel helpless and victimized. Focusing on the challenges will encourage you to mobilize your resources. Potential traumas *can* be converted to strengthening experiences.

- If you are not making satisfactory progress in controlling your anxiety despite using these techniques, set a smaller goal for yourself. Try to go just a few hours without worrying. Each time you are successful, praise yourself lavishly. You may need to schedule two shorter periods each day to deal with your worries and problems. However, as soon as you can manage, cut back to one. Remind yourself that the most effective way to deal with problems is step by step, just as you are doing.

- Seek professional help to deal with pervasive anxiety that is unresponsive to self-help measures. Don't hesitate to initiate counseling. You may also wish to consult your physician to see if medication may be advisable.

FEELING LIKE A ROBOT: IS THERE A PERSON IN THERE?

When Meg told Hank their marriage was finally over after years of fighting and months of counseling, he was incredulous. "It will be okay, Meg," he kept saying. "We'll work it out." Meg packed her things and flew to Chicago three days later, where she hoped to start a new life close to her family. Each evening, Hank came home and hoped to find her there. He stayed close to the phone whenever he could, expecting her to call and say she was coming back. He continually tried calling her, reasoning she wanted him to make the first move. But all he ever got was an answering machine. Hank continued with his daily schedule, telling people Meg was visiting her folks. "This isn't happening," he repeatedly told himself. "She'll come back. She's got to come back." Even after he was finally contacted by Meg's divorce attorney, it took Hank another month to accept that Meg was serious. But what was he feeling? Why wasn't he upset? He wasn't angry. He wasn't panicked. He wasn't depressed. He wasn't anything! "A robot," he thought. "I'm just like a robot. I go to work. I do what needs to be done. I go through all the motions. And I don't seem to feel anything at all. A robot."

Frequently the first response to the end of a marriage is denial. This is not only true for those who are left; leavers can also go through a period of denial. ("I can't believe I would walk out on 20 years. I can't believe after all this time that there is just nothing left.") Emotionally, many are in a state of shock. They are simply numb, feeling very much like robots, just as Hank did.

Denial and emotional numbness are not only common but also useful, *if* they do not continue for too long. Denial allows you to stall, so to speak, providing you with time to gain your strength so you can face the inevitable turmoil ahead. To *continue* to deny the end of your marriage, however, is self-defeating. Many an ex-spouse becomes stalled indefinitely, unable to get on with his or her life because to do so would be an acknowledgment that the marriage *is* indeed over.

If your spouse has told you the marriage is over and you are refusing to accept it, it's time you do so. Allow yourself a very good cry, and start to mourn its loss. If you find you cannot get past the denial stage, get some professional help from a divorce therapist. You cannot get on with your life until you accept that the marriage is over.

SADNESS AND GRIEF:
THE IMPORTANCE OF MOURNING

Sadness is a normal, expected, and healthy emotion in divorce. Even when a relationship has seriously deteriorated in recent years, there is plenty to be sad about at its end. At one time the relationship had been good, the partner had been cherished, and hopeful plans had been made for a lifetime together. These past good memories are mixed with the recent bad ones, and usually there is some wistfulness about what was and what might have been. Besides this, a past and a whole way of life has been left behind, as well as a good chunk of each partner's identity. A home, possessions, continuous contact with children, and other relationships may have been left behind as well.

For many divorcing men and women, the sadness is overwhelming. They feel out of control. They can't eat, sleep, or concentrate. They feel drained and helpless and fear they will never stop crying. The worst of the pain is likely to peak during the first several months. It is likely to have leveled off by the end of the first year.

Some people shut out their feelings of sadness and loss. "Why should I be sad? I'm happy to be out of a bad marriage." They dismiss their losses as insignificant, bury their sorrow, and assume an air of nonchalance. These are folks who are likely to have problems completing their emotional divorce (see Chapter 10).

When any marriage ends, there are *inevitable* losses. Before the door can be completely closed on the marriage, these losses need to be acknowledged and good-byes said to them. The death of a relationship needs to be mourned just as any death does. Doing so does not mean you have to be sad the marriage is over. It simply helps you close the door permanently and get on with your life. Chapter 10, "Your Emotional Divorce," will help you with the mourning process.

If your sadness and grief are overwhelming, here are some coping tools to get your feelings under control while still mourning your losses:

- Set aside a designated time each day (no more than an hour) to fully experience your sadness and losses and shed your tears.

Setting aside this time will help you control your emotions for the rest of the day and help you through the mourning process as well.

- Try writing in a journal during this scheduled time. Write about the way you feel, the things you are struggling with, and the things you have learned.
- When sadness overwhelms you outside this scheduled time, force yourself to think instead of an unpleasant memory about your former spouse. You can also use distraction and thought stoppage, already discussed. Of course, you can talk your feelings out with friends, but don't overdo it to the point that they begin avoiding you. Overindulge yourself during your designated time each day.

THOUGHTS ABOUT YOUR EX:
"AM I GOING CRAZY?"

I couldn't understand what was going on. I didn't love Peggy anymore. I wanted the divorce. Yet I missed her! I would call her on the phone and her voice would sound so damn comforting. I would drive past the house and become uneasy if she wasn't home.—*Frank*

For months after we split I drove myself and everyone else crazy. I was completely obsessed with thoughts of my marriage. I went through each year, each fight, over and over again. Why did it go so wrong? When did things start going sour? First I blamed myself for everything. Then I blamed him for everything. People would tell me to put it all behind me. But I couldn't. I couldn't concentrate on anything else. I thought I'd go mad!—*Jessica*

Attachment and Ambivalence

For many divorcing men and women, one of the most incomprehensible and frustrating feelings they experience is the continued pull toward an ex-spouse. Ex-partners think and wonder about one another and seek news about the other's activities. Some make excuses to call or stop by, some actively miss their former mates, some even pine for them. It is not only those who are left who experience this pull. Leavers experience it, too, and many find it incomprehensible.

University of Massachusetts sociologist Robert Weiss first identified this phenomenon more than two decades ago. He called it *attachment*. Research suggests that lingering attachment is somewhat more common among those who are left and somewhat more common among men than women.

Just what is attachment? It is a sort of emotional bonding and a feeling of connectedness, a feeling of ease in the other's presence and restlessness when the other is inaccessible. Attachment can paralyze a spouse with fear when he or she even thinks about leaving the unhappy marriage. It can cause a spouse to fight any and all settlement agreements in order to delay the final divorce. It can prevent a spouse from taking steps toward starting a new life.

Attachment persists far longer than does love, and it persists despite conflict and antagonism. Proximity alone appears to be enough to sustain it. It seems to fade only gradually, without contact and sometimes with the help of a new love.

Given the widespread feelings of attachment, it is not surprising that divorcing partners so often have intensely ambivalent feelings about one another. They vacillate between longing and anger, between love and hate. What does it all mean? they wonder. Are they doing the right thing by divorcing? Some go through periods of dating each other again. Some resume sexual relations. In a University of California study, one-third of the study group had had sexual relations with their ex-spouse during the first year following their legal divorce. People tell the couple to make up their minds, but this advice is easier said than followed. It is a difficult time to get through, but it's easier when you know it is normal. Lingering attachment and ambivalence contribute to the ups and downs and the confusing turbulence of the emotional roller coaster, as do the obsessive thoughts of the marriage, experienced by so many people and described earlier by Jessica.

Obsessive Thoughts of Your Ex: The "Account"

After marriages end, divorcing men and women usually have an urgent need to think and talk about their marriages. They go through the same events over and over again: what each partner said and did; what triggered each significant event and fight; what each partner could have done differently; where it may have gone wrong; who was to blame. Often it becomes such a consuming obsession that people question their sanity, as did Jessica.

This kind of obsessive thinking is your search for an explanation. Retrospectively you can put events in perspective, search for missed clues, and make sense of events you did not understand at the time. Each time you go through the events of your marriage, more of the pieces fall into place. Constructing *an account* of your marriage's collapse will help you achieve closure on that chapter of your life. Without it, you are likely to continue to wonder years down the road what went wrong. There is more on the importance of constructing an account in Chapter 10.

It may take several months before you no longer have the urgent need to ruminate about your marriage all the time. Until then, here are a couple of ways to gain control of your thoughts so your ruminations will not consume your waking hours:

- Restrict your ruminations to a scheduled time, using thought stoppage and distraction techniques during the rest of the day.
- Behavioral therapists Zev Wanderer and Tracy Cabot, co-authors of *Letting Go*, have come up with a different and ingenious solution. You can ruminate all you want, but at a price. Force yourself to write down *each* thought you have *every* time you ruminate about your marriage. Keep your notes together in a journal. Why is this method effective? Your natural inclination will be to rehash the same events over and over again. However, if you have to write down the same things repeatedly, it will be a boring hassle. Pretty soon you will be less tempted to rehash the same old events and be quite satisfied just to fill in the missing details as they occur to you.

FEELINGS OF REJECTION, WORTHLESSNESS, AND FAILURE

This trio of feelings is such a common component of the emotional roller coaster that divorced members in singles groups often refer to themselves as the "walking wounded."

It is common for those who are left to feel rejected. It may help to know that frequently the leaver is not rejecting the *person left* as much as *the person the leaver once was and no longer wishes to be*. A leaver frequently has moved in a new direction that may be incompatible with the direction the spouse desires. People move in new directions for any number of reasons, ranging from personal growth to a reaction to some life event such as a trauma, a new job, a religious experience, or relocation. Whatever the reason, the leaver may feel that the only two choices are sacrificing his or her new direction or leaving the relationship. Although at one time society clearly pressed people into the first option, it now openly accepts the second. Terms such as self-fulfillment, growth, being true to oneself, and irreconcilable differences have become familiar. However, society sends a double-edged message. At the same time it openly accepts divorce, it refers to "failed" marriages and extends very little support to the divorcing, who often feel as if they were sinking in quicksand. It is no wonder that so many divorcing men and women, caught in the middle of these double-edged messages, feel like failures.

How do you deal with feelings of rejection, worthlessness, and failure? Try the following:

- Work on rebuilding your self-esteem using the strategies in Chapter 11. Divorce is usually very hard on self-esteem. As it is rebuilt, feelings of rejection, worthlessness, and failure diminish.
- Don't write off your *entire* marriage as a failure because it ended in divorce. Look for the successes over the years.
- Don't put all the blame on yourself. Try to identify *all* the causes contributing to your divorce.
- Look at the broader picture. Ask yourself, "Because my marriage ended, does it negate my worth as a *person*? How does the end of my marriage make me into a different person than I was before? Does it detract from my other successes?" Think about the more than two million people each year who divorce in this country alone. Do you think they are all worthless failures? Then why are you?

EUPHORIA: WHY CAN'T IT ALWAYS BE LIKE THIS?

You do not need special coping tools to deal with your periods of euphoria, but no coverage of the emotional roller coaster would be complete without a discussion of the highs as well as the lows. Euphoric periods are the sunshine between the storms, when you may be delirious with feelings of freedom, brimming with self-confidence, and certain that your world abounds with unlimited opportunities. However, as suddenly as your euphoria appeared, it can be cruelly whisked away—

often at the slightest hint of personal failure. It is all part of the emotional roller coaster. As you progress through the transition-restructuring period and become more confident in your new state of life, you will be less susceptible to these emotional ups and downs.

Take full advantage of the extra energy you have during euphoric periods to start a new self-change program. If you can get going when you are feeling good, the momentum can help you continue it through the low times. This book is full of ideas for self-change programs. Follow the steps in Appendix A, but don't get carried away because you are feeling good. *Always* set your goals in small steps so you will be successful. The more successful you are, the fewer low times you will have!

The following chapter focuses on these low times, when you are feeling defeated and immobilized. It discusses depression and how to get yourself out of it.

4

Feeling Defeated and Immobilized: How to Combat Depression

Sometimes overwhelming sadness and grief drag on week after week, or even month after month. It may be a struggle to carry on with your job or care for your children. You may feel worthless and hold little hope for your future. The activities you once loved may no longer give you pleasure. Your world may seem joyless, and you may spend your time in passive, solitary activities such as watching television. Your appetite may be poor and you may be chronically fatigued, perhaps unable to sleep. Sometimes even the most mundane tasks require supreme effort. This is serious depression.

In one major study, roughly 30 percent of both men and women were seriously depressed after separation. Another third of the men and three-fifths of the women were mildly to moderately depressed. Depression hits both leavers and those who have been left.

Depression usually peaks during the early stages of separation. A short-lived depression is nothing to be concerned about; some people need a period of withdrawal before they can begin to face the new demands of separation. However, it is never too soon to learn some tools to cope with depression—it can become a long-term problem that does not get better with time. In fact, the longer depression continues, the more likely it is to perpetuate itself.

If your depression has gone on for days, begin today to use some coping tools. You *can* turn your depression around, and you *can* begin to get on with your life. However, if you do not feel that you can handle your depression by yourself, if serious depression continues week after week, and certainly if you feel suicidal, please get professional help *immediately*. Do not try to cope alone with depression at this level. Supportive divorce therapy is likely to be a lifeline. There is also effective antidepressant medication now available.

Many people have a second period of depression much later in the transition-restructuring stage of divorce. In fact, in a carefully conducted University of Virginia study, the majority of men and women in the study group reported they were at an all-time low one year after their divorces were final. If you have this second bout of depression, don't be discouraged. You are not going backward after so many months of hard work. In fact, this second depression is sometimes called the "darkness before the dawn."

The coping tools in this chapter can be used anytime you are depressed. In fact, if you continue to follow their principles, they are likely to *prevent* periods of depression in the future. Many of these methods have been developed by either psychiatrist David Burns, author of *Feeling Good: The New Mood Therapy,* or Dr. Peter Lewinsohn and his associates, who have devoted years to the study of depression. The methods have had a lot of success.

TAKING ACTION

One of the most effective cures for depression is so deceptively simple that you may be skeptical that it will work. It is *activity*. The more you get yourself going, the less depressed you will feel.

You see, your feelings and your behavior are intimately bound together: Feelings affect behavior and behavior affects feelings. When you are depressed you don't feel like doing anything. (Your feelings affect your behavior.) But the less you do, the more depressed you become. (Your behavior affects your feelings.) It is a vicious cycle!

Increasing Your Pleasurable Activity

Increasing your *pleasurable* activity is more effective in combatting depression than increasing activity at random. Dr. Lewinsohn finds that compared with most people, depressed people engage in very little pleasurable activity from day to day. Most depressed people put off doing pleasurable things until they "feel better." What they don't realize is that taking the opposite approach is a much quicker way out of depression. Usually, when depressed people start increasing the pleasurable activities in their lives, they begin to feel better, their mood begins to improve, and their depression begins to lift. The vicious cycle is broken. Their better mood enables them to do more, which boosts their mood and morale still higher. Instead of a downward vicious cycle in which their depression worsens, they begin an upward spiraling cycle in which their depression lifts.

The trick is to get yourself started. Lewinsohn and his associates have developed many effective methods to help you do this. Try the following.

Step 1. Start making a list of activities that you might find pleasurable. If you have a handy list, you can refer to it each day and choose some activities that appeal to you at the time. In Lewinsohn's book *Control Your Depression,* he lists more than three hundred widely varied activities that give people pleasure. It is a great source of ideas. I'll give you some examples here to get you going on your own list: reading, solving puzzles, listening to music, building or watching a fire, bicycling, enjoying nature, hiking, painting, sculpting, making crafts, restoring antiques, gardening, going to a health club, having coffee with a friend, repairing something, taking part in a discussion group, attending a club or church function, doing volunteer work, participating in or watching sports, attending concerts, photography, meditation, yoga, and treating yourself to a facial or massage.

There are also some very simple activities that make most people feel good, which you may not think of on your own. Examples are praising or complimenting someone, smiling at people, thinking about people you like, doing a job well, breathing clean air, taking in some beautiful scenery, becoming involved in a project, planning a trip, and learning to do something new. You may find they give you pleasure, too. Notice that a pleasurable activity does not have to be time-consuming.

You can add to your list as new things come to mind. Be sure to include things that are not time-consuming: sitting in the sun, taking a hot bath, putting your feet up and drinking a good cup of coffee or tea, purchasing a plant to brighten up your home, taking the children for an ice cream. Let your imagination roam. Eventually you will want a long and varied list of about one hundred pleasant activities from which to choose.

Step 2. Rate your mood *right now* on a scale of 1 (the pits) to 9 (feeling great). Keep track of your mood each day and record it daily on a "daily mood chart." Graphing your mood like this will allow you to track it visually and notice small improvements. Starting immediately will give you a baseline measure of your mood *before* you increase your daily pleasurable activities. Then you can enjoy watching it rise.

Step 3. Determine how many pleasurable activities you need to do each day to feel better. How? Lewinsohn suggests you keep track for a few typical days of the number of activities you usually do that give you pleasure. (The small number may surprise you.) Then start by increasing that number by three to five each day. (Remember, pleasurable activities do not need to be time-consuming.) By keeping a daily mood chart, you will be able to tell exactly how many pleasant activities *you* need to do to relieve your depression. It varies from person to person.

If you are having difficulty motivating yourself, try following the simple self-change method discussed in Appendix A. With it you will be able to successfully break your do-nothing pattern. Without it, you may continue to take the path of least resistance—nothing!

Combatting Depression via Other Kinds of Action

Increasing your pleasurable activities isn't the only way you can lift your depression through action. Try the following:

- Regular aerobic exercise is a great antidote to depression. You don't believe it? According to a University of Kansas study of people who were confronted with serious life change (divorce, death of a loved one, and so forth), those who were physically fit experienced less depression than did their less physically fit counterparts. You say you don't have the energy to exercise? Force yourself to go for a brisk 20-minute walk. If you record your mood on your mood chart before and again after your walk, I think you will be surprised at the improvement. Set a goal for yourself each day and reward yourself for achieving it.
- Work on building your self-esteem using the methods in Chapter 11. As you begin to feel better about yourself, it will automatically lift your mood.
- Reach out to other people. Social support can be a real boost to your morale. People who have gone through divorce can be particularly helpful; try joining a divorce support group or a singles social group.
- Make a special effort to do some nice things for yourself and for someone else, too. Take more care with your appearance,

get a new outfit, do a favor for someone. It will make you feel good, and it's difficult to feel good and depressed at the same time.

- Think of one thing that would make you feel good to accomplish—writing a long-owed letter, spending some quality time with your child, getting your desk organized, making a good meal for a change. Then get started doing it. If it is a big task, break it down into small steps, such as spending 15 minutes organizing your desk each day. Reward yourself for sticking to your goals. Notice how much better you feel with each small accomplishment.

- Some of your depression may come from feeling deprived of many things that you routinely enjoyed in your marriage. Make a list of the things you now miss. Then try to figure out some other ways you can fill at least some of those voids.

- Keep a journal of your feelings, and reread it frequently. It's often an eye-opener and a morale booster to realize how much you have improved over time.

DOING A TUNE-UP ON YOUR THINKING

If you cannot combat your depression sufficiently by taking action, you may have to do a tune-up on your thinking. There is a very logical reason for this. Not only are your *feelings* and *behavior* intimately bound together, your *feelings* and *thinking* are bound together, too. How you think influences the way you feel, and how you feel influences the way you think. Let me give you a hypothetical example.

Two couples, Phil and Maureen and Andy and Sheila, had been in marital counseling for several months, trying to save their rocky marriages. Both women were committed to trying indefinitely, but Phil and Andy gave up and told their wives they wanted a divorce. How did Maureen and Sheila feel?

Maureen chastised herself. "I should have tried harder. I should have been a better wife. I was too involved doing my own thing. Now it's too late. He's gone. I'm such a failure. What will I do? Life will be so meaningless and empty. I'll never find someone to love me again." Maureen felt depressed, guilty, unlovable, and like a failure. She went through a period in which she withdrew from life, continuing to chastise herself and sinking further into depression.

Sheila, on the other hand, blamed Andy. "He never even gave the counseling a chance. That self-centered, inconsiderate jerk. Well, I'll be damned if I'm going to wither up and die. I'll show him." Sheila was angry and bitter. In a rage, she threw his belongings in the backyard, working herself into a frenzy. For the next two months she went to singles bars three or four times a week, determined to show Andy she didn't need him.

Maureen and Sheila reacted very differently to their husbands' divorce plans. How they felt (depressed and guilty, or angry and bitter) was profoundly influenced by how they thought. Their ongoing thoughts were also influenced by how they felt (depressed or angry).

Dr. Aaron Beck, a leading expert in the area of depression, has focused his attention on how depression and thinking affect each other. He discovered that when people are depressed, they lose their ability to think clearly and put things in perspective. They magnify their mistakes and imperfections, as well as the negative events in their lives. Negatives clearly dominate their reality. This is evident in some of the typical thoughts people have when they are depressed: "I'm such a loser." "I'm so worthless." "What's the use?" "It's all my fault." "Life is so unfair." "Why does everything bad happen to me?" Dr. Beck describes depressive thinking as the four Ds: *defeated, defective, deserted,* and *deprived.* Who wouldn't be depressed if such thoughts filled their minds all the time?

This is why you may not be able to combat your depression effectively by *only* taking action (although many people can). You may also need to do a tune-up on the self-defeating thoughts that fill your mind. Let me guess what you are thinking: "That's okay for other people, but *my* thoughts aren't self-defeating. *I'm* just being realistic!" *All* depressed people feel this way *when they are depressed;* they are convinced that they are thinking objectively. However, when they are not depressed, their thinking is not nearly so negative. Negative thinking is both caused by depression and causes further depression.

Combatting Depression by Reprogramming Your Thinking

One way to combat your depression is to break your negative thinking pattern. To break it, you must be aware of it. So a first step is to tune into your *self-talk* for a day or two and write down the negative things you say to yourself. You will find that you say some things over and over again. Mark the thoughts that seem to be most important in contributing to your depression.

Jaime Anderson kept track of his self-talk for two days and felt that these thoughts were having the most impact on his mood:

"You're such a loser, Anderson."
"No wonder she dumped you. Who wouldn't?"
"What a screwup I am. I'll never be able to get anywhere in life."
"Why bother? It's all so pointless."
"God, this is awful. I can't cope with losing her."
"I'll never find anyone else who could love a jerk like me."

Jaime Anderson sounds like a real loser and would probably be able to convince a stranger that he was, too. But anyone who knew him would have been shocked at his self-talk. Jaime is a well-liked and respected associate in a prestigious law firm. For 8 of the past 10 years, his marriage had been fairly successful. He is a good father, and his children adore him. Jaime's thinking had become his own worst enemy.

Here are some ways to break your negative thinking pattern. Choose the ones that make the most sense to you.

- Use the "pat-on-the-back" technique. Get into the habit of giving yourself a pat on the back throughout the day at every opportunity you can. ("That was a good report I wrote." "That was a good meal I fixed." "I organized my time well today." "I was really patient with the kids today.")
- Focus on what you *do* accomplish rather than what you fail to accomplish. Make a list each day of all your successes, however small.
- Keep a daily journal in which you focus on the *positives* in your life. Include everything positive that occurred that day, no matter how small. And don't forget the big things—your health, children, friends, family, job. Your journal will counteract your tendency to focus only on the negatives.
- Make a list of your good points, and write each one on a small index card. Don't stop until you have at least 10. If you're so depressed you can't think of any, ask a trusted friend for help. Post a few cards someplace where you will see them frequently, and rotate the cards from week to week. When you read the card, take some time to think about it. In this way, you can *sys-*

tematically implant some positive thoughts in your mind and break the continuous pattern of negative thoughts. Be sure to make a new card each time you think of another good thing about yourself. You will be surprised at how your card collection grows.

- When you catch yourself in negative self-talk, replace it with some positive self-talk. The suggestions above will give you a plentiful supply of positive self-talk to use.
- You can also use thought stoppage (see Chapter 3) to stop your negative thinking.

Combatting Your Distorted Thinking

Some people find they can fight depression most effectively by combatting their *distorted* thinking. Remember that when people are depressed, they lose their ability to think clearly and put things in perspective. Invariably, their self-talk is not only negative but *distorted or illogical* as well. Let me give you two examples.

One of the most common types of distorted thinking used by divorcing people who are depressed is what Dr. Albert Ellis, the father of Rational-Emotive Therapy, calls *catastrophizing*. Catastrophizing means interpreting a very unfortunate event as the end of the world. ("This is horrible!" "I can't stand it anymore!" "I can't live without him (her)!") When you use words and phrases like "awful," "terrible," "I can't stand it," and "I can't live without _____," you are probably catastrophizing. Why is catastrophizing a distorted kind of thinking? Because you are confusing what you would like *very much* with what you *need to survive*. You may hate what is happening to you, but it is not the end of the world, as more than two million people who divorce each year learn. Catastrophizing is not only distorted thinking but self-defeating thinking as well because it tends to immobilize you. It makes you feel the situation is too difficult to do anything about. If you stop catastrophizing and start using some good coping tools, you will survive quite well.

A second type of distorted thinking commonly used by depressed people is *all-or-nothing* thinking. In all-or-nothing thinking, you use blanket labels to define yourself. ("I'm such a jerk." "I'm a fool." "I'm worthless." "I'm a complete failure." "I never do anything right.") Why is this distorted thinking? Because people fail in *some* areas, not in *all* areas of their lives, and they make mistakes at *some* times and in *some* situations. Defining yourself with a blanket negative label ignores everything in your life that is positive and everything you do well. It is unrealistic and will always make you feel bad.

How can you attack your distorted or illogical thinking? There are some general changes you can make in the way you think that will help you combat your depression. Here are three methods Dr. David Burns recommends:

- *Think in shades of gray.* This is an antidote for much of your distorted thinking. Avoid slapping negative labels on yourself or your problems ("I'm a blunderer." "I'm a jerk." "I've ruined my life."). Instead, Dr. Burns recommends you evaluate your shortcomings, mistakes, and problems on a scale from 0 to 100. Be as honest as you can. Before you use the scale, consider *all* the evidence. What evidence is there to confirm the label you've given yourself (loser, failure, worthless, imbecile, jerk)? What evidence is there to refute the label? Spend time thinking about each area of your life, and write down everything you think of that counteracts the label so you can't forget about them. Then use the 0-to-100 scale.

  When Jaime Anderson did this exercise, he had to admit he was far from a loser. He had many successes professionally. He was a good father and his kids loved him. He had friends. He kept himself in shape. This realization made him feel so much better that he vowed he would never again tell himself he was a loser. And once he stopped telling himself he was a loser, he began to feel better!

- *Look for partial successes.* Remember the old dilemma: Is the glass half empty, or is it half full? The optimist is happy because he perceives his glass as half full; the pessimist is sad because his is half empty. When you are depressed, you are bound to be a pessimist. Rather than looking at situations as failures, start looking for the partial successes. For example, if you have been married for 10 years and you get divorced, does that make your *entire* marriage a failure? What about the good times? What about the things you brought away from the marriage? In what ways are you different now than you were before you married?

- *Watch those emotionally loaded words.* This is a good antidote for catastrophizing. Replace your catastrophizing language with language that is *less* emotional. Here are some examples:

Instead of: "My life has been *terrible* since we split up!"

Try: "My life has been *difficult* since we split up."

Instead of: "It's just *awful* that Mary left."

Try: "It's *very unfortunate* for me that Mary left."

Instead of: "I just *can't* cope with this divorce."

Try: "I *don't like* having to cope with this divorce."

Instead of: "I *can't stand* Ted living with someone else."

Try: "I *really wish* Ted weren't living with someone else."

Instead of: "It *shouldn't* have turned out this way."

Try: "I'd *certainly prefer* that things had turned out differently."

You might be thinking, "Okay, this sounds better, but isn't this just a word game?" No, it isn't. When a situation is difficult, unfortunate, and not what you prefer, you tend to try to do something to improve your circumstances. But when a situation is disastrous, you tend to feel that it is out of your control and that you *cannot* help yourself. You become frozen in self-pity, misery, and despair. Spending your time catastrophizing saps initiative, time, and energy that would be better used getting on with your life.

While you are trying to combat depression, do not try to do everything at once. You will set yourself up for failure and disappointment, which will make you more depressed. Make your goals small ones and increase them very gradually, step by step. Start with increasing the number of pleasurable activities in your life or with other positive action. This is probably the easiest way to get quick results. If this doesn't do the trick, then work on giving your thinking a tune-up. Don't forget to use the self-change program in Appendix A to keep yourself on track. Dr. Burns's and Dr. Lewinsohn's books, listed in Appendix D, offer many more methods for relieving depression.

Sometimes depression saps your motivation and energy to such an extent that it is difficult to get yourself going without some external support. If you find this to be the case, initiate some counseling to see you through this tough time. This is likely to provide you with the energy, support, strength, and primary relationship you need right now to get yourself back on your feet. You may also wish to check into the advisability of short-term antidepressant medication. A third possibility is suggested by Dr. Andrew Weil, author of the bestsellers

8 Weeks to Optimum Health and *Spontaneous Healing.* Dr. Weil recommends an herbal treatment, Saint-John's-wort, but reports it may take two months to see its full benefit.

The emotional roller coaster does not end here. Missing is the emotion of anger. One of the biggies in divorce, it is the subject of the following chapter.

5

What Do I Do with All This Anger?

Early on a Sunday morning in November 1989, a prominent attorney and his newlywed wife were found shot to death in their beds in my hometown of San Diego. Later that day the attorney's distraught ex-wife called a friend and admitted to the shooting. As the story unfolded, it told of bitter acrimony between the formerly married pair since their divorce several years earlier. In fact, the attorney had been quoted as saying, "It is not going to end until one of us is gone."

One of the interesting things about the incident was the compassion that many in the community seemed to feel for the ex-wife, despite their horror at what she had done. What had happened to this once well-functioning woman, whose smile had frequently graced our local paper's society pages and who had entertained our city's finest? How could her anger have gotten so far out of control?

As you come to accept that your marriage is truly over, a dam may seem to break inside you, spilling out a torrent of anger—or perhaps even rage, more intense than you had thought yourself capable. Unfamiliar feelings of bitterness and vindictiveness may become your new companions, consuming a good share of your thoughts and energy each day. You may become obsessed with old hurts you had almost forgotten, reliving each as vividly as if it had occurred yesterday, each memory pouring fuel on your seething anger. Your friends may notice that you have added some very graphic language to your vocabulary, and you may find that you are unable to have a conversation with your former spouse without the anger erupting into a full-blown battle.

Researchers Judith Wallerstein and Joan Kelly found that 80 percent of the men and a somewhat higher percentage of the women they studied experienced such anger and bitterness after separation. Both leavers and those they had left became victims of their own rage. Frightened children heard their dads called disgusting, crazy, liars, and bastards, while they heard their moms called whores, drunken bitches, greedy, and grasping.

WHERE DOES IT ALL COME FROM?

Where does all this anger come from? From frustration and resentments that have been bottled up over the years. From unfulfilled expectations. From the losses and disappointments. From broken commitments that were supposed to be forever and "for better or worse." From thwarted needs for love and affection. From uncertainty about the future. From feelings of being exploited and betrayed. From hurt and humiliation. From wounded self-esteem. From feelings of helplessness. And, of course, from genuine conflicts of interest over property settlements, support payments, and parenting arrangements. It may be of little comfort to know that the intensity of your rage is likely to reflect the importance the relationship had in your life. If the relationship did not matter to you, you would have little reason to get so angry when the marriage ended.

Anger and divorce go together about the same as do love and marriage. But your anger may have a useful aspect. It can make it easier to distance yourself from your former spouse so you can get on with your life, but only under one condition: that you do get beyond your anger and *let it go*. As long as you hold onto your anger, you will be bound to your ex as surely as if you were still in love; the only difference is that the bonds will be negative rather than positive. For your own sake, you need to eliminate both the positive *and* negative bonds with your former partner. You have the potential to create a future in which your former spouse will no longer have power over you and will no longer trigger an emotional reaction within you. Your anger and resentment can be exchanged for indifference and perhaps even concern. This is a goal toward which, I hope, you will be motivated to work.

Many divorced men and women *do* hold onto their anger, however. In their large-scale study, Morton and Bernice Hunt found that for one-third of their study group of almost one thousand, anger was the *predominant* feeling toward the ex-spouse months after divorces had been *finalized*. But far more surprising was Judith Wallerstein's report that one-half of the women in her study group and one-third of the men were still intensely angry at their former mates *10 years after* they had divorced. Shocked by how little effect the passage of time had, she reported that she sometimes felt as if she had wandered into a play with the same cast of characters relating the same story, delivering the same script with the same fervor.

Who is hurt when a spouse holds onto anger? The spouse who will not let the anger go, as well as his or her children. Investing emotional energy in anger and revenge saps the time and energy needed to build a new life. The still-angry spouse can become stalled in the past, bound with scars to the dead relationship. He or she may become one of the embittered divorced who are unable to have a meaningful present or hopeful future, who go into a tirade at each new encounter with their former partners, who attempt new court actions year after year, who sometimes resort to physical violence, and who draw their children into a quicksand of emotional turmoil.

Letting go of your anger is *critical* to your divorce adjustment. This chapter discusses a number of methods to help you deal with your anger and finally let it go. But before we begin, it may be helpful to take a brief diversion and note some important distinctions about your anger that you may otherwise find confusing.

WHEN ANGER IS SELF-DEFEATING

All anger is not necessarily self-defeating. In addition to making it easier for spouses to distance themselves from one another so they can get on with their lives, anger can also be a strong *motivator*, propelling people to take constructive action to improve a situation. Let me give you an example.

George Frieze had never been able to assert himself with his wife, Eugenia. She always seemed to have the upper hand, and he had always given in to her demands. Now that they were divorcing, she called him constantly—demanding more money, demanding most of their joint possessions, dictating how he spent time with the children, dictating how much he should spend on his new apartment. "Who does she think she is?" fumed George. Frustrated on every front and fueled by 15 years of resentment and anger, George felt ready to kill. Fortunately, members of George's divorce support group encouraged him to take an assertiveness training class. The class gave George a new feeling of confidence, and he diligently worked on using his new skills to communicate and negotiate effectively with Eugenia. "Maybe if I had taken this class earlier, I wouldn't be getting divorced," mused George. "Funny, I knew about assertiveness training for years and never did anything about it. I guess I just wasn't angry enough before to get myself off my duff."

To determine whether your anger is useful or self-defeating, ask yourself these questions: Can my anger be useful in improving the upsetting situation? Can I channel it constructively in some way to achieve a positive end? George's anger motivated him to learn effective ways to deal with his ex-wife. Some people who have been angered by the legal system during their divorces have channeled their anger into becoming activists so others may avoid similar problems.

But what about situations that you cannot change or influence? Anger about these situations is self-defeating. You are investing emotional energy in making yourself miserable! It is far better for you to realistically accept, or at least tolerate, situations you cannot change. Take your emotional energy and invest it in rebuilding a new life instead of in self-defeating anger. This is what Betty Johnson did.

Betty Johnson was devastated when her husband of 30 years left her for his young assistant. For months she was in a deep depression, unable to function. She had no idea what she would do now that he was gone, and she didn't care. Then her anger surfaced, and Betty was filled with rage. She yelled, screamed, swore, and threw things. She'd never before realized she had the capacity for such anger or violence. Then gradually she came to a conclusion: "I'll be damned if I'll let him ruin my life. Who the hell needs him? I'll show him I can get along just fine without him." That was the beginning of a new life for Betty. She took her anger and channeled it constructively; it provided her with the motivation to reconstruct her life. Once she had successfully launched herself in school, she let go of her anger; it no longer served a useful purpose.

Your anger probably has two sources right now. The first is what divorce expert Judith Wallerstein calls "old anger," left over from the relationship you are no longer in (all the injustices, hurts, frustrations, betrayals, and losses in your marriage). Your old anger is about situations you clearly cannot change. You can never change the past hurts, and since the relationship is over, there is no purpose in bringing up all the past resentments, injustices, frustrations, and betrayals. To do so is likely to incite your former partner to retaliate and set into motion a spiraling cycle of angry accusations and escalating conflict. Before you can adjust successfully to your divorce, you will need to let go of your old anger. The methods discussed in this chapter will help you to do this.

What is the other source of your anger? Wallerstein calls it "new anger," and it is caused by definable situations in the here and now (such as your ex-wife making it difficult to see the children, your ex-husband not making his child support payments, your ex going on your dream vacation with a new love). Some of this new anger is likely to stem from situations in which your rights are being disregarded (for example, missed support payments or barriers that prevent you from seeing your children). These are situations that you *may* be able to improve. Later, we will look at how to use your anger constructively to help bring about desired change.

But some of your new anger may be about situations that do not affect you directly and are clearly out of your sphere of influence (such as that upcoming vacation with the new love, whom your ex dates, or how he or she conducts life from now on). The only thing that anger about these situations will accomplish is to make yourself miserable. It is *self-defeating anger,* and the best way to deal with it is to treat it like your old anger—*let it go* by using the methods discussed in this chapter. *It is self-defeating to hang onto anger over situations that you cannot change, whether they are past or present situations.*

HOW TO DEAL WITH
SELF-DEFEATING ANGER AND LET IT GO

How do you let go of your self-defeating anger? First, be sure you recognize your anger and acknowledge it. This may sound like a joke to those who are acutely aware of their anger. But some among the divorcing do not recognize anger as part of the turmoil they are feeling. This is especially true about their old anger.

In their book *Letting Go,* psychologist Zev Wanderer and co-author Tracy Cabot suggest a useful technique for those who feel only sadness and depression rather than any anger. Compile a "crime sheet," listing every specific incident you can think of throughout your marriage in which your former partner was guilty of lies, hurts, humiliations, coldness, thoughtlessness, selfishness, or cruelty. Write down each incident, and include how you felt at the time. Then, when your sadness begins to erupt, block it by dwelling on some of the incidents on your crime sheet, and especially on your feelings at the time.

If you do not acknowledge your old anger, you are likely to find it popping up in all sorts of ways—snide comments, overreacting to your ex's behavior or mannerisms, resenting your children having a good time with their other parent, "forgetting" to mail support payments, heightened anxiety. Your unacknowledged anger could stand in the way of freeing yourself completely from your former spouse and your marriage. As researchers Morton and Bernice Hunt point out, *expressed* anger tends to *break* the bonds between former spouses, whereas *suppressed* anger tends to *maintain* the bonds.

Effective Methods of Diffusing Self-Defeating Anger

Once you've acknowledged your anger, you have at your disposal a number of safe and constructive ways to diffuse that pent-up anger so that you can let it go. (Slashing your ex's tires is not on the list.) Try some of the following:

- Tell your former partner off in a letter. This is your time to let him or her have it about all your past hurts and the injustice inflicted on you. Go ahead and use the meanest, nastiest language you can think of, and be as critical as you like. *BUT DO NOT MAIL IT!* The unmailed letter technique will not only help you ventilate and diffuse some of your anger but also help you sort out your feelings in your own mind and acknowledge them.
- Exercise is a wonderful way to drain the emotional energy created by your anger. Join a gym or take up fast walking, jogging, bicycling, swimming, or some other aerobic activity. And do it *regularly*! Most people who exercise fairly strenuously when they are angry feel invigorated afterward rather than angry. Activities such as strenuous housework and chopping wood can also dissipate some of the extra adrenaline your anger pumps into your body.
- Rechannel your excess emotional energy into constructive activities that will help you rebuild your new life.
- Talk out your feelings with a supportive friend or therapist. This allows you to vent some of your anger and helps you sort out some of your feelings, such as the pain underlying your anger. A word of caution, however: Though talking is good, unlimited talking is not better. Ranting and raving about the same list of grievances over and over again is likely to have negative

repercussions. Why? Social psychologist Carol Tavris, author of the well-documented book *Anger: The Misunderstood Emotion,* reports that with each new recitation of your grievances, your emotional arousal tends to *increase.* You experience your anger all over again, often right down to a flood of adrenaline, a rise in blood pressure, tightened muscles, and quickened pulse. Instead of reducing your anger, you increase it! Find a compromise between holding your anger in and talking about it to death. If you begin to find yourself feeling angrier *after* talking than you felt before, try a different anger-releasing method. At a later date, you may want to talk again, but for the purpose of either gaining perspective or acknowledging your pain rather than rehashing old injustices one more time.

- Keep a journal in which you can release your feelings.
- Some people, men as well as women, find that some good, hard crying is an effective emotional release from their anger.
- Some find they get an emotional release from screaming or pounding something. These methods are not for everyone, however. Studies find they can escalate rather than diminish feelings of anger in some people. Watch your own response. It's probably best to use these methods strictly as a release. For example, if you punch a pillow strictly to release your pent-up rage, you may feel better afterward. If you punch a pillow while pretending it is your ex-spouse, you may wind up feeling angrier afterward.
- Do you have an *uncontrollable* urge for revenge? You say there is *no* way you can resist mailing a letter about your ex to the IRS or calling his or her new love? If so, behavioral psychologist Zev Wanderer suggests you play out this vindictive behavior in *fantasy.* Vividly create the whole sequence of events you would like to have happen. Studies find that fantasizing gives you almost as much gratification as does the actual act. And you will not have to worry about retaliation, legal repercussions, or feelings of regret or guilt. However, Wanderer wisely points out, your sweetest revenge will be to build a good life and be happy.

Finishing the Job: Doing a Tune-Up on Your Thinking

The preceding methods will help you vent your anger, but they may not do the whole job. If you want to let go of your anger, you must do more than lower your pulse rate, points out anger expert Carol Tavris. You must also "rearrange your thinking."

How can you let go of anger by rearranging your thinking? People, including your ex-spouse, do not *make* you angry. What makes you angry is the interpretation or meaning that you give to their behavior. Let me give you an example. Suppose a superior tells you, in a not very kindly way, that something you did was really stupid and then storms off, leaving you red-faced. Think for a minute how you would feel if you believed the criticism was justified. If you are like most people, you would feel humbled. But how would you feel if you believed the criticism was *unjustified*? Now, if you are like most people, you would probably get rather hot under the collar. But who is making you feel humbled or angry? Your superior, who has said exactly the same thing in each case? Or is it you, because of the way you appraise the situation and evaluate what is said? In reality, *your interpretation of the situation influenced your feelings more than the situation per se.*

Dr. Albert Ellis, the father of Rational-Emotive Therapy, refers to this phenomenon as the A-B-C of emotions. Think of it like this: The A is the actual event (your superior calls you stupid). The C represents your feelings of being upset. Most people assume the event (A) causes the feelings (C). But in fact, something intervenes between A and C, and this is the real culprit that causes anger. That culprit is B, your *beliefs* or *interpretation* of the event. After your superior storms off, you may think further about the criticism and hold a conversation in your head ("God, how could I have been so stupid? I'm such a jerk!" or "The more I think about it, the more I'd like to tell that witch off!"). As you are talking to yourself, your feelings may become even more intense. Who is escalating your upset? Your superior? She has already left the scene. Or is it yourself via your thoughts?

Now try something else. Vividly imagine the times you really get angry with your former partner, and allow yourself to get as upset as you can. If you need to recall a single situation that angered you, go ahead. Let yourself go with your vivid imagery for five minutes before you continue reading.

If you did this exercise, you probably had a rather elaborate conversation running through your mind. Get a pencil and paper and write down the things you were saying to yourself. Rick did this exercise. These were the thoughts he wrote down:

> She shouldn't have just walked out. What right did she have? I didn't
> deserve this. She should have told me she was unhappy. But no, what

does she do? Walks out! On ten years! No discussion. No nothing! Oh, there was something, all right. She had it all planned down to the last detail. Apartment all lined up. I wouldn't be surprised if she had a boyfriend all lined up, too! Conniving! Says she can't take it anymore. Can't take *what* anymore? She should have said something. What ever happened to "till death do us part"? It isn't fair! She had no right to just unilaterally walk out like that. This isn't the way marriages should end!

After Rick worked through this exercise, he reported he was very angry, his muscles were tense, and he had a tightness in his chest and throat. After you complete this exercise, take a brief audit of how *you* feel right afterward. Had Rick been hooked up to some monitors, they probably would have indicated elevated blood pressure and a quickened pulse rate. Was it Rick's ex-wife that made him this angry? She wasn't even there!

Psychiatrist David Burns, author of the best-seller *Feeling Good,* points out that we create our *own* anger by our beliefs that an incident was unjustified or that someone behaved unfairly toward us. This was certainly indicated in the thoughts running through Rick's mind, that is, in his *self-talk*. Take an audit. Were these beliefs evident in your self-talk?

When people are angry, usually their self-talk has been full of *should* and *should not* statements. ("Marriages *shouldn't* end this way. She *shouldn't* have walked out. She *should have* said something.") Sometimes, of course, the *shoulds* and *should nots* are implicit. For example, "I don't deserve to be treated like this" really means "She *should not* have treated me this way." "She had no right" means "She *should not* have acted in this way."

The trouble with using *should* statements is they give you the illusion that your *personal* standards of behavior are *absolute* standards. What you really are saying is, "My ex-spouse *should* behave the way that *I* think is right." Then, if you are like most people, you go one step further: When your former partner violates your personal "rules," you think of him or her in derogatory terms ("The creep!" "What a louse!" "Can you believe that conniving shrew?" "Only an inconsiderate, self-centered jerk would have done that."). Of course, you would *prefer* your ex (and everyone, for that matter) to behave the way that you think is right, and it would be a better world if everything were fair. But unfortunately, there are no universal laws dictating either fairness in human relationships or fairness in the world. Using *should* statements only sets you up to become angry, frustrated, resentful, and blaming. They are what Dr. Burns calls "hot thoughts." The more you use them, the angrier you become. The angrier you become, the more you get carried away with hot thoughts ("I could kill her!" "Just let me at the bastard!"). Emotions and thoughts form a two-way street.

Tune-Up Tools

Watch your anger further dissipate when you use the following five methods to tune-up the way you think about your former spouse.

First, note your self-talk when you are angry, and replace your hot thoughts. When you feel yourself becoming emotionally aroused, focus on the sentences that are running through your mind, and jot them down. Once you are aware of the hot thoughts that keep your resentments alive, you can more easily replace them. Probably the easiest way to replace them is eliminating your *should* statements. Dr. Ellis suggests that you replace the *shoulds* with statements about your preferences and dislikes ("I wish ... I would have preferred ... I'm disappointed ... I do not like the fact that ..."). This is not a simple exercise in semantics. Avoiding *shoulds* will help you keep in mind that your personal rules are just that—they are personal, *not* unbreakable laws. Avoiding *shoulds* also markedly changes the emotional tone of an event. Suppose we give Rick's thinking a tune-up and replace his hot thoughts, which were full of stated and implied *shoulds,* with preferences and dislikes. His self-talk might go something like this:

> I don't like it one bit that she just walked out like that. I certainly would have preferred that she give me a chance to work on our problems. I wish she had just told me she was unhappy. We could have discussed things. Worked on some changes. I'm certainly disappointed she arranged for an apartment the way she did. I would have preferred some semblance of honesty from her. This isn't my idea of a marriage.

How would you rate Rick's emotional state now? Perhaps very annoyed, disappointed, hurt. But do you suppose extra adrenaline is pumping through his system? Are his pulse and breathing becoming faster as he is talking to himself? Are his muscles tightening? You can learn other approaches to changing your self-talk in Dr. Burns's and Dr. Ellis's books listed in Appendix D.

This next tune-up technique is the "ultimate anger antidote," says Dr. Burns. Try to put yourself in your ex's shoes and see the world through his or her eyes. Try to think of as many varied reasons as you can to explain your former partner's behavior. If you do, you may find that his or her behavior is not as unreasonable as it once seemed. This technique frequently dissipates anger, as Dan discovered.

Dan received what he believed to be unreasonable demands for a property settlement from Mary Beth's attorney. Dan saw red. He immediately called her to tell her off, but she had bought an answering machine and wouldn't return his calls. After several days of phoning, he went over to her house, but Mary Beth wouldn't answer the door and had changed the locks. Dan was livid. He pulled up the new flowers she planted. "Who the hell does she think she is? I don't deserve this kind of treatment. Live with someone for fifteen years and you think you know them. Hah! Now her true colors come out. I won't stand for being treated like this. She doesn't want to play fair. OKAY. She'll be sorry she ever started this game."

After talking to his lawyer, Dan learned that Mary Beth's lawyer instructed all his clients not to talk to their spouses and to change the locks on the doors. Furthermore, he had a reputation for demanding high property settlements so he would have more negotiating room. With some help from a close friend, Dan realized that Mary Beth had always depended on him to make all the decisions and had never questioned them. It was one of the things he had found so infuriating about her. Perhaps she had become just as dependent on her attorney and was accepting his instructions blindly. It would be just like her. Dan was surprised that his anger drained away when he finally was able to look at the situation through Mary Beth's eyes.

Third on the list of tune-up tools is realizing that some anger will dissipate on its own if you refrain from making an issue of each new annoyance. For example, if your ex makes a snide comment, refrain from responding and learn to occupy yourself with some pleasant activity rather than thinking about it. Remember the age-old advice of counting to 10? It works!

Fourth, if you are not successful in tuning up your negative self-talk, derail it. There are several ways to do this. If you focus on autogenic breathing or deep relaxation (see Chapter 3) when you feel your tension begin to rise, you will not only interrupt your negative self-talk but obstruct the physiological arousal that accompanies anger. You can also derail negative self-talk by using the distraction and thought stoppage techniques discussed in Chapter 3.

Fifth, remember that *you* are the only person who can make *you* angry. Your emotions are yours. Don't let someone else control them!

TOOLS FOR LETTING GO OF YOUR SELF-DEFEATING ANGER*

ANGER DIFFUSION TOOLS

✓ Unmailed letter technique.
✓ Physical exercise.
✓ Rechanneling emotional energy into constructive activities.
✓ Talking out your feelings, but not excessively.**
✓ Releasing your feelings in a journal.
✓ Having a good cry.
✓ Screaming; pounding a pillow.**
✓ Carrying out uncontrollable urges for revenge in fantasy, *not* reality.

FINISHING UP THE JOB: GIVING YOUR THINKING A TUNE-UP

✓ Replace "hot thoughts." Reframe *shoulds* into preferences/ dislikes.
✓ Examine situations from your ex's perspective.
✓ Don't make a big issue of annoyances; use distraction or count to 10.
✓ Derail negative self-talk with autogenic breathing, deep relaxation, distraction, or thought stoppage.
✓ Remember, *you* are the only one who can make *you* angry.

*Anger that cannot be channeled into improving an upsetting situation.
**Can sometimes increase angry feelings. If you feel angrier afterward, use another tool.

If your self-defeating anger continues to consume you, please initiate some counseling. Don't let yourself and your children become casualties of divorce.

DEALING WITH "NEW" ANGER CONSTRUCTIVELY

It is likely that you have some new anger mixed in with the old. Recall that new anger is about definable situations in the here and now—chronically late support checks, an ex badmouthing you to your family and friends, the other parent always being late to pick up or return the children. If you have gripes like these, they are probably accompanied by frustration and anger.

How do you deal with new anger? You could diffuse it by using one of the methods discussed earlier. If your new anger is about situations that do not directly affect you and you cannot change, this is exactly what you *should* do. (Examples include whom your ex dates and what your ex does with his or her life from now on.) However, if your new anger stems from situations in which your former partner is infringing on your rights (such as the examples in the preceding paragraph), why not try to do something about them? Your anger can be a great motivator to take positive action to find a solution to an upsetting situation.

You say you've tried everything? Yelled? Threw tantrums? Threatened? Called your attorney? *Nothing* worked? "Nothing works" is a common complaint of angry divorced spouses. But let's look at the way most former partners express their anger at one another. Many do not express it directly. Instead, they hang up on each other, slam doors, "forget" to send support payments, or needle one another. Many others do express their anger directly but in destructive ways, such as physical violence or verbal attacks. ("You witch! Why did you tell Johnny I wasn't sending you enough money?" "You irresponsible bastard! Where the hell is the check?")

How do you suppose tactics such as these affect former partners' interactions with one another? Listen to some typical reactions: "I give it right back to him." "It gives me pleasure to make her so mad." "I really get ticked off." "I become defensive and strike back." "I ignore the dope."

The best way to change these upsetting situations is to enlist your former spouse's *cooperation*. Impossible, you say? Don't bet on it! Chapter 12, "Communicating with an Ex-Spouse: Ten Tools That Will Make the Difference," provides you with the resources to express your new anger constructively and communicate in a nonaggressive and nonthreatening way. Using these tools will create an atmosphere conducive to cooperation rather than hostility. Chapter 19 will be a further help. It is a step-by-step approach to ending the conflict with your former partner. Although it is in the co-parenting section of the book, much of the chapter is applicable to ex-partners who are childless.

In short, if a situation in the present is having a negative impact on your rights (or your children's), don't become a helpless victim of either your anger or your ex-spouse. Express your anger directly and *constructively,* so that you might bring about a change for the better. If, after all your efforts, it seems certain the situation will not change, use the tools to deal with self-defeating anger. There is no sense in hanging onto anger about situations that you cannot change.

Through your divorce and new beginnings, you have the potential to take nearly full control of your life. But you will not do so unless you can let go of your self-defeating anger and learn to deal with your new anger constructively. To let your former spouse anger you is to allow him or her to still control you. Remember, your emotions are yours, and you are the only person who can make you angry through your "hot thoughts." You will find that taking control of your own anger is taking a gigantic leap forward on the path to your new beginnings.

II

Children and Divorce

6

Divorce through a Child's Eyes

During the London blitz of World War II, the British carried out mass evacuations of their children to safe rural areas. An estimated 25 to 50 percent of the evacuated children, separated from their families during this stressful time, developed emotional problems. The children who had good relationships with their parents from whom they were now separated generally handled their exile well. Children who had poor relationships with their parents generally fared poorly. However, the children who fared the best of all emotionally were those who remained with their parents right through the terror of the German bombings! Apparently, the security provided by their parents offset the trauma of the air raids, the bombs, and the rubble surrounding them.

The point of this anecdote is to illustrate the powerful role that parents can play in buffering their children from severe and prolonged stress. If you understand this very significant function that mothers and fathers play in children's lives, you will be better able to fully understand children's divorce experience.

It is easy for parents to downplay their day-to-day importance to their children, particularly if their youngsters are already involved with peers, school, and their own activities. But to children of all ages, parents are very much like a reserve bank account. When all is well with the world, a reserve bank account may go unnoticed and have no apparent influence on day-to-day activities. However, it provides a safety net that allows its owner to explore and enjoy new horizons without the threat of peril hanging overhead. If a disaster does strike, the reserve account can take on enormous significance; it could mean the difference between the survival or the demise of the person's way of life.

You are no doubt concerned about how your divorce may affect your children. To give you a straight answer, parental divorce is very painful to children, and most do experience problems for a while. Does divorce cause *long-term* problems? A significant minority of children do develop long-term emotional, behavioral, social, or academic problems, even some who appeared to be doing well during the crisis itself. The majority, however, are not troubled with lasting problems, and some even develop greater psychological strength because of the divorce. Which path will your children take?

The last two decades of research have taken much of the guesswork and uncertainty out of why some children emerge from their parents' divorce unscathed while others develop long-term problems. With this information, you can engineer a situation that is likely to enable your children to thrive despite your divorce. The following chapters will guide you in doing this.

In this chapter, we take a look at divorce through a child's eyes. You may find the chapter discouraging in spots, but this and the following chapters will help you to avoid many mistakes that other parents have made. Many problems can be short-lived when handled well. While reading the chapter, try to keep in mind the experience of the British children who remained with their parents through the wartime bombing and the protective role parents can play in buffering their children from stress.

CHILDREN'S DIVORCE EXPERIENCE

To children, divorce does not mean the second chance that it so often means to one or both parents. Rather, it means the loss of their family— the entity that provides them with support, stability, security, and continuity in an often unpredictable world. Children assume that their family is a given and that their parents are permanent. After all, their family and parents are what provide for their needs. In their eyes, their family is intricately woven with survival.

Studies uniformly find that divorce is a jolt to most children. Even youngsters who have lived in tense, conflict-ridden homes for many years seldom think of divorce as a remedy for unhappiness; the remedy would be for parents to stop fighting. Among children for whom verbalized threats of divorce have loomed for many years, the actual happening most often is perceived not as an expected event but as a nightmare that becomes a waking reality. Suddenly the assumptions children have accepted as givens and the structure they have relied upon fall apart. They feel not only vulnerable but powerless to have any influence on a situation that profoundly affects their lives.

The inevitable anxiety children feel is intensified when they are given little information—a situation that occurs with alarming frequency, especially for younger children. "What will happen to me?" "Who will take care of me?" "If my parents don't love each other anymore, will they continue to love me?" "Where will I live?" "Who will I live with?" "Will I have to give up my school and friends?" "What will my life be like now?" "Will I still see my other parent? How? How often?" "What will that parent do now?" "Will we have enough money to live?" "Can I still go to camp?" "Can I still go to college?" Children's unanswered questions are endless and their worry intense. It feels more precarious having only one parent on whom to rely. Can that parent manage? What will happen if something happens to that parent, too? Will that parent find someone else and get remarried? "Will I get lost in the shuffle?"

Children's Feelings

Many children feel rejected, perceiving that the parent is leaving them as well as the spouse. "He (she) wouldn't have left if he (she) cared about me." Fears of abandonment are not uncommon. In the California Children of Divorce Study, Judith Wallerstein and Joan Kelly found that one-half of the children they studied (who ranged from preschoolers to adolescents) were afraid of being abandoned by their fathers, while one-third feared abandonment by their mothers. A few children even feared they would be placed in foster homes. Not surprisingly, children's self-esteem frequently takes a plunge after divorce.

The majority of children are intensely sad and feel a deep sense of loss—of their family, their security, even their daily routines and family traditions. Even most of those who never had a close relationship with their departing parent now long for that parent. Many children have little control over their tears. Fourteen-year-old Meredith described how she felt when her parents were divorcing:

> The divorce really affected me emotionally. I just felt bad all the time. I used to cry a lot, and when I wasn't crying, I would feel like crying. . . . [I]t was just a terrible time in my life.[1]

Anger is a fairly common reaction among children. Many feel betrayed by the very people they have trusted to protect and care for them. They feel no one is considering their needs, and they feel powerless to alter the situation that is completely disrupting their worlds. Some angry children hide their anger, fearing it will further upset or alienate their parents. Others have explosive outbursts. Some act out their anger in temper tantrums, noncompliance, aggressiveness, destructiveness, rebelliousness, or sexual promiscuity.

Some youngsters are haunted by gnawing feelings that they are responsible for the divorce. In a recent Boston University study of 6-to-12-year-old children, one-third of the children felt that the divorce was partly their fault. Preschoolers are even more prone to blaming themselves. Some children will remember parental fights they overheard about child-rearing differences. Others will remember their parents' exasperation over sibling quarrels. Some turn into model children, hoping they can undo the damage they think they have done. One child confessed to her mother years later, "I felt I was being punished by God for being really bad, so I tried being really good so God would change His mind ... and let Dad come home."[2]

Some children feel relief when parents separate, although it appears they are a small minority. One widely cited study found that fewer than 10 percent felt this way—most often older children who lived in fear that the violence in their homes would end in physical injury. Several studies have reported that initial feelings of relief are sometimes temporary and are later replaced by sadness and anger.

If children have *only* their parents' divorce to contend with, their situation is not so bleak, and their poor functioning is usually short-lived. But for most children, the divorce is only the beginning of what they must contend with.

Will the Fighting Ever Stop?

From children's perspectives, the one positive aspect of divorce is that it may put an end to the fighting and tension with which they have been living. But studies find that conflict between parents usually escalates after separation, as hurt and embittered parents must work out details about parenting arrangements, support, and property, and as many begin to date. Distressed and bewildered children hear their mothers called whores, drunken bitches, and rotten mothers, and their fathers called liars, bastards, and terrible fathers. In the widely cited

California Children of Divorce Study, over one-half of the children witnessed at least one incident of physical violence between their parents, many of whom had never had such incidents prior to separation. Even worse, some children found themselves blatantly used as weapons by one parent to punish the other.

Children caught in this parental cross fire become frightened and angry at the incomprehensible behavior of their parents; they wonder if the conflict will ever stop. Many feel unremitting tension created by conflicting loyalties; any move toward one parent is a move away from the other. If they remain loyal to one, will their relationship with the other be jeopardized? Some children offer themselves as mediators or even scapegoats, some withdraw from both parents, and some align themselves with one parent. Children often feel as if they were being torn apart or split in two (see Chapter 8).

Is Anything the Same Anymore?

When parents separate, the world as their children know it begins to change and often ends. Daily life is transformed. Children lose daily contact with one parent, and the great majority long for that parent, whether or not the relationship had been close. Often early visits are infrequent and follow no predictable schedule on which children can depend, increasing their fears of abandonment. Will this visit be the last?

At the same time, many youngsters also experience a sharp drop in contact with busy and overwhelmed custody-retaining parents, leaving children feeling isolated and intensely lonely at the very time they need reassurance and support the most. Many children find themselves for the first time spending long hours in day care or alone after school. Even some rather young children must get themselves off to school and prepare their own meals.

Studies find that in most postseparation homes, established rules and routines fall by the wayside, discipline becomes inconsistent, family meals become infrequent and erratic, and general disorganization prevails. Many children could take these disruptions in stride at another point in their lives. But when so many disruptions coincide with their family's collapse, children's insecurity is compounded. They become more convinced that life is in complete chaos and wonder if it will ever become normal again.

Money also becomes tighter, now that two homes must be maintained, and often becomes a source of conflict between parents. Anxiety over money is easily transmitted to children, whose vigilance alerts them to each new problem in their lives. Things once taken for granted can no longer be afforded. What will the future hold? What plans will no longer be possible? It is not uncommon for families to move and for children to be forced to find a way to cope with losing their home, school, and friends at a time when their lives are already in turmoil.

Each of these changes requires children to adapt anew at a time when many of them are already taxed near the limits of their capacities. However, the worst changes from children's perspectives are the dramatic changes in their mothers and fathers and in their relationships with them.

Will My Old Parents Please Return?

For many children, the parents they come to know after separation do not seem to be the same people they have known all their lives. Many parents' behavior becomes unfamiliar and unpredictable. Bewildered youngsters commonly observe rage, tirades, wide mood swings, lethargy, new pursuits, changed appearances, increased drinking and smoking, and drug use. Some become painfully aware for the first time of their parents' sexuality, as a number of new "friends" share their parents' beds. Some keep a vigilant watch on a parent who they fear may commit suicide.

The rapid and dramatic changes in parents, occurring at the same time that children's lives are in turmoil, are bewildering and frightening to children—younger and older alike. Ordinarily when children are in crisis, they can rely on the security, stability, and support offered by their families—these provide a protective cushion that softens the impact of the crisis. This is what happened with the British children who stayed with their parents throughout the wartime bombings. The children looked to that "reserve account" of theirs—their parents—to help them through the turmoil so they could emerge unscathed.

During the stressful postseparation period, however, a large percentage of parents are so overwhelmed by their own stress, emotions, and new demands for rebuilding their lives that either they do not recognize their children's neediness and distress or they simply do not have the emotional resources to tend to them. In one study, only 10 percent of the children felt that their fathers were in tune with their feelings, and only 15 percent believed their mothers were. Moreover, one-half believed their fathers were *completely* unaware of their distress, while more than one-third believed their mothers to be completely unaware. Studies report that a significant percentage of parents, both those with custody and without, become markedly less available, less supportive, less nurturant, and less sensitive to their children's needs. They communicate with their youngsters less, enjoy them less, and are less affectionate. They are inconsistent in their discipline and provide fewer rules and guidelines. At the same time, parents' stress makes them more negative and volatile with their children.

One woman, who worked long hours while trying to maintain an active social life, tells this story:

> I was too needy myself and too self-involved.... I have a great sadness about the kids and my relationship with them, even though they're nearly grown now. In many ways, they were emotionally neglected. I was under a lot of stress, and they added to it. So they became targets for my outbursts and my anger. That's the worst part of all this, and I wish I could do it over again.[3]

Generally, younger children, who are obviously more needy, tend to receive more attention than do their siblings who are eight or older. But good parenting is disrupted for many a younger child as well.

Whatever children's ages, if they lose their parents' support at this critical time in their lives, they usually feel rejected, abandoned, and profoundly hurt. They lose their most powerful buffer from the severe stress they are experiencing and must face it alone, feeling exposed and vulnerable.

Twenty-nine-year-old Sean, who was 16 when his parents separated, recalls how he felt when both his parents shut down emotionally.

> I was so scared.... I was at a point in my life where I just longed for someone to talk to about life and growing up.... After the divorce, I had no orientation about my life. I felt that everything that went on outside got into my insides. There was nothing between me and the outside world. My parents were gone emotionally, especially my dad, and I never felt safe or protected from that time on. In fact, I still don't and I'm almost thirty.[4]

How Can Anyone Expect Me to Act the Same?

Very often, children's behavior is an expression of their feelings. With their lives in turmoil, is it surprising that children's behavior is affected, at least for a while?

The children of divorce studied by British researcher Yvette Walczak reported, in retrospect, being unhappy, insecure, and apathetic at the time of their parents' divorces. They were no longer able to appreciate or look forward to things they had once enjoyed. They lost their appetites, had difficulty falling asleep, and were restless throughout the night as well. Tears, withdrawal, and bad tempers were common ways to express the misery they felt.

A significant percentage of children have a hard time maintaining friendships and a social life. They become tense, irritable, demanding, and bossy. They smile less and scowl more. They seek attention, pick fights, antagonize people, and drive friends away.

Declining academic performance is another frequent fallout. Children's preoccupation with difficulties at home makes it difficult if not impossible for them to concentrate. Some children report being so distracted that they are unable to make sense of what teachers say. Children's anxiety and restlessness compound their learning difficulties, as does the disruptive behavior that some develop in the classroom.

Many children act out their distress in unmanageable behavior. They are angry, irritable, cranky, unruly, and rebellious. Younger children are more likely to become aggressive, noncompliant, demanding, clinging, or whiny. Older children are more likely to become rebellious about rules and discipline. Some turn to truancy, delinquent activities, or precocious sexual activity.

Parent-Child Relationships Recast

As you might suspect from the foregoing findings, relationships between parents and children usually fall victim to the fallout caused by separation and divorce. In fact, studies find that frequently parent-child relationships after separation bear little resemblance to their preseparation patterns.

Changes in relationships are frequently in the form of increasing distance between parent and child. Sometimes the change is temporary, but sometimes it is permanent, as it was for Kim.

Two years ago Kim basked in the warmth of her parents' attention, feeling loved, protected, and treasured. Unhappy with one another, both parents showered their only daughter with all their time and affection. But once they divorced, Kim's storybook life came to a screeching halt. Her dad embraced his new single life with the same devotion he had once shown his daughter. Her mom, who had not worked since Kim's birth, now juggled a full-time job and classes. Kim went from coming home to a stay-at-home mom and home-baked cookies to spending every afternoon and many evenings alone, with a neighbor looking in on her. Now, two years later, Kim's parents' lives have changed for the better, but Kim is still a very lonely child. Her dad has remarried and has a new stepfamily. She sees him alternate weekends, which generally means four days each month. They have never regained the closeness they once had. Usually he and her stepmother take her someplace with her stepsiblings. "It's okay, I guess," she says sadly when asked about her relationship with her father. "It's just that I wish I could spend more time with him, and I wish we could spend some time alone so we could talk. It feels like he just lets me tag along when he takes his *real* family places." When asked about her mother, Kim reports in a flat voice, "Mom has a job she likes and lots of new friends. She always talks about how close we are. I guess we are. She tells me all about her friends and dates and all the things she does. But she's pretty busy with her life and I'm more like someone on the outside looking in than a real part of it. I guess we're more like roommates than a family."

Many parents and children find themselves in a vicious cycle that strains their relationship beyond limits. Anxious, angry children often become increasingly demanding and defiant. Their emotionally overwhelmed and fatigued parents are generally unresponsive to their children's outbursts to a point, but once parents' limits are reached, they respond with yelling and nagging and by becoming less nurturing. But such reactions make children even more anxious, angry, and doubtful of their parents' love. And so the cycle begins anew.

University of Michigan research, studying the perceptions of custody-retaining mothers and their children, found that mothers do not understand that their children's angry outbursts stem from the stress of the divorce. Neither do they understand that what children need is understanding. Instead, mothers misinterpret their children's outbursts as a series of isolated incidents that require disciplining. At the same time, children do not recognize their mothers' fatigue but misinterpret it as disinterest or anger, which of course fuels youngsters' feelings of hurt and isolation. The University of Michigan study found that mothers who reported feeling the most overwhelmed typically had children who felt unloved and angry at their mothers' perceived "indifference."

There are other ways in which parent-child relationships are recast after separation. Some overwhelmed parents draft their children as stand-ins, assigning them excessive responsibility for their years—for housework, cooking, and the care of younger siblings. Some parents suddenly become overly protective and possessive of their children. Some become emotionally dependent, clinging to their children for their own emotional survival and treating youngsters as companions and confidants; these children basically parent their parents and frequently become emotionally overburdened themselves.

Not all parent-child relationships change for the worse. Some parents and children develop a very close and healthy relationship after divorce. Leaving the unhappy marriage allows the parent to focus more on the children's needs than was previously possible.

IS IT BETTER TO DIVORCE WHEN CHILDREN ARE ONE AGE VERSUS ANOTHER?

Many parents who are struggling through a bad marriage wonder whether the divorce may be harder for children at one age rather than another. Preschoolers generally have a more difficult time initially than do older children, and some research has found that children under age five are at greater risk for developing long-term problems, as well. In many ways, this makes intuitive sense. After all, preschoolers are more dependent on parents for their care and nurturing and are less able to reach out for support outside their families. Moreover, young children are more likely to fear abandonment, more likely to blame themselves, and, of course, spend more years growing up in a disrupted family. But contrary to intuition, other studies have found that younger children are no more likely to develop long-term problems than are older children. Researchers generally conclude that age is not a critical factor in children's *long-term adjustment*. However, age does affect children's *reaction* to divorce, and it appears that each age group is faced with its own unique set of problems.

Infants and Toddlers

Even infants are affected by divorce because of the upset and tension transmitted by their parents, disruptions in their routines, and lapses in their care due to their parents' distress. It is common for infants to become fretful and have eating and digestive problems.

Toddlers' most common reactions to the stress in the home and sudden disappearance of a parent are irritability and aggressiveness, temper tantrums, and regression to behavior they formerly outgrew.

Preschoolers

Children between the ages of three and five and a half are the youngest children to be studied in any detail and show the most dramatic changes in behavior in response to the family's disruption. Having a poor grasp of what is happening, they are bewildered and frightened. Preschoolers perceive their parents as a single unit; therefore, once one leaves, they become terrified the other will abandon them, too. Routine separations become traumatic. So do bedtimes, because these panic-stricken little ones fear waking up to an empty home. For the same reason, they wake up fretful and crying in the night.

Because of their intellectual stage of development, preschoolers believe the world revolves around them. This explains why they so often believe that the divorce is, in some way, their fault and that the departing parent is rejecting them personally. "My mommy and daddy are getting divorced because I was bad." "My daddy left because I was too noisy." "My mommy left because she didn't love me anymore." Consider the following interchange between a three-year-old and a researcher. The child is obviously confused about his father's absence and believes that, somehow, the confusing events revolve around him.

> Researcher: Will you tell me your story?
> Child: Somebody stole the daddy.
> Researcher: Somebody stole the daddy?
> Child: Yeah, someone took him away.
> Researcher: Why did they do that?
> Child: So the little boy would feel bad. The daddy doesn't love the little boy.
> Researcher: Why doesn't the daddy love the little boy?
> Child: 'Cause he went away.[5]

Preschoolers are overwhelmed with anxiety and express it in ways most parents find aversive: irritability, clinging, whining, increased aggressiveness, and temper tantrums. Due to their insecurity, these youngsters also generally lose their most recently acquired skills and regress to earlier behavior. A return to security blankets, thumb sucking, masturbation, and lapses in toilet training are common. Regressions to younger behavior are transient and generally last from a few weeks to a few months.

Interestingly, in her 10-year follow-up of the California Children of Divorce Study, Judith Wallerstein was surprised to find this youngest group seemingly the best adjusted a decade after the divorce, despite their greater vulnerability at the time of separation. These youngest children tended to receive better care and more love throughout the years following divorce than did their older siblings. Wallerstein felt this was the critical factor in their better long-term adjustment. In her 25-year follow-up, Wallerstein's interviews with this youngest group were again notable. What they vividly remembered was the abrupt loss of feeling nurtured and protected that accompanied the separation, and they said it continued throughout their childhoods. Wallerstein believed that this sense of diminished nurturing and protection was their legacy as children of divorce.

Six-to-Eight-Year-Old Children

Generally, children at this age, particularly boys, are the most openly grief-stricken, feel the most loss and despair, and yearn the most intensely for their absent parent. Six-to-eight-year-old children believe their intact family is vital to their survival. This perception is epitomized by one panic-stricken six-year-old in the California Children of Divorce Study who sobbed inconsolably, "I don't have a daddy! I'll need a daddy!" Their despair is so deep that they can't concentrate in school or relate to playmates. In fact, they can't seem to find any way to distract themselves from their grief.

These youngsters also are very susceptible to feelings of abandonment and rejection and worry they will be replaced ("Will my daddy get a new little girl?"). They also have a very rough time with parental conflict; they so desperately want to be loyal to *both* parents that they feel they are literally being pulled apart. Those who experience anger usually express it indirectly rather than directing it at their parents; they may clobber their peers or refuse to do homework, go to bed, or do routine chores.

Nine-to-Twelve-Year-Old Children

The 9-to-12-year-old's distress is frequently expressed in physical complaints, such as headaches and stomachaches. Many immerse themselves in vigorous activity that helps offset their feelings of powerlessness. A shaken sense of identity and of right and wrong plague them. At this age they are already grappling with these issues, and children usually rely heavily on their parents' identity and values in defining their own.

The most distinguishing reaction for a significant percentage of 9-to-12-year-olds is to direct intense anger at one or both parents, usually whomever they blame for the divorce. Children at this age reason that parents could reconcile their differences if they tried hard enough and bitterly accuse their parents of selfishness and indifference to their children's needs.

Some children at this age are easily swept into a bitter and open alliance with one parent (usually the one who was hurt) against the other. Generally these alignments are short-lived. When they continue, they are often fueled by a very angry parent who is making poor progress toward closing the door on the divorce. Their youngsters often end up feeling guilt, anguish, and regret over their behavior. Many ultimately resent the parent with whom they aligned themselves for using them as weapons to hurt the other parent.

Adolescents

Many parents are surprised at how deeply their teens are affected by divorce. Adolescents tend to react with a deep sense of loss, grief, anger, feelings of emptiness, difficulty concentrating, and chronic fatigue—even many who shrug off the divorce as inconsequential. Teens also become acutely concerned about their own futures. Does their parents' divorce forecast a similar fate for their own future relationships?

Some researchers identify adolescence as a particularly vulnerable time for children to experience family disruption. You may wonder why, since teens are already becoming independent of their parents anyway. The answer lies in the way adolescents move away from their families and achieve independence. Progress toward independence does not follow a steady course. Teens take several steps forward and then a step backward; they move toward independence and then temporarily move back to the security of the family to refuel and regroup. The family is their safe haven to which they can retreat. If homes are disorganized, parents make themselves less available, and structure and supervision fall by the wayside, adolescents lose their safe haven and feel as if they have been set adrift or pushed out into the world before they are ready.

Adolescents who are ready to be launched ahead in their development can cope well with divorce. Some even thrive and become mature, insightful, and empathetic. They assume additional family responsibilities while achieving a good balance in their own lives. But when teens are not ready to be thrust ahead, their development can get derailed in one of several ways. Many abandon friends, interests, and adolescent activities. Some regress to younger ways of behaving. Some become far older than their years and assume the role of family protector at the expense of their own needs and lives. Others take another path, which is the most alarming. They express their distress, anger, and internal conflicts in potentially dangerous ways not available to younger children: alcohol, drugs, delinquent activities, or precocious sexual activity—this last is more prevalent in girls. What makes a teen take this potentially dangerous path? Usually it is some combination of several circumstances, including lax supervision and rules, poor parenting, anger, poorly developed internal controls, poor coping skills, loss of their safe haven, and exposure to parents' sexual behavior. Some studies have reported that adolescents from divorced families are two to three times more likely to engage in serious delinquent activities. Sometimes these problem behaviors are transient, but they can become long-term problems if the postdivorce environment is a poor one.

> Holly's parents divorced three years ago when she was 13. Deserted by her father and ignored by her mother, who had an active social and sexual life, Holly turned to the liquor cabinet at age 14. Drinking allowed her to bury her feelings, she confided. "It was the only way to make the pain go away." At about the same time, she became sexually active. Feeling abandoned and alone, she thought that sex might be a way to have someone of her own who would care. "But I just seem to go from guy to guy," she admits. "I think I'd rather reject them before they reject me like my parents did."

In the 25-year follow-up of her study group, Judith Wallerstein reported that the incidence of drug and alcohol abuse, which started in early adolescence to midadolescence, usually subsided by the time her study group reached their early-to-mid-20s and ran its course by the end of their 20s.

Many adolescents cope with their parents' divorces by distancing themselves from the crisis at home and looking for support on the outside—from peers, parents of friends, teachers, and so forth. Unless this outside support is detrimental (for example, troubled or delinquent peers), this distancing usually helps teens cope successfully with the divorce, and most become reinvolved with the family once the turmoil subsides.

HOW LONG ARE CHILDREN LIKELY TO EXPERIENCE PROBLEMS?

Frequently the duration of children's transient problems roughly coincides with the duration of acute turmoil and disruption in the family. Youngsters' problems fade as parents begin to regain their own emotional equilibrium and are able to provide more nurturance and support, as parental conflict subsides, as parenting arrangements become stabilized, and as new routines, rules, and discipline become established. A substantial number of families regain their equilibrium enough to at least get children back on the right track sometime within the first year after separation; very young children tend to take longer.

However, the prognosis is not rosy for all children. When Judith Wallerstein and Joan Kelly reassessed their study group 18 months following separation, they were shocked to find that 25 percent of the children (all ages) still had symptoms that had developed in response to the divorce, such as depression, withdrawal, acute anxiety, poor self-esteem, poor school performance, sexual promiscuity, and delinquent behavior. The researchers were even more surprised to learn that many children had *worse* problems at this point than they had had early after the separation. Would these problems gradually fade? Or would they become long-term problems?

Three and a half years later (five years after the parents separated), Wallerstein and Kelly assessed their study group once again. Thirty-seven percent of the children were now functioning poorly, many of whom had been functioning adequately when previously assessed. In fact, one-third of the children who had been functioning *very well* were now doing poorly. Common problems for these poorly functioning children were moderate to severe depression, acute unhappiness, poor learning, intense anger, sexual promiscuity, and delinquent behavior such as drug abuse, alcoholism, and petty stealing.

Based on *many* studies, most experts now agree that *the majority* of children do adjust successfully to their parents' divorce, but a statistically significant minority develop long-term problems. It has become clear that children's divorce adjustment is affected not only by what happens at the time of the divorce but also by what takes place in the years following divorce. For some families, divorce sets in motion a chain of events that results in the family becoming stalled in a chronic state of stress, instability, and turmoil. Children whose relationships with parents are close, nurturing, supportive, and dependable are buffered from many (though not all) of the blows inflicted by chronic stress, just as the British children were buffered during the wartime bombings. But a sizable minority of parents and children never achieve this kind of relationship after divorce, robbing children of this powerful buffer.

"SHOULD WE STAY TOGETHER FOR THE CHILDREN'S SAKE?"

About now you may be wondering, "Should we stay together for the children's sake?" Research suggests that the majority of divorcing men and women have thoughts of reconciliation at one time or another. In one study, 23 percent of the study group actually withdrew their divorce petition and reconciled. Some couples go through a number of separations and reconciliations, and some remain separated for an extended period before filing for divorce. Whether they should stay together for the children's sake is a question that plagues many parents.

What is the answer to this often asked question? The following well-established research findings will be enlightening:

- At least some of the problems often found in children from divorced families, and usually attributed to the divorce, can be identified in the children several years *prior* to the divorce, probably due to the conflict and turmoil in the family.
- Children's adjustment improves with divorce *if* the divorce ends the conflict.
- Children from conflict-free divorced families are usually *better* adjusted than children from conflict-ridden intact families.
- Continued parental conflict is more damaging to children who have gone through divorce than for children who remain in intact families.

These compelling findings have led researchers and mental health professionals to conclude that divorce provides a better environment for children when their alternative is living in a conflict-ridden intact family, *providing the conflict ends* and the postdivorce family does not become stalled in a chronic state of turmoil and instability.

After reading this chapter, you are probably better able to understand divorce from a child's perspective and why divorce *can* have very negative repercussions for children. For children, divorce casts its shadow for a large fraction of their young lives. Unlike their parents, who have a lifetime of experience to fall back on, children have no map or experience to lead them out of this mire. And unlike their parents who made the decision, they have no vision of a better life because of the divorce. Indeed, many children never *do* experience a better life after divorce, and for some, divorce is a turning point that thrusts their lives in a downward spiral.

At this point, you probably feel that you have been bombarded with a confusing array of information. What do you do with it? How do you use it so your child will be among those who successfully adjust, in both the short and long terms?

The following chapters will directly address these issues and provide you with very concrete guidance. Chapter 7 identifies the *specific* conditions found to be critical to children's long-term divorce adjustment. Chapter 8 focuses on one of these critical conditions, conflict, because it is the number one predictor of children's poor adjustment. Chapter 9 is a step-by-step guide to show you *how* to engineer each of these critical conditions so your children can thrive. If you follow this guide, you will create an environment that will allow your children to bounce back from divorce rather than become its casualties.

7

Critical Ingredients
for Children's Adjustment

All divorced parents worry about the repercussions the divorce may have on their children. The good news is the majority of children bounce back from divorce. Some even become stronger because of it.

But there is disconcerting news as well. The negative repercussions of divorce continue to affect a significant minority of children throughout their childhoods. Divorce places children at greater risk for developing emotional problems, long-term behavioral problems, academic difficulties, and problems with heterosexual relationships during adolescence and young adulthood.

Interestingly, how well or poorly children adjust at the time of the divorce does not necessarily forecast their *long-term* adjustment. In the groundbreaking California Children of Divorce Study, about one-third of the children who adjusted well at first developed problems later. Some youngsters who had serious initial difficulties showed marked improvement over time. Of the children who were doing moderately well initially, some were doing very well and others very poorly five years later.

Why do some children bounce back while others seem to be set on a course of long-term problems? Why isn't children's adjustment consistent? Why do some children start out doing well but subsequently do poorly? You may wonder how much children's eventual adjustment is determined by their emotional adjustment before the divorce or by some inner qualities, such as their temperament or resourcefulness.

Such factors certainly play a role. However, studies find they are only part of the picture.

We now know that youngsters' *long-term* divorce adjustment is influenced not only by their inner strength, by how well parents prepare them, and by how well they cope in the early postdivorce months, but also by the circumstances they encounter in the years *following* divorce. We've learned that the long-term problems children sometimes develop are not caused by the divorce *itself* but by events set in motion by the family disruption. Researchers have identified a number of conditions following divorce that prove to be so critical for children that they may overshadow circumstances at the time of divorce or immediately thereafter.

You and your children can now benefit from this research. With it, you can engineer these critical conditions to be favorable for your children. The quicker you can create these conditions for your children the better, and Chapter 9 provides you step-by-step help to do this. All these critical ingredients will not be in your control, so you will not be able to create completely favorable circumstances for your children. However, you can compensate by working harder at those you can control.

PARENTS' PROLONGED CONFLICT VERSUS COOPERATION

Perhaps one of the most startling discoveries of divorce research is the devastating repercussions that *prolonged* parental conflict can have on children. Most children can cope well with short-term conflict between their parents. However, children who are exposed to chronic strife are more likely to be emotionally troubled children with problems such as depression, withdrawal, poor self-esteem, poor grades, aggressiveness, rebelliousness, and delinquency. Moreover, the negative effects of long-term parental conflict often continue into adulthood.

Research findings on the effects of prolonged conflict are so damning that there is now wide agreement that it is preferable for children to live in a conflict-free single-parent home than in a conflict-ridden two-parent home.

Unfortunately for many children, their parents' conflict does not end with the divorce. For a substantial minority of divorced parents, conflict becomes a way of life, and their children live with intense parental bitterness throughout much of their childhoods. Escaping from parental conflict is one of the few benefits children can derive from their family's rupture. When the battles go on and on, children are dealt a double whammy from which many do not recover.

Parents' verbal and physical battles are not the only conflict children experience after divorce. Some children must find a way to exist on both sides of a cold war, shuttling back and forth between hostile, distrustful parents who refuse to communicate about their child's well-being. Many children feel caught in the middle and torn in two by conflicting loyalties. Parents pump them for information about the other parent, ask them to carry messages between the two warring homes, pressure them into an alignment with one parent against the other, or badmouth the other parent. Feeling caught in the middle like this can be *more* destructive to children's well-being than witnessing parents' open fighting. Children caught in the middle feel guilty and torn no matter what they do. Any move toward one parent is a move away from the other. And if they try to remain neutral, both parents are hurt! It's a lose-lose situation.

Children have graphically compared their parents' conflict to a spider's web that ensnares them. They have compared themselves to a tug-of-war rope being yanked at both ends. Many wish they could cut themselves in half so both parents can have their "fair" share.

Prolonged conflict is the number one predictor of children's poor adjustment after divorce. It is so critical that I have devoted the following chapter to it alone.

On the other side of the coin is parents' cooperation, and it is children of cooperative parents who fare the best after divorce. Parents who cooperate create a wide safety net for children, enabling them to adjust better not only to the divorce but to their parents' remarriages. In fact, everyone wins when parents work together as parents after divorce: Parents report being happier and more satisfied in their new lives, and they are found to have better relationships with their children as well. Chapter 18, "Making Co-Parenting Work," guides you in developing a workable co-parenting relationship with the other parent.

CHILDREN'S RELATIONSHIPS WITH *BOTH* PARENTS

Studies find that parent-child relationships often begin to deteriorate during the failing marriage and become even more troubled after separation because parents are so consumed by their own crises. These deteriorating relationships are a blow to children because their relationships with parents play a key role in how successfully they adjust to divorce.

When children have close, supportive, and reliable relationships with both parents, they have most of the emotional benefits of an intact family. But even more important, close relationships with parents play a powerful role in buffering children from stress. You can think of these relationships as a protective umbrella that shelters children from much of the fallout caused by stress. Children who have a poor relationship with one or both parents are more vulnerable.

Children reap a long list of other benefits when they have good relationships with both their divorced parents. These fortunate youngsters do not have to wrestle with feeling unloved and unlovable. They do not need to fear abandonment by a parent—an issue with which many children of divorce struggle. They are more likely to be supported financially by both parents and, therefore, to be shielded from the sudden severe financial hardships experienced by so many children after divorce. They can also draw from the psychological resources and guidance of both parents.

Each Parent's Unique Contributions

A relationship with two parents is not just "more of the same" as a relationship with one parent. Traditionally, much has been written about mothers' contributions to children's lives. It may interest you to know how fathers uniquely contribute to children's development. Studies find that children who have good relationships with warm, supportive fathers tend to be less anxious and fearful, more highly motivated, and more successful in school. They are also found to have a better sense of humor, to have more self-control, and to get along better with peers.

Furthermore, sons look to their fathers to provide a prototype of male behavior and help them develop a stable and valued sense of their own masculinity.

Girls also need their dads. Girls from divorced homes are found to be more vulnerable to problems with heterosexual relationships as teens and young adults, including inappropriate attention-seeking behavior toward the opposite sex, drifting from one relationship to another, early marriage, and divorce. Girls who are most vulnerable appear to be girls who have had little contact with their fathers over an extended period. Interaction with an attentive and loving father, particularly during adolescence, can be very important to a girl, giving her confidence in relating to men and a sense that she can be valued as a female. Both will put her in good stead in her future dating, courtship, and marital relationships.

Relationships with Resident versus Nonresident Parents

A good relationship with the parent who has primary custody is found to be particularly critical to children because of the amount of time they spend with this parent. This relationship is a key to good adjustment for children of *all* ages, and it is *vital* for younger children. A close relationship with a resident parent who is nurturing, supportive, and dependable can be *particularly* effective in buffering children from the stress of divorce and can help compensate for an indifferent nonresident parent.

You may hear or read in the popular press that children's relationship with the nonresident parent is unrelated to their adjustment after divorce. Don't be misled! A good relationship with the parent without custody, *particularly* when that parent is warm, nurturing, and has good parenting skills, is found to be positively related to children's well-being. And several studies have reported that the benefits of a good relationship with an involved and caring nonresident father continue to have a positive impact right into adulthood.

However, research findings about the role of the noncustody parent have been inconsistent. Why? Because the importance of a good relationship with this parent has sometimes been *masked* in studies. There appear to be two reasons for this. One is the way some studies have measured the relationship: by *frequency* of contact rather than *quality* of contact. Although the two may be related, they are far from the same. There are many parents who have frequent contact with their children but who are not responsive to their needs, cannot communicate with them, and are not in touch with their feelings, concerns, and interests. A good relationship requires more than frequent contact!

The second reason the importance of this relationship is sometimes masked is that old bugaboo, *conflict*. Children who have a good relationship with their nonresident parent usually see that parent more frequently, which usually means parents also have more contact. Unfortunately, increased contact often means increased conflict. Conflict creates so many problems for children that it markedly detracts from the benefits children would ordinarily derive from their noncustody parents' involvement in their lives. Sometimes, it completely overshadows these benefits!

Unfortunately, the relationship between children and their nonresident parent is a fragile one after divorce. Keeping involved in children's lives is often easier said than done (see Chapter 15). Studies find that a significant percentage of noncustody parents who fade out of children's lives do so out of frustration, feeling they have become such peripheral players in their children's lives that they are inconsequential. Although many parents are depressed and feel a sense of loss after dropping out of their children's lives, the children are the real losers. A parent's abandonment is a trauma from which many of them do not easily recover. The California Children of Divorce Study dramatically demonstrated the plight of children whose noncustody fathers were indifferent. Even after five years, many still felt anguished, rejected, and depressed. They felt both unloved and unlovable, and they had low self-esteem. Some children are troubled with feelings of loss, rejection, and abandonment throughout their childhoods. Some are angered over a parent's abandonment and act out their anger in behavior problems such as noncompliance, aggressiveness, rebelliousness, or drug use.

THE QUALITY OF PARENTING AND STABILITY IN THE PRIMARY HOME OR HOMES

Studies find that children are likely to be parented poorly during the first year after separation and often for longer. Children tend to receive less attention, less affection, less support, less supervision, and erratic discipline—much of which is punitive. Most postdivorce homes are in a state of chaos; communication is poor, and children frequently find themselves the target of their parents' angry outbursts. Children who are already overwhelmed by their family's rupture feel devastated by the lack of support they receive just at the time they need it the most. Many other children find themselves thrust in the role of miniature adults, trying to shore up their emotionally fragile parents when the youngsters themselves feel as if they are sinking in quicksand.

Children can't get back on their feet while they are being parented erratically, their home lives are in turmoil, and the future is precarious. They anxiously look to their resident parent to see if he or she will be able to take control of the crisis and chaos that have taken over their lives. When it appears that their parent has little control over day-to-day life,

---

KEY ELEMENTS OF GOOD PARENTING
IN DIVORCED HOMES

1. Children are shown *warmth, nurturance,* and *respect.*
2. Parent encourages *open communication.*
3. Parent is *supportive* and *responsive* to children's needs.
4. Parent provides *clear expectations, limits* and *rules.*
5. Parent *monitors* children's behavior and consistently follows through with *positive discipline.*
6. Children are provided with consistent and predictable *routines.*
7. Children can function as children; they aren't burdened with adult worries and responsibilities.

---

children's anxiety and distress escalate further. A resident parent's poor adjustment is usually a good predictor of children's poor adjustment.

The quicker the parent with custody begins to get his or her own life together, creates some stability in the home, and provides good parenting, the quicker children are able to get back on track and resume the course of normal childhood development. When parents share physical custody, both play critical roles because of the amount of time children spend with each. Chapters 9 and 14 will help you create stability in your home and develop good parenting practices. Chapters 10 and 11 will help you get your own life together.

Just what is "good parenting," you ask? Researchers have been able to identify key elements, which appear in the accompanying table. These parenting practices help children adjust better both to the immediate crisis of divorce and to life in a one-parent home. You can learn how to implement these key elements in Chapter 9.

The parenting practices of parents without custody can also contribute to children's adjustment and development. In a sophisticated statistical analysis of 63 studies of nonresident fathers, Penn State researcher Paul Amato and his colleague Joan Gilbreth discovered that noncustody parents' use of an *authoritative parenting style* was strongly related to children's good adjustment and academic success. An authoritative parenting style incorporates numbers 1 through 5 in the table above.

AMOUNT OF ADDITIONAL STRESS
IN CHILDREN'S LIVES

The amount of stress children encounter during the years following divorce is the fourth major contributor to their long-term divorce adjustment. Virtually all children find their parents' divorces highly stressful, but groundbreaking research in the field of stress has demonstrated that children can usually deal with a *single* source of stress, such as their parents' divorce, quite well. However, if the divorce is accompanied by other major sources of stress, the risk of long-term problems *multiplies.* Each additional source compounds youngsters' already-difficult task of reconstructing their lives. The cumulative effect of stress can be compared to a person receiving a second punch while still dazed and weakened from the first. Although the second punch may not have been very hard, it makes his recovery more difficult. If a third punch immediately follows, it may very well do him in. After all, how much can he take?

What would be considered additional major sources of stress? Several have already been discussed: parental conflict, poor parent-child relationships, and poor parenting. When experienced for prolonged periods, each compounds the stress children already feel from the divorce itself. There are two other major sources of stress that are found to have an impact on children's adjustment.

Numerous Other Changes in Children's Lives

A series of studies conducted at Virginia Commonwealth University found that the more changes children experience while they are trying to cope with the divorce, the more likely they are to develop problems such as depression, social withdrawal, low self-esteem, and aggressiveness. The more changes with which children must cope—weakened relationships with parents, disruptions in parenting and routines, a move, a new neighborhood, a new school, a loss of friends, parents' new significant others—while they are trying to cope with the divorce itself, the more likely they are to feel that their world is out of control. An exception appears to be changes that significantly improve the child's or family's situation.

Some children in divorced families are subjected to multiple disruptions to their lives *throughout their childhood years:* new adults moving in and out of the home, multiple divorces, new stepfamilies, outright abandonment or rejection by a parent, or multiple moves involving changes in school, friends, community, and further separations from the parent left behind. A chaotic home life may accompany each subsequent change, as might an overwhelmed parent and poor supervision.

Some children do not have the opportunity to regain their equilibrium from one stressful life event before being bombarded with another. They are in a chronic state of stress, and the continuous demands made upon them to adapt and readapt far exceed their capacity. Even highly resilient children with startling psychological strength can stand only so much stress and adversity before their resources are overtaxed. Dr. Neil Kalter, of the Department of Psychology and Psychiatry at the University of Michigan, suggests that the conditions some children experience during the years after divorce are like multiple land mines to be encountered along the path to adulthood.

Dramatic Drops in Standard of Living

Studies uniformly find that the economic circumstances of mothers and children typically decline markedly after divorce, while those of fathers usually decline only slightly or even improve. That there is a disparity is clear; the magnitude of the disparity is less clear. In a 1999 study, Suzanne Bianchi and her colleagues from the University of Maryland reported that during the year following divorce, the average total income for women was 75 percent of their former husbands'. When needs were taken into account, such as children living in the home, it was estimated that mothers' total income averaged 56 percent of their former husbands'. Only one-fifth of the mothers saw their standard of living improve compared with two-thirds of the fathers.

One reason for the disparity is the gender gap typically found between men's and women's salaries. Another is that divorcing women who return to full-time employment after a hiatus often must start out in low-paying jobs. If child support is not paid, the economic plight of mothers and children can be chilling. It is no wonder that payment of child support is found to be positively related to children's well-being.

With divorce, some children suddenly find themselves living in low-cost housing, attending inferior schools, and having a very different peer group than they formerly had. Some live under a cloud of anxiety about their daily financial survival. For many children, windows of opportunity that were formerly open are suddenly shut. Even many who are able to remain in their middle-class neighborhoods *perceive* their economic situation as tenuous due to the marked discrepancy between their pre- and postdivorce standard of living, made more evident by the relative affluence of their peers.

Although children's standard of living typically drops after divorce, the lower standard of living per se is not the culprit in some children's poor adjustment. Rather, it is the pressure and stress it causes the family and the resultant ripple effects, such as when parents are so focused on making ends meet that their parenting and relationships with children are disrupted. Close, loving relationships between the resident

---

CHECKLIST FOR GUIDING CHILDREN'S LONG-TERM DIVORCE ADJUSTMENT

✓ Are our children exposed to any of our conflict?
✓ Do I refrain from putting my children in the middle? From—
  • Bad-mouthing my children's other parent?
  • Enlisting my children to be message carriers?
  • Pumping them for information about their other parent?
  • Pressuring them to side with me, even subtly?
✓ Am I building a *good* relationship with my children?
✓ Do I support my children's relationship with the other parent?
✓ Am I returning stability to our home and following routines?
✓ Do my children and I communicate openly?
✓ Am I nurturing and supportive? Do I show them respect?
✓ Am I providing them with clear expectations and limits?
✓ Am I monitoring their behavior?
✓ Am I providing consistent discipline in a loving manner?
✓ Do I avoid burdening them with adult responsibilities, roles, and worries?
✓ Am I keeping their lives as much the same as I can?
✓ Am I making my child support payments to minimize financial problems for my children?
✓ Am I finding other sources of social support for my children?

parent and children can buffer youngsters from a good deal of the stress caused by reduced economic resources. Interestingly, a 1997 Boston University study found that only 3 percent of the children in the sample said having less money was one of the things that made their lives worse after divorce, even though two-thirds of the mothers reported their financial situation had worsened.

SOCIAL SUPPORT

Frequent contact with supportive adults outside the family, such as grandparents, a teacher, parents of friends, a youth leader, a coach, or a therapist, can be an invaluable asset for children when they are under stress. Children need extra doses of time, support, sensitivity, and understanding during the lengthy period of upheaval after separation and divorce. But because parents themselves are distressed and depressed, they are often unable to meet these extra needs. Even after parents are back on their feet, they are sometimes so stressed from single-handedly juggling the mechanics of home, work, children, and a social life that youngsters still don't receive the nurturing they need. Supportive adults outside the immediate family are found to be valuable resources, helping to buffer children from some of the negative effects of the stress in their lives.

TEMPERAMENT AND PREDIVORCE ADJUSTMENT

Early in the chapter, I mentioned that inner qualities contribute to whether a child bounces back from divorce or experiences long-term repercussions. These inner qualities are discussed last because they are givens, rather than conditions that you can engineer to be favorable to your children. But knowing what they are will help you better understand why all children don't respond similarly to what appear to be the same life events.

If you have a child with an easy-going, adaptable temperament or one with a very difficult temperament, it will not surprise you to learn that temperament plays a role in children's divorce adjustment. An easy-going nature cushions the impact of stress for a child. Easy-going children are more likely to roll with the punches. They adapt more readily to change. They focus more on the positives in their worlds.

They are more likely to receive social support because others respond positively to their pleasing natures.

Children with difficult temperaments usually have a much rougher time with divorce. These children feel stress more acutely. Their emotions are more fragile and labile. They find change and uncertainty difficult. Their naturally cranky and demanding natures are exacerbated by the stress, and people tend to respond more negatively to them. It is not difficult to see why they are more likely to be seriously affected by divorce and its repercussions.

Similarly, children who are well adjusted prior to the separation have more resources to cope with the divorce and bounce back from it than do poorly adjusted children who are already stretched thin with few coping skills.

Don't be disheartened if you have a child with a difficult temperament or prior adjustment problems. And don't feel you can "skate" because you have a child with an easy temperament or a history of good adjustment. All children need to be protected from the conflict. Good relationships with both parents are important to all. All children will thrive more readily with a stable home life and good parenting. All will benefit from outside social support. But these critical ingredients will be even more pivotal for children with difficult temperaments or prior adjustment problems, as will minimizing the stress and change in their lives.

Now that you know which postdivorce circumstances are so important for your children's long-term well-being, your job becomes making favorable conditions a reality for them. Chapter 9 is a step-by-step guide to help you create the kinds of conditions that will enable your children to get through the divorce unscathed and thrive afterward. But first, the following chapter is devoted to conflict and its devastating repercussions for children. Living with their parents' conflict is a reality for many children after divorce, and it is the number one predictor of children's poor adjustment.

8

Conflict!
The Number One Predictor
of Children's Poor Adjustment
after Divorce

Children whose parents are locked in conflict have been described as psychological double agents living in a militarized zone, negotiating perilous crossings from one warring camp to another.[1] An analogy has also been drawn between these children and a tiny child who wanders onto a battlefield in which opposing enemy armies, each consumed with tension and animosity, are poised for battle—their weapons drawn. Of those who notice the tiny, innocent child, none want him hurt. But neither do they risk laying down their weapons to save him, fearing the other side will get the upper hand. The battle begins, and the tiny child freezes in terror, trying to protect himself as best he can from the cross fire.[2]

You may wonder whether the above analogies are a bit overdramatic; unfortunately, they are all too apt. Perhaps the most chilling discovery made by divorce researchers concerns the trauma caused children when their parents are in chronic conflict and its devastating impact on their lives. Research findings are so damning that prolonged parental conflict is now considered by most experts to be the number one predictor of children's poor adjustment after divorce.

I hope this chapter helps you understand how your children experience the conflict between you and their other parent, and the long-term impact it is likely to have on them. Chapter 19 shows you how you can protect your children from the conflict and put an end to it.

The period after separation is typically fraught with anger, bitterness, and conflict (See Chapter 5). Many parents are so absorbed in their battles that they are blind to their distraught youngsters, who stand by helplessly watching the two people they love most in the world seemingly try to destroy each other. One study reported that children witnessed more than half of their parents' verbal and physical confrontations and that only 5 percent of parents consistently protected their children from their conflict. Well-known divorce researcher E. Mavis Hetherington and her colleagues found that 66 percent of parents' interactions after separation were fraught with anger and conflict. Among physically abusive couples, physical attacks typically continue even many months after separation.

How long, then, does conflict continue? For the great majority of parents, conflict noticeably subsides, or is at least contained, within the first year or so. However, studies suggest that approximately 25 percent of the divorced population are embroiled in conflict for years, and many of these remain fraught with bitterness and hostility for most of their children's growing up years.

HOW CHILDREN EXPERIENCE CONFLICT

Parents' shouting, pushing and shoving, name-calling, threats, insults, put-downs, and accusations most often play out during exchanges of children from one parent's home to the other. Sometimes they take place when a parent calls to talk to a child, whose phone call is wrecked before it even begins. Sometimes they take place at soccer and Little League games, at music recitals, at school open houses or award ceremonies, and even at graduations—much to the horror of their mortified children.

Children of all ages, even those under a year, become emotionally distressed by their parents' anger and conflict. Children's distress is evident physiologically—in changed heart rate and blood pressure. Their distress is unmistakable in their overt reactions. Children cry, hold their ears, or appear to freeze. Their distress is evident in their faces—if only someone would notice. Children become anxious and apprehensive. They report feeling fearful, helpless, sad, and angry. Some develop stomachaches or headaches. When the conflict is somehow related to them (visitation, child support, parenting disputes), children feel guilt and shame as well. Generally, the more intense the conflict, the more intense are children's reactions. As children get older, they try to avoid their parents' battles if they can; they escape to a bedroom or to a friend's home, or they make themselves scarce in situations that bring parents together. Children never get used to the fighting. In fact, studies show that the more children are exposed to parents' conflict, the more they become *sensitive* to it and the more vulnerable they become.

Children under five are particularly upset, confused, and frightened. Even when they can't understand what the battles are about, they respond to their parents' angry voices and intense emotions. These young children are dependent upon their parents to keep them safe, but it is these very parents who seem to be out of control! Young children emotionally fall apart, crying and clinging. Some two- and three-year-olds literally panic—running aimlessly about or throwing tantrums.

When conflict is chronic, children often try to intervene to stop the fighting. Children as young as one or two years old have been known to try to distract their angry parents by frantically calling, "Mommy, mommy," or "Daddy, daddy." Toddlers also try to comfort a distraught parent. By the time children are five or six, they are increasingly more likely to try to intervene between their battling parents, either directly, such as by yelling at them to stop, or indirectly, by trying to distract them. Children will hit a sibling, hurt a pet, or otherwise create a disturbance to interrupt the fight and divert parents' attention elsewhere. Of course, physical confrontations are even more terrifying to children than are verbal ones. Children commonly fear that arguments may turn physical and worry that either they or a parent may be injured.

THE MANY FACES OF CONFLICT: THE TRAUMA OF BEING CAUGHT IN THE MIDDLE

Although parents tend to be shocked at their toddlers' and preschoolers' attempts to stop their fighting, many parents are only too happy to draw their young school-age children into their conflict, actively soliciting them to take sides.

Young school-age children can grasp a basic understanding of what the arguments are about, and they start to struggle with trying to figure out what is true and what isn't. Their loyalties are unstable and shift from one parent to another because they can only grasp one parent's perspective at a time. So, when parents badmouth one another, these confused young children believe the parent they are listening to at the time and appear to align themselves with that parent.

As children are able to grasp both parents' conflicting views simultaneously, they have no way to reconcile them. If children question parents on these inconsistencies, they risk either angering the parent or being pressured to "see the truth." Children's anxiety escalates. They feel *caught in the middle* and develop painful *loyalty conflicts*. But how to cope with them?

In their groundbreaking study of children with divorced parents in chronic conflict, Janet Johnston and Linda Campbell found that children attempt to cope with these painful loyalty conflicts in a number of ways. Some become obsessed with fairness, insisting that everything must be exactly equal between their two parents. Others guard every word they say for fear that one parent may use it as a weapon against the other. Some keep their lives at each parent's home completely separate, even refusing to talk to one parent while with the other. Others try to please both parents by telling each what he or she wants to hear. Some unfortunate children learn that the only way they can find temporary relief from their loyalty conflicts without alienating a parent is by exaggerating the negatives at each parent's home when talking with the other parent. In their consuming drive to keep their relationship with each parent, children become oblivious to their own needs and feelings.

When children chronically feel caught in the middle, the endless tension becomes unbearable. In a Boston University study of 160 separated or divorced families with 6-to-12-year-old children, Abigail Stewart and her research team found that loyalty conflicts were the *best* predictor of the children's poor adjustment. And a Stanford University study found that feeling caught in the middle was a better predictor of adolescents' poor adjustment than was the actual level of the parents' conflict. Children with loyalty conflicts say they feel as if they are being torn apart. Some wish they could cut themselves in half and give half to each parent. Some say they feel like a rubber band that is about to snap from the persistent yanking. Ten-year-old David told me, "I think the reason I've gotten so tall lately is because they're tugging so much at my heart—one tugs from my head and one tugs from my feet." Some children even say they wish they were dead so the fighting would stop.

Many children with long-term, intense loyalty conflicts eventually form an alliance with one warring parent as a way to relieve their constant tension and anxiety. Alliances are especially common for 9-to-12-year-olds and are usually formed with the parent who shows them the most empathy. With an alliance, the child finally decides which parent to believe—which parent is "right" and which is "wrong." The more protracted and intense the conflict and the more children are exposed to it, the more likely they are to form such an alliance.

Once an alliance is formed, the child's tension and anxiety does diminish, but at a price: Aligned children are found to be angrier, are at risk for emotional problems, and of course, have cut themselves off emotionally, and sometimes physically, from a parent they once loved.

Some alignments are very enduring, but most do not last through the teen years. Older teens are better able to distance themselves from parents and less likely to perceive life in the black and white terms of the right and wrong parent. Many teens come to the realization that they have been exploited by one or both parents in their quest to hurt one another. Some teens will actively seek out a parent whom they formerly rejected. Some will withdraw from both parents.

Battling parents place their children in loyalty conflicts in a number of ways. The following sections present the most common. Please read them carefully to determine whether you are engaging in any of these activities. If you are, you need to stop immediately! It's critical for your child.

Pumping Children for Information

Parents often pump their children for information about the other parent's home, activities, friends, and new significant others. Some parents sit children down and literally grill them. Others fish for information subtly: "So what's your mother's new boyfriend like?" However, except for the very youngest children, the agenda behind this more subtle approach is not lost on children. They are torn between trying to please the parent they are with and feeling disloyal to the other parent. Children constantly feel as if they are walking on eggs. "Will Mom be angry if I tell Dad this? Will Dad be angry if I don't?"

Enlisting Children to be Message Carriers

Parents who don't speak to one another often ask their children to carry messages between their warring homes. "Mom said to tell you I need new shoes and she doesn't have the money." "Dad said to tell you if your boyfriend spanks Johnny again, he'll take you back to court."

"Mom said to tell you if you bring your girlfriend, I can't go." Children who are asked to be message carriers are in a no-win situation. If they deliver the message, they risk incurring the wrath of the parent who receives it. If they don't, they risk incurring the wrath of the parent who sent it. And when they are enlisted to carry a message back to the original parent, both parents are likely to be angry with them.

Thirteen-year-old Jill's distress at being a go-between is evident:

> Whenever my dad is late with the child support check, my mom makes *me* ask him for it. I just hate it! It's so humiliating, and I never know what he'll say. Sometimes he really acts embarrassed and says he just doesn't have it this month. Or sometimes he gets mad and asks me what she does with all the money. If I mention things like the rent, he acts like I'm taking my mom's side, and he gets hurt. Sometimes he starts ranting that she's probably spending it on new boyfriends and wants to know whether she's had anyone over to dinner. What do I say? If I say yes, I feel like a rat to Mom. If I say no, then I lie to Dad. It's bad enough they got a divorce. Why can't they just leave me out of it?

Disparaging the Other Parent

Many children hear from one parent that the other parent is a liar, a slut, conniving, money grubbing, neglectful, an alcoholic, or a host of other disparaging names. Sometimes a parent's extended family also join in the badmouthing. Sometimes badmouthing is done directly to the child. At other times, children overhear it, which is no less destructive.

Disparaging the other parent is one of the most destructive forms of conflict because its consequences for children are twofold. First, it creates serious loyalty conflicts for them. Children feel disloyal to the disparaged parent and feel they should come to his or her defense. But to do so is likely to anger or hurt the parent doing the badmouthing. Children, once again, are in a lose-lose situation, and many feel guilty no matter which course they take. Second, children's self-esteem is whittled away when they hear a parent badmouthed. Why? Children identify closely with their parents and see themselves as composites of each. When children hear negative things about Mom or Dad, they wonder what that says about them. "If my dad is no good, how can I be good?" "If he is so despicable, what does that say about me?" "If my mom is a slut, will I become a slut when I grow up?" "Will I become a liar and a cheat like my parent?"

Asked what she would tell parents who were getting a divorce, seven-year-old Shauna replied:

> I would tell them never to say anything about their kid's mommy or daddy. I try not to listen when my mommy says bad things about my daddy. Sometimes I hold my hands over my ears. But she yells so loud, I hear it anyway. It gets me so confused. I love my daddy! I don't want to hurt him. Sometimes I wonder if the things my mommy says are true. Sometimes I don't even understand what she's saying, but they sound bad. My daddy doesn't seem bad, and I don't think I'm bad. But I don't think my mommy would lie either. I don't know what to think. Tell other parents not to do that!

No matter how bad a parent is, a child needs to know some positive things about him or her. It is okay to let your children know in passing that you are angry or disappointed, but it's not okay to degrade their other parent under any circumstances.

Attempts to Align Children with a Parent

Once children hit school age, many belligerent parents actively attempt to procure a commitment of a child's loyalty. One study reported that a full two-thirds of the study group of divorcing parents exerted demands on their children for allegiance to them and disloyalty to the other parent!

Parents encourage these alignments in a number of ways, some of which are blatant. Some insist that children listen to tales about the other parent's transgressions, sometimes telling a child, "You're old enough to know about this now." Some make comments so the child will question the other parent's love and commitment: "If your father didn't spend so much time with his girlfriend, he might have some time for you." Some entice children to be spies at the other parent's home, asking them to report back about the other parent's activities. Some openly criticize the other's parenting and draw comparisons with their own: "I don't understand why your mother doesn't go to your games and practices like I do. I guess she just isn't interested in what you do." Others pounce on a child's passing complaint about the other parent and escalate it into a catastrophe, such as labeling a swat on the rear as child abuse. Some undermine the other parent by telling children they do not have to do what he or she says. Or some tell a child to call if the other parent does something the child does not like.

Sometimes parents' attempts to align children are more subtle, but they are abundantly clear to a youngster. Some children find that any expression of positive feelings toward one parent is treated by the other as a slap in the face. Any indication of a good time had with one parent is greeted icily by the other. Children learn that to enjoy one relationship is to risk the other.

THE NIGHTMARE OF TRANSITIONS

Children's transitions from one parent to the other can best be described as nightmarish for many children whose embittered parents exchange them directly. At this time all-out warfare is likely because this is the only time that many parents see one another. Some insist on discussing volatile financial or emotional issues. Many can't resist lashing out with stored up digs. Some parents take along new significant others or family members who are entrenched in the conflict, and all too often a free-for-all erupts with name calling, shouting, and shoving. Parents who have not gotten the last word may pursue their former partners, screaming insults out the car window, without regard for the distraught child in the car. Some parents insist on being accompanied by a police officer when exchanging children, which may preserve the peace but frightens the children.

But it is not only when conflict is so blatant that transitions from one home to the other can be nightmares for children. Hostile parents often begin to feel anxious and tense hours and sometimes days prior to an exchange of the children, in anticipation of having to see one another. Their tension is palpable and easily transmitted to children, who begin their own countdown to potential disaster. By the time of the exchange, all parties are so highly charged that children are frequently grabbed roughly by one parent from the other, without opportunity to say a calm good-bye. Many children are denied the comfort of taking along a favorite toy or piece of clothing because one parent bought it and believes the other may not return it. Some children are put through a ritual of completely changing their clothes upon arrival and before leaving the second home because of parents' chronic arguments over who owns what clothes. Although this ritual may provide a solution to battling parents, it robs the child of even the most basic sense of continuity between his disparate lives with each parent.

Although some children with highly contentious parents handle transitions between homes without obvious distress, the majority do not. Some become quiet and withdrawn before and after exchanges. Some develop somatic problems, like stomachaches, headaches, and asthma. Many resist going from one parent to the other: Some cry and cling to the parent they are leaving, while others run away, hide, or protest verbally. Some have nightmares or can't sleep. Others regress to behavior they had outgrown, such as bed-wetting, thumb sucking, and the need to sleep with a parent. Some act out their distress in temper tantrums, irritability, aggressiveness, or defiance.

It is not only the direct exchange between parents that is difficult. It is all the adjusting children must do each time they switch homes. Contentious parents rarely strive for consistency between their homes, and children must adapt to different rules, different schedules, different routines, different expectations, and different discipline with each transition.

Sometimes transition-related problems are short-lived—tapering off soon after the exchange between parents takes place. For other children, it can take hours or even days before they regain their equilibrium and they are back to "normal." For these children, making frequent transitions between their battling parents is particularly harmful because they are always feeling anxious, distressed, and out of kilter.

As you may guess, children's transition-related problems often fuel new conflict between battling parents, as each blames the other for the problems. Many parents with primary custody return to court in an attempt to stop visits because they are "obviously" harmful to the children. Other parents go to court seeking primary custody because they assume something must be going on in the primary home to cause such problems.

CONFLICT'S REPERCUSSIONS FOR CHILDREN

For years now, study after study done in the United States and other countries has documented the powerful impact that prolonged parental conflict has on children of all ages—boys and girls alike. The more protracted and hostile the conflict, the more likely children are to be emotionally troubled and poorly adjusted.

You may be interested to know that children in divorced families are not the only youngsters who suffer from their parents' conflict. Children from *intact* conflict-ridden families are harmed as well.

In fact, it is now widely accepted that children fare better in a conflict-free divorced home than in a conflict-ridden intact home. If divorce ends the conflict, children usually benefit. However, when conflict continues despite the divorce, children's risks for long-term problems multiply. They not only have to deal with the painful conflict, but they must do so without the security of their family and while their lives are falling apart. To make matters worse, conflict after divorce is far more likely to be focused on them, in the form of custody, child support, and parenting disputes, which leads children to blame themselves for the ongoing battles.

Adjustment Problems

Compared with their peers, children whose divorced parents are in chronic conflict are more likely to be impulsive and aggressive. They are more likely to have behavior and delinquency problems; to be anxious, withdrawn, and depressed; and to have lower self-esteem, poorer school grades, and poorer relationships with their peers.

Parents sometimes acknowledge that their sons seem to be affected by their conflict but believe that their daughters are not affected. There is, in fact, no evidence that parental conflict has a greater impact on boys than on girls. However, boys' distress is more evident to the outside world because they are more likely to act it out in aggressive, impulsive, and defiant behavior, while girls are more likely to turn their distress inward and become withdrawn, depressed, and anxious. For this reason, girls from very conflicted divorced families generally present to the outside world as better functioning than do boys. In fact, girls sometimes strike people as being "too good." In reality, studies find that boys and girls seem to suffer equally from their parents' conflict—just in different ways.

Children's Fragile Emotional Security

When parents are in prolonged and intense conflict, day-to-day life can feel very fragile to children. When the very people they expect to keep them safe are out of control, the world can become pretty scary. When their most important role models cannot begin to solve their own problems, are problems hopeless to solve? Without role models to lead the way, how can children learn to deal with their own intense and confusing emotions? When they are struggling just to survive in the family's chaos, how can they develop effective coping skills? And when parents rely on them for emotional support, how can children keep their own meager emotional resources from becoming depleted?

It has long been suspected that chronic and intense parental conflict can threaten children's emotional security. But this is no longer speculation, thanks to an in-depth study, spanning many years, conducted by Drs. Janet Johnston and Vivienne Roseby at the Center for the Family in Transition in Corte Madera, California.

Their study group consisted of school-age children and their divorced parents, who were in very severe and protracted conflict. The conflict was so severe that the researchers estimated the parents to be among the 10 to 15 percent most highly conflicted parents in the divorced population. Thus the study group does not represent *all* children from conflicted families, but the study does shed light on the potentially devastating repercussions children can suffer when conflict is severe and prolonged.

As a group, these children lacked a basic ability to trust themselves, other people, and the world in general. Their perceptions of the world were distorted. Many of them invested a tremendous amount of energy in being hypervigilant—constantly on the alert for danger erupting in their small worlds.

The children sacrificed a lot of themselves to their parents' conflict. Many were so intently focused on the emotional and physical welfare of their needy parents that they had shut down their own emotions. They had difficulty asserting their own needs until their neediness became so overwhelming they exploded in distress. The majority had no strong, or even consistent, sense of who they were. They also lacked spontaneity and flexibility because of their strong needs to feel safe and have a sense of control. Not surprisingly, the majority had a good deal of intense anger, much of it unexpressed.

Although some of these children put on a confident front to their parents and the outside world, testing indicated they secretly felt inadequate, bad, or damaged in some way. They seemed to have a confused sense of their importance: On the one hand, they were the center of the conflict, but on the other, they were completely helpless to do anything about it. In general, the majority did not feel valued or important in relationships.

Other researchers report that children from conflict-ridden homes are more likely than their peers to blame *themselves* when anything negative happens. They are more likely to remember negative events in their lives than positive events. They are also more likely to perceive other people to be unhappy or angry.

Children who witness physical violence between their parents are at particularly high risk. These children are more likely to suffer with feelings of helplessness and hopelessness, fears, anxiety, depression, nightmares, low self-esteem, and anger. They also learn that coercion and violence are acceptable ways to influence people they love.

It is difficult enough for children in today's world to grow up and keep on track so that they become healthy, well-functioning adults. But when children must divert time and emotional energy to deal with their parents' ongoing conflict, their own development and well-being is at serious risk.

SURVIVING THE CONFLICT

Research can serve as a guide. Studies can demonstrate how children, as a group, experience and are affected by conflict. Researchers can point to the hazards for your children. However, research cannot predict how your particular children will be affected. *All* children do not develop *all* the problems cited above. Even when children do develop similar problems, they do not do so to the same degree. While conflict is distressful to all children, it can have a wide range of repercussions. Just as conflict has many faces, its effects are multifaceted.

The more intense, pervasive, open, and chronic the conflict, the greater the risks for children. Children who are exposed to physical violence are at greater risk than those exposed to ongoing verbal battles. Children exposed to ongoing verbal battles are at greater risk than those who live with the tension of their parents' cold war. Children in intense loyalty conflicts are at risk at least as much as children exposed to frequent verbal battles, and probably more so. It may interest you to know that when children witness arguments that end in resolution, they are not negatively affected as they are by the endless battles that are never settled.

Even prolonged and severe conflict, however, is not devastating to *all* children. Some are highly resilient; they can survive the harsh reality of their lives and emerge intact. Children are resilient to varying degrees, just as they are vulnerable to varying degrees. Where does their resiliency and vulnerability come from? Some comes from within, while the remainder stems from life circumstances. Researchers have been able to identify a number of conditions that can mitigate or exacerbate the hazards of conflict for a child.

The first is *temperament*. Children who have easy-going, adaptable temperaments are found to focus more on the positives in their worlds and to react less to the negatives. You may remember from the last chapter that a child's easy-going temperament can help buffer him or her from the stress of parents' divorce. An easy-going temperament can also help buffer a child from the impact of parents' conflict. Unfortunately, the reverse is true for children born with difficult temperaments: These children are far more vulnerable to conflict's emotional fallout.

It probably won't surprise you that *children's prior adjustment* is important. Children who are initially well-adjusted and successful in other areas of their lives, such as school, sports, or social lives, are more likely to survive the conflict because they have more resources to cope with it. Conversely, children who have a history of problems are already stretched thin, and the chronic conflict can be the final blow from which they cannot recover.

Just as prior adjustment is important, so is *prior family functioning*. A child whose family functioned well prior to the divorce is likely to have developed more resources and coping skills to rely upon than a child who has lived for years in a poorly functioning family.

Having *siblings* can also cushion the impact of conflict, particularly if the siblings are older. In fact, often the oldest child in a family takes the brunt of the emotional fallout from parents' conflict. In contrast, only children are found to be particularly vulnerable, perhaps because they are usually the focal point of the battles.

Finally, youngsters who have a strong and healthy *support system outside their immediate family* are likely to fare better than children who are more reliant on their parents for support. A support system provides children a safe haven and strength to bolster their sagging coping resources. Sometimes a child is lucky enough to have grandparents who can support him or her *while maintaining their own neutrality*. Some children have the inner resources to seek support from a willing teacher, coach, neighbor, or the family of a friend. Still others have parents who are savvy enough to put them into counseling. These fortunate children have more than a safe haven: They have someone to advocate for them and teach them coping skills to deal with the conflict. Both parents should be in contact with the therapist so the therapist can help them *both* to better meet their child's needs.

CUSTODY BATTLES: THE MOST DAMAGING OF POSTDIVORCE CONFLICTS

Litigation over custody is commonly referred to as a custody *battle*, and battles they are, with few families prepared for the ensuing trauma. Parents forge ahead, day by day and month by month, mired in the escalating animosity, with little thought other than winning. Each parent plans a battle strategy with his or her attorney, and if one or the other attorney is a highly adversarial one, the situation can get out of hand rapidly.

Each parent tries to amass the greater number of allies among family members, mutual friends, neighbors, and therapists, asking them to write declarations in support of their bid for custody. Parents sometimes try to involve teachers, day care providers, coaches, and doctors. Each side arms itself with a stack of declarations, many of which are likely to be highly inflammatory. All too often every minor shortcoming of the other parent is embellished into a major detriment to the children, and occasional mistakes are presented as if they were routine occurrences. For it is typically part of the battle strategy to make one parent look bad so the other will look better.

When parents are served with this verbal assault, many can barely recognize the person described as him- or herself or the marriage described as the marriage they have lived. They are furious with the other parent and devastated by the betrayal of the former spouse, in-laws, former friends, and occasionally even members of their own family, who for one reason or another have aligned themselves with the other parent. Partly for protection and partly for revenge, that parent retaliates with a new round of escalation. "I wasn't going to say anything about this, but as long as we're going to play dirty..." The battle strategy extends its reach to the other parent's past or to tangential issues that can cast him or her in an unfavorable light, even though they are not germane to either custody or parenting.

This is only the preliminary battle leading up to the court trial. Before the ultimate battle, private investigators may be hired, witnesses are deposed, and new charges and countercharges may be leveled. Attorneys posture and maneuver, so that if a settlement can be negotiated, their client will fare favorably. In many jurisdictions, parents are ordered into mediation to attempt to resolve their differences. There may be one postponement after another, requiring new trial dates to be awaited on crowded court calendars. The waiting is excruciating, and both parents and children live in limbo. Anxieties mount, as does distrust, and parents feel their control over their lives slipping away. Many parents find the courts to be objectionably intrusive, as they may be ordered by the court into counseling, parenting classes, anger management classes, or drug treatment programs, or to undergo psychological evaluation or drug testing. Many parents deplete their financial resources and put themselves and their extended families into long-term debt.

The majority of parents settle somewhere along this long, torturous road. However, the small percentage who make it to the ultimate battle, the trial, suffer the final indignities of having their lives scrutinized, with the most intimate details aired in open court, where anyone can walk in off the street. And when the judge makes a ruling and declares a "winner," bitter parents are left to pick up the pieces of their lives and those of their children. Even more difficult, they must continue to deal with one another in parenting their children, despite all the animosity, bitterness, resentment, and distrust engendered by the custody battle.

Even more depressing, frequently the battle does not end with the judge's ruling. Some parents appeal the decision. Others pounce anytime there is the slightest change of circumstances and petition the court to reconsider the matter in this new light. Meanwhile, embittered parents, made more bitter by the prolonged legal battle, continue their battle outside of court. The parent who "lost" the battle often engages in a campaign of passive aggressive behavior, pushing the other parent's buttons at every opportunity. Parents who supposedly "won" begin to think that they have won the battle only to lose the war. The arguments continue over every minor issue related to their children—clothes, haircuts, hygiene, nutrition, television, homework, bedtimes, exchange times, discipline, friends—the list is endless.

The Children

After reading this chapter, you don't need to ask how children survive a custody battle and its aftermath. Children are typically drawn into the battle in all the usual ways, now familiar to you. But many are drawn in far more directly. Some parents keep children apprised of the court action, showing them court papers and letting them read inflammatory declarations. Some children are even asked to talk to a parent's attorney or to write a letter to the judge. Angry parents bring the battle to the child's world outside the family—badmouthing the other parent and sharing slanted information with teachers, coaches, day care providers, and other parents. Many parents do not watch what they say in front of their children, so even if a parent does not directly involve the children in court issues, many youngsters become very knowledgeable about them.

The immediate and long-term repercussions for children who experience prolonged custody battles were documented by research conducted at the Child and Family Divorce Counseling Service at Children's Hospital of San Francisco by Drs. Janet Johnston and Linda Campbell. During the course of the lengthy custody battles, the children in the study generally presented as sweet, docile, eager to please, and highly controlled. Absent were the acting-out, aggressive, defiant behaviors so characteristic of children from high-conflict homes. Why? The researchers believed it was because these children dared not express any aggression, emotion, or even preference that may be unacceptable to one parent or the other because they feared being abandoned. Two to three years after the custody battle, these children looked very different. They were two to four times more likely to be seriously disturbed, both emotionally and behaviorally, than were their peers! Depression, withdrawal, aggressiveness, and other behavior problems—all at a serious level—were common. Researchers speculated that once the protracted court battle was over, the children felt safer to express their distress.

The Parents

It is ironic, the San Francisco researchers commented, that under the guise of fighting for their children, parents can inflict so much suffering on them. Some custody battles cannot be avoided, but it appears that most *prolonged* custody battles are less about the *children's* needs than they are about one or both *parents'* needs. Since litigious parents typically have a pervasive distrust of one another, it is easy for their animosity to be couched in terms of the children's needs.

This may strike you as an outrageous claim. However, in their study at Children's Hospital in San Francisco, Drs. Johnston and Campbell found a number of commonalities in families engaged in prolonged custody conflicts. Generally families were characterized by at least two of the commonalities they identified.

For many of these parents, the conflict was a continuation of years of marital conflict. Very little changed for them with the divorce, other than the forum for the conflict.

A large proportion of the litigious parents were psychologically fragile and unable to deal with the loss, sadness, feelings of helplessness, and plummeting self-esteem that go hand in hand with divorce. The only way they found to cope was by masking their grief with anger. As long as they could remain focused on their fierce anger, they did not have to deal with their pain and they felt empowered. By taking matters to court and being oppositional, they could regain a sense of control and ward off their feelings of helplessness. By obtaining a custody award, they could be publicly acknowledged as the better parent—a boost to their sagging self-esteem. For a minority, the custody battle was a retaliatory maneuver to punish the other parent.

For other families, the primary instigator of the prolonged legal battle was a very unexpected and traumatic separation. These traumatic separations often had startling repercussions that not only gave birth to the conflict but infused it with a life of its own (see Chapter 10, "Your Emotional Divorce").

Finally, the researchers found that many of the litigious parents had outside support systems—people who were embroiled in the conflict, who embellished a parent's distorted perceptions, and who added fuel to the fire.

The more prolonged the battle and the more parents repeatedly return to court, the more likely it is that the agenda of one or both parents is something other than the children.

Better Alternatives

Although parents believe that they are battling in court for the best interests of their children, the adversarial court system is the worst place to determine children's futures. If your children's needs are your legitimate agenda and you cannot agree on custody, there are better alternatives than a court battle.

The notion of "custody" is an unfortunate one. We use the term when we talk about prisoners and property that we own. Rather than getting hung up on the issue of who will *get* the children, think of the custody issue from a different perspective: "When will the children be with each of us so we can each continue to parent them in a meaningful way?" That, after all, is what children need for their emotional well-being.

Following are three alternatives to a court battle to determine future parenting arrangements. With each successive option, you will receive a greater amount of help.

The first option is to seek the help of a family mediator with expertise in custody and child development issues who can help you sort out different parenting options in a safe environment. You and your former spouse, as the children's parents who know them best, will be the sole deciders of future parenting arrangements. Any concerns you may have about the other parent's home or parenting skills can be discussed and solutions sought. Mediation is discussed in Chapter 2.

A second alternative is to seek the help of a mental health professional with expertise in child custody matters who can help you *assess* your children's specific needs and *guide* you in how to best meet those needs. You might try different parenting schedules to see how they "fit" the family, evaluating them along the way with the counselor. The counselor can also help shore up a parent's parenting skills and recommend resources for additional help. Keeping the mental health professional on board for an extended period is likely to help everyone through the adjustment period.

The third alternative is appropriate for the most contentious parents who are entrenched in their own positions and unlikely to reach any agreement, even with help. This is a *psychological* or *custody evaluation* by a mental health professional who has court-recognized expertise in child custody matters. An evaluation may consist of psychological testing, interviews, observations of you and your children, home visits, and contacts with people who can provide additional information. The evaluator will come to know both you and the other parent, your strengths and weaknesses as parents, your children's needs and attachments, and the family dynamics. Based on that data, he or she will make an informed recommendation about the specific parenting arrangements that would best meet your children's needs. At times, parents use the evaluator's recommendations as a starting point from which to negotiate their own, somewhat different, parenting arrangements. Although evaluations can be costly, they are far less so than custody battles, they avoid the animosity created by the adversarial system, and they offer solutions that are tailor made for your family—benefits that can't be measured in dollars.

Remember, some conflict during the first year or so after separation or divorce can be expected. But if you take steps now to control it, it is less likely to get out of hand. And if you protect your children from it, they are less likely to be harmed by it. Chapter 5 will help you manage your anger constructively. Chapter 19, "Ending the Conflict: A Step-by-Step Approach," will show you how to protect your children from conflict and then to end it. There are many steps that you can take *immediately*. Start taking action today!

9

Fostering Children's Long-Term Adjustment: A Step-by-Step Guide

"T he parents are divorced" is a phrase routinely used to "explain" children's long-term troubled behavior. The good news is that a convincing body of research shows that divorced homes *can* provide an environment that enables children to thrive. If parents can provide certain critical conditions, children can usually bounce back from divorce with remarkable resilience.

This chapter will help you set the stage for your children's successful divorce adjustment and provide them what they need in the years to come. There is no "quick fix" formula. Divorce is painful and is likely to affect your children adversely for a period of time. Starting out right makes children's long-term adjustment more likely but does not guarantee it. It is not only what you do to help your children at the time of the divorce that will determine whether they bounce back or develop lasting problems, but what transpires in the months and years following divorce. This is because divorce is not a single event: It sets in motion a chain of events that spans an extended time.

If you've read Chapter 7, you already recognize the factors that play a powerful role in children's *long-term* divorce adjustment. However, knowing what you *should* do and knowing *how* to go about doing it are two different things. How can you create a stable home life for your children when the entire family's world is upside-down? How do you stop your conflict with the other parent when you are both so angry? How can you shore up your relationship with your children so you can successfully buffer them from the stress created by divorce? How can you get your children to open up to you? How can you limit the stress and change in your children's lives when divorce, by its very nature, inevitably causes so much of both?

This chapter guides you through specific steps to create the kinds of conditions that enable children to bounce back from divorce. Notably missing from this chapter is a guide to ending the conflict with the other parent. Ending conflict is so critical to your children's well-being that it warrants a separate chapter, Chapter 19.

STARTING OUT RIGHT

How you tell your children about the pending divorce will help set the stage for the difficult months ahead. Your ongoing reassurance, your openness to talk, your answers to their questions, and your acceptance of their feelings will all contribute to their *initial* adjustment.

How to Tell Children about Divorce

Think through what you are going to tell your children and how you will do it. Use the following guidelines to create the most favorable conditions that you can.

Wait until your decision is *definite* before telling your children. Children have more difficulty adjusting when they face prolonged periods of uncertainty. Telling them roughly two weeks before one of you leaves the residence is a guideline. This gives them enough time to adjust to the idea, but not enough to fuel their natural hopes for a reconciliation, which will simply prolong their tension and turmoil. If the children will be moving from the home at the time of separation, they may need to know earlier so they can prepare.

If you have already separated, continue reading. It is not too late to provide your children with the information, clarification, and reassurance they need.

Ideally, both you and the other parent should break the news *together*. Your children are likely to feel more reassured when they see you working together for their benefit, and they are less likely to deny the reality of the decision if they hear it from both of you. Each of you will also know exactly *what* your children have been told.

It is usually a good idea to tell *all the children together* because doing so is more likely to create feelings of closeness among them. Children can provide invaluable support for one another. Many parents neglect to give any information to very young children, believing they are too young to understand what is happening. However, young children have a very difficult time adjusting when one parent simply disappears without explanation. Their active imaginations can concoct frightening reasons for a parent's disappearance. One three-year-old who was given no explanation for his mother's sudden departure was terrified that she had "been burned up in a fire." If your children are of markedly different ages, have a lengthier talk with the older children later.

Ideally children should hear the decision in a warm, loving, and calm manner. (Right after a fight would be a poor time.) Children need to have *some* reason for the divorce in order to deal with it. However, use caution. Don't bombard them with grievances, and don't provide specific details or embarrassing information. Keep it simple. Give them a general explanation they can understand, such as, "Mom and Dad have been very unhappy for a long time, and we feel that we can't go on living together like this any longer."

Don't get into blaming, even if the divorce is completely the other parent's idea. Blaming creates a good parent/bad parent scenario that places children in painful loyalty binds, and this only *adds* to their distress and turmoil.

Give children concrete information about how the divorce will affect them personally. How will their lives be different? How will they be the same? If major changes are close at hand (moving, a new school, Mom taking a full-time job, a serious need to cut back on expenses), children should be prepared. If you foresee no other dramatic changes in the family's life, let them know that, too.

It is important for your children to have details about the departing parent. When will the parent move out? Where will he or she live? Particularly critical is information about how, where, and when they will see the departing parent in the future. These details will make the future less frightening to them.

Be sensitive to your children's reactions. Exactly how many details you cover in the initial session should depend on how well they are absorbing the information and how receptive they are. Don't overwhelm them. Children may need several discussions prior to the actual separation.

Provide Continuing Reassurance

Your children will need an abundance of reassurance about your continued love and concern for them, both at the time you announce the di-

---

GUIDELINES FOR TELLING CHILDREN ABOUT DIVORCE

✓ Wait until the decision is definite.
✓ Let children hear it from both parents together.
✓ Tell all children together so they can support one another.
✓ Provide a *basic* reason.
 • Don't bombard them with details.
 • Don't assign blame.
✓ Provide specifics about—
 • How children will see the departing parent.
 • When the parent will leave.
 • Where the parent will live.
 • Changes to their lives.
✓ Reassure them that—
 • They will still have two parents.
 • The divorce is not their fault.
✓ Encourage questions and sharing concerns and feelings.

---

vorce and during the ensuing months. The anxiety most children feel at the news of their family's rupture provides a fertile ground in which misconceptions and fears can breed. "If Dad and Mom don't love each other anymore, maybe they'll stop loving me, too." "If Daddy leaves, we won't have any more money for food." Make it clear that divorce is just between parents, not between parents and children. Reassure them that they will still have two parents, that both of you still love them, and that both of you still want to take care of them, if this is so. And they definitely need to know that it is all right to still love both of you. It is very harmful to children's well-being to feel they must choose between their parents.

If the other parent has disappeared or is adamant about not being involved with the children in the future, it will be even more critical to reassure them frequently of *your* love and concern. How to handle the situation of an absent parent is discussed later in the chapter.

Your children also need reassurance that the divorce is *in no way* their fault. This is a fear among many children, particularly younger ones, but sometimes older ones, too. Children will sometimes sob, "What did I do wrong?" They will often beg their parents to stay together, promising they will be good from now on. Some become model children after the announcement, hoping they can now alter the decision for which they think they are responsible. Some won't verbalize their fears but will agonize over their past misdeeds.

Encourage Questions and Discussion

Your decision to divorce will probably throw your children's once well-ordered lives into a tailspin. It almost inevitably stirs up a myriad of questions and causes a welling of strong emotions.

Encourage your children to ask questions, and let them know you will always answer them the best you can. Children who bring questions to their parents generally are found to adjust earlier than those who do not. But many youngsters will not ask questions unless they are given a great deal of encouragement. In fact, Boston University researcher Abigail Stewart and her colleagues found that most of the children in their study group tended *not* to ask questions—even those who were visibly distressed.

Encourage your children to share their concerns and feelings about the divorce, as well. A study reported by British researcher Yvette Walczak found that good communication around the time of separation was vitally important to children's successful coping. When their feelings are understood, children become emotionally stronger and are more likely to be able to close the door on the divorce and move on with their lives.

Allowing children to express their feelings freely may be exceedingly uncomfortable for you. It's natural to want to stop their tears and to convince them otherwise when they say you are ruining their lives. It's understandable to become defensive at their angry outbursts. But it is important to allow them their feelings and to understand them as best you can. Remember, they are hurting. Life as they know it has just fallen apart. It will help you to know that these early feelings and outbursts are not indicative of their future adjustment. They are merely your children's way of temporarily dealing with their pain.

Gauging Children's Early Reactions

Children's initial responses to the announcement of their parents' divorce vary widely. Some respond with seeming indifference, as did David, whose only comment was, "Oh, can I go out and skateboard?" David's response did not reflect his lack of caring; his way of dealing with his pain and distress was to block out the reality of the news. Some children retreat to their bedrooms, not to be heard from again for hours and refusing to talk about the impending separation when they emerge. Many are very open about their pain, distress, or anger. One study reported that half the children reacted with visible distress and 9 percent were visibly angry, according to their parents. Some younger children literally panic, as did one child, who ran out of the house screaming for help.

Sometimes parents are puzzled about children's reactions and are uncertain how their children feel. Although children's overt reactions vary greatly, studies find that most share *similar feelings*. Generally, children faced with the news of their parents' divorce are intensely sad and anxious. They feel rejected, vulnerable, and powerless to stop their world from crumbling to pieces. Many feel angry and betrayed. Some feel guilty, afraid they are responsible for the rupture in some way. Children's self-esteem commonly tumbles. Most fear they will lose their departing parent, and some worry about complete abandonment. You may wish to refer to Chapter 6 for a more detailed discussion of children's reactions, as well as of children's typical feelings and behavior at different ages.

Your children are likely to show some kind of changed behavior in the weeks or months after separation. One may become withdrawn and temporarily lose interest in school, friends, and normal activities. Another may become aggressive and rebellious. A teen may withdraw from the family and spend every free moment at friends' homes or in outside activities. If you have young children, they may become very demanding or whiny, throw temper tantrums, and sob uncontrollably when things don't go their way. Your children's changed behavior is a symptom of their distress and reflects their anxiety, fears, and anger about what is happening in their lives.

If you notice *no* behavior change, don't automatically assume your child is "doing just fine." Research suggests that the majority of divorcing parents are unaware of the extent of their children's difficulties. There are many reasons for this. Parents are self-involved because of their own distress. They also *need* to feel that their children are coping well. Some children appear to be completely unfazed because they are dealing with their distress through denial. Others send out subtle signs of their distress that parents don't recognize, such as a lower tolerance for frustration, refusals to complete tasks, a lack of self-direction, a drop in self-confidence, or poor impulse control. One University of Michigan study found that parents automatically assumed their children were fine if the youngsters' reactions were subdued rather than dramatic. But those parents greatly underestimated the extent of their youngsters' distress, as described by the children themselves. When journalist Linda Bird Francke was writing an article on divorce for *Newsweek* many years after her own divorce, she interviewed her two daughters about their reactions at the time. She was shocked at each child's revelations. Said Francke after interviewing the first of her two daughters:

> I was struck dumb by my maternal ignorance. How could I have failed to pick up the distress signals that she must have been sending out? I could have comforted her, reassured her, at least listened to her. And why hadn't she told me all this before? "Because you never asked," she said.[1]

Helping Children Sort Out Their Feelings

Throughout the months following separation, continue to be accessible to your children, reassuring them of your love and reminding them you are always there to answer questions and talk about their feelings, concerns, and fears. Children may be confused about their feelings and about why they are acting as they are. If a child is having difficulty opening up and talking about his or her feelings or concerns, there are a number of things you can do:

- Children's books on divorce can be used as springboards to talk about feelings. Read them with your preschoolers and elementary-school-age children, and make them available to teens. You may find your children want to read them over and over again. Each reading helps them to process what is happening and how they feel. You can find many good books listed in Appendix D.
- Talk with your child about the way *other* children feel and see if you can form hunches together about how he or she might be feeling. For example: "Lots of kids feel angry when their parents divorce. They're upset they can't live with both their parents anymore and they think it's really unfair their life is in such a mess and they can't do anything about it." Talks like this may help your child sort out his or her jumbled feelings and see that they are normal and do not threaten you. Chapter 6

discusses children's typical fears, feelings, and reactions in detail.

- Some children find that expressing their feelings on paper is less threatening than verbalizing their fears out loud. It is good therapy for them, too. This is something you can encourage. Angela found it very comforting to write her thoughts in a diary each day. Jimmy wrote many letters to his father who never visited him. Even though he never mailed them, he felt better "telling" his father how he felt.
- Preschoolers will often thinly disguise their fears and feelings in the stories they tell, in the pictures they draw, and in their imaginative play. For example, preschoolers whose parents are divorcing will commonly draw pictures of children who are looking for their homes and for their parents. They tell stories about disasters occurring to people and about animals who are very needy. Give your preschooler plenty of opportunity to draw, tell stories, and engage in imaginative play. Then you can use these as springboards for talks. Talking about how *other* children feel is particularly important for preschoolers because often these very young children find their fears too scary to face head-on. You can alleviate your preschooler's fears by correcting the misconceptions that preschoolers often have. For example: "Many little children feel that something they did caused their mommy and daddy to get a divorce. But divorces are just between mommies and daddies. Children don't cause them." You can learn about the misconceptions and fears preschoolers have in Chapter 6.
- A couple of family counseling sessions around the time of separation can be very beneficial, allowing parents to address children's questions, anxieties, and fears with the help of a counselor.

When talking to your children, be sure not to make negative comments about their other parent; keep your comments about their parent positive or neutral. Allow them their feelings without influencing them with your own.

You may be wondering if you shoud allow your children to see how upset you are. Expressing your own sadness may help your children express their sadness. But achieving a healthy balance can be tricky; you don't want to overwhelm them. Seeing a few tears and hearing that you are sad, too, is healthy. Seeing you fall apart and hearing you dwell on your sadness and anger is not! Your children need to know that you are in control and can help them.

The remainder of the chapter guides you in creating the conditions that have been found to be vitally important to children's *long-term adjustment*. All these conditions will not be in your control. Work on the ones that are. Start right away. The quicker you can provide them the quicker your children are likely to bounce back to their old selves.

HOW TO CREATE A STABLE HOME LIFE

Life as children know it falls apart with divorce. To children, their family was a given—the entity that provided them with stability, security, and continuity in a sometimes unpredictable world. Now this structure in their lives has crumbled.

A stable home life is important to all children, but for children going through divorce, it assumes enormous importance; it can be their lifeline. The quicker you can create stability for your children, the better it will be for them. If your children live with you a significant share of the time, your ability to provide them a stable home life will play a vital role in their adjustment.

Following are specific steps that you can take immediately to create a stable and secure home for your children—whether your home is their primary or part-time residence.

Set Predictable Routines and Schedules

Set up regular and predictable routines and schedules, and make every effort to stick to them. The structure provided by routines and schedules is reassuring to children because it provides a sense that life is in control despite the apparent chaos around them. In fact, sometimes routines and schedules are the only sources of stability and predictability on which children can depend during the early months after separation!

Routines can be used to regularize each of the following parts of a child's day: school mornings, after-school activities, homework time, play time, chores (make a list), mealtimes, and bedtime (be sure to make going to bed at a specific time part of this routine). Regular school attendance is itself an important routine. Very important as well is a predictable routine for children to spend time with the parent who is not in the home.

Predictable routines are *critical* for infants, toddlers, and preschoolers. When under stress, very young children function far better in highly structured, organized, and predictable environments. In addition to the routines mentioned above, make every effort to have consistent sitters and a consistent schedule for naps and snacks.

If you are a parent whose children live with you part-time, try to incorporate some of their familiar routines into life at your home to provide them this consistency.

Create Clear Expectations and Limits and Consistently Follow-Through

These three parenting practices typically fall by the wayside in divorcing homes, but their absence only compounds the chaos and confusion children feel. Clear expectations (rules) and limits are a sign to children that some order remains in a world that seems to be falling apart. They provide an additional benefit as well: Children have a more difficult time exercising self-control during times of stress, and clear expectations and limits provide them with *external* controls to compensate for their lapses in *self*-control.

Please note, and this is very important: Expectations and limits should be enforced in a *loving but firm manner, not a cold, punitive manner.*

Divorcing parents are especially hesitant to impose limits on very young children because children already have so much stress in their lives. They usually find their preschoolers regressing to inappropriately immature behavior, such as whining, thumb sucking, and temper tantrums. Many divorcing parents respond by overindulging little ones, making no demands on them, and enforcing no limits. Contrary to parents' instincts, studies find that preschoolers adjust better when parents make appropriate maturity demands of them, *providing they are made lovingly and firmly, not punitively.* These very little ones have even more difficulty with self-control during times of stress than do older children, which makes their need for external controls even stronger.

Studies find that divorcing mothers are more reluctant to enforce rules and limits with their sons than with their daughters. Another mistake. Boys from divorcing homes are found to need clear rules and firm limits even more than girls do. When limits and follow-through (discipline) are lax, boys function particularly poorly. Rules and limits should be enforced in a calm and caring manner. The key is to be firm but kind.

Read Chapter 20, "How to Discipline Effectively and Still Be a 'Good Guy,'" to learn how to provide your children with clear expectations, limits, and consistent follow-through in a *positive* way. You will also learn why a warm but firm approach is so important. Please don't confuse discipline with punishment and spanking. Discipline is *teaching* self-control, responsibility, and how to behave appropriately.

Establish a Set Parenting Schedule

As quickly and as amicably as you can, work out a parenting schedule with the other parent on which your children can rely. Chapter 17 will help you do this. There is no greater instability for children than not knowing where they will live and when they will be with each of their parents. Mark the parenting schedule on a calendar and post it so children will know which parent they will be with at any given time.

Many parents with primary custody use their children's needs for stability as an excuse to limit the time they spend with their nonresident parent. However, the stability and continuity of their relationship with *both* parents is an important ingredient of a stable environment for children! It should be given a high priority.

Protect Children from Parental Conflict

Children's home life is not stable when they must deal with the turmoil created by battling parents. Make every effort to end the conflict with the other parent, and until you can do so, protect your children from it. Prolonged parental conflict is the number one predictor of children's poor adjustment after divorce. There will be more on this later in the chapter.

Don't Make Your Child Your Confidant

Don't lean on a child to fulfill your needs for emotional support, adult companionship, or a confidant, no matter how mature your child *ap-*

pears to be. Children do not have the emotional capacity to shoulder adult burdens or the intellectual capacity to solve adult problems. Children who are placed in the role of confidant, companion, or absent parent tend to develop a *pseudomaturity*. But, inside, many become overwhelmed with anxiety, depression, and worry—and eventually develop problems such as physical symptoms, plummeting grades, and substance abuse. There is more on this in Chapter 14.

Your children are in crisis themselves. Find an adult to be your confidant and companion. Don't rob them of their childhoods and adolescence.

Don't Overburden Children with Adult Responsibilities

As the only parent now in the home, you are likely to need your children to assume some additional responsibilities to lighten your load. It's fine to encourage children to be *helpers* in the home. Children who contribute to the family grow in self-reliance and self-esteem, particularly when they understand their contribution is important to the family's smooth functioning. However, don't make your children *stand-ins*. Many children in divorced families become overburdened with responsibilities far beyond their age and are robbed of their childhoods. How do you know if you are overburdening them? A good rule of thumb is that children and teens should not have so many responsibilities that they do not have time for normal activities enjoyed by other children their age, such as friends, play, and some scheduled after-school and weekend activities. Neither should their schoolwork suffer because of home responsibilities. Be especially aware of this with teens and preteens, who are sometimes expected to be "on call" at all times in one-parent homes. Thirteen-year-old Andrea is such an overburdened child.

> Andrea rushed out of class with a quick good-bye to her friends. She never lingered after school and had dropped out of drama and choir long ago. She didn't have time for such kid stuff anymore. Her mom really needed her. Danny had to be picked up from his afternoon kindergarten and Tommy from the day care center. She had her hands full until her mom got home at 6:30, taking care of her two brothers, who had become so ornery since Dad left, doing chores, and making dinner for the family. "You're amazing," her appreciative mother said each night. While her mother spent time with her younger brothers and put them to bed,

---

CHECKLIST FOR A STABLE HOME LIFE

✓ Create predictable routines and schedules.
✓ Provide clear expectations, limits, and consistent follow-through in a loving but firm manner.
✓ Establish a set parenting schedule with the other parent.
✓ Protect children from parental conflict.
✓ Do not make your child your confidant.
✓ Do not overburden children with adult responsibilities.
✓ Resolve indecision about reconciliation.

Andrea did the dishes and straightened the house. It was usually after eight when Andrea could begin her own homework and school projects.

Chapter 14, "How to Create a Successful One-Parent Home," offers practical suggestions for dealing with the many new demands in your life so you will not have to overburden your children.

Resolve the Issue of Reconciliation

Avoid impulsive reconciliations that may end in another separation. If there is a chance of reconciling with your spouse, initiate some marriage counseling to help resolve your indecision and help ensure that the reconciliation will be a stable one if initiated. Both long separations and repeated separations are hard on children, placing them in a state of limbo—hoping for a reconciliation, fearing a divorce, and unable to get on with their lives. Both place stumbling blocks in the path of children's adjustment.

HOW TO SHORE UP YOUR RELATIONSHIP WITH YOUR CHILD

The quality of the relationships children have with both their mothers and fathers is a powerful determinant of whether they adjust well to divorce. Nurturant and dependable relationships with parents help protect children from stress. It may help you to visualize such a relationship as a cushion that softens the emotional blows of stress. Children with a poor relationship with one or both parents are found to be more vulnerable.

Unfortunately, parents' relationships with children frequently deteriorate after separation because parents are so involved with their own crises and with rebuilding their lives. In fact, recent studies have discovered that parent-child relationships begin to suffer in the months or even years *prior* to divorce as a result of the troubled marriage.

Make your relationship with your children a high priority. Start today, whether you need to rebuild a relationship or simply maintain an already good one. What is the foundation of a good relationship, you wonder?

- Warmth, nurturance, and emotional support.
- Sensitivity and responsiveness to children's needs.
- Empathy and respect shown to children.
- Good communication.

The following suggestions will help you build a solid relationship with your children. You can use them whether you are a parent with primary custody, joint custody, or part-time custody. If you see your children infrequently, you can find additional practical suggestions in Chapter 15 specifically for your limited time together.

- Talk with your children every chance you get. Get in touch with their feelings, concerns, and interests. Learn about their friends, school lives, and day-to-day activities. Car time provides golden opportunities for talking, as do mealtimes. Eat together at dinner, and turn off the television! After dinner, share the cleanup with a child, using the time to talk.
- Become an active participant in your children's lives. Attend their sporting events, ask a child if you might sit in on a gymnastics class, and get to know your children's friends. Talk with their teachers and coaches, and volunteer to help out as your time permits. Support your children in their interests and help them achieve what is important to them.
- Spend some one-on-one time with each child every day your children are with you. It doesn't need to be a long time as much as it needs to be consistent. Find things to do with each child that you both enjoy—read a book together, play a game, work on a hobby or school project, go for an ice cream. Develop some mutual enjoyments. Let your child know that he or she has your undivided attention during this special time.

- Institute weekly family meetings so you and your children have a forum to share ideas, concerns, and problems related to the family. Family meetings are discussed in Chapter 14.
- Give children plenty of reassurance that you love them and they are important to you. Then back up your words with action!
- Permit your children to have their own feelings, thoughts, and opinions, *and respect them!* Watch that you don't become defensive or judgmental. ("There's no reason to feel that way." Or, "Don't be angry at *me*. This divorce wasn't *my* idea!").
- Let children know you understand their struggles and feelings. When children feel that a parent understands them, they become closer to that parent.
- Be positive! Look for opportunities to praise your children and show that you appreciate them. ("That was a great job you did." "I liked the way you waited so patiently." "That was such a thoughtful thing you did for Johnny." "Thank you for doing your chores without being asked.")

HOW TO BECOME A COMMUNICATION-FRIENDLY PARENT

An important part of a good relationship is open communication. The two go hand in hand; as you improve one, the other automatically follows. Good communication around the time of divorce can draw parents and children closer together, even when relationships were distant previously. Here are some concrete steps you can take to open up the lines of communication with a child. Don't try to tackle them all at once—try working on a few at a time.

- The first step to good communication is good listening. *Really listen* to your child; don't just act as if you're listening. Resist distractions, ask questions, and give feedback ("I see." "Go on." "What else?"). Paraphrase what your youngster has said in your own words to be sure you understand and to assure your child you understand.
- Use "door-openers" to encourage children's talk, suggests Dr. Thomas Gordon, the father of Parent Effectiveness Training. For example: "Tell me about it." "I'd be interested in your point of view." "Shoot, I'm listening." "Sounds like you've got something to say about this."

- Is your child usually too guarded to share his or her feelings? Take the attention off the fact that you are looking for meaningful communication. Get involved together in an activity that is engrossing but doesn't take all your child's concentration, such as playing a board game or baking cookies. Then, while attention is focused on the activity and defenses are down, subtly sneak in a probing question.
- Avoid questions that children can answer with one word, because one-word answers are all you are likely to get. Instead, phrase questions in an open-ended manner that encourages children to elaborate. For example: "What do you think about..." "Tell me about..." "Tell me what you did at..." A word of caution here: *Be specific*. Too general a question, such as "Tell me about school" is likely to get you a blank stare, a shrug, or a "What do you want to know?"
- If you have a tendency to lecture, interrogate, or criticize, work very hard on changing these habits. They are sure to break down the lines of communication.
- Tune into any questions that are divorce-related and use them as an opening to talk about your child's concerns and feelings. Remind youngsters that you are always willing to answer their questions and talk about their feelings and concerns.

FOSTERING YOUR CHILD'S RELATIONSHIP WITH THE OTHER PARENT

Having a good relationship with *both* parents is an important ingredient of children's long-term divorce adjustment. Even if you would like nothing better than to see the other parent out of your life, you need to support your children's relationship with him or her. There is wide agreement that, with few exceptions, the relationship between a child and the nonresident parent should always be fostered, and their time together should be of sufficient duration to develop and maintain a meaningful relationship. Even in those exceptions, if the child can be protected by visitation under supervision, this is usually recommended rather than no contact.

Please don't erect barriers to make it more difficult for your children to spend time with their other parent. Some studies have reported that up to one-half of the custody-retaining parents studied made visitation difficult, even though many did not realize they were doing so.

Common examples were "forgetting" about scheduled "visits" and refusing to reschedule a "visit."

A court-ordered program in Maricopa County, Arizona, offers compelling evidence of the negative repercussions for children when visitation is frustrated. This program enforced visitation orders that had been disregarded by custodial parents. Just in the six-month duration of the study, improvement was noted both in children's overall adjustment and in school adjustment, particularly when children's access to their nonresident parent became frequent.

Ideally, you will encourage the other parent to function as a full-fledged parent in the children's lives. Children appear to do better when they have two parents who function *as parents* rather than when one becomes a "visitor" or "activities director." It also cuts down on the "Disneyland Dad" syndrome, so often complained about by custody-retaining parents.

You may be interested to know that many formerly uninvolved parents develop an appreciation for their parenting role after separation and go on to develop very close relationships with their children. Youngsters literally beam when they talk about spending more time with a parent than they ever did before the divorce.

In contrast, parents who become peripheral players in their children's lives are more likely to drop out of their lives and fall behind in child support payments as well. A parent dropping out of a child's life is devastating to most children and has long-term repercussions. Meet Billy, one of the children in the California Children of Divorce Study:

> Billy was five when his parents separated, and over the years, his dad became convinced that Billy didn't need him. When Billy was interviewed five years after the divorce, he broke down and cried uncontrollably for 35 minutes when asked how often he saw his dad. By the time Billy was reinterviewed in another five years, he had developed more self-control, as is typical of 15-year-old boys. However, at the mere mention of his father, his eyes immediately filled with tears. Billy was unable to regain his composure for the remainder of the interview and sheepishly apologized afterward for being "so emotional."

Here are some steps you can take to support your children's relationship with their other parent:

- Give your children permission to love their other parent. Their love for him or her is not a threat to you.

- Keep the other parent informed about the children, and encourage him or her to participate in decisions about them. In a large-scale Arizona State University study, the best predictor of whether nonresident parents remained involved with children *and* paid child support was their perception that they had some control over their children's upbringing. In fact, a growing body of research indicates that participating in decisions, remaining involved with children, and paying child support are all strongly linked to one another.
- Respect the other parent's relationship with the children, right to parent the children, and autonomy with the children when they are together. If you have trouble doing this, please read Chapter 18, "Making Co-Parenting Work."
- Honor parenting schedules. *Never* use access to the other parent as a reward or punishment, and *never* deny a visit because of missed child support. The other parent's time with the children is not a privilege but a *necessity* for your children.
- Suppose your children do not want to go? Treat the other parent's time with them as a top priority and a normal routine for your children to follow. Realize that all children occasionally do not feel like going; this is nothing to be concerned about. When it occurs, be positive and matter-of-fact about their going. If they have conflicting activities, follow the principle of the "on-duty/off-duty parent," discussed in Chapter 18. If they persistently do not want to go, become a detective and try to identify why. First, critically look at what messages you might be sending them—perhaps implicitly or nonverbally. Also be sure you're not making fun plans (and letting them know about them) during the other parent's time. Watch to see if they are always negative about going, or just when the time is near. Many children find the transition from one household to the other very difficult but are fine once they are with the other parent. In the case of a younger child, refer to Chapter 17 to make sure the parenting schedule is appropriate for your youngster's developmental capabilities. In the case of an older child, encourage him or her to talk to the other parent directly. If you decide to talk to the other parent about the problem yourself, use the communication tools in Chapter 12.
- Don't mistake your children's upset or problematic behavior before or after spending time with their other parent as signals that their time together is harmful. Making the transition from one parent to the other is difficult for most children,

particularly when there is tension between the parents (see Chapter 8). Most likely, the transitions themselves are the root of your children's upset. Refer to Chapter 19 to learn how to make transitions easier for children.

- Put your objections to the other parent in perspective. Some parents feel justified in not supporting their child's relationship with the other parent because of the "harm" caused the child by too much junk food, lax discipline, loss of sleep, exposure to different values, or difficulties transitioning between homes. Whatever "harm" these may cause pales in comparison to children's distress if a parent drifts out of their lives.
- If a child's physical or emotional safety is at risk, visitation can be under supervision until the parent addresses his or her problems. You may need court assistance to implement this.
- Strive to build a workable co-parenting relationship with the other parent (Chapter 18). It will become a tremendous asset to both you and your children in the future.

IF THE OTHER PARENT HAS DROPPED OUT

If the other parent has dropped out of your children's lives and you are unsuccessful in reinvolving him or her, help your children see that the problem is inside the missing parent and not a reflection of any shortcomings in them. They need to understand that they did not do anything wrong and that they are not unlovable or unworthy. As much as you would like to, do not disparage the other parent. Children identify with their parents, even an indifferent one. "If my dad's no good, will I grow up to be no good, too?" Hearing disparaging remarks about their parent will make them feel worse about themselves.

Reassure your children frequently of your commitment and love and that you will always be there for them. A good relationship with you can go a long way in buffering them from the stress of losing the other parent. Try extra hard to obtain social support for them from outside sources, especially other men if the missing parent is the father, or women, if it is the mother. See if the other parent's extended family is willing to be involved. Sometimes grandparents feel their involvement will be unwelcome and are reticent to initiate it themselves.

Counseling is an excellent way to help children deal with feelings of abandonment or rejection and come to terms with an indifferent or rejecting parent.

LIMITING THE AMOUNT OF CHANGE IN CHILDREN'S LIVES

You may remember from Chapter 7 that children can usually handle one source of stress (your divorce) quite well. However, exposure to *additional* major stresses at the same time multiplies the difficulty of reconstructing their lives as well as the risk of developing long-term problems. Examples of additional major stresses are prolonged parental conflict, prolonged poor parenting, chronically poor parent-child relationships, and a marked drop in economic resources that leaves the family in duress.

Having to cope with considerable change and instability is another source of major stress. When children must cope with many other changes at the same time they are trying to cope with the divorce, they receive a double whammy. How do you limit the amount of change in your children's lives?

- Strive for continuity and predictability. As much as you can, keep details of your children's lives the same after divorce as they were before.
- Contact between the children and the parent who is not in the home should start *immediately* after the separation and should be *regular and reliable*. The more extensively the parent has been involved with the children, the more extensive his or her contact should continue to be. It is preferable for the nonresident parent to continue in a parenting role and continue doing things with the children that he or she did previously. Frequent phone contact is also a good idea to facilitate continuity in this relationship.
- If at all possible, temporarily delay any major changes for your children during the first year, such as moving or attending a new school.
- When major changes *must* be made, make them as gradually as your situation allows. If you must move, try to keep your children in the same school, at least for a year. Try to continue with familiar routines. Incorporate as many things as you can from the family home into the new home. (Now is not the time to toss out all your furniture and "get a fresh look.") If you must return to work, can you get along on a part-time job for a while? Children whose at-home parents suddenly return to full-time employment experience a double loss—both father and

mother. If a full-time job is necessary, try to make up for your lost time with your youngsters by giving them some undivided attention each night and on weekends.

- If you have a new significant other, don't introduce him or her into your children's lives while they are still trying to cope with the divorce (see Chapter 13). Let them deal with one thing at a time.

- If many negative changes in your children's lives cannot be avoided, work to offset them by providing some positive experiences. The negatives are more detrimental if there are few positive events to offset them. Give your children extra love, time, support, and sensitivity. Remember, a good relationship with you can soften the impact of stress.

ARRANGING SOCIAL SUPPORT FOR CHILDREN

You may be able to give your children's adjustment a considerable boost by arranging for adults outside the family to provide children some of the extra support and nurturing they need, not only during the divorce but during the time you are rebuilding your life. Outside social support can help buffer children from the stress in their lives.

You will probably have to ask for help. In one major study, only 25 percent of the youngsters were given support by anyone in the extended family, and only 10 percent received support by someone outside the extended family. People were simply hesitant to intrude.

Who can you ask? Grandparents and other extended family members are likely candidates. Don't forget your children have *two* extended families! Teachers can be good resources. Many a child has pulled through the rough postseparation months because of the support offered by a sensitive teacher. Family friends, neighbors, school counselors, coaches, scout leaders, youth group leaders, or the parents of friends are also good candidates to show your children some extra caring. So is a mature baby-sitter who is nurturing and sensitive. A professional counselor or therapist can be an invaluable source of support for your child. Helping your children to get involved with after-school activities will not only open up new sources of support but will help them get their minds off the divorce and distance themselves from the turmoil.

CONTAIN THE CONFLICT!

If you come away with only one message from this book, I hope it is that you need to protect your children from parental conflict. If this message is stamped permanently in your mind, then reading this book will have been well worth your while. Please be sure to read Chapter 8, "Conflict! The Number One Predictor of Children's Poor Adjustment After Divorce."

Conflict refers not only to open battles between you and the other parent. Loyalty conflicts (that is, when children feel caught in the middle between their parents) are every bit as destructive as is open conflict, and often more so. Parents often put children in the middle without realizing it. They may pump children for information about the other parent, badmouth the other parent, ask children to be message carriers, ask children to spy on the other parent, or pressure children, even subtly, to take sides. Protecting children from conflict and loyalty binds is so critical to their well-being that Chapter 19 is devoted to steps you can take to contain the conflict and then to end it. It is full of practical suggestions. Please don't put off reading it.

Although containing the conflict is the biggest factor in preventing children's poor adjustment, the opposite of conflict (that is, working together) is a major contributor to children's *good* adjustment. Children whose parents work together *as parents* after divorce adjust better to both the divorce and to their parents' new relationships. These children are found to have better relationships with their parents. Their parents are happier in their new lives, too. Everyone wins!

SHOULD YOU SEEK PROFESSIONAL HELP?

If you keep in mind how children experience their parents' divorce, children's distress, which is so often expressed in changed behavior, is very understandable (see Chapter 6). Children need to mourn the loss of life as they know it and adjust to the many changes in their lives.

Some counseling sessions are very common for children going through their parents' divorce, and for some, counseling can be a lifeline. Usually children welcome the chance to unload their anxiety and fears in a safe and confidential place, sort through their confusing feelings with a neutral person who is their advocate, and learn good coping skills to deal with the upheavals they are facing. Even young children can benefit. (Therapists use play therapy with a young child.) Counselors are also good resources for parents: to answer questions, to offer practical suggestions, and to be on call if problems arise in the future.

Many parents take their children to a few counseling sessions early on to ensure that they have appropriate coping skills and are on track handling the pending divorce. "She's doing as well as can be expected" is very reassuring to a parent who doesn't know whether a child's lowered tolerance for frustration, lethargy, renewed bedwetting, or clinging is within normal limits or a sign of problems that need addressing.

Most children's problems fade as the turmoil in their lives subsides, particularlty if they are able to alleviate their fears and talk about their feelings. This chapter is full of steps you can take to provide an environment that will enable your children to bounce back to their old selves, and Chapter 19 guides you through protecting children from conflict—the number one predictor of children's poor adjustment.

During the months after separation, be alert to your children's behavior and signs of distress. You will probably have to make a special effort to do this because of all the stress you are dealing with in your life. Be especially sensitive to a child who was already having adjustment difficulties prior to the separation and to a child with a difficult temperament because they will likely be the most vulnerable (see Chapter 7). It will be invaluable to keep in touch with your children's teachers to see how they are functioning in school—emotionally, socially, and academically. If a child is doing well in school, it is a good sign. Ask the teachers to contact you if they notice anything of concern.

There are no hard-and-fast rules dictating when you should seek counseling for a child. With some problems it will behoove you to seek professional help quickly. Some red flags that warrant *immediate* attention are *dramatic* changes in behavior or behavior that can cause harm either to your child or to others, such as serious aggression, severe depression, or experimenting with drugs, alcohol, or sex. A radical drop in school grades or a shift to new and undesirable friends are other red flags calling for some immediate crisis intervention.

What if a child's problems are not this serious? Watch to see how long and how intensely problems continue. If troubling behavior continues for six to eight weeks with no improvement, and certainly if it becomes worse, give your child the gift of couseling—particularly if the child appears to be bottling up his or her feelings. But listen to your instincts. If a child is in obvious distress, such as overwhelming sadness, and your reassurance, extra attention, and talks do not seem to help, don't wait this long. Basically, if you have doubts, do the safe thing and seek some professional advice. Not only do you want to help your child through this tough time, you want to be sure that any difficulties he or she is having are short-lived and do not become long-term problems. A few sessions now may get your child back on track and avert future problems.

Children may also need to shore up their coping skills in counseling if they are making poor progress in bouncing back to their old selves after a couple of months, if the conflict between you and the other parent cannot be contained, if they feel caught in the middle, or if you are unable to get life under reasonable control for them. Many children can manage quite well early after the separation but find their coping skills taxed beyond their limits when the turmoil in their lives is prolonged.

It is preferable for both you and the other parent to keep in contact with the counselor so he or she can provide both of you with suggestions and answer your questions.

Children's divorce adjustment groups are now available in many communities, and virtually all children can benefit from them. They provide a forum for children to share concerns and feelings with other youngsters their age from divorcing families. Many help children identify and talk about their feelings, communicate more openly with parents, and develop good coping skills. See if there are any in your community.

For leads to good child counselors and for children's divorce adjustment groups, ask your child's pediatrician or teacher or other divorced parents. You might also contact your local family court agency, a local child guidance clinic, or community agencies. Many health insurance programs cover a specific numbr of counseling sessions, and some have lists of counselors who are covered by the insurance. If counseling is not covered by your insurance, it is often available on a sliding scale fee, based on your income.

DIVORCE AND THE STEELING EFFECT

Guilt is not an uncommon feeling in divorcing parents. Most parents want to do well by their children and experience anxiety about the repercussions of their divorce. The fact that you are taking the time to read these chapters suggests that you are a conscientious parent. As such, you are likely to do a good job bringing your children through this stressful time. But as a conscientious parent, you may feel lingering guilt and uncertainty.

It may encourage you to know that some children emerge from their parents' divorce with *greater* psychological strength. How can this be, you wonder? It is now known that the most effective way to foster resilience in children is not to shield them from stress and adversity, as many parents assume. Rather, it is to allow them to encounter stress in doses that are moderate enough for them to handle. In this way, the stress does not overwhelm them. Instead, they are challenged to learn how to cope with a difficult situation and master it. If they are successful, they will likely emerge from the experience with new self-confidence, an increased sense of competence, and the ability to successfully handle a greater amount of stress in the future. This phenomenon is called the "steeling effect."

The key, of course, is for the stress to be moderate enough so a child can handle it rather than be overwhelmed by it. How do you know how much stress is moderate enough? Remember that children can usually cope with a single stress, such as parental divorce, as long as its effects are not compounded by other major stresses, such as prolonged conflict, chronically poor relationships with parents, poor parenting, overwhelming change, or severe financial hardships (see Chapter 7).

Carol's parents divorced when she was 8. She is now 16 and appears to be convinced that the steeling effect actually does occur. About the divorce, she says, "I've gained, I'm more aware, independent and a strong person because of the divorce. ... I've learned a lot."[2]

III

Rebuilding a
Rewarding Single Life

10

Your Emotional Divorce: Stepping-Stone to a Rewarding New Life

On the evening of January 10, 1990, John Faller came home to a house devoid of half its furniture and found a note on the kitchen table from his wife, saying she had left him. Now, years later, he is still very bitter. He continues to tell his story to willing listeners and does so with such detail and anger that the unsuspecting person is inevitably shocked to learn the incident occurred years ago. John defends his feelings as most appropriate. "I did NOTHING to deserve this. She ruined our lives, and I didn't even have a part in it. Why shouldn't I be bitter?" John and his two college-age sons still live in the same home. Little has changed in it over the years, other than some needed replacements for what was taken all those years ago. John's life consists of his construction job, his sons, and his preoccupation with the past. He refers to his former wife as "that woman." His sons are concerned about what will happen to their father when they leave home. They have never told him they are now seeing their mother on a regular basis.

Ann is an attractive, vibrant, 48-year-old successful businesswoman. Six years ago her husband left her to marry a co-worker. Ann shakes her head at the memory of the shocked, angry, depressed, and suicidal homemaker she had been at that time. "It's only been six years, but it seems like a life-time ago," she says. "There is so little left of that Ann now. After a year of hell and four months of therapy, I worked up the energy and nerve to go back to school to take some business courses. It was the best thing I could have done. I found a wonderful support group in a reentry women's organization on campus. In fact, that's where I met my partner, Phyllis. After we finished our course work, we took the money from our respective divorce settlements and invested it in this franchise. I suppose it was risky, but it's been a wonderful success. I found I have a real head for business, and she is wonderful on the PR end. I love being out in the world and feeling competent and successful. I've made a number of very dear friends, both men and women. I've developed so many new interests. My children are doing well now and freely float back and forth between their father's house and mine. After several years of bitterness and conflict, we now have a quite civilized relationship. His leaving turned out to be a blessing in disguise!"

Your emotional divorce is completely separate from your legal divorce. For some it does not take place until long after the legal divorce is finalized. For some, it is an elusive goal, never reached.

Your emotional divorce is accepting the end of your marriage, recognizing both its strengths and shortcomings over the years, and acknowledging the role you played in its demise. It is letting go of the sadness, anger, and resentments and laying your past to rest. It is feeling only indifference, concern, or tenderness for your former partner rather than anger, hatred, resentment, regret, sorrow, longing, love, or dependency. It is getting on with a future of your own design.

People achieve their emotional divorce to different degrees; not everyone is a glaring failure like John or a dazzling success like Ann. Those with moderate success may still harbor strong feelings but may be able to compartmentalize them so they do not interfere with their day-to-day lives. Others may successfully co-parent their children but not without a constant struggle to avoid conflict.

The guidelines in this chapter will help you through the process of completing your emotional divorce, so you can move on to your new life, unencumbered by leftover emotional baggage.

SETTING THE STAGE: SEPARATION

How the separation is handled can have repercussions that reach far into the future, affecting each family member's ability to adjust and move on.

In studies at the Child and Family Divorce Counseling Service at Children's Hospital of San Francisco, psychologists Janet Johnston and Linda Campbell discovered that a very unexpected or traumatic separation (such as desertion, discovering a devastating affair, or first-time violence) tends to set the stage for prolonged conflict between former partners and to thwart their attempts to emotionally divorce.

In these traumatic separations, the common scenario is for the hurt spouse to *redefine* the character of the leaver in the context of the sudden betrayal and to conclude that the leaver's *true* nature has been discovered for the first time. ("How could I have been so blind all these years?" "His true colors certainly came out." "I guess I never really knew her at all.") Friends or relatives, who usually spend hours with the devastated spouse, often validate this new perception of the leaver's character, and it becomes the more firmly entrenched.

The situation can turn from bad to worse. The events of the separation often destroy the hurt partner's belief that the leaver *ever* valued the marriage. Now, all the years and energy invested in caring for the leaver seem wasted. Feeling enraged and exploited, many hurt spouses set out either to retaliate, seek "justice," or capture *some* power in the situation. Maneuvers may include snatching bank accounts, making threats, turning children against the leaver, or destroying the leaver's clothing. Many leavers, under emotional distress themselves, also redefine the hurt spouse in light of this new unexpected behavior. A vicious cycle of attack and counterattack is launched.

Because the situation has gotten out of control, the former partners do not talk to one another rationally. If they were to do so, they would likely discover the inaccuracies in their new perceptions of one another. Instead, the new negative perceptions each has of the other become frozen for years to come. If one spouse does behave in an altruistic way that is incompatible with the other's distorted image, it is likely to go unnoticed or to be reinterpreted as somehow self-serving.

The best way to avoid a crisis is with preparation, discussion, and sensitivity before separating. The left partner needs time to process the decision and make some plans for the future. Decisions need to be made about how you will separate your entwined lives and share parenting if you have children. If you need help, a few conjoint sessions with a family therapist may be helpful, both in cushioning the impact of the final decision and in providing a forum to discuss plans for a smooth transition.

If you are already enmeshed in a crisis separation, such as that described, understanding the dynamics underlying it may help to extricate yourself from it. Could there be explanations for your former spouse's behavior other than those you have assumed are fact? You may need help in sorting out your feelings and gaining some perspective. A good divorce therapist could be an invaluable help to you.

As long as you cling to your unrealistic perceptions of your former spouse and the end of your marriage, you are likely to feel victimized.

And as long as you feel victimized, it will be more difficult for you to put the marriage behind you. Your efforts to complete your emotional divorce will be further thwarted if you become enmeshed in conflict.

EARLY STEPS

Immediately after separation, you can begin to take steps to help your divorce adjustment.

The Announcement

Telling people about your separation or pending divorce is a difficult step that many people delay. However, University of Oregon psychologist and researcher Stephen Johnson, author of *First Person Singular,* has found that announcing the separation contributes to early adjustment. Tell each family member, friend, and associate directly, says Johnson. Your explanation does not have to be extensive, particularly with acquaintances. Plan in advance what you will say.

Making your new status public will help you to start feeling and acting like a single person rather than a married one. It serves as a sort of ritual to mark the end of your marriage and the beginning of your single life.

Announcing your separation also opens the door to your receiving a good deal of social support when you need it the most. People, particularly family and friends, usually rally around a newly separated person. However, most people are hesitant to intrude and will not make an overture unless they know it will be welcome. Johnson suggests that you have some suggestions ready should people ask how they can help. You might ask them to be available to talk or to go out for an evening. You may prefer they invite you to their homes or introduce you to some single people. Or perhaps you would like help with some new skills you will need to learn (cooking, child care, car and home maintenance, financial advice, and so on).

Balancing Change and Continuity

Studies find that people seem to adjust better if they create *some* changes in their environment yet at the same time maintain some continuity and stability in their lives. If you remain in the home you shared with your spouse, you might make an effort to put your own stamp of individuality on it. However, if you have children living with you, do not make the changes too drastic. Their need for continuity is much stronger than yours.

If you are the spouse who leaves, you will have plenty of change, perhaps too much. You need to guard against feelings of rootlessness and a loss of identity, which are common for spouses who leave home, particularly when there are children in the home. Most people do better when they take some favorite things from their home with them. Take time to find a place you like and begin right away to make it look and feel like a home.

What the great majority of departing parents miss most is daily contact with their children. If you have children, be sure to see them regularly and talk to them by phone in between visits.

Painful Memorabilia

You may have enough sorrow in your life after separation without being surrounded by things that automatically trigger sadness because of their strong association with your spouse. Collect them all—photos, gifts, clothes, wedding ring, mementos, special records, or whatever causes you particular sadness—and put them away where you will not see them for the time being. However, don't throw them away yet.

Symbols of Your New Beginning

There are likely to be many negative things going on in your life right now, so guard against slipping into the twin modes of lethargy and feeling bad about yourself. Do some things for yourself that will make you feel good, boost your feelings of self-worth and self-confidence, and symbolize your new beginning. This will help you get started on the right foot in your single life. Pamper yourself by getting a massage, facial, or new haircut; buy some new clothes; take a trip, join a gym, or develop some new interests.

DISENGAGING FROM YOUR SPOUSE

For most people, disengaging from one another is an important step in completing their emotional divorce. Many people balk at the idea of disengaging, feeling that it is unnecessary. However, in the long run, relatively few people find they were correct. For most people it is a *must!*

The following steps will help you in the disengaging process:

- If you are a departing spouse, take everything with you and change your mailing address; do not keep keys to the family home.
- Limit all contact and discussions with each other to *necessary* matters only, such as children, dividing belongings, and resolving financial matters.
- Formalize how you will communicate from now on; set prearranged meetings or phone calls.
- If your former partner persistently tries to make unnecessary contact, get an answering machine and screen calls.
- Send support payments through the mail.
- Do not rely on your ex-spouse for any of the functions (other than parenting) that he or she took responsibility for in the marriage (cooking, laundry, car or house repairs, bill paying, financial planning, and so forth). Falling into these familiar patterns will keep you in a state of limbo—no longer a part of your old world but unable to enter a new one.
- If you have children, establish a set schedule for them to see the departing parent (see Chapter 17). This eliminates the need for ongoing contact to arrange for exchanging the children, and it allows each of you to make plans independently. It is also good for your children.
- Respect one another's privacy; do not ask about or offer personal information.

Please don't misunderstand. Disengagement does not mean you must *permanently* terminate your relationship with your spouse. A good relationship with your former partner can be a real asset in the future, particularly if you have children. However, to have a good relationship in the future, the spousal relationship needs to be *redefined* and *restructured*. You need to stop interacting in your old ways and find mutually acceptable new ways of relating. Because of the emotionally charged atmosphere of separation, a period of noninvolvement is usually necessary before a new and different relationship can develop successfully. How to restructure the marital relationship is discussed at length in Chapter 18, "Making Co-Parenting Work." Whether or not you have children, the process of restructuring is the same. The only difference is that divorced couples without children have the option of permanently severing the relationship rather than restructuring it.

DISLODGING YOUR SPOUSE FROM YOUR MIND

Disengaging from your spouse physically will be far easier than dislodging him or her from your mind. If you've read the preceding chapters, you know that intense sorrow, bitter anger, and obsessive thoughts about your former spouse are likely to be familiar companions for a while. However, sometimes a former mate influences one's behavior long after divorces are final. Some people continue to buy clothes their former partners would have liked. Some continue to act in ways an ex-spouse would have expected. Some continue to frequent places because of their association with happier times in the marriage. Many cannot "move on" because of their hopes of reconciliation. Many others are so consumed with anger at their ex-spouses that it dominates their postdivorce lives. For your own future happiness, you must dislodge your former partner from your mind. Return to Chapters 3, 4, and 5 and use some of the coping tools to deal with overwhelming sadness, obsessive thoughts, and anger.

As tempting as it will be, don't seek out or listen to information about your ex or his or her activities. It is only likely to upset you anyway. You may need to tell well-meaning friends that you don't want to hear any information or news about what he or she is doing. If you have an uncontrollable urge to call your former partner, *don't*. Distract yourself instead, either with some activity or by going somewhere. When you think of something you *must* discuss, write it down and save it for your scheduled discussions. Writing it down will get it off your mind so you can go on to something else. Keep all your notes together in a note pad so you can take care of all the loose ends during your next meeting.

A critical step in dislodging your spouse from your mind is getting rid of your hopes of reconciliation. Psychologist Zev Wanderer, co-author of *Letting Go,* calls hopes of reconciliation the "hope trap," because they keep you hooked to the past and prevent you from moving on to the future. Many divorcing men and women refuse to give up their hope trap because they believe that doing so will ruin their chances of reconciliation. Nothing could be further from the truth. In fact, many leavers decide they want a reconciliation only *after* they notice dramatic changes in their former partners and see how well their ex-spouses are doing without them. Giving up the hope trap is a necessary prerequisite to getting on with your new life as a single person.

YOUR ACCOUNT

Most divorcing men and women are obsessed by thoughts of their spouses and their marriages. What went wrong? What led to the breakup? Who was to blame? What could have been done differently? Each potentially significant event and fight is replayed and examined over and over again. Very gradually, most people construct a subjective account of the history of their marriages and their breakups.

Constructing this account moves you a step closer to coming to terms with the end of your marriage and completing your emotional divorce. Without understanding what went wrong, it is difficult to lay the marriage to rest. Many men and women who have not worked through the confusion of events and have not found an explanation for the breakup are unable to put the marriage behind them. Some continue to lament years later, "If only I knew what happened"; some continue to feel victimized; some continue to rage at the perceived injustices dealt them.

Since accounts are subjective, the accounts that two divorcing spouses construct sometimes bear little resemblance to one another. However, the account you construct can have important implications for your future. It is important to achieve a *balanced* version—you should neither assign all the blame nor take all the blame. It's unusual for a marriage's collapse to be completely the fault of a single partner, although many former spouses place the entire blame on their ex's nagging, inability to communicate, neglectfulness, selfishness, dependence, frigidity, or sloppy housekeeping. It is also rare for a single factor outside the marriage to be completely at fault, although some place all the blame on a third factor—a spouse's job, an affair, or in-laws.

What difference does it make if you place all the blame elsewhere and fail to recognize any personal responsibility? People who continue to place all the blame outside themselves are more likely to continue to feel victimized and remain bound to their former spouses in some way, whether it be in anger, conflict, hate, or lingering attachment. The specific nature of the bond is less important than is its existence. The bond keeps them chained to the past and thwarts them from fully moving on to the future.

Constructing an unbalanced account may affect your future in other ways, too. First, failing to recognize the role you played increases your chances of repeating the same patterns in future relationships. Second, if you are a parent, your ability to successfully co-parent your children will be influenced by whether you have a balanced view of your former partner's strengths and weaknesses. If you recognize only the other parent's faults, you are less likely to respect your children's relationship with him or her, more likely to blow minor incidents out of proportion, and more likely to have ongoing conflicts about your children's parenting and rearing.

When constructing your account, try out all the possible reasons for your marriage's end. Although you may go through periods when it appears to be all your spouse's fault, all someone else's fault, or even all your fault, do not get stalled at this point. Work toward a balanced view of both your marriage and your former partner. Try to identify the following:

- Why you married.
- What difficulties contributed to your marital problems.
- What sequence of events led to the divorce.
- How each of you contributed to the problems.

After much struggle, the woman in the following example came to terms with the role she played in her husband's affair and the end of their marriage.

Who could ever imagine anything like that happening to my marriage? My husband was the squarest, straightest of men—a deacon in the church, a Little League Dad, a Cub Scoutmaster, a non-drinking, crew-cut junior executive. But I let it happen. Our marriage had become nothing but a kind of corporate enterprise without my ever taking time to wonder about it. How it got that way I don't know. It seemed as if we were so busy with children, the house, and local activities, that we never paid any attention to each other; we never said anything real to each other. As for sex, I was bored by it. I felt I could live nicely forever without it, and tried to avoid it as much as possible. I hardly ever thought about any of this, but when I did, I told myself that every marriage goes through phases of this sort and there was nothing to worry about. I was living in never-never land, refusing to see the truth or do anything about it. [1]

If you have trouble identifying why your marriage ended, you may find it helpful to learn about unhealthy love relationships that frequently end in divorce. Yours may have fallen into one of these patterns. Read Bruce Fisher's book *Rebuilding*, listed in Appendix D.

MOURNING AND RITUALS

When you divorce, you not only part with a spouse—you also leave behind your past, your whole way of life, the future plans and expectations you once had, and a good chunk of your identity. Part of the process of completing your emotional divorce is mourning your losses and the death of your marriage, just as you mourn the death of a person who has been an important part of your life. Once a death is mourned, the pain eases, memories of the departed person lose their power to provoke tears and sorrow, and the mourner feels that he or she can let go of the past and get on with life once again. The same happens when people mourn the death of their marriage and the inevitable losses it entails. It is widely maintained that mourning the death of the marriage and one's losses is necessary in order to completely let go and get on with life, free of an ex-spouse.

Even if you are happy to be out of the marriage, there are always losses you need to mourn. Many people flippantly dismiss the idea that they have lost *anything*. "Good riddance," they scoff. "There's nothing I'll miss." But in so doing, they risk carrying leftover emotional baggage from the relationship into their future, never completely putting the marriage behind them.

Psychotherapist Bruce Fisher, author of *Rebuilding*, suggests that you write letters of good-bye to each loss in your life—to your former spouse, to the relationship, to your home, to your way of life, to your past times together, to the dreams you had for the marriage, to the future you planned together, and to your identity as a husband or wife. Include all the things you will miss as well as the things you will be glad to leave behind. Dr. Fisher's research suggests this method moves people closer to their emotional divorces. They are not easy letters to write, warns Fisher. Begin with a superficial loss and gradually work your way to more important losses.

You might also try writing a letter to your former spouse (but do not mail it). Write everything in the letter that you would like your former partner to know—all those things that have been going through your mind but you have been unable to say. Include your feelings, your thoughts about the marriage and the past, and your hopes for the future. Getting the thoughts out of your head and on paper will help you close the doors on them.

Going through the painful memorabilia you put away early in the separation can also help you mourn your marriage's end. If you haven't been able to get in touch with your sadness, this will help. If you are very much in touch with your sadness, wait until you have had time to release much of it before tackling the painful mementos. Take out the mementos one by one and vividly replay in your mind the good memories associated with each one, allowing yourself to cry and grieve over the memories. After grieving like this, you will find that the mementos have less power over your emotions and that you have moved that much closer to closing the door on the relationship for good.

More and more mental health professionals are now recommending participation in some type of *ceremony* or *ritual* to mark the end of your marriage and help you reach closure. Every major event in our lives has some type of ritual to mark it, with the exception of divorce. The impact that such a ceremony can have was vividly described by this woman, who watched one several years after her own divorce:

> I clearly remember the day of my divorce and my anger that this "letting go" process had none of the elements of my marriage ceremony. . . . I remembered thinking that had one of us died, we would have at least received support in our grief. . . . Years later, when I watched . . . a divorce ritual, my children and I cried our tears and relived our own situation. I envied that couple and their children, for they had a chance to participate in the letting go process. I watched the woman remove her ring and give back the obligations that he had given to her. I listened to her tell what she would remember that was good and what she would forgive and forget. . . . The couple cried, their children cried, and we all mourned the passing of an important event in their lives.[2]

The couple she described had already been divorced for two years but had continued in bitter conflict with one another, refusing to let go until that day.

Some couples participate in rituals that reverse their marriage ceremony—each releasing the other and returning wedding rings, much as the divorced couple above did. University of Southern California professor Constance Ahrons, author of *The Good Divorce,* suggests a parting ritual in which each person acknowledges the positives they took from the marriage and the need to end the marriage at this time. If the divorcing couple are parents, she suggests they each pledge to raise the children together in a healthy divorced family and never badmouth one another. Ahrons suggests involving children in the ceremony and, perhaps, inviting extended family and close friends.

If a ritual with your former spouse is not for you, well-known divorce therapist Florence Kaslow, director of the Florida Couples and Family Institute in West Palm Beach, suggests you write your own divorce decree as a sort of divorce ritual. In the decree, she suggests you include what went wrong with your marriage in some detail, what is likely to lie ahead for you in the next two years, and what your future goals are. Dr. Kaslow finds that such a written decree, which can be reread often, helps people finally accept the end of the marriage and move forward to restructure their lives.

LETTING GO OF YOUR ANGER

Letting go of your anger is critical to a successful emotional divorce. Your anger keeps you emotionally bound to your former partner just as much as love does. It is the *intensity* of your emotions about your former spouse that tells you if you are still hooked in emotionally. Regardless of whether your professed emotion is love or hate, it binds you to the relationship and to the past. Until you let go of your anger you will be unable to complete your emotional divorce and move on to your future unencumbered.

Many divorced couples who continue to battle year after year have never acknowledged their losses or dealt with their underlying feelings of rejection, hurt, failure, and wounded self-esteem. Instead they mask their underlying feelings with anger and cling to it. As long as they can be angry at their former partner, they do not have to face the inevitable pain created by divorce and its losses.

If you find you can't let go of your anger, realize you have work to do. Return to Chapter 5, "What Do I Do with All This Anger?" Take another stab at constructing your account, trying for a more balanced accounting of the marriage and its end. Permit yourself to go through the mourning process. As difficult as that may be, it will allow you to heal and move on. Don't hesitate to seek professional help from a divorce or family therapist who can help you sort through your feelings and provide some perspective. If you are entrenched in conflict with your former spouse, read Chapter 19, "Ending the Conflict." Although the chapter is in the co-parenting section of the book, a good deal of it applies to couples without children or with grown children.

THE POWER OF FORGIVENESS

Even after you feel that your anger is spent, you may be left with lingering resentment: "I'll never forgive her (him) for what she (he) did to me." How many times have you said that, or heard it said by other divorcing men and women? Some people hold on to their resentment as if it were a badge of honor, feeling they should never let it go. Many repeatedly replay past injustices in their mind, physically reliving their pain as they do. Some cling to their desire for revenge as if it were a lifeline, biding their time and dreaming of the glorious day of retaliation.

What you may not realize is that your resentment or desire for revenge keeps you entangled in the past and prevents you from closing the door on the marriage completely. Forgiving your spouse for past wrongs will allow you to lay the past to rest and move on, free of the emotional baggage that has been weighing you down. *The person you set free by forgiveness is yourself*!

In forgiving, you are not saying the wrongs were okay. Forgiveness is not even something you do for your spouse. Forgiveness is something you do for *you*.

Dr. Kenneth Cloke, director of the Center for Dispute Resolution in Santa Monica, California, eloquently states that forgiveness is a gift you give yourself for your own peace of mind, your own self-esteem, and your own future.[3] Cloke points out that it is your choice whether to forgive, and when you make the choice to forgive, you take back control of your life. You release yourself from feeling victimized and from the pain created by your spouse.

It may be your own guilt that is crippling you—"I'll never forgive myself for my mistakes that led to this divorce. If only I could take them back." You may berate yourself repeatedly for everything you have done or left undone. Your guilt will keep you entangled in the past just as resentment will. If you are loaded down by guilt, forgiving *yourself* will set you free.

Cloke suggests you write a list of reasons why you should not forgive your spouse (or yourself). Then list the reasons why you should, being sure to include the benefits of forgiveness that you have just learned. Which better serves your self-interest? Forgiveness? Or hanging on to the pain, anger, resentment, and need for revenge?

It may help to act out a ritual revenge, suggests Cloke. What is the ultimate revenge you can imagine? Either act it out in your mind in great detail, or you might act it out with an inanimate object. Afterward, make the choice to let go of the anger, the pain, the resentment, and the desire for revenge. You might even create a ritual to signify your letting go and forgiveness. Remember, forgiveness is a choice, and only you can make it.

THE ROLE OF SOCIAL SUPPORT

Many divorcing men and women are convinced they never would have made it through the divorce without the support of friends and family. The caring, warmth, and reassurance of others seems to serve as a cushion that softens the impact of divorce-related stress. A study conducted at the Center for the Family in Transition in Corte Madera, California, found that social involvement helps to diminish attachment to a former spouse. Social involvement also offers temporary distractions, something to anticipate, a relief from loneliness, a lift from depression, and perhaps encourages some new friendships as well.

Reach out to others. Don't make the mistake of withdrawing into a shell because you do not want to "bother" people. Usually family and friends are only too willing to provide moral support, and sometimes financial support and services, too (baby-sitting, errands, home repairs). If you remember to give something of yourself back to those who offer their support, you will not feel like a burden.

When you are with others, however, don't fall into the trap of always dwelling on your divorce and your former partner. Some talking is healthy, but *continually* talking about your ex can become addictive and fuel your anger. It can also frustrate and alienate friends who otherwise would be supportive.

If you do not already have a support system, it's important to develop one. Accept the overtures of others. Many people report their best source of support during divorce came from an unlikely person, such as a co-worker, acquaintance, or attorney who had also gone through a divorce. Divorce support groups can be of great help; they are often available through community colleges, churches, counseling centers, community agencies, and singles groups such as Parents Without Partners. How to build new social support networks is discussed in Chapter 11.

A word of caution: Sometimes social support, particularly from family, can be a double-edged sword. In addition to the many benefits families can offer, they are sometimes a source of problems. Family members are more likely than friends to openly voice their opinions, including displeasure, about the divorce and each partner's behavior. But more important, family members are sometimes drawn into the dispute in full force. Family outrage has been known to fuel conflict between divorced couples for years. And prolonged family sympathy may encourage a divorced person to feel victimized, which may impede progress toward closing the doors on the marriage and completing an emotional divorce. Whether or not you have this type of family involvement, studies suggest you are likely to do better if your social support network includes friends in addition to your family.

REINVOLVING YOURSELF

Many divorcing men and women make a common mistake: They put off reinvolving themselves with life until they can rid themselves of their sorrow, depression, and anger. "There's no point in doing anything when I feel this bad," they say. This is tantamount to putting the cart before the horse. Here is something many people do not realize: Once you reinvolve yourself, you will feel better! The woman in the following example tells how she floundered in misery until she finally reinvolved herself.

> I hated him. Yet I couldn't ignore him. I could see his face in my son's eyes; I saw him in the house, remembering the rooms he painted. For a while I tried to suppress every nice remembrance. This hurt more than it helped. It was only after I went back to school and stopped pitying myself that I could face the good memories and accept what was.[4]

The importance of reinvolving yourself was clearly illustrated in a well-known study conducted by Dr. Graham Spanier, of the State University of New York at Stony Brook, and his research team. These researchers found that creating a new lifestyle is *the most critical factor* in people's successful adjustment after divorce. Perhaps the best example of this surprising finding is offered by the story of Grace:

Grace was 65 when her husband uprooted her and moved to the Southwest, supposedly for the climate, but in reality for the liberal divorce laws. Within several weeks of their move, he shocked her by moving out of their rented apartment. Within days, a uniformed marshal banged loudly on her door and handed divorce papers to the stunned woman. Grace had nowhere to turn. She had not yet made friends since her move and was too embarrassed and ashamed to talk to her friends back home. She sat in her apartment for months, depressed and bewildered; fortunately for her, her religion precluded suicide. The divorce became final too quickly for her to assimilate all that was happening. She was given a small share of her husband's modest Social Security check, but the couple had no assets and little savings. Grace's situation had all the makings of a disastrous divorce and a bitter lifetime ahead. But she met a woman at church who worked in a program for abused children. One day the woman convinced Grace to come along for a few hours, and Grace discovered that, for the first time in many months, she was able to take her mind off the nightmare she had been living. She signed up as a volunteer that day, and within several months was receiving a stipend for her dedicated work. One year later, Grace was a smiling, cheerful woman. She had met several good friends and was congenially sharing an apartment with one. She loved the children and experienced a new sense of fulfillment working with them. "Never have I felt so needed, so loved, or so productive," she beamed. Grace never sees or talks about her husband and, to all around her, seems to have completely closed the door on her marriage.

The principle of reinvolvement is simple: It is easier to give up the past and your old identity when there is something to replace them with in the present. So quit investing your emotional energy in a dead relationship, and begin investing it in yourself. Begin today to reinvolve yourself with life and to forge a fresh identity separate from that of your spouse and your marriage. You will get plenty of help with this in Chapter 11. Remember that it will be easier to get yourself going and keep on track if you follow the five-step self-change program in Appendix A.

FINAL RESOLUTION

Divorcing men and women are commonly advised to "resolve" the relationship and the end of the marriage. You have probably heard that advice a number of times. What exactly does it mean to resolve your relationship? The phrase is sometimes used interchangeably with letting go of the relationship and completing your emotional divorce.

Resolving your relationship and the end of your marriage means truly accepting both the end of your marriage and the role that you played in its breakdown. It means laying your past to rest. It's being able to distance yourself from your former partner—so you can see him or her *objectively* and recognize his or her weaknesses *and* strengths. It's being able to distance yourself from your divorce—so you can objectively recognize your hurts and disappointments without them triggering the emotional turmoil they once did. It's feeling and acting like a single person and getting on with a future of your own design. It means acknowledging your feelings of loss, sadness, anger, and resentment and letting them go, so you no longer harbor them. Don't misunderstand. Resolving your relationship does not mean that you should never get angry with your ex. If your former spouse is doing things in the here and now that are infringing on your rights (failing to pay ordered support,

---

STEPS TO HELP YOU COMPLETE YOUR EMOTIONAL DIVORCE

✓ Set the stage at separation: sensitivity and discussion.
✓ Take these early steps:
  • Make your separation public.
  • Achieve a balance between change and continuity.
  • Temporarily remove painful memorabilia.
  • Do something to symbolize your new beginning.
✓ Disengage from your partner in all but parenting roles.
✓ Take steps to dislodge your spouse from your mind.
  • Avoid information about his or her activities.
  • Avoid the "hope trap."
✓ Construct a *balanced* account of why your marriage ended, acknowledging your role.
✓ Thoroughly mourn the end of your marriage and your losses.
✓ Mark the end of your marriage with a ritual or ceremony.
✓ Let go of your self-defeating anger.
✓ Take back control of your life through forgiveness.
✓ Seek out social support.
✓ Reinvolve yourself; don't wait to feel better.
✓ Work on developing a new identity of your own.
✓ Work on rebuilding your self-esteem.

arranging other activities for the children during your scheduled time, or badmouthing you to your family), of course you will be frustrated, irritated, and angry. But your anger will be tied to *current* situations. (Chapter 12 suggests ways to help you handle these.) When anger is left over from the past, however, your relationship is not yet resolved.

Chapters 3 through 5, and of course this one, were designed to help guide you to this final resolution. Chapter 11 is devoted to the rebuilding of your life. In reality, there are no such arbitrary boundaries as there must be in books. You will start to rebuild your life while you are still trying to resolve the end of your marriage. So please go on to read Chapter 11.

In her book *Coming Apart: Why Relationships End and How to Live through the Ending of Yours,* therapist Daphne Kingma suggests one last thing to do in the letting-go process, and I think it is a good thought with which to end. It is to acknowledge the "gifts" you took away from your marriage. Kingma is not referring to material gifts, but rather to the changes in yourself, the lessons you learned, the needs that were fulfilled, and the accomplishments that your marriage made possible. Even if you feel as if you were the one who did all the giving, spend some time analyzing your marriage and comparing the person you are now with the person you were before. Every relationship is enriching in some way.

Kingma suggests that you write a letter to your former partner (it need never be mailed) thanking him or her for all the gifts you received from your marriage. Having a written record of the benefits you derived from your marriage and an acknowledgment of your former spouse's contribution to them is a wonderful idea. It will not only dissipate your resentments, but in the future it will allow you to view your marriage from a fresh and positive perspective—a giant step toward completing your emotional divorce.

11

Rebuilding

Georgia's husband left her three years ago. "She had a rough time," says a close friend, "but she's fine now. The depression and anger seem to be gone, and she's feeling better about herself. They had lots of assets, so she got a great divorce settlement—the house and plenty of money to invest. She doesn't even have to work. She's very involved with the kids and PTA. And her friends are very good. They still have her to dinner from time to time— many couples don't do that, you know. She certainly landed on her feet!"

But life doesn't seem quite so full to Georgia. She feels fortunate to have been able to keep the house and have no money problems. And it is a relief to have life on an even keel after the upheavals of the last three years. But she frequently wonders, "Is this all there is from now on?" She feels an emptiness inside her and a feeling of estrangement from her world that she finds hard to put her finger on. Sometimes she dreams that she is bobbing around in the ocean in the dark alone, without a compass and with no land in sight.

Most people think of divorce adjustment as coping with the divorce itself—weathering the stormy emotions, dealing with the disruptions and problems, helping children adjust, and learning to let go. But divorce adjustment has a second facet: building a rewarding new life. Unfortunately, the importance of building a new life often goes unrecognized. Many people emerge from the stormy crisis still frozen in old patterns. They "get over" their divorce, but they do not grow. For them, life after divorce is no more, and sometimes far less, satisfying than was married life. Both leavers and reluctant partners are represented in this group.

Life after divorce *can* be rewarding and satisfying, if you invest the time, energy, and planning to make it so. This chapter focuses on the ingredients necessary for building a rewarding single life.

REBUILDING SELF-ESTEEM

During the last 5 years of their 15-year marriage, Bonnie and Dale grew further and further apart. Because of conflicting interests and dissatisfaction with their marriage, they became increasingly more negative and critical with each other. They never really fought, they criticized. "Nothing I do pleases her. I've given up trying," Dale frequently griped. "I can't do anything right in his book," Bonnie likewise complained. Generally, their exchanges were peppered with put-downs and name-calling—inept, selfish, jerk, shallow, prima donna, immature. What wasn't said directly was communicated by innuendo. Throughout the final year of their marriage, each was taking full advantage of the other's vulnerabilities. By the time they finally separated, both Bonnie and Dale were emotionally drained and their self-esteem was seriously eroded.

By the time a marriage ends, each partner's feelings of self-worth have generally taken a plunge. Sometimes, as with Bonnie and Dale, self-esteem is damaged over time because of the steady barrage of negative feedback received from a spouse, some of which is inevitably internalized. Sometimes it is damaged by feelings of rejection, other times by feelings of failure. Yet this blow to self-esteem comes at the very worst time for divorcing people—when they must go out on their own and build new lives. This is a tall order for anyone, but it is overwhelming when self-esteem is shattered. Feelings of self-worth are critical to you right now. With high self-esteem, your task of building a new life is more likely to be challenging than overwhelming. Psychiatrist David Burns compares self-esteem to faith: Both can move mountains!

Don't wait for your self-esteem to miraculously reemerge. It may, but it may not. After interviewing her study group 10 years after divorce, researcher Judith Wallerstein wrote of her constant amazement at how many of these long-divorced people continued to carry around the negative self-images formed during their poor marriages—negative images that impaired their ability to create satisfying lives. Your self-esteem can be shaped, and you can be the shaper. Here are some things you can do. Choose a few that make the most sense to you:

- Your feelings of self-worth are closely tied to your perceptions and thoughts about yourself. For a few days, keep track of the things you say to yourself and write them down. You may find you are telling yourself a lot of negative things ("God, I'm such a jerk." "I never do anything right." "I'm worthless."). No wonder your self-esteem is low! Once you become tuned in to your negative self-talk, you can begin to talk back to yourself and break this self-defeating habit. When you catch yourself in negative self-talk, firmly tell yourself to STOP! Then replace your negative thought with a more positive one. Try, "So I made a mistake. That makes me human, not a jerk." Or, "I may not have done *this* right, but I've certainly done lots of other things right." (Then force yourself to think of some examples as evidence.) How do you know how to talk back to yourself positively? Talk to yourself as you would to a friend. Would you tear down a friend constantly? Don't do it to yourself either. Wouldn't you help a friend see the folly of his destructive negative thinking? Do the same for yourself. A second way to talk back to yourself is to remind yourself of your *positive* attributes.

- Write down everything you like about yourself and everything you have going for you. Include all your good qualities, strengths, skills, talents, hobbies, and goals. Keep a running list until you have *at least* 20 to 25 positive attributes (the more, the better). You can use your list of positive attributes to counteract your negative self-talk. Go through your list of positive attributes often, especially before social events, so you will project a positive image. How you feel about yourself affects your behavior, which in turn influences the way people respond to you.

- Self-esteem is enhanced by new accomplishments. Develop some new interests or hobbies. Or learn some skills you need to live independently: Home repair or decorating? Investing? Car maintenance? Cooking? Additional parenting skills? Your self-esteem will be boosted not only by your new accomplishments but also by the confidence you'll gain in being able to live independently. Be sure to tackle new pursuits in *small* steps so you feel successful and not discouraged. Follow the program in Appendix A.

- Make a list each day of everything you accomplish. All too often, people focus on all they *haven't* accomplished and never give themselves credit for the things they *have* accomplished.

- Think about the things you do well and make room in your schedule to do them frequently.

- Whenever you can, socialize with people who are supportive, who like you, and who make you feel good about yourself. Limit the time you spend with people who are critical or unaccepting.

- Begin to behave assertively. Allowing others to take advantage of you chips away at your self-esteem. Learn to express anger and things that concern you in a constructive manner by practicing the communication skills in Chapter 12. They can be used with anyone. Each time you speak up for yourself, you will feel more like a person worthy of respect. The book *Your Perfect Right* listed in Appendix D is a good source of assertive techniques. Many workshops teach assertiveness, as well.

- Make a list of five adjectives that best describe you, suggested the late Virginia Satir, a very well known therapist. Indicate next to each adjective whether you consider it a positive or negative trait. Now take each of your negative traits and see if you can find something positive about it. One man realized that what he defined as "weakness" made him a more sensitive person. Another decided that his "tunnel vision" was also responsible for his determination. When Becky described herself to her divorce adjustment group as "wishy-washy," she was surprised that other members thought of her as flexible.

- Begin to give your needs a higher priority and pamper yourself a little. Take time to do things for yourself that you will enjoy. Get a new hairstyle. Buy some new clothes. Take off some weight. Get in shape. You will begin to feel better about yourself.

- Pay attention to the compliments others give you, and start to incorporate them into your view of yourself. Stop yourself from automatically assuming that compliments are not sincere.

- It is an interesting fact about people that our behavior affects our feelings. Think about how you would treat a *very* special person who came for a visit. Then begin to treat *yourself* the same way—not for an hour, but all the time. Watch yourself begin to feel better about yourself.

- If there is something you *really* want to change about yourself, follow the self-change program outlined in Appendix A. Only work on *one* thing at a time.

- If you are a single parent and are overwhelmed with parenting, work on improving your parenting skills. A study conducted at the University of Virginia found this to be an effective way of boosting single parents' self-esteem. Be sure to read Chapters 14 and 20. You might also try taking a parenting class where you can meet other people.

- Join a divorce support group. The caring and empathy usually offered in these groups can do wonders for self-esteem. Check local churches and community agencies for a support group in your area. Alternatively, a therapeutic relationship with a counselor may be just what you need at this time to enhance your self-esteem.

OVERCOMING YOUR IDENTITY CRISIS

Mark Ballinger had been a family man. He and Kate had grown further apart over the past few years, but he loved his two daughters and had spent a good deal of time with them each day. When he wasn't spending time with them, he had kept himself busy with home repairs, gardening, or helping one of his neighbors with a project. Kate had planned their social activities, and he had gone along. Now Mark sat in an unfamiliar and barren one-bedroom apartment 10 miles from his home. He was able to see his daughters only on alternate weekends and one evening each week, and he missed them terribly. He had lost his "girls," his home, many of his worldly possessions, his neighbors, his customary social activities. Instead of home repairs, he had to tackle cooking, cleaning, laundry, and ironing shirts—tasks distinctly out of character for him. He had not realized how thoroughly he had become entrenched in the roles of married man, father, handyman, and neighbor. Now, without wife, children, and home, he had no idea what to do with himself. In fact, sometimes he didn't know who he was anymore. What was he like before he married Kate? What did he do? How did he feel? It was all so long ago. That person seemed to be gone. And the person he had become during the last 12 years seemed to be gone as well. What now? he wondered.

An identity crisis almost always accompanies divorce. Over the years of married life, spouses inevitably relinquish some of their individuality and pursuits in the interest of the marriage. And because of their shared years, children, home, commitments, and activities, their lives become interdependent, as if the two are woven into a single fabric. With divorce, couples must disentangle the threads of their lives, and the process may leave each with a shaky identity, in need of reworking before it can stand on its own.

There are other contributors to the postdivorce identity crisis. Most people lose many of the material possessions that have become part of "who they are." Most have to assume new tasks that are out of character for them. Many feel as if they are no longer part of society's mainstream.

People commonly feel they have been left adrift without an anchor. Questions believed to be settled long ago now resurface: Who am I? What do I want out of life? Where do I go from here?

Your job now is to forge an identity separate from that of your former partner and from your marriage. You no longer have to be the person your spouse expected you to be. You can create a lifestyle of your own design, speak with your own voice, and pursue your own interests. But it will take time, and until you decide who you are, what you like, what you want to do, and where you are going, you will be between "selves," in a sense, and this may be uncomfortable for you.

Well-known University of Massachusetts sociologist Robert Weiss reports that many divorcing people become upset because they cannot seem to make decisions. They cannot decide what kind of clothes, furniture, house, neighborhood, or lifestyle is right for them because they cannot separate their own likes and dislikes from those they developed as a compromise with their former partners. Others behave very impulsively because one option seems just as good as another. Many are suddenly open to behaving in ways they would have found unacceptable previously. Some become highly suggestible—flip-flopping their self-images in response to others' reactions to them. The divorcing commonly feel as if they are different people from one day to the next. To the bewildered people around them, they seem indecisive, inconsistent, unstable, and impulsive.

In your quest for a new identity, you may make a number of false starts. You may follow along one path for a time, only to find it unsatisfying; then you may switch your focus to a second and to a third. The process of carving out a new identity is not a quick one. Most people seem to need several years before they achieve the stability of a consistent self once again. For some, the identity they develop after divorce has little resemblance to the identity they had within the marriage. This is particularly true for women, whose identities are usually more closely tied to marriage and family than are men's. Studies find that women frequently use divorce to launch themselves on an entirely new life track—often a more confident, independent, and professional one. Sometimes men also use divorce as an impetus to self-assessment and dramatically change the course of their lives.

The following suggestions may be helpful to you in overcoming your identity crisis:

- Rather than focusing on losing your old lifestyle, focus on the challenge of developing a new and more rewarding lifestyle of your own design. Work to overcome the mentality that you are somehow incomplete without a partner, and consciously try to break the habit of perceiving the world from the perspective of a married person. This may not come easily.
- Rely less on your old sources of fulfillment and develop a variety of new ones to supplement them (new interests, new hobbies, new skills, and some new friends).
- Think back and try to reconnect with your old roots to see if they might feel comfortable once again. Who were you before you married? What did you like to do? What types of people attracted you?
- Try not to make major decisions that will lock you in. Flexibility and exploration are more likely to lead to a rewarding single life.
- Take some time to seriously examine what direction you would like to take—in both the short and the long terms. Then try to take at least *one small step* each week to move closer to one or two of your most important goals. Make a "to do" list each week to keep yourself focused and on track. It might help to follow the steps in Appendix A.
- Keep a journal, and record your progress and setbacks in developing your new identity. What new directions have you taken? How satisfying has each been? Can you identify what made it satisfying or unsatisfying? Your notes may teach you a good deal about yourself and suggest future directions that may be rewarding. Every few months, reevaluate by asking these questions: "What are my strengths and weaknesses?" "What do I want?"
- "Try out" a new identity or self among people you meet in a new setting, such as a club or organization. For example, you may wish to try out being more adventurous, confident, or assertive. Experimentation will be easier if you do not have to buck the expectations of others. And if you happen to fall on your face, you can do so among people you never have to see again.

COPING WITH THE LONELY TIMES

Loneliness, or the longing to feel interconnected with others, is generally a fact of life for the recently divorced. Loneliness is usually accompanied by a long list of negative feelings—sadness, depression, vulnerability, boredom, restlessness, self-pity, and self-deprecation. No wonder recently divorced men and women find it so distressing! When asked what loneliness feels like, people commonly respond: "I feel empty inside." "It feels like a hole in my stomach." "I feel depressed, unwanted, left out."

There are two types of loneliness, and each must be remedied differently. The first, *emotional loneliness,* stems from the absence of a close emotional relationship. Even a very socially active person can suffer from this type of loneliness if his or her social network consists exclusively of superficial acquaintances. Feelings of anxiety and emptiness generally accompany emotional loneliness. The second, *social loneliness,* stems from the absence of a social network. Even a close confidant cannot protect you from social loneliness if you have no other friends or acquaintances. Usually feelings of restlessness, boredom, and not belonging accompany social loneliness.

Many divorced men and women jump to the incorrect conclusion that the only way to cure their loneliness is to remarry. In their haste to end their distress, some make poor choices, only to find themselves in an unhappy second or third marriage. You can cure loneliness by building a new social support network that includes a very close friend or two and a number of people with whom to do things. More on this shortly. But until you develop a new social support network, there are steps you can take to manage your loneliness. Try some of the following:

- Plan ahead for weekends and other potentially lonely times by scheduling some activities you can look forward to—a class, a singles activity, a support group, an interesting lecture, a day trip, a movie.
- Begin to develop some new hobbies or interests, and develop a repertoire of enjoyable activities that you can do by yourself. Try the things you always wanted to do but never had time for, return to some hobbies or talents that you let slide while married, or take a chance with something completely new. Think of your time alone as an opportunity to develop yourself. Becoming more comfortable with being alone is one of the most valuable assets you can develop to help you live a rewarding single life.
- Try doing some things by yourself when there is no one to accompany you. You might find them surprisingly enjoyable.

- Share a *few* private thoughts and feelings with one or two people with whom you would like to become closer. Self-disclosure is often the first step toward a close relationship. However, making a habit of talking about your problems is likely to drive people away.
- Work on increasing your self-esteem. Low self-esteem makes people feel more lonely and marginal.
- Complete your emotional divorce (see Chapter 10). Being absorbed in the past will increase your feelings of isolation and loneliness.
- Join a support group.
- Common methods people use to relieve their loneliness include caring for pets, pampering themselves, calling others on the telephone (even if the conversation is superficial), sharing their home with another person, spending time with other lonely people, or reaching out to others in need (volunteering at a nursing home, taking a shut-in shopping, serving meals to the homeless). You may find these helpful, too.

Some words of caution: Some activities involving others may increase your feelings of loneliness rather than decrease them. Singles sometimes report increased feelings of loneliness and marginality after spending time with a happily married couple or eating alone at a restaurant, surrounded by couples or families. Second, don't rely on your children to reduce your loneliness. Not only is it an unfair burden on them, but most adults find that children do not reduce their feelings of loneliness to the same degree that other adults do.

BUILDING A NEW SOCIAL SUPPORT NETWORK

Jan related that it wasn't until she moved from the suburbs that life began for her. After the divorce she had rented a small house for herself in her familiar neighborhood. She had been comfortable there, so it seemed logical. But it was a bad four years, she later concluded. Initially, her married friends had been very supportive and literally bombarded her with invitations. But after several months, they assumed she was over the worst, and the invitations grew more sparse. For almost four years she felt that she was on the fringe of life, not fitting in anywhere. She felt uncomfortable at the few married social gatherings she attended because she wasn't part of that world anymore, and she had no new world to replace it with. She didn't even know other singles. Feeling close to no one, she became more isolated, emotionally barren, and depressed with each passing month. Then the doctor she worked for invested in a condominium and needed a reliable renter. Since there were so many professional singles in the building, he asked Jan if she would be interested. In less than a year, Jan had found a good support system. She had three very close friends she cared about and could count on, as well as some acquaintances—both men and women—with whom she occasionally did things. Jan's eyes sparkled as she related how the building manager recently remarked to her that he couldn't believe she was the same person who had moved there just 10 months previously. "You always looked so forlorn," he said. "Now you're always smiling!"

If single life is to be rewarding, you need to develop a new social network in which you can feel accepted, receive support, and be socially involved. Your married friends are likely to drift away as your lives diverge. As soon as you can, get started reaching out to new people. Aim to have at least one or two close confidants. For many singles, the friendships formed after divorce are the closest and most rewarding they have ever had. Some have friends who are basically surrogate families, always there ready to help. Ideally, the social network you build will include many acquaintances as well. The larger your network is, the richer your life is likely to be.

Following are ways to get started. Try what is comfortable for you. The more things you try, the more success you are likely to have:

- Make contact with old friends and acquaintances from your past.
- Approach other singles at work and in your community. Use any basis to get an acquaintanceship started. Take a chance—ask people to join you for lunch, coffee, or a movie. Most singles are open to new friendships.
- Begin entertaining in your home. Ask a few singles over for a casual evening. They are likely to reciprocate.
- Start a monthly group with some other singles, such as a gourmet group, a potluck dinner group, a discussion group, a support group, or a theater group.
- Invite a few singles to a party at your home and have them each invite a few other singles.
- Most communities now have numerous interest clubs or groups for singles—theater groups, ski clubs, hiking clubs, gourmet groups, dance groups, professional groups, art groups, and so

forth. You are probably more likely to meet kindred spirits in interest groups than at open singles events. Usually singles groups and events are listed in the local newspaper once or twice a week.

- If you have an interest for which there is no existing group in your community, place an ad in a newspaper and see if you can get a group going. You don't need to open up your home to strangers. Try to use a room at a local church, community organization, or possibly a recreation room in an apartment complex. One woman started a French-speaking singles club this way; one man started a bowling club for singles; and another started a group for people from his home state.
- Try joining a volunteer organization, community group, political organization, church group, or softball team.
- Keep in mind that you are more likely to develop friendships in groups that provide an opportunity to work with others on projects over a period of time.
- Take some classes, particularly ones that encourage projects and participation—gourmet cooking, photography, drama, laboratory classes, discussion classes.
- Join a divorce or singles support group, now sponsored by many churches and community organizations. Many people who have reluctantly joined support groups are now enthusiastic proponents of them.
- Many women find wonderful support networks in women's groups that are available in most communities. Many women's groups help members discover their own strengths and create a strong sense of solidarity and friendship.
- If you are a parent, try a singles-with-children group. Many churches now have these. Parents Without Partners is an old standby with chapters across the country.
- Don't forget your married friends. Some may continue to be good friends for life. Others may become good friends again after a lapse of time if they know that you are still interested in the friendship.

OPPORTUNITIES FOR PERSONAL GROWTH

As is true of so many things in life, being single has the potential to be as rewarding as you work to make it. You may not be single by choice, but that isn't germane to whether your life as a single will be satisfying.

Many others before you have been devastated by divorce, believing it was the end of their lives. Instead, many have found it was their second chance, providing opportunities they would not have had otherwise. One woman commented:

> I thought I would die, I mean really, literally die, when he told me he was leaving. I just couldn't conceptualize life without him—after 24 years. And then one day I realized, hey, I'm still alive....
>
> That was the turning point. Suddenly I stopped feeling like a victim and I had this wonderful sensation that someone had given me another chance, a chance to experience life in a way I had never expected ... as the architect for all my choices....
>
> I discovered that the life I wanted to lead on my own was very different from the life I'd been living with him. His leaving was the beginning of my development as a person. In a way, I really thank him.[1]

Too often, single life is treated as a transitory period to be endured until one remarries. *You* are the one who needs to make your life right. Don't wait around hoping for someone else to do it for you. Use your single life as a time to explore and develop the many facets of yourself that lie undiscovered. Open yourself to new experiences. Develop new interests. Forge a new identity. Learn the skills necessary to live independently as a single. Build a large and varied social support network. Develop goals and keep yourself moving toward them. Learn to become a better person because of your divorce. Don't waste this time as a single. Structure it to be rewarding and growth-promoting.

And what of the ambition of having another committed relationship? People are most likely to meet a new partner when they are involved with life and the things that interest them. It is when people are absorbed and enthusiastic about what they are doing that others are most likely to be drawn to them. Don't wait for someone to make you happy. Happiness is an inside job.

12

Communicating with an Ex-Spouse: Ten Tools that Will Make the Difference

"We could never communicate" is one of the most common reasons couples give for their marriage's failure, and many divorcing spouses look forward to never having to communicate with one another again.

Unfortunately, divorce opens a Pandora's box of issues that need to be settled as you separate your entwined lives and joint possessions. If you have children, you will need to communicate throughout their growing-up years. Impossible, you say? Many others feel exactly as you do.

The good news is that the kind of communication needed between divorcing spouses and divorced co-parents is very different from the kind needed between spouses. While a marriage calls for intimate communication, divorce and co-parenting call for businesslike communication that is restricted to concrete and practical issues in the here and now.

The bad news is that divorce engenders anger, mistrust, and new conflicts of interest that can easily impede constructive communication.

Fortunately, you can learn communication tools that will make all the difference between communicating effectively and ending up in a frustrating shouting match with nothing resolved and anger ignited. Each of the 10 communication tools in this chapter is adapted from tools used by mediators to facilitate communication. Each is very useful when relationships are strained or the respective parties' interests are in conflict. Each is a skill you can master with practice. You will find them useful with many people, not only your former partner.

You may notice that many of these tools have something in common: They help you communicate in a nonthreatening way that does not place the other person on the defensive. People on the defensive focus on protecting themselves rather than on the issue at hand. In fact, they often decide that the best defense is a strong offense and counterattack with a barrage of their own. Instead of the problem being resolved, it escalates into a conflict.

USE "I" MESSAGES

"I" messages, or *"I" statements,* are a way to express your anger and frustration in a way that encourages the other person to cooperate rather than respond with an argument, sarcastic response, or tit-for-tat retaliation.

Think for a minute about some of the more frustrating things your former spouse does that affect your rights or those of your children. Is the support check always late? Perhaps he or she shows up late to pick up the children and ruins your plans? Or perhaps the other parent frequently seems to have the children involved in other activities when it is your time to pick them up?

Now think about the way you usually respond. If you're like most people, you respond with "You" messages: "You're so inconsiderate!" "You're irresponsible!" Or how about, "You make me so furious, I could scream!" Or you may communicate your anger nonverbally, such as by slamming a door, hanging up the phone, or retaliating at a future time. None of these responses will inspire goodwill or cooperation, and they are likely to ignite yet another battle.

Learn to use "I" messages. "I" messages are deceptively simple but effective, and they can take several forms. When used with a former spouse, I prefer the following form because it reminds you what kinds of things are legitimate to complain about to an ex-spouse, specifically, behavior that infringes on your rights (or your children's).

To use an "I" message, start a sentence with "I," say how you feel, and describe how your ex-spouse's behavior is negatively affecting you. "I get so frustrated when the kids aren't ready on time." (How you feel.) "I have such a short time with them, and I want to use all of it." (How it affects you.)

What's so good about "I" messages? They allow you to express your feelings in a nonaggressive, nonthreatening, and nonblaming way and set the tone for a constructive solution to be found. In contrast, "You" statements blame the other person for your anger, put that person on the defensive, and encourage a counterattack.

Think about how you would feel if you were greeted by your former spouse in the following way: "Your irresponsibility is infuriating! The judge ordered those support payments and you'd better pay them on time!" Now think about an "I" statement. "I get so angry when I don't get the support check." (How your ex feels.) "I'm in a real bind when the landlord is on my back and the bills go unpaid." (How it's affecting your ex.) Do you feel the difference? Would you respond differently?

Here's another example. "You are so inconsiderate and selfish! Where were you on Saturday? Your kids were in tears when you didn't show. And you made me miss my plans." Compare that with this: "I'm irked you didn't come or phone on Sunday." (How your ex feels.) "The kids were in tears and I had to cancel my plans." (How it affected him or her.)

Try this one: "You knew very well I was supposed to have Kerry this weekend. You planned something else so I couldn't see her" versus, "I get so irritated when Kerry is scheduled for other activities on my weekend. How can I keep a relationship with her if I don't see her regularly?"

Learn to use "I" statements whenever you are angry or frustrated and your rights (or your children's) are affected. Make a very conscious effort to avoid "You" statements, no matter how tempted you are to "blame."

TURN COMPLAINTS INTO REQUESTS

Do you complain about certain things to your former partner over and over again, only to never see the situation improve? Here is a good tool for you. Instead of complaining or accusing, turn your complaint into a request. It is a lot easier to respond to a concrete request than to a vague complaint. And because a request is less negative, it is less likely to put the other person on the defensive.

Instead of, "You always send the kids in ragged clothes," try, "Could you routinely send one good outfit in case I take the children somewhere special?"

Instead of, "You don't brush Jenny's hair all weekend," try, "When Jenny's hair doesn't get brushed, it gets tangled in knots. Can you be sure to brush it every morning and evening?"

Instead of, "Communicating through our attorneys is absurd, and I won't do it," try, "Communicating through our attorneys is expensive and unreliable. Can we set aside a specific time each week for a business phone call and take care of things directly? We can make a pact that we won't raise personal issues."

Keep in mind that you are making a *request* to deal with a problem that you see. There may be other solutions as well, so be open to a *different* solution that the other person may suggest.

ATTACK THE PROBLEM, NOT THE PERSON

When you raise a problem with your former spouse, do the two of you usually get into an argument rather than tackling the problem? If so, perhaps the way you're stating the problem is getting things off on the wrong foot. Divorced spouses are particularly prone to present problems in ways that blame or criticize the other person. And in so doing, the chance to resolve the problem evaporates before it ever reaches the table for discussion.

For example, imagine the following scenario: The children spend Wednesday evenings with the other parent, and they've been arriving home tired, and without their homework completed. How would you handle it? You might be tempted to state the problem like this: "You never take care of the kids' homework Wednesday evenings. What are they supposed to do, stay up all night to get it done?" Hearing that, the other parent is likely to go on the defensive and to counterattack: "Well anytime you want to change roles, I'd be happy to have the kids with me during the school week and their homework would always be done. You think it's easy doing homework in a restaurant or arcade?" Immediately, you both get off track and the problem is never tackled, let alone resolved.

To avoid this scenario, attack the problem not the person. Focus on finding a solution rather than assigning blame. How? State the problem in *neutral* terms, and avoid using the word *you*. Take the stance that there is a problem and you would like to find a solution. How does this sound rather than the blaming statements above? "There's a problem with the kids not getting their homework done on Wednesday nights. It's too late to do it after they get home. How can we handle this?" Now the other parent won't feel the need to defend him- or herself, and both of you can focus on solving the problem.

Here is another example. Take a minute to think of how you would feel and how you might respond if you were on the receiving end of each statement. "Why didn't you tell me about Billy's award ceremony? You never keep me informed about what's happening at his school!" Compare that blaming statement with this: "There's a problem with information reaching me about Billy's school activities. If I had known about the award ceremony, I would have taken time off to be there. How can we handle information in the future so I don't miss Billy's special events?"

Phrasing problems in neutral terms is not likely to come naturally to you. Take time before raising a problem to think about how you are going to word it. Remember to attack the problem, not the person. Before raising the issue, put yourself in your former partner's shoes. Would you feel attacked? Or would you be motivated to tackle the problem?

OFFER SUGGESTIONS, NOT SOLUTIONS

Many divorced spouses fall into the trap of assuming that a problem has only one solution, which they then present to their former spouse as a "done deal." "You'll have to miss this Saturday with Sarah. She's got a birthday party." "You'll have to get a job. I can't afford the amount of money I've been sending you." "You'll have to buy your own clothes for the kids. I'm tired of clothes not being returned."

Even if you state a problem in neutral terms, it is unlikely to be resolved successfully if you present the solution, rather than make a suggestion. When you mandate a solution, you set yourself up as "the authority," which is bound to draw resistance from your former spouse. Presenting solutions in this fashion slams the door on constructive discussion before it begins!

Consider the scenario in which Jeanne tells Brad, "There's a problem with Scott getting to bed on time Sunday nights because he comes home from the weekend dirty and hungry." So far, Jeanne is doing okay—she's stating the problem in neutral terms. But then she ruins it by saying, "You'll have to have him home by five from now on." Whoops. Instead of a constructive discussion of how the problem might be handled, Brad's ire is raised and there's an argument. "My time is short enough with him. It doesn't hurt him to get to bed late one night. How much time do you need to bathe him anyway?" Had Jeanne *suggested* a 5 P.M. return time as a *possible* solution, she may have learned that Brad would love to do the dinner-and-bath routine with Scott on Sunday but just never thought of it. Or Brad may have proposed a compromise return time, with him feeding Scott a good dinner and Jeanne bathing him.

Remember, the "suggestion-not-solution" rule also applies when you are turning complaints into *requests*.

TUNE UP YOUR LISTENING SKILLS

You can't be a good communicator without being a good listener. Practice listening—*really* listening. Here are some *do*s and *don't*s that may help you:

- *Don't* interrupt. If you think you might forget a point, jot it down so you can address it when it's your turn.
- *Don't* rehearse how you will respond while the other person is still talking. You can't listen and plan your response at the same time!
- *Do* try to put yourself in your former spouse's shoes to understand his or her point of view. Ask questions to better understand.
- *Do* offer cues that you're listening, such as eye contact, a nod of the head, or a quick comment, such as, "Go on" or "I hear you." When couples work on this principle in counseling, their communication is found to improve. Joellyn Ross, who works with couples at the Penn Council for Relationships, has coined the sports term "pitchbacks" when teaching couples this valuable skill. Get in the habit of giving the other person pitchbacks (nods, eye contact, etc.) when you are conversing. The person will feel heard, and communication will go more smoothly.
- *Do* summarize the other's point of view as you understand it. ("Let me make sure I understand what you're saying" or, "So you feel that...") This is a more advanced form of pitchback. It not only offers a clear signal that you are listening; it prevents misunderstanding, too.

AVOID BUTTON-PUSHING LANGUAGE

Divorced couples are very tuned in to how to push one another's buttons, and there's nothing that will short-circuit constructive communication as fast. Undoubtedly you are well aware of what pushes your former spouse's buttons. Avoid doing it, no matter how tempted you are.

Some words are likely to push virtually *everyone's* buttons, and you need to watch these, as well. These universal button pushers are *should, shouldn't, always,* and *never.* Not many people respond well to being told by a former spouse what they *should* or *shouldn't* do. It sets one person up as the authority, and grates on the other. The most likely response? Resistance, active opposition, or a counterattack. Try stating what you would like to see *both* of you do, rather than telling the other person what he or she should or should not do. Instead of, "You shouldn't be allowing MaryBeth to stay up so late on weekends," try, "I know MaryBeth likes to stay up late on the weekends, but it gets her off schedule for the school week. Can we both follow a 10 P.M. bedtime on weekends?"

What are some other words that are universal button pushers? How about the exaggerations we so often use? "You're *never* on time." "I'm *always* the one who has to compromise." "*Every* week, you bring Andrew home hungry." Avoid these exaggerators. They are sure to turn the discussion into a recitation of incidents that contradict them. They are also sure to irritate the other person, who will feel that his or her efforts have gone unnoticed.

BE RESPECTFUL

Avoid put-downs. This one is so obvious it doesn't need elaboration. Everyone knows what a put-down is and how it feels to be on the receiving end. Unfortunately, divorcing spouses are notorious for hurling put-downs at one another. Have they ever inspired you to be cooperative? Just the opposite!

Sometimes put-downs are not explicitly stated but are implicit in the lack of courtesy or respect shown the other person. People with difficult ex-spouses often feel disdain for them and let it show. This is the worst thing they can do because difficult ex-spouses are often acting out of weakness and wounded self-esteem. When treated with disrespect, they feel even *more* dismissed and devalued. Their most likely response? To dig in and not give an inch! "I'll show her. She won't push *me* around!" It's their way of protecting their self-respect. In contrast, when treated with courtesy and respect, they are not put on the defensive, are likely to let their guard down, and are more open to constructive discussion.

Put-downs and disrespect invariably have disastrous consequences. Avoid them.

USE DISARMING TOOLS

Disarming tools cause people to falter when they are on the attack and to change gears. They de-escalate the conflict and can even have a calming effect. For example, if your former partner begins to yell or goes on the attack, *listen*. Don't attack back! Why? Because people find it difficult to continue attacking someone who is listening to them instead of yelling back. Listening forces the other person to regroup and change tactics. It is a great disarming tool. As an extra benefit, listening, rather than counterattacking, provides time for you to think and for both of you to calm down.

When you do speak, find a way to offer some support—another effective disarming tool. "You're a good parent and I know you want what's best for Jamie." Or, "I can see you're very upset." Offering a touch of support increases the likelihood of the other person calming down and changing tactics. Once your former partner is calmed a bit, try to address his or her concerns. "It sounds like you're worried about ever getting ahead financially because of the legal bills and support payments."

HOW TO KEEP YOUR COOL

You say that despite your best intentions, you always wind up exploding at your former spouse because he or she is a master at pushing your buttons? If so, you have probably learned that losing your cool is a sure way to douse constructive communication. Here are some things you can try that might help:

- Use autogenic breathing or deep relaxation (see Chapter 3) before and during encounters to keep yourself calm.
- Coach yourself each step of the way through tense conversations by talking to yourself ("Take it easy. Just breathe deeply and keep calm." "I won't let myself get as excited as she (he) is, or we'll get into a shouting match.")
- Keep your focus on the issues. Don't allow yourself to focus on your former partner, who may be in an abusive mood.

- Try giving the other person the benefit of the doubt. Anytime he or she does something that irritates you, force yourself to come up with at least one alternative explanation that has nothing to do with pushing your buttons.
- If your former partner is so angry and emotional that battles seem to be inevitable, humor may help. Try a technique developed by psychologist Albert Bernstein of Vancouver, Washington. Dr. Bernstein points out that our thinking brain retreats when we become emotional, and our more primitive lower brain centers—which he calls our "lizard brain"—take over. Any guesses as to how you might add some humor the next time your former partner flies off the handle? You've got it: Picture him or her as a lizard brain. You will be surprised at how this will help you keep your cool.
- If your former spouse constantly criticizes you, try a technique suggested by Dr. Marian Mowatt, a clinical psychologist and divorce therapist in Seattle, Washington. Try keeping a scorecard handy (out of sight). Divide it into two columns (negative and positive comments) and keep a tally for each "conversation" you and your former partner have together. The ratios of negatives to positive are usually rather lopsided. Some people get so caught up in the "game," reports Dr. Mowatt, they no longer get drawn into defending themselves. Instead, they make a game of seeing if old records will be broken. And since former spouses don't find it nearly as satisfying to criticize when they get no reaction, criticism often starts to decline!

USE EFFECTIVE NEGOTIATING TOOLS

Divorcing and co-parenting involve negotiation, and it behooves you to learn some good negotiating strategies. There are some excellent books on the market, such as *Getting Past No,* listed in Appendix D. Following are a few basic negotiating tools that you may find valuable:

- Be prepared. Don't try to negotiate if you have no direction. Be clear about your own needs, preferences, and priorities. Know where you can compromise and what your bottom line is. Think through several reasonable proposals in advance. When thinking about possibilities, remember that any problem can be attacked from many angles. Don't get stuck on one!

- Agree with your former partner on an agenda of issues to be discussed, and write it down.
- Break issues into small, manageable pieces. As an example, take a look at Chapter 17 and notice how each issue in a parenting plan is broken down into many separate parts.
- Start with the easiest issues to resolve. It's easier to build on success than failure.
- Avoid getting sidetracked. This can be tough. There are four key ways to succeed:
  1. Keep referring to your agenda to be sure you are still on track, and keep your focus on what you want to get out of the meeting.
  2. If other issues arise, agree to write them down for later consideration.
  3. Avoid talk of the past—it's sure to get you off on a tangent.
  4. Avoid putting the other person on the defensive; it will most likely result in a counterattack. Let me give you an example: Sue blames Phil for missed homework assignments when the children are with him. Phil feels attacked and counters with, "Yeah, well at least I go out and do things with the kids and don't use the TV as a babysitter." Suddenly the conversation shifts to who does what with the children and who is the better parent!
- Avoid positional bargaining. In positional bargaining, each party becomes fixated on a position and tries to force the other into agreeing. Positional bargaining invariably deteriorates into power struggles and a contest of wills.

  If you are set on a position, figure out *why* it is so important to you. What do you think it will give you if you win? Will it meet some strong need you have? Will it solve a critical concern? Will it somehow quell your fears?

  If your former partner is set on a position that you cannot accept, try to figure out why you can't. Perhaps you are rejecting a good proposal because you can't separate the proposal from the source. Try to put yourself in your former partner's shoes and understand his or her perspective. What important needs might this proposal meet for your ex?

  Once you've identified *why* your respective positions are so important to each of you, you may find a solution that will address the most important concerns *each* of you have.

Identifying each of their concerns allowed Rob and Mariless to resolve their dispute.

Rob and Mariless were stalled on the issue of legal custody—that is, who had the right to make the major decisions about their son, Gary. Mariless insisted she have sole legal custody so she could make all the decisions independently. Rob insisted that major decisions be made jointly. Each threatened to take the issue to court. Instead, they agreed to shelve the issue until they both had time to figure out why their position was so critical for each of them. When they met again, Mariless, who is a teacher, pointed out that she has always made the decisions about Gary's education and has always done the research and legwork that went into them. How could Rob make as informed decisions about Gary as Mariless could with all her research and training? Rob explained he feared being cut out of Gary's life. He would feel like an uncle, rather than a father, if he had no say in Gary's upbringing. Rob agreed that he had always deferred to Mariless on educational issues, and he saw no reason this should change. He suggested that if they could not agree about an *educational* issue, Mariless would be the decision maker. However, in areas other than education, they would make major decisions jointly. Although the solution was not what either initially wanted, it addressed their major concerns and was a solution with which each could live.

Learning good communication skills takes time and *practice*. Don't demand too much of yourself too quickly or you are likely to get discouraged and give up. Try one or two of these tools at a time until you master them. Then try one or two more. Before a discussion, practice them in your mind. Afterward, assess how you did. If you were successful, congratulate yourself. If you blew it, don't chastise yourself. Resolve to practice more and do better next time.

13

New Romantic Relationships

For six months, Mike kept all his relationships strictly platonic. "I didn't want anything more than company," he reported.

When people asked Penny if she would like to date, she told them she just got rid of one man from her life and certainly didn't want another.

Jackie couldn't understand what happened to her after her divorce. "I never thought of myself as the one-night-stand type, but for six months, I had this insatiable appetite for sex. I went to singles bars several nights a week and often wound up spending the night with someone I met." She is grateful this is behind her. "Now I'm very selective about whom I share my bed with," says Jackie.

Ross reports that after his wife left, he felt so empty and lonely he couldn't cope. Then he met Cheryl and they married within months. "I thought I was head over heels in love with her," confides Ross, when discussing his subsequent divorce. Now he is determined to be very careful next time.

Bruce has been in three live-in relationships since his divorce a year ago. "Each relationship seemed so right in the beginning," says Bruce. "Maybe I'm just not cut out for long-term relationships."

Most people find that divorce seriously influences their relationships with the opposite sex, although its impact assumes a number of different forms.

You may experience several of the patterns just described as you progress through the postdivorce months. Immediately after separation you may have no interest in either dating or sexual intimacy, proclaiming to all that you have sworn off the opposite sex for life. This is sometimes referred to as the "walking wounded" stage. It is a temporary adaptive reaction that protects you from involvements for which you are not ready.

Do you have an insatiable appetite for sexual intimacy? Have you had a string of casual sexual partners? Many divorcing men and women are completely baffled by their newly aroused needs and uncharacteristic behavior ("I don't know what's gotten into me."). However, this aspect of postdivorce adjustment becomes less baffling when some of the major motivating forces underlying it are understood. It seems to be largely an attempt to prove one's attractiveness and desirability, bolster sagging self-esteem, quell loneliness, and test sexual capabilities. Confidence in these areas is usually wounded during a poor marriage and the trauma of divorce. Casual partners have the advantage of requiring neither commitment nor trust, which is appealing to many who still feel vulnerable after divorce. But a series of casual partners is not for everyone, particularly in this age of AIDS and other sexually transmitted diseases.

Therapist Bruce Fisher, director of the Family Relations Learning Center in Boulder, Colorado, and author of *Rebuilding*, suggests that many of the needs underlying this compulsive sexual behavior can be satisfied in ways other than direct sexual contact. Since a strong motivating force behind the behavior is the need to bolster self-esteem and quell loneliness, he suggests that efforts be focused on *building* self-esteem and coping with loneliness in other ways. Chapter 11 will help you do both. Typically, the divorcing also have a strong need for physical touching, and many use sexual intimacy to meet this need. However, this need can be satisfied by nonsexual touching as well, says Fisher, such as getting and giving lots of hugs. Many relieve their sexual frustration during this time by masturbation.

BUILDING A STRONG FOUNDATION

At some point, people become bored with revolving partners and shallow relationships and look for something deeper. It is at this time that a new permanent relationship becomes very tempting—it would be so much more comfortable than being out there alone, having to forge a new identity and life. By all means, develop deeper relationships, *but* resist the temptation to enter a committed relationship at this time.

Relationships built when you are feeling needy and vulnerable are usually built on shaky ground. A relationship that seems serious at this point in your life may feel like an albatross around your neck once you are back on your feet. Right now you are likely to need someone who will teach you to trust again, bolster your self-esteem, fend off your loneliness, and distract you from your pain and anxiety. But these temporary props would be a poor basis for a *permanent* relationship. Once you are feeling confident and whole again and are ready to try new directions, you may feel completely out of sync with the person who once seemed so necessary.

When will you be ready for a new permanent relationship? You need to complete two major tasks first. One is your emotional divorce (see Chapter 10 for a complete discussion). You will start your new relationship with two strikes against it if you are weighed down with emotional baggage from your last one. If you have not figured out the role you played in the last relationship's collapse, you are less likely to be successful in the new one. If you still have lingering guilt or attachment to your former spouse, your new partner is likely to feel insecure and competitive. If you still feel vulnerable, you may keep your new partner at arm's length, denying him or her needed intimacy. If you still feel needy, you are likely to have unrealistic expectations for your new partner—that he or she will somehow make up for all your past hurts. If you have not achieved emotional distance from your former spouse, you may find yourself flaring up at your baffled new partner when he or she does something reminiscent of your former partner.

Many people falsely assume they are completely over their marriage because they hate their former spouse. "She's nothing to me anymore. I can't even stand the sound of her voice." They couldn't be further off base. It is the *intensity* of your emotion that determines whether you are still hooked in with your former partner, not whether you identify that emotion as love or hate. Continued fury and conflict with a former spouse creates havoc in the relationship with the new partner. It also saps the emotional energy needed to build a life with your new partner.

Your second task to attend to before you are ready for a permanent relationship is your own sense of identity, direction, and self-worth. Your contribution to a new relationship will be meager if you are still struggling to feel whole again. You should first feel that you can make it on your own. Chapter 11 will help you with this.

You might be thinking you know many people who remarry without completing these steps. You are right, many do. However, the divorce rate is 10 percent higher for second marriages than it is for first marriages, and 25 percent of second marriages never make it past their fifth year. If statistics were available for the demise of cohabiting relationships, they may very well be astounding.

If you are looking for a time frame, it seems to be the consensus of experts in the field that people who *rapidly* progress through the transition-restructuring stage of divorce and also make good progress in the recovery-rebuilding stage might be ready to enter a long-term committed relationship about two years after divorce. For most people, it would be longer.

Most mental health professionals suggest you experience a number of relationships after divorce *without* concerning yourself with permanency. Become a person who is interested in people and aim to get to know as many people as you can. Resist sizing up each new date as a potential marriage partner or comparing each against some ideal standard. If you do, you will deny yourself many potentially rewarding relationships. You might also spend much of your life feeling disappointed.

WHAT IF THERE ARE CHILDREN?

The reality is that a large proportion of divorcing men and women embark on a serious relationship—often a cohabiting one—within months or even weeks of the separation. Stories such as Ross's and Bruce's, in the beginning of the chapter, are common.

If there are no children involved, you can only hurt yourself, and it is your option whether to do so. But an alarming number of parents move a new significant other into their beds and homes while their children are still reeling from the collapse of their family. Dazed children feel as if they are caught in an avalanche, with too many momentous changes coming at them too quickly. Just when they need stability the most, their world is shaken again. Just when they need reassurance and one-on-one time with each parent, they are expected to share both time and affection with this intruder.

And who is this person anyway? Where does he or she fit in? Is this a replacement for their real parent? How can their parents possibly get back together with this new person in the picture? How can their parent expect them to simply accept this person with a smile? Can't their parent see how upset they are? Does their parent even care how distressed they are?

Older children experience anxiety on another front. The new relationship forces them to acknowledge their parents' sexuality, when they would prefer to think of parents as nonsexual beings. Adolescents, who are trying to deal with their own sexual thoughts and feelings, can be particularly troubled by the implications of the new relationship.

It is not unusual for children to feel abandoned and to be fearful, insecure, resentful, or angry. Anger often masks children's other emotions. Some express their anger indirectly—becoming uncooperative and sullen. Some act it out in obstreperous behavior. Some explode directly at a parent.

Some children align themselves with the other parent, especially if that parent treats them with sensitivity and provides them the one-on-one time they so desperately need. Such an alignment increases the likelihood that the rift between the children and the new couple will solidify into a long-term cold war.

The majority of children seem to develop painful loyalty conflicts, reflecting the lose-lose situation into which they have been thrust. It's obvious their parent wants them to like this new person. If they reject the person openly, their parent will be angry, and they will risk their own relationship with the parent. If they give the person a chance, they will betray their other parent.

To escape this dilemma, many children tell each parent what they know the parent wants to hear. Some are so conflicted, they don't know how they feel. If asked by a neutral person, they simply shrug their sagging shoulders.

Children are devastated still further if the "left-behind" parent vents his or her fury to them about the new relationship, demanding their loyalty and pumping them for information. These children feel they have no safe haven.

Go Slowly

The key when you have children is to *go slowly*. Give them time to adjust to their family's collapse before you introduce another person into their lives. For children, their family was a given—the entity that met their needs and provided them support, stability, and security; now that family is gone. If you remember from Chapter 7, children can usually deal with one significant source of stress at a time, such as their parents' divorce. But if the divorce is accompanied by other significant sources of stress, children will find it that much more difficult to reconstruct their lives. With each additional significant stressor, the risk for long-term problems multiplies.

Going slowly does not mean bringing a new person into your children's lives will be easy. Children often equate having less of their parents' time with having less of their love, and they have already witnessed their parents' love for each other wane. "Will I be the next one to be shut out of my parent's new life?" Children are still likely to be conflicted and to have loyalty binds. They still must face up to their parent's sexuality. They still must deal with dashed hopes that their parents will reconcile. They still may be fearful, jealous, angry, and feel abandoned.

However, going slowly will help ensure that you do not throw your children into a tailspin, especially when they are still trying to regain their equilibrium from the divorce. It will also give you time to prepare them for a new significant other in your life.

Laying the Groundwork

Many potential problems can be avoided with some *advanced* preparation. In her book *Sex and the Single Parent,* psychologist Mary Mattis provides a wealth of ideas. Here are some to get you started.

- Set aside regular time to spend with friends and build a social network, conveying to your children that adults need a social life with other adults just as children need a social life with friends their own age. When you are ready to date or become involved with someone, it will be a natural transition and will be less disruptive of their time with you.
- Evaluate your relationship with each of your children and begin to make changes now. Are you treating one or more of them as a confidant, companion, or equal partner? Not only is that detrimental to your child (see Chapter 14), but it will complicate bringing a significant other into your life some day. Understandably, your child is likely to feel replaced and become resentful. Allow your children to be children. Seek out adults for your companions.
- Build a strong relationship with your children that can weather future changes. (Chapter 9 will help you.) A child who feels secure about your love is less likely to feel abandoned when someone new enters your life. However, even a secure child will need reassurance, time, and attention. All children feel threatened when a stranger displaces them in their parents'

lives. Watch that your behavior toward them does not change dramatically.

- One day you may have a companion spend the night, and you will not want your children barging in on you. Begin now to teach them to have respect for your privacy. Start by respecting theirs. Always knock before entering their rooms, and teach them that when your door is closed, it is your private time.

Introducing a New Partner to Your Children

Don't make a companion part of your children's lives unless you think there is a strong possibility for a long-term relationship. If your children develop a bond with this person and the relationship ends, as relationships often do, they must endure yet one more loss in their lives. Children who suffer multiple losses because of parents' failed relationships are likely to conclude they are better off not to become attached. Some children become cynical about relationships; others become untrusting. "People can't be counted on. They are always disappointing me and leaving."

This does not mean there should be *no* contact. Once you begin to see someone frequently and after children have regained their equilibrium from the divorce, you might introduce your significant other to your children and involve them in an occasional *short* outing. Outings can gradually become longer if it looks as if the relationship will be a long-term one.

Before you introduce your significant other to your children, tell them you hope they will get to know the person as a friend. Make it clear your companion is not a replacement for their other parent. Children are more likely to accept someone who is not a threat. Be sure to reassure them of your love, and follow your assurance up with action. Parents often assume it is sufficient to include their children in activities with their companions, but this sends the message to children that the parent no longer has time for them *alone*.

Your New Partner's Authority

Companions (even live-in companions) should avoid trying to take on any kind of parental role. Children, and especially teens, usually become very resentful when a parent's new partner tries to exert any type of authority over them (disciplining, giving orders, assigning chores, siding with the parent against them). "You're not my parent and you have no right to tell me what to do" is an often-heard cry. Some children express their resentment openly, some become uncooperative, some act out their anger, some simply withdraw—none of which makes for a pleasant atmosphere in the home.

It is best for parents' companions to develop a relationship with children before attempting to move into any kind of parental role. This is discussed in Chapter 23.

When a Relationship Becomes Intimate

It is very anxiety-arousing and stressful for a child to have a series of men (or women) share his or her parent's bed. Many become angry, embarrassed, and withdrawn. Save intimacy for nights your children are staying with their other parent, grandparents, or a friend.

Most experts agree, however, that long-term committed relationships are a different matter where children are concerned. With time, most children are able to gradually accept a parent's sexual intimacy with one person for whom the parent deeply cares.

Prepare your children *before* you start having a significant other spend the night in your home. Don't be explicit; what you do behind closed doors is your private concern. Do watch for your children's reactions, and try to address their concerns calmly and warmly. Be forewarned: Parents are often startled to learn how aware of sex their elementary-school-age children are and how strict their moral codes are.

If you are a parent without custody, please be sensitive to your children's need to spend time alone with you during your limited time together.

When Teens Are in the Home

Teenagers present a unique problem that you must address. As mentioned before, teens are dealing with their own emerging sexuality, and having to acknowledge their parents' sexual behavior complicates their task considerably. Many become stimulated and curious, yet repelled, reports psychologist Neal Kalter of the Department of Psychology and Psychiatry at the University of Michigan. Girls can become particularly troubled, uneasy, and self-conscious. Sometimes there is a fallout that many single mothers do not consider: They become a role model for their daughters' sexual behavior. Teens find it difficult to understand why there should be a double standard for parents and for them. Girls will sometimes defiantly confront their mothers with, "If you can have your boyfriend spend the night, why can't I have mine?" Some mothers become intimidated and allow their teenage daughters far more freedom than is good for them. As a group, girls from single-parent homes are found to be more sexually active at an earlier age and more likely to become pregnant before marriage than are girls from two-parent homes.

You need to draw clear boundaries between the acceptability of sex for adults and for teens and you need to do so with conviction and confidence. Point out that sex is an adult behavior meant for long-term relationships and has a number of responsibilities tied to it that teens are not mature enough to handle: Teens are neither emotionally nor financially ready for parenthood; teens may not be emotionally ready to handle the end of a sexual relationship, which can be far more devastating than other breakups; teens are also unlikely to have the maturity to either question a partner about or adequately assess a partner's risk for exposure to AIDS or other sexually transmitted diseases. Making such distinctions will not necessarily solve the problem. For many teens, distinctions such as these won't hold water.

It would be less disconcerting to you if there were a pat solution to this dilemma, but each single parent must work out his or her solution individually.

The message of this chapter is to proceed slowly and thoughtfully with new committed relationships. Haste can leave a trail of turbulence that is likely to exacerbate problems in the long run and further delay successful new beginnings. When children are involved, the stakes and risks are higher. Please be sure to read the three chapters on stepfamilies before making a new significant other part of your children's lives.

14

How to Create a Successful One-Parent Home

The transition to parenting solo is seldom easy. New single parents talk of feeling estranged and displaced. They have lost their familiar role of "married parent" and now must assume the unknown role of "single parent" in their own household. Change always causes stress, but in this case, the stress is intensified by the feelings of loss, upset, and confusion that usually accompany separation and divorce. New single parents have fewer emotional resources to cope with the seemingly unending new demands.

You must carve your own path in this unknown new role. This chapter will lead your way. Its principles are based on what research has found to be successful for single parents and their children and can be used whether your children live with you all of the time, the majority of the time, or part of the time.

CREATING A HOME IN WHICH YOUR CHILDREN CAN THRIVE

Your children have lost their family as they knew it. It is now up to you to replace it with a new family unit in your home. Now that there is only one parent in the home, family members may need to assume new roles and responsibilities, learn new skills, and adapt to new routines. A new sense of "family" needs to be created. Reduced financial resources may further complicate an already complicated picture. But

193

children can and do thrive in one-parent homes. Following are steps you can take to ensure that yours are among those who do.

Adopt an Authoritative Parenting Style

Children are found to be better adjusted and to function more successfully when their parents use an *authoritative* parenting style rather than either an indulgent or an overly strict parenting style. This is particularly true for children in one-parent homes.

An authoritative parenting style is one whereby parents are warm, nurturing, and respectful of their children. They encourage open communication, seek their children's input, and are sensitive to their children's needs and opinions. At the same time, the parent is clearly in charge of the family and provides children with clear expectations, rules, and consistent follow-through. Let me give you an example:

> Sixteen-year-old twins Mike and Debbie complain to their mother, Janice, that they no longer want or need a curfew. Janice discusses the issue with them. What is their reasoning? What do they propose instead? What curfews do their friends Jack, Andy, Bill, Jeannie, and Marcia have? Janice feels they have some valid points. Perhaps their curfew is too strict. However, she thinks that not having a curfew is unreasonable for teenagers and shares her concerns with them. Janice compromises, saying that she can live with extending their 10 o'clock curfew to midnight on the weekend, but it remains in effect on school nights. They exert additional pressure on her, hoping she'll give in further. Janice remains firm, reminding them that as the adult and parent, her judgment has to be the one to prevail.

DEVELOP AN AUTHORITATIVE PARENTING STYLE

✓ Provide children with warmth, nurturing, and respect.
✓ Encourage open communication.
✓ Be supportive and responsive to children's needs.
✓ Provide clear expectations, limits, and rules.
✓ Follow through with consistent *positive* discipline.
✓ Remember, you are in charge.

Chapter 9 provides practical suggestions for how to improve communication with your children and how to shore up your relationship with them—both important ingredients of an authoritative parenting style.

Consistent Positive Discipline.

Studies find that consistent positive discipline plays a critical role in whether one-parent homes function well or poorly. Please don't make the mistake of confusing discipline with harshness and spanking. *Discipline is teaching children responsibility, self-control, and how to behave appropriately.* An authoritative parent sets clear rules and limits for children, monitors children's behavior, and consistently follows through with consequences *in a calm and caring manner* when limits and rules are broken. Ideally, the consequences should make sense to children and be known in advance.

> Four weeks after Janice extended the weekend curfew to midnight, Mike came home at 12:30 A.M., assuming Janice would be asleep. Janice calmly grounded him, despite Mike's pleas that he couldn't miss the school football game the following evening. Janice said she was sorry he would miss the game, but pointed out the decision had been his. She reminded Mike that they had both agreed to the consequences for breaking curfew.

Chapter 20, "How to Discipline Effectively and Still Be a 'Good Guy,'" will help you develop an effective system of discipline. You will also learn why an authoritative parenting style is so beneficial to children.

Family Meetings

A good way to help you develop an authoritative parenting style is to institute weekly *family meetings*. Family meetings can be used to air and discuss family problems, make some family decisions, and plan family activities. Make it a policy that every member of the family is listened to with respect. Family meetings will foster children's feelings that everyone in the home is respected, needed, and working together.

When you involve children in finding solutions to family problems, you are likely to have a smoother-functioning family. Children are generally more committed to adhering to decisions they help make. For example, children may be slacking off on chores or you may be getting too many calls at work about arguments. What can be done about the problem? Try some brainstorming to find solutions.

In *brainstorming,* everyone is encouraged to come up with as many solutions as they can, no matter how silly they sound. Assign one person to write down *every* idea, and make the rule that no one is allowed to comment on any idea, even if it is silly and totally impractical. To do so will stifle creativity. One idea usually leads to another, and a totally impractical idea may stimulate a workable idea that would not have been thought of otherwise. When you are done brainstorming, go over each idea and mark the ones that seem to have strong possibilities. Once the list is pared down, discuss the pros and cons of each and decide on a solution to try.

However, as the parent, some decisions are yours alone. You might use family meetings to democratically divvy up chores, but you need to provide guidance about the age appropriateness of different chores. You might even use a family meeting to decide on consequences when rules are broken, but you yourself need to determine if the suggested consequences are appropriate.

Maintain Generational Boundaries

The importance of maintaining "generational boundaries" between parent and children is a theme that consistently emerges in studies of one-parent homes. We've already seen the importance of parents being in charge of setting and following through with limits. But maintaining generational boundaries is important in areas other than discipline. Children and teens need to function as children and teens both emotionally and in the responsibilities delegated to them.

Unfortunately, in one-parent homes generational boundaries often become blurred. The reason is that overburdened single parents usually rely on children to fill some of the gaps left by the other parent. The implicit or explicit message is that "we are all in this together," and a coalition between parent and children generally evolves. Having been promoted to the status of "junior partners," children are also typically given a larger say in family and household matters. Family decisions and rules, once jointly made by parents, become more open to negotiation. In many homes, the authority distinctions that once existed between parent and children become fuzzy, as do the distinctions between the parent's and children's rights and responsibilities.

It is fine for children to become *junior* partners in the family—for parents to share *a few* of their concerns with their offspring and to enlist children to help with *some* family responsibilities. Such an arrangement can have many benefits. However, many single parents go a step further and either explicitly or implicitly grant the role of *equal* partners to their children. In so doing, they effectively (although not intentionally) relinquish their parental role and authority. This is a real mistake, frequently leading to one of two related problems, each of which can spiral out of control.

The Parent-Becomes-Peer Family.

Families in which single parents become peers of their children are seen with regularity in child guidance clinics and community mental health centers across the country, report Dr. David Glenwick of Fordham University and Dr. Joel Mowrey of Kent State University. In these families, one typically finds a very bright, articulate older child (frequently 9 to 13 years old) who appears to be far more mature than he or she actually is. These children's precociousness lures overwhelmed single parents into treating them as peers, confidants, and companions rather than as the children they are. Parent and child become extremely close, with the parent regularly sharing personal and financial problems, frustrations, and loneliness with the youngster, as if the child were another adult. In some cases, the child functions as the parent's chum. At other times, children begin to parent their parents, providing nurturance, support, and advice. Sometimes these youngsters are the prime forces holding the household and family together.

Although these children appear to have great inner strength, many are stretching themselves beyond their psychological limits. They marshal all their resources to hold a vulnerable parent together because they are well aware that children cannot make it on their own. In the process, they suppress their own needs, fears, concerns, and feelings of loss surrounding their parents' divorce. These children's outward appearance of maturity belies the overwhelming anxiety and insecurity they generally feel. But many eventually express their anxiety and fears indirectly in symptomatic behavior, such as stomach pains, sleeping and eating problems, academic and school problems, drug use, and promiscuous behavior.

Sometimes problems do not become evident until the parent develops a new romantic relationship. A new person on the scene threatens the child's special relationship with the parent and the prestigious position he or she has earned in the family. Feeling cast off, youngsters are often filled with jealousy and anger and begin to act out their feelings in problematic behavior.

If you are treating your child as a peer or confidant, find an adult friend to confide in, and encourage your child or teen to develop friends and outside interests. Allow your child to worry about childhood or adolescent concerns rather than adult ones. Shift the focus from you, and help your child adjust to the many losses he or she has had.

The Child-Competing-for-Power Family

A second problem commonly develops when a parent promotes a child to the role of *equal* partner in the family: a subtle struggle for leadership and power in the family. This pattern is particularly likely when a parent sends the child competing messages—sometimes accepting the child as an equal partner and other times expecting the child to submit to parental authority. The parent often loses this power struggle, although he or she is seldom aware of it until the situation is out of control. Usually the parent drifts into the pattern of deferring to a child in areas where parents should be in control, including authority over younger siblings. Children in these families also routinely make their own decisions without guidance or input. However, because of their lack of maturity, their decisions are often poor ones.

Once again, children are functioning in an adult role for which they are unprepared emotionally. A parent has effectively relinquished his or her parental role of providing the child with discipline, guidance, and protection, and the situation often goes amiss. Common problems that eventually bring these pseudomature youngsters to therapists' attention include rebelliousness against authority, drug abuse, sexual promiscuity, truancy, or a number of other behavior problems. Their single parents, throwing up their hands in despair, report, "I give up. I can't do anything with him, and I have no idea what happened!" The underlying problem is not only that children have insufficient guidance and too much power in the family. They are also under too much stress from functioning in an adultlike role before they have the maturity to handle it.

If you have been treating a child as an equal partner, begin to exert your authority in areas that naturally separate parents and children, such as allowances, chores, homework, curfews, and types of television programs that are acceptable for them to watch. Read Chapter 20 on discipline, and begin to set and enforce limits and rules. Be prepared for protests and resistance; it is only natural. But don't back down on your resolve. Children need their parent to be in charge.

If your home is out of control, don't hesitate to see a family thera-pist who will help you get it back on track. Most communities have agencies that provide family counseling on a sliding scale rate in ac-cordance with a parent's income. If you have health insurance, it may also cover counseling.

Create a New Identity for Your New Family

Make a conscious effort to create a new identity and a bank of good memories for your family. This will help minimize your children's feel-ings that your new family is somehow incomplete now that it has only one parent. Here are some ways that you can create a distinct family identity:

- Arrange frequent family activities that everyone enjoys doing together.
- Try to discover some *new* activities and interests that everyone enjoys that can come to symbolize your new family. Brain-storming is a good way to come up with new and creative ideas.
- Develop some new family traditions and rituals. Examples might be weekly family meetings, spending individual time each day with each child, a weekly family night, outings with a local "singles with children" group, and yearly Thanksgiving dinner with other single parents and their children.
- Consider getting a new pet that will always be associated with your new family.

Provide the Critical Ingredients for Children's Long-Term Divorce Adjustment

Chapter 9 focuses on how to create an environment that will foster children's long-term adjustment. If you incorporate these basics into your one-parent home, your children can thrive. Children's long-term divorce adjustment depends not only on what transpires at the time of the divorce and shortly thereafter, but on what transpires during the *years following divorce*. Take time to review Chapter 9 and to look at the table that appears here, which summarizes these important ingre-dients. You will notice that some have already been discussed in this

---

HOW SUCCESSFULLY ARE YOU INCORPORATING THESE BASICS INTO YOUR HOME?

✓ Are you protecting children from parental conflict?

✓ Are you protecting children from loyalty binds?

✓ Are you shoring up your relationship with your children?

✓ Are you supporting your children's relationship with their other parent?

✓ Is there a dependable schedule for children to be with each parent?

✓ Are you trying to develop a workable co-parenting relationship with the other parent?

✓ Have you created predictable routines and schedules in your home?

✓ Are you providing clear expectations, limits, and consistent *positive* discipline?

✓ Are your children free of adult responsibilities, roles, and worries?

✓ Are you careful not to overwhelm children with many changes simultaneously?

✓ Do your children have outside sources of social support to supplement the support you provide?

---

chapter. Check the table to see whether you are integrating these fundamentals into your home.

CREATING A HOME IN WHICH A SINGLE PARENT CAN THRIVE

Single parents often feel as if they were jugglers, trying to keep four balls in the air—their jobs, their children, the household, and their personal lives. Competing demands steadily vie for their immediate attention, and in the absence of an involved co-parent or willing relative, no one is likely to step in when a single parent is fatigued or in trouble.

Successful single parents have many of the same problems as do their less successful counterparts: dealing with divorce-related emotional stress, financial pressures, and time pressures; coping with ex-spouses;

dealing with children's divorce-related emotional problems; and, of course, the responsibilities of parenting solo while children are with them. What distinguishes successful single parents from less successful ones is the way they learn to handle these problems.

A number of researchers have been able to identify coping strategies developed by successful single parents. Here are some effective strategies that are well worth developing.

Develop a New Social Support System

It may surprise you to learn that social support plays an important role in your being able to parent successfully solo. Studies find that single parents with good social support systems are more likely to have good parenting practices, good relationships with their children, good morale, and better mental and physical health.

Strive to develop a wide network of people who can provide you with many different types of support, such as emotional support, companionship, relief child care, help in emergencies, and practical help. It will be a boon to your morale, and exchanging services, talents, and practical help can relieve you of some of the varied responsibilities you shoulder. Perhaps you can divvy up tasks (taking turns doing errands) or exchange services (some grocery shopping for clothes alterations). Home sharing is another possibility that many single parents enthusiastically recommend. It provides them with an extended "family" and significantly cuts down on costs and workload.

Social support is not likely to fall at your doorstep. Most likely you will have to seek it out actively. Chapter 11, "Rebuilding," has many suggestions to help you build a new social support network.

Keep Your Expectations Realistic

Remind yourself that you are only one person and you can't do all that two people can. No matter how competent you are, you are only human! Consciously look for your successes rather than your failures.

If you get in the habit of making a mental list of your accomplishments each day, you will be less tempted to berate yourself for all you did not accomplish and more likely to remain upbeat.

Household responsibilities usually offer the most flexibility when something has to slide. In fact, time studies report that employed single mothers spend considerably less time on household tasks than do their married counterparts. For example, an Ohio State University study found that single working mothers spent an average of one and one-third hours less each day on house chores than did married working mothers. A Boston study reported similar findings.

How can you save time on household tasks despite having to shoulder them without a partner's help? Here are some suggestions:

- Prepare simpler meals, which also means less time spent shopping and cleaning up; meals don't have to be fancy to be balanced and nutritious.
- Try entertaining simply; casual potlucks are favorites for many single parents.
- Get out of the perfection trap and lower your standards. Some things just aren't worth the time it takes to do them perfectly. Save perfection for the important things. This means consciously evaluating how well a task really needs to be done and whether you need to do it yourself or can delegate it to someone else.
- Work out arrangements with other single parents that are mutually supportive for each of you, such as setting up baby-sitting co-ops and car pools, or taking turns doing errands.
- Enlist children's help.

Children and Chores

Enlist your children to assume *some* new responsibilities that are appropriate to their ages, remembering not to overburden them. Since every member of the family enjoys the use of the home, eats the food that is bought and prepared, and wears clean clothes, every member should pitch in and share some of the household responsibilities. Generally, children who do chores become more responsible and have higher self-esteem than children who do not contribute to the family.

To enlist children's help with chores, try calling a family meeting and discuss what needs to be done. Then jointly decide how to divide jobs. Be realistic. Chores need to be appropriate for children's ages, as well as for their daily schedules. Make children responsible for themselves as much as possible (picking up after themselves, cleaning their rooms, and, if they are old enough, washing and putting away their laundry). Children will cooperate more readily if they have a say in the chores they do. If some jobs are either very popular or unpopular, they might be rotated, or children may find it more fun to choose them out of a hat. Some families have a job list with each chore assigned a point value. Then children take turns choosing chores until they total a certain number of points. Make up a chart so everyone can remember his or her jobs for the week.

Be sure to remember not to overburden children. They should have time for normal childhood activities, friends, homework, and some unscheduled time.

Match Chores with Fun Activities

Set a time aside for the entire family to do chores together, and follow it with an activity everyone will enjoy, such as a trip to the ice cream store, a video, a picnic, or an hour playing games that the family enjoys. It is a good idea to set a time by which jobs must be completed in order to participate so that one slow child does not deny the others their reward. ("Everyone who is finished with their chores by noon gets to play the new game.") For children who resist doing chores, consequences should be clear. For example, chores must be completed before children are free to do fun activities (go out with friends, watch television). Some parents tie the completion of chores to receiving an allowance. Others withhold privileges (television, use of the car) or favors (chauffeuring). However, never make the consequence that they cannot go with their other parent! That relationship is a necessity, not a privilege, and it is not your right to deny the other parent's time with the children. Read Chapter 20 to learn more about setting appropriate consequences.

Don't Neglect Your Personal Life

Your well-being is integral to your children's well-being. Successful single parents generally have learned the importance of taking time to recharge their batteries. They realize the difficulty, if not impossibility, of effectively tending to children's ongoing needs when their own lives are barren. In fact, studies find that a poorly functioning single parent usually forecasts poorly functioning children. In the long run, denying your own needs may lay a guilt trip on your children as well. Young adults raised in single-parent homes often report a reluctance to create a life of their own, feeling they are abandoning a parent who has sacrificed so much for them. Here are a few goals to target:

- Set aside a minimum of a half-hour a day to do something that you will enjoy, and try for one evening a week.
- Get involved with at least one pursuit that will bring you personal fulfillment. Single parents are generally happier if they have outlets they find rewarding, besides parenting.
- Aim to incorporate as many single parents into your support group as possible. If they have children the ages of yours, all the better. You will find it immensely helpful to have people with whom to share ideas and perspectives, obtain feedback, and seek advice. Parents Without Partners and other single-parent support groups are excellent ways to meet other single parents. So is your children's school. Either your children or their teachers may know of other single parents you can contact.
- If you have not already done so, work on completing your emotional divorce (see Chapter 10) and dealing with your leftover anger (see Chapter 5).
- Work on rebuilding your self-esteem and your life (see Chapter 11).

A word of caution: Don't be lured by the advice to "focus on your own adjustment and your children's will *automatically* follow." While a poorly functioning single parent usually forecasts poorly functioning children, the reverse is not necessarily true. Research has identified many custodial parents who have adjusted exceptionally well to the divorce but whose children's adjustment is exceptionally poor. This is because the parents were so involved with their own lives that they had little time for their children. In what little time they spent together, parents were preoccupied, emotionally distant, and unresponsive to their children's needs and distress.

Juggling Finances, Employment, and Family

It is important to find a way to secure a stable income, sufficient to provide for your family's needs, and then to find creative ways to live within it. Studies find that once income is at a level that meets basic necessities and allows independence, its *stability* is more important than its *size*. Successful single parents do not necessarily have large incomes.

If you are reentering the workforce or dramatically increasing your work hours, you are undoubtedly experiencing a good deal of work overload. It may reassure you to know that new single parents who have always worked have a less difficult time juggling all they have to do. You, too, should find it easier with time and experience. You may also find it reassuring to learn that many single parents find work to be an important source of self-esteem, fulfillment, and social contacts. Studies find that both job satisfaction and job performance are high for single parents.

Although a full-time job is a fact of life for most single parents and does provide them satisfaction, many do trade off the better job for one that is less demanding, is closer to home, or has more flexible hours. Many single parents accept that they will be passed over for promotions because they cannot travel or put in overtime. Often, careers are simply put on the back burner until children are raised.

You will feel more comfortable at work if you are satisfied with your child care arrangements. Alison Clarke-Stewart's book *Daycare,* listed in Appendix D, provides guidelines for what to look for.

If you have older children who will be on their own after school, make sure you set up strict rules to ensure their safety and have them practice how they would handle different emergencies. Ask your children to call you at work when they get in from school or if a serious problem arises that they cannot handle themselves. You can also establish the routine of calling them.

Find one or two backup sitters who can stay with a sick child. Parents who do not have an extended family member, friend, or co-parent on whom they can rely often search for a neighbor they can depend on, or their child may have a friend whose parent does not work outside the home. Repayment with another type of favor or service is a good trade-off. The key is advance preparation so you do not have the dilemma of losing a day of work, sending a sick child to school, or leaving a sick child home alone.

Put an End to the Conflict with the Other Parent

Work on ending the conflict with the other parent and building a workable co-parenting relationship. Studies find that an acrimonious relationship with a former spouse takes a toll on single parents' health and well-being, in addition to being destructive for children's well-being. Ongoing conflict creates a pervasive atmosphere of chaos, emotionally ties you to your former partner, and hinders you from moving on with your life. In Chapter 19, you can find many practical tools to help end the conflict. Even if you wish the other parent would disappear from your life, his or her participation in your children's lives is important for their well-being. Chapter 18 guides you through the steps to develop a workable co-parenting relationship. You may find, as have many other single parents, that once you develop a workable co-parenting relationship, you have a new resource to call on in a pinch.

THE CONSEQUENCES OF GROWING UP IN A ONE-PARENT HOME: FACTS OR MYTHS?

If you are like many single parents, you may have lingering concerns about whether being raised in a one-parent home will negatively affect your children. You may have heard that single-parent families are a cause of psychological problems, academic difficulties, truancy, and delinquent behavior. How true is all of this? Are your children at risk? How much is fact and how much is myth?

Children from one-parent homes are indeed overrepresented in the population of children who are troubled, have academic problems, are truant, and have encounters with the law. But studies have discovered that one-parent homes, per se, do not create children's problems. It is what happens *within* the home that is important, not whether that home has one parent or two. Is the home happy or unhappy? Is it conflict-free or conflict-ridden? Does it radiate love or breed insecurity? Is it stable or unstable? Is an adult in charge to provide guidance, supervision, and discipline, or are children on their own without rules or limits? Can children partake in normal childhood activities and live from day to day without shouldering adult problems and responsibilities?

The reason that children from one-parent homes are more often in the population of children who develop problems is that *statistically* fewer one-parent homes are stable and conflict-free. *Statistically* fewer single parents provide supervision, rules, and limits. *Statistically* more one-parent homes are in a chronic state of stress. *Statistically* parent-child relationships are poorer in divorced families. And *statistically* more children from one-parent homes are overwhelmed with feelings of abandonment, adult responsibilities, and adult worries.

A one-parent home *can* provide children with as healthy an environment as can a two-parent home. Children can and do thrive in one-parent homes, and so can yours.

15

The Parent without Custody: Dilemmas and Solutions

The noncustodial role thrusts parents into a dilemma that commonly goes unrecognized. Unfortunately, many nonresident parents who find no satisfying way to solve their dilemma allow themselves to drift along in a way that has serious repercussions for their children. Most don't realize the seriousness because they believe they have become inconsequential to their youngsters. With few exceptions, they are wrong. The issue is not whether parents without custody have an impact on their children, but whether their impact is positive or negative.

THE "VISITATION" DILEMMA

What precisely is the nonresident parent's dilemma? Researchers find that after separation, the great majority of parents without custody intensely miss being involved in their children's daily lives and report overwhelming feelings of loss and being shut out. Even many previously uninvolved fathers become distressingly aware of what they have missed.

Instead of opportunities for a meaningful relationship, however, most parents without custody are restricted to what is known in most states as "visitation." Visitation? With your own children? What are you supposed to *do* during "visitation"? Do you take the children to your home? Will they be bored? Do you try to do something spectacular?

Play tour guide? Take them on a shopping spree and shower them with presents? After all, you have so little opportunity to show your love these days, and you want them to look forward to seeing you. Perhaps they might even stop coming if you don't show them a good time. Do they want to see you as much as you want to see them? Parents whose children differ widely in age or interests have more complicated problems with how to spend their allotted time. Studies suggest the most common visitation pattern for noncustody fathers is interacting with children as an adult friend and spending time in recreational activities— a pattern that often develops by default rather than by design.

Few parents without custody are satisfied with the "visitation" arrangement or the role of "recreation director." They complain there is too much to compress into a limited time and simply no time to let things happen naturally. How do you pass on your values and hard-earned wisdom to your children on a Sunday outing? How do you get children to share their feelings, fears, and inner lives with you? Getting children to open up takes time, the right situation, and the right mood— luxuries often not enjoyed by nonresident parents and their youngsters.

It is not only *meaningful* communication that is difficult in this strange new "visiting" situation, say nonresident parents. They and their children often report an awkwardness with one another never before experienced; they often have the feeling of not knowing what to say, what to do, or how to act with each other. And if a parent and child do finally establish some rhythm between them that feels comfortable, it is usually lost in the interim before they see one another again.

Too often, whatever sense of intimacy the parent once had with a child feels tenuous at best, and the parent begins to feel like a peripheral player in his or her child's life. Many parents eventually ask themselves whether "visitation" is worth it. If their child seems to be doing okay, many wonder how much they are really needed. They wonder how much influence they can possibly have on their child's development. To many, "visitation" seems futile, and the role of noncustodial parent feels like a sham.

How do parents without custody resolve the "visitation" dilemma? Many resolve it poorly: They begin to distance themselves from their youngsters. As they do, their children become less central to their lives, and with the passage of time, spending time together, phoning, and letters drop off. Some eventually join the ranks of parents who have drifted out of their children's lives completely.

But fading out of children's lives has high emotional costs. Everyone loses. Many nonresident parents who withdraw from their children report feeling anger and a continued sense of loss for years afterward—quite a contrast to the uncaring, indifferent parents others assume them to be. But children are the real losers.

THE IMPORTANT ROLE
OF THE NONRESIDENT PARENT

In the aftermath of divorce, youngsters cling to their "visits" with the parent who has left the home, and the "visits" assume tremendous symbolic importance. To youngsters, these contacts are not only evidence of a parent's love, but a gauge of how lovable and worthwhile they are. After all, the parent *chooses* to see them regularly, despite the hassles involved. It must prove the child is loved, lovable, and worthwhile.

Infrequent and unreliable contact with the nonresident parent is also symbolically significant to children. They feel rejected and abandoned, and they look for some explanation for the parent's seeming indifference: "I'm not lovable enough." "I'm not good enough." "I've done something wrong." "How terrible I must be if my own dad (mom) doesn't even want to see me!"

Most noncustody parents who drift out of their children's lives would be shocked to learn of the anguish they cause their youngsters and of the prolonged impact their absence has. Although many realize they will be missed initially, they generally assume their children will get over it. After all, children are resilient. They have their other parent, and sometimes a stepparent. They have their friends, activities, and lives. "How important can I be?" they wonder. How important are noncustodial parents? Meet Debby and Kelly.

Debby is a teenager who has not seen her father since a very young age. Says Debby,

> I sit sometimes for hours and think of what it would be like to have a father hold me, take me places, and tell me he loves me. If only I could have that feeling once more. I always see pictures with him holding me, and I get so mad at myself because I can't remember that feeling.[1]

Kelly, now 12, was only 2 when her parents divorced. It is not surprising her dad felt he was inconsequential to her life. But one gets a very different impression from Kelly herself. Kelly has had little contact with her dad over the years. In fact, during the previous two years, she had spent a total of three hours with him. Yet she confides to the interviewer,

> Once a couple of years ago ... he invited me to spend a weekend. I had the best time of my life, because I love him more than anyone in the world.... I miss him. I miss him so much.[2]

The fact that Kelly has a stepfather with whom she is very close makes her idealization of her father and the intensity of her feelings that much more striking.

Researchers who interview children from divorced families frequently report being stunned at children's fierce attachments to parents who have done little but disappoint them. The interviewers report being deeply moved by children's anguish and distress at their parents' disinterest. They have commented on children's grateful acceptance of whatever little attention they receive from errant parents. They have marveled at how important a relationship with an absent parent is to a child when, to the outside world, there appears to be *no* relationship. One writer, after interviewing hundreds of children from divorced families, commented that the loyalty these children had for their parents, regardless of circumstances, made man's landing on the moon seem commonplace by comparison.

To children, a parent is a parent forever, not someone casually forgotten. Although children are usually quite resilient, a parent's abandonment is a unique trauma from which many do not easily recover. Some continue to be troubled with intense feelings of rejection, abandonment, and loss throughout their childhoods. Some continue to feel unlovable and to have poor self-esteem. Some respond with anger and act out that anger in behavior problems such as aggression, drug abuse, or delinquent activities. Some, after having seemingly adapted for years, develop a renewed intense desire for their missing parents when they reach adolescence. Children who had a close relationship with a parent before divorce are the most hard hit. To such a child, the parent's disinterest and abandonment are utterly incomprehensible and devastating.

SOLUTIONS FOR THE "VISITATION" DILEMMA

Nonresident parents *can* maintain good relationships with their children despite constraints on the time they have together. In fact, some parents without custody develop *better* relationships with their children after divorce than they had while living with their children full-time. Once freed from the problems in the marriage, some previously uninvolved parents get to know their children as individuals and form warm and close relationships with them. So can you.

The first thing you need to do is a tune-up on your thinking. Eradicate the terms *visitation* and *visiting parent* from your vocabulary! Your time with your children is your *parenting time* and you are a *co-parent*.

Usually the most satisfying relationships between parents without custody and children are found when parents create a second home and family for their children. Within this more natural environment, parent and children can continue more genuine relationships. They can spend relaxed time together, which all people need to really know one another. They can continue doing many familiar activities together. Parents can feel like parents rather than aunts and uncles, and children can feel like they still have *two* parents.

But what about the fun outings and presents? Isn't that what children expect, you wonder? What they really want, say most children, is to feel *loved* and *valued*. They want to feel that their parents are interested in them and in what they do. *They want their parents to be involved in their lives.* It is usually only if parents make entertainment and presents the focus of their interactions after divorce that children come to expect these things. Of course, fun outings can be interspersed with at-home time.

Don't be overly concerned if your place is very small. Size is less important to most youngsters than you might think, providing a parent does a few simple things (discussed shortly) to make it feel like a home for them, too. All your time together does not have to be spent there, but at least it is a home base.

If you feel that creating a second home for your children is simply not feasible, there are still ways to build good relationships with them and have a positive impact on their lives. The following pages are full of suggestions for how to successfully parent your children part-time in a variety of circumstances.

Creating a Second Home for Your Children

Immediately after separation is the best time to begin setting up a second home for your children. That way you can avoid interrupting the continuity of your relationship. You can even involve them in helping you set it up.

However, it is never too late to start creating that second home. Here are some guidelines that will help:

- Try to make your home feel like a home to your children, too. Find some niche for their belongings, even if it is only a drawer.

Have them leave some of their things or purchase a few things for them to leave, such as a toothbrush, pajamas, a few changes of clothes, and some special toys, books, or games that they will look forward to using when they come. The less they have to carry back and forth in a suitcase, the more they will feel that they have two functioning homes. Display the things they make or give you (pictures, crafts, gifts, and so on). Have some of their favorite foods on hand.

- Continue doing things you have always done together, and get involved in other activities that full-time parents do. Ask your children when they come if there is anything they need to do—homework, school projects, picking up school supplies. Then help them do it. Have long talks. Play games. Enlist their help in fixing meals, grocery shopping, or a fix-it project, but be sure these are things you do together. The idea is to make them an enjoyable part of your time together.

- If your children are old enough (see Chapter 17), spend regular overnights together. If you don't have lots of room, buy some sleeping bags and inflatable air mattresses, and have your children "camp" on your living room floor. Overnights provide special bonding time for parents and children that daytime visits do not.

- Establish some routines—bedtimes, a bedtime story or talk, a morning routine, homework time, and some minor chores (setting the table, helping with dishes, feeding a pet, picking up after themselves). Try to keep some routines consistent with their familiar routines in their other home.

- Establish some house rules. Provide your children with clear limits and expectations of unacceptable behavior. Aim for some consistency with their other parent.

- Try to live close enough to your children so they can get to activities from your home. This generally creates a more natural situation and allows longer stretches of time together.

- Explore your neighborhood together. Establishing ties to the neighborhood will help your children feel they belong there. Meet some neighbors. Learn if there are children to play with, places that interest them, or activities they might enjoy. Invite neighborhood children to join activities you initiate.

- Encourage your children to invite friends to your home.

- Develop some new traditions that symbolize your children's second family. Try having family meetings to discuss plans, house rules, feelings, and problems. Discover some special ways to spend holiday time together. Get involved in some new fun activities that each of you will enjoy—start a hobby together, build something, cook special meals, find games you all enjoy. Be sure to solicit your children's ideas. Brainstorming is a fun and effective way to come up with new and creative ideas. (Family meetings and brainstorming are discussed in Chapter 14).

- Read Chapter 18, "Making Co-Parenting Work," and start following its principles. Chapter 14, "How to Create a Successful One-Parent Home," is also for you.

Building Good Postdivorce Relationships

If you have not already done so, arrange with the other parent a set schedule that allows your children to see you frequently and regularly. (See Chapter 17 and Appendix C for ideas about appropriate parenting schedules.)

Frequent and reliable time together shows your youngsters that you are giving them a high priority in your new life. It also provides them concrete evidence that their relationship with you is stable and can be counted on. If you have teens, asking for their input in scheduling time together will show them you are sensitive to their needs and busy schedules.

The following suggestions will be helpful whether you create a second home for your children *or* see them away from your home. You can build a good relationship with them either way.

- Be dependable and be sure to keep the promises you make.
- It helps to begin your time together with some kind of ritual to get everyone past the early awkwardness created by lapsed time—stopping for ice cream, playing a word game in the car, stopping at Grandma's or at a park.
- Involve children in planning your time together so they will have input in what you do. This is especially important to older children. If you run out of ideas, brainstorm.
- Keep abreast of your children's interests, activities, and school progress. Make every effort to attend their plays, music recitals, sports games, school open houses, and parent-teacher conferences. See if you can take them to their activities from time to time. Learn the names of their friends and teachers. Ask them about their activities since the last time you talked, books they've

been reading, their favorite television programs, and new interests they've developed. (You might try some of them yourself.)

- Make it a point to remember what your children talk about from one time to the next. If they need to tell you the same things over again, the lines of communication will gradually shut down.

- Keep in touch between your scheduled times together with phone calls. Even if your children are very young, hearing your voice will provide continuity in their relationship with you. Encourage older children to call you, too.

- Relationships are a two-way street. Share what you have been doing, and introduce them to some of your interests to see if their interest might be sparked.

- See each of your children individually when you can so each can have one-on-one time with you, especially if they are of markedly different ages.

- When children's special activities conflict with your scheduled time together, be flexible to accommodate their needs. It goes a long way in relationship building when your children see that you respect their individual needs and wishes. Can you take them to the activity yourself? It would give you time together and further involve you in their lives. If not, see if you can reschedule time together at a different time, even if it is a shorter time. The older the children, the more flexible you will need to become.

- Create an atmosphere of open communication with your children. Refer to Chapter 9 for ideas. If you want to penetrate your child's inner life, you need to make a special effort to do so.

- Avoid creating loyalty conflicts for your children by putting them in the middle of issues between you and their other parent (see Chapter 8). Not only is it harmful to your youngsters, but you are likely to lose a contest with their other parent since they spend most of their time with that parent.

- Accept the fact that you will not have as much influence on your children's development as you would have if you were living with them full-time. You may be able to broaden their horizons, but don't spend your limited time together lecturing them or trying to change them.

- Limit the number of times you invite an adult companion to join you. Taking along a companion denies your child the exclusive time he or she needs with you and usually creates strong feelings in children, as it did with eight-year old Celia.

Celia used to anticipate her dad's visits with excitement. She never cared what they did; she was just happy being with him, holding his hand, and telling him about her week. Now visits make her angry and sad. Two months ago Jan moved into Celia's dad's apartment and has come along on their days together ever since. Celia can't understand why Jan has to come when she sees her dad so seldom and Jan sees him all the time. She was ruining everything. It was so unfair. Half the time her dad and Jan talked to each other and left her out. One day, in frustration, she blurted out, "Why does she always have to come?" But her dad became angry with her. So now she keeps her frustrations to herself, afraid he will stop coming at all if he learns how angry she is.

If a significant other lives in your home, arrange to spend some time alone with your children while they are there.

- If the relationship with one or more of your children is going poorly, hang in there. Some children are very angry because of the divorce, and although they may not verbalize it, their anger can create some stormy times together. Other children try to cover up their fears with arrogance, while still others continually test the sincerity of their nonresident parents' love by being obnoxious and ornery.
- If you find your time with your children falls apart during the last hour or so, it is probably due to the tension everyone is feeling about the impending separation. It is much easier to say good-bye when everyone is angry at one another. Try talking with them about how hard it is to say good-bye. You might try spending the last half-hour in an activity that will allow you and your children to get some emotional distance from each other before you have to part physically.
- Review the suggestions in Chapter 9 for shoring up your relationship with your child.

PARENTING AT A DISTANCE

If you live so far from your children that you can only see them a few times a year or less, there are two excellent books listed in Appendix D that will give you lots of help with keeping a relationship with them even though you live at a distance: *Long-Distance Parenting* and *101 Ways to Be a Long-Distance Super Dad—Or Mom Too.* Following are some suggestions to get you started:

- *Continuity is critical!* Make frequent and regular phone calls. Try to establish a regular time that is convenient for your children's schedule to be sure they will be home. If they are old enough, encourage them to call you when they need you. Teach them how to reach your pager, use prepaid phone cards you provide, or reverse the charges.
- The more you keep abreast of your children's daily lives, the easier phone conversations will be. Encourage them to keep a list of things they would like to talk to you about, and be sure to do the same.
- Send mail frequently—letters, postcards, small items, pictures—anything to preserve your presence in their lives and let them know you are thinking about them. Many long-distance parents don't write to their children because they don't know what to say in letters. A California-based organization has developed a program called The Write Connection. It consists of kits of materials that include ideas for topics to write about and inexpensive things to send, developmental information about children, stationery, and return mailers for your children. It's a great way to get yourself started. Send for information to The Write Connection, P.O. Box 293, Lake Forest, CA 92630. Or you can call 1–800–334–3143. Those with e-mail can contact them at WriteBack4@aol.com.
- Let your children know you want to hear about their activities, interests, and lives. Ask your older children to send you reports they've written for school and ask younger ones to send pictures they've drawn. Be sure to provide them with self-addressed, stamped envelopes and write back to them about the things they send. Get a real dialogue going.
- Try to spend some time in their home community so you can be a part of their lives.
- Send self-addressed stamped envelopes to your child's teacher and request to be kept up-to-date on your child and school activities. Ask the teacher if you may call or e-mail.
- Be sure your child has a lot of photos of the two of you doing things together. You may even want to make up a special photo album together.
- If you have a new family, encourage them to communicate with your children.
- Before your children visit, talk with them about things that you will be doing during the visit; get their input. Be sure to get

them caught up on what you (and your new family if you have one) have been doing if you haven't done so on an ongoing basis. During the visit, have family meetings so everyone can openly discuss feelings and concerns (see Chapter 14).

PARENTING YOUNG CHILDREN AT A DISTANCE

If you have young children, you have a special challenge in keeping a relationship with them when you cannot see them frequently. Young children have difficulty developing and maintaining bonds with a parent when their contact is infrequent. While your children are young, it will be important to keep a very active and ongoing presence in their lives. Here are some suggestions in addition to those given in the previous section:

- Make audiotapes or videotapes of yourself reading stories to your children, and add a personal message at the end. Be sure they have a child's tape recorder so they can play the audiotapes. Your child can hear you read a bedtime story every night! If you send along the storybook you read from, your child can read along with the tape—a wonderful learning-to-read tool. Encourage preschoolers to make tapes for you, too—telling you about their day or telling you a story. If you send stamped, self-addressed envelopes, the other parent is more likely to cooperate in helping them.
- Your toddler or preschooler would be thrilled to have a little book to "read" consisting of pictures of the two of you with a few words underneath each. ("Dad and Jimmy having a picnic at the lake. Remember the big fish we saw that day?") You can easily make the pages of the book out of sturdy, colorful poster board and hold them together with yarn.
- Whenever you see your young children, give each of them something they can associate with you, preferably something that each has grown attached to. Tell your youngsters, "Every time you look at this, it will remind you of me and the good times we had together." It will help you maintain a presence in their lives despite the distance between you.
- Be sure to read about children's developmental needs in Chapter 17, and don't push your child to visit you before he or she is developmentally able. Unless the more familiar par-

ent is along, young children, at least till age 3, need to be visited in their home community, where they are comfortable and where they can return to their more familiar parent and surroundings at night. Your visits should be as frequent as possible, so your child can develop strong bonds with you.

- When can your child visit you? A widely used rule of thumb is that a young child can be continuously away from his or her primary resident parent for *one day for each year of age,* providing the child is comfortable with the parent he or she is visiting—in other words, three days for a three-year-old. This can be longer if the more familiar parent is in the area and the child can have contact with that parent during the visit. I have seen more liberal guidelines suggesting that a three or four-year-old child, who is very adaptable, might be able to visit a parent for up to one week, providing there has been lots of contact between the parent and child and the youngster is very comfortable with the parent. There should be daily phone contact with the more familiar parent. Having a sibling along would make it easier on the child. If your child does make out well with one week, you might try extending it a few days the following year. However, cut back if your young child shows signs of stress. It will only harm your relationship if your youngster is stressed and anxious when visiting you.
- Before your young child does visit, it would be helpful to spend a day or two with him in his home community so the two of you can become reacquainted in his familiar surroundings and he can return home to spend the night.
- Prepare carefully for a visit with young children. Ask the other parent about their familiar routines and favorite foods (as well as favorite brands of food). The more you can make your environment feel familiar, the more comfortable your youngsters will be and the more likely they will be to enjoy the visit. Ask their other parent to pack a few things that each is very attached to, such as a stuffed animal, blanket, doll, or favorite toy. It would be comforting for them to have a picture of their other parent with them because of their difficulty maintaining an image of the parent in their minds. While your children are with you, be sure they have daily phone contact with their other parent, and help them keep track of the days on a calendar so they can have some idea when they will be returning home.

THE MYTH OF THE INCONSEQUENTIAL PARENT

Contrary to what you may have feared, you need not be a peripheral player in your children's lives, and your influence on them need not be superficial. A combined research effort between Iowa State University and the University of North Carolina reported that nonresident parents were successful in influencing their children's development when the parents engaged in positive *parenting* behavior, such as helping children with their problems, providing encouragement, setting clear expectations of acceptable behavior, and following through with consistent discipline. A 1999 study, headed by Penn State sociologist Paul Amato, who statistically pooled data from 63 studies of noncustodial fathers and their children, revealed that a consistent predictor of children's adjustment and academic success was nonresident fathers' use of an *authoritative parenting style*. You may remember from Chapter 14 that an authoritative parenting style is one that combines parental warmth and support, open communication, firm limits, and consistent *positive* discipline.

In other words, you can have a positive impact on your children by assuming the role of an effective parent rather than a pal or recreation director. This is undoubtedly why nonresident mothers are generally found to have a greater impact on their children's well-being than do nonresident fathers. Nonresident mothers are more likely to take on the role of supporter, adviser, and disciplinarian than are nonresident fathers. Generally, noncustody moms are also found to be more involved in their children's lives and to communicate better with them.

If you read Chapter 7, you know that both mothers and fathers make *unique* and important contributions to their children's lives and development. But your impact extends even further. Your continued involvement as a warm, supportive parent is likely to influence your children's lives in two *additional* important areas.

The first is their self-esteem. When nonresident parents stay positively involved in their children's lives despite the hassles, children's self-esteem, which is usually damaged from the divorce, often climbs. Self-esteem is one of the most powerful gifts you can give a child. With high self-esteem, life's obstacles become challenges; with low self-esteem, they become stumbling blocks.

The second area in which you can have a positive impact is your children's ability to handle stress. If you read Chapter 7, you may recall that good relationships with parents act as a protective cushion for children that buffers them from many of the blows inflicted by stress. True, your children have their other parent, but a good relationship with one parent usually does not afford children the same protection from stress as do good relationships with *both* parents.

Your children's development and adjustment, academic success, self-esteem, and ability to deal with stress—having a positive influence in these areas is like throwing a stone into a pond. The stone makes a ripple that gradually spreads over the entire surface. So, too, will your positive influence in these areas have a ripple effect in your children's lives. Be sure, however, to protect them from conflict between you and their other parent (see Chapters 8 and 19). The damage caused them by conflict could significantly weaken the benefits of your involvement (see Chapter 7).

Some of the benefits of your involvement with your children will be more immediately tangible to you. You will be able to enjoy the relationships you build with them, which will last a lifetime. And you can forge a role for yourself that both you and your children will find satisfying. It may not be the role you had planned or the role you would have played if you lived with them full-time, but it does not have to be any less meaningful. When asked about their noncustody parents, many children talk fondly of a caring parent who is always ready to provide a warm and safe haven, to be a sounding board, to offer a fresh perspective, or to simply listen and empathize. Listening to these children, it is obvious their nonresident parents have become special resources they can draw upon. These parents have added another dimension to their children's lives that has certainly enriched them—and this is something that some parents in intact marriages never accomplish.

IV

Co-Parenting Children after Divorce

16

Custody: What's the Real Scoop?

For many parents, custody arrangements are the source of as much anxiety as is the divorce itself. "What custody arrangement," they ask, "is best for children?" "Do children need a stable home base?" "Should children spend equal time with each parent?" "Is it disruptive for children to go between homes during the school week?" "Can my children benefit from all I have to offer them if they don't spend at least half the time with me?" "Shouldn't siblings always stay together?"

What is the answer to the often asked question "Which form of custody is best for children?" If you read Chapter 7, "Critical Ingredients for Children's Adjustment," you may recall that custody was never mentioned in the chapter! What is critical for children's adjustment is an end to parents' conflict, good relationships with both parents, and good parenting and stability in the primary home or homes. Social support and not having to deal with stress from multiple sources are found to be very important, as well.

So where does custody fit into children's adjustment, you wonder? The answer is, as a general rule, one form of custody is no more preferable than another. What is best depends upon the children, the parents, and the circumstances.

This chapter looks at different custody arrangements. It is not meant to be a legal treatment, for laws differ from state to state, and there is no shortcut for learning the laws and terminology of your state. Our focus will be the distinctions between the different forms of custody and what the research finds about each.

LEGAL CUSTODY VERSUS PHYSICAL CUSTODY

Most states now make the distinction between legal and physical custody. Legal custody is concerned with *decision making* about the children, and physical custody is concerned with *where the children live.* The two are independent. In many states, it is common for parents to have joint *legal* custody but for one parent to have sole *physical* custody.

Legal Custody

Sole legal custody means that one parent has the authority to make all the major decisions about the children. When parents share *joint legal custody,* they make *major* decisions about their children jointly. Some states have a preference for joint legal custody and award it in the majority of cases, even if one parent objects.

The types of decisions encompassed under legal custody are usually those related to education, religious training, nonemergency health care (such as elective surgery or controversial medication), and significant issues related to the child's general welfare. Check your jurisdiction for issues that might fall within this last category. Examples of more clear-cut issues may be whether a child is placed in counseling or whether an underage child is allowed to marry.

Regardless of who has legal custody, the minor day-to-day decisions are usually left to the parent whom the child is with at the time. Examples of day-to-day decisions are those related to playmates, nutrition, discipline, and house rules. You can find specific help on the issue of decision making in Chapter 17, "Parenting Plans," and Chapter 18, "Making Co-Parenting Work."

The Pros and Cons of Joint Legal Custody

The benefits of joint legal custody are obvious: It affirms that both parents have a right to have a say in how their children are raised. Several studies report that nonresident parents are more likely to keep involved with their children when they have input into child-rearing decisions. When one parent has sole legal custody, the other parent often feels disenfranchised or like an aunt or uncle rather than a parent.

Obviously, joint legal custody works best when parents do not have major philosophical differences about child rearing, when they are able to communicate and focus on their children, or when there is an accepted decision maker in the event of a disagreement. When none of these are the case, joint legal custody has the potential to throw a child's life into limbo, as important decisions are left hanging. However, the great majority of parents seem able to negotiate joint legal custody without major problems. It appears that most parents do not have major philosophical differences over the kinds of major decisions that must be determined jointly. Additionally, a number of studies suggest that in many divorced families, parents with sole *physical* custody actually become the de facto decision makers, whether or not they have joint legal custody. Researchers find that at times the parent without custody is asked for input beforehand but at times is told about the decision only after the fact. For many families, this is merely a continuation of the roles parents played during the marriage and feels natural to them. Interestingly, in one large scale study, 40 percent of the nonresident parents felt that they were equal partners in decision making, while most of the resident parents felt that they made decisions themselves. For these parents, there appeared to be a general sense of satisfaction in the way decisions were being handled.

Even when parents have philosophical differences and both insist on being involved in making decisions, joint legal custody does not necessarily forecast problems. Some parents agree to take disputes to mediation to help resolve them. Others agree that the resident parent will make the decision in the event of an unresolved dispute. Some agree that each parent will make the final decisions in specific areas. For example, Mom makes the final decisions about school issues, while Dad makes them on religious issues. In another family, Dad trades final decisions about religious issues for final decisions about the children's sports and music lessons. A very small percentage take disputed issues to court to be resolved. Joint legal custody is contraindicated in cases of stalking, serious domestic violence, or the impaired mental functioning of one parent.

Whatever else joint legal custody accomplishes or fails to accomplish, it has a high *symbolic* value, making it clear to both parents that in the eyes of the law, nonresident parents have both the right and the responsibility to be involved in their children's upbringing.

PHYSICAL CUSTODY: JOINT VERSUS SOLE CUSTODY

Physical custody designates where children primarily reside. In sole physical custody, one parent provides the child's primary home and usually has the major responsibility for the child's day-to-day upbringing. The other parent sees the child either on a specified schedule or has "reasonable visitation"; what is "reasonable" is open to interpretation.

In joint physical custody, children spend substantial time in each parent's home, and parents actively share in their day-to-day upbringing. (For the sake of brevity, joint physical custody is also referred to as dual residence or simply joint custody for the remainder of the chapter.)

Parents often assume that joint physical custody means that children are with each parent 50 percent of the time. In fact, few children divide their time equally between parents, and there are no generally accepted hard-and-fast rules about what time share should be considered joint physical custody. Definitions and interpretations differ depending upon the state and jurisdiction.

Researchers generally define dual residence as the children spending between one-third to one-half of their time in one home and one-half to two-thirds in the other. Even with this more liberal definition, dual residence arrangements are relatively rare. In a 1999 research review, divorce expert Robert Emery of the University of Virginia estimated that fewer than 10 percent of postdivorce child-sharing arrangements fall into dual residence arrangements.

In the eighties, there was a flurry of research on joint physical custody, and some considered it to be a panacea for all divorced families. The obvious benefits of joint custody were touted: Parent-child relationships would more closely resemble the intact family; children could have strong ties to both parents; both parents could play an active role in their children's upbringing; and neither parent would be overburdened with the stress of full-time parenting.

Early research on joint custody generally reported positive findings. Compared to sole custody children, the joint custody children were often found to have higher self-esteem, reported more positive experiences in their lives, and felt very valued because of both parents' determination to remain in their lives. Some studies reported the most satisfied children to be those in joint custody arrangements. Parents, especially fathers, also reported a high satisfaction, and parents' stress levels were lower than those reported by sole custody parents. However, the parents in these early studies also *chose* joint custody and were very committed to making it work. Research results are not as positive in all studies, particularly when joint custody is imposed upon parents.

When the research is looked at in its totality, there is no evidence that joint custody is *either better or worse* for the *majority* of children than is sole custody. Some experts have concluded that joint physical custody can be the *best* as well as the *worst* alternative for children.

When Can Joint Physical Custody Be Beneficial?

It is now widely agreed that the question is not "Does joint physical custody work?" Nor is it "Is joint custody good for children?" Rather, we need to ask, "For *whom* does joint custody work, and under *what* circumstances does it work?"

The Parents

Joint physical custody works best when parents—

- Can separate parenting issues from spousal issues, focus on their children, and keep the children out of parental conflict.
- Are able to communicate and cooperate with one another about their children.
- Respect one another as parents and one another's importance to the children.
- Fundamentally agree on child rearing.
- Are willing to coordinate schedules, standards of behavior, expectations, and discipline for their children.
- Are flexible and adaptable.

The Children

Particularly when parents do not work together in their parenting, it is the children who shoulder the brunt of dual residence demands. It is the children who must continually adapt to the differences and demands of two homes, move back and forth, and keep schedules and belongings straight. Many children shoulder the burden of coordinating the logistics, such as when team uniforms are needed and the progress of long-term homework assignments so things will be at the right home at the right time. Depending upon how different the homes are and how contentious the parents, some children feel as if they change lives each time they change homes.

Still, various studies have reported that between two-thirds and three-quarters of the children in their study groups reported being satisfied with their dual residence arrangement. Who are the youngsters for whom joint custody works?

They are children with the developmental capability of handling the demands of living in two homes. Although there is negligible research on the issue, generally there is concern about the ability of infants, toddlers, and preschoolers to handle dual residence. These young children thrive on consistency and generally need a stable home base. Some, however, do well. Researchers Rosemary McKinnon and Judith Wallerstein, were able to identify a very small group of toddlers who appeared to successfully adapt to a dual residence arrangement, but their parents worked very hard to make the arrangement work. These parents were exceptionally sensitive, communicated with one another *daily*, and coordinated all aspects of their youngster's life to provide a stable environment *within and between* both homes. They also kept their child out of any conflict. The Joint Custody Study Project, sponsored by the Jewish Family and Children's Services of San Francisco, found that children under five did well with dual residence when parents were exceptionally able to work together, remain child focused, and value one another's contributions to their child's life.

However, even such impressive parents are not *always* successful in paving a smooth road for their children in dual residence arrangements. In a different study conducted at the Jewish Family and Children's Services with similar parents, 25 percent of the children were found to be confused and anxious about switching homes and about their schedules of going from one home to the other. Half of these were the youngest children in the study—four- and five-year-olds. Interestingly, they had already lived in dual residence arrangements for a minimum of two years. This study group was very small, however.

Teens often prefer having a primary home base, even many who have grown up in equal child-share arrangements. Many teens, particularly older ones, simply find it too difficult to negotiate two homes with the demands of their busy social, school, and work schedules.

Children's temperaments also play a role in how well they adapt to a dual residence arrangement. Some children have very easy-going, adaptable temperaments and adjust to change easily. These children can usually negotiate the demands of two homes in their stride. In contrast, children who have a hard time with change and need consistent routines in order to function well are likely to have more difficulties.

The Circumstances

For dual residence to work for children, parents must live in close enough proximity to one another so children can consistently attend one school. Preferably, children should be able to participate in their activities from each parent's home and have consistent friendships. The more equal the child-sharing schedule, the more necessary this is for a child.

Some parents arrange dual residence around vacation times, so the parent who lives further away has a larger share of school breaks. This works well for many families. As children grow older, most want to spend some time during vacations in their more familiar community with their close friends, however.

There is another type of joint physical custody arrangement, called "nesting," which works for some parents who work *very* well together. The children remain in the home, and the parents move in and out, whether weekly, biweekly, monthly, bimonthly, or in several-month blocks of time.

When Can Joint Custody Be Damaging to Children?

When parents are locked in conflict, distrustful of one another, and cannot separate children's needs from their own, joint physical custody is found to be the worst alternative for children. It appears that the more equal the child-sharing schedule and the more frequently children go back and forth between the warring homes, the more likely they are to be negatively affected: to be withdrawn, depressed, aggressive, or to have somatic symptoms.

Why should this be? The more that both parents are actively involved in day-to-day child rearing, the more contact is needed between them and the more there is for embattled parents to fight over with children caught in the middle. Even worse, antagonistic parents are also more likely to become locked in power struggles over managing their children's lives when children spend more equal time in each home. Sarah's parents are an example.

Eight-year-old Sarah had been spending equal time with both her parents for three years when her father remarried and moved to a community 40 minutes away from Sarah's school. For the next year, he transported Sarah back and forth to school during his parenting time with her, but then he enrolled her in *his* neighborhood school. He informed the mother of Sarah's new school by letter, stating it was a better school and Sarah's preference. Sarah's mother was furious and strenuously objected to a change in Sarah's established school. Both homes were in an uproar with Sarah caught in the middle. The matter finally ended up in court.

When parents are embroiled in conflict, children in dual residence arrangements usually become enmeshed in the ongoing battles, get caught in parental cross fire, and feel emotionally torn by conflicting loyalties. As researchers at the Center for the Family in Transition so aptly put it, these children are double agents living in one warring camp or another and continually crossing between the two. They have no safe haven. Please read Chapter 8 to learn about the devastating repercussions conflict has for children.

MOTHER CUSTODY VERSUS FATHER CUSTODY

Despite the popularity of fathers' rights groups across the country, the great majority of children in sole physical custody arrangements continue to live with mothers. Of single-parent homes, 15.9 percent are headed by fathers, according to the 1998 Current Population Survey, published by the U.S. Bureau of Census. Fathers would find the raw numbers far more impressive. Between 1988 and 1998, homes headed by dads grew from 1.8 million to 3.1 million!

Studies find that the great majority of divorcing parents make custody decisions themselves without court intervention. For example, the Stanford Custody Project reported that 51 percent of 1,100 divorcing families completely agreed on custody, while an additional 29 percent settled custody arrangements without going to court. Another 11 percent reached agreement in court-mandated mediation. Only 9 percent of the families remained in dispute! What arrangements did the parents agree upon? Seventy percent agreed to mother custody, while 10 percent agreed to father custody. Another 17 percent agreed to joint physical custody. Three percent decided to split custody (each parent having custody of at least one child).

The Stanford researchers also asked their large study group what custody arrangements they had wanted *initially*. Interestingly, one-third of the fathers reported they initially wanted sole physical custody, but fewer than half of them actually pursued this in court. Some realized their work commitments would not accommodate full-time parenting. Some felt that the children were closer to their mother and that she was also the more experienced parent. Some did not want to engage in a custody fight. Others assumed the odds would be stacked against them in court.

Is There Gender Bias in the Courts?

"Courts always give the children to mothers" is a belief expressed by many fathers. At one time, courts did show a preference for maternal custody. However, most, if not all, states now have gender-neutral custody laws in which mothers and fathers are equal before the law. The criterion now used by courts is "the best interest of the child," and custody is determined on a case-by-case basis.

Many parents continue to believe, however, that judges' rulings demonstrate a strong bias for mothers. In an attempt to assess the validity of this belief, Berkeley professor Mary Ann Mason and her colleague Ann Quirk undertook a comparison study of a random sampling of appellate court decisions across the country, along with their rationale. The years 1960, 1990, and 1995 were compared. (Appellate courts hear appeals.) Professors Mason and Quirk reported a significant shift in court reasoning between 1960 and the 1990s. By the nineties, the concept of maternal preference had disappeared from judicial rationale for custody. In its place was the concept of the *primary caretaker.* The primary caretaker is the parent who has had the *major* responsibility for meeting the children's needs on a day-to-day basis. The primary caretaker is usually determined by such criteria as intimate parent-child interactions, including comforting, nurturing, feeding, bathing, dressing, teaching elementary skills, and caring for children when sick; managing children's schedules and routines; overseeing school work and arranging activities; and dealing with schools, child care, and doctors. The rationale is that children will be provided with more continuity and stability in their postdivorce lives if they remain with their primary caretaker. A second rationale is that the postdivorce family is likely to function more smoothly with the more experienced parent in charge.

The primary caretaker criterion explains why mothers are still more likely to be granted custody than are fathers. Despite the prevalence of two working parents in the home, studies are continuing to find that mothers assume *most* of these parenting responsibilities, and fathers usually play a secondary role.

Although primary caretaking was the most common factor stated in judicial custody decisions in the nineties, it is certainly not the only criterion courts use. The broader criterion, the *best interest of the child*, considers what a particular child needs at this time, given the totality of the current circumstances. The primary caretaker is usually only one consideration, albeit a very important one. Other considerations are likely to include a child's individual needs, attachments, and emotional ties; parents' emotional stability, parenting competence, and life style; parents' willingness to share the child; parents' ability to provide continuity with school and community; domestic violence and abuse issues; and substance abuse issues.

How frequently are mothers being granted sole physical custody in the courts? The best statistics available are those from the Stanford Custody Project mentioned earlier. If you remember, only 9 percent of the 1,100 divorcing families did not resolve the custody issue themselves or as a result of court-mandated mediation. Of these, 44 percent of mothers received sole physical custody. Of fathers, 11 percent received sole physical custody, 40 percent received joint physical custody, and 5 percent received split custody. For cases that reach a court of appeals, a far greater percentage of fathers receive sole custody. In the 1995 appellate court decisions reviewed by professors Mason and Quirk, 45 percent of mothers and 42 percent of fathers were granted sole physical custody. The remainder of families were granted either joint physical custody or split custody. If you are wondering why there is such an increase in father custody awards in appellate cases, it is because fathers are likely to have a very substantial case for custody by the time a case reaches an appeals court.

How Do Children Fare in Mother versus Father Custody?

In a widely cited mid-1990s study conducted at the University of California at Irvine, researchers Alison Clarke-Stewart and Craig Howard reported that children in father custody homes were doing *better* than those in mother custody homes. Their study group consisted of 5-to-13-year-old children, 72 of whom were in their father's custody and 187 in their mother's custody. Those being raised by fathers were generally found to have higher self-esteem, less anxiety, less depression, and fewer behavior problems. Boys fared particularly well, although girls were doing better, too.

Before you conclude that fathers make better single parents than do mothers, read on. There are several reasons children may do better in father custody homes. Custody-retaining fathers are found to be a very select group. Most are well educated, have a higher than average income, actively chose their nontraditional role, and are eager to make it work. Perhaps even more important is that mothers without custody are generally found to be more involved with their children than fathers without custody typically are. After reviewing the research, well-known divorce expert E. Mavis Hetherington reported that nonresident mothers have two to three times more contact with their children than do nonresident fathers. When children's perceptions of their nonresident parents are compared, mothers without custody are perceived to be more supportive and sensitive, more responsive to children's needs, more interested in children's activities, and to have more influence on children's lives than do fathers without custody. It appears then, that children in father custody homes are more likely to have *both* parents involved in their lives and to have good relationships with *both* parents, which, of course, contributes immensely to these children's well-being.

All studies have not found that children do better in father custody, as did the University of California study. In a thorough review of the research, Dr. Robert Emery, director of the Center for Children, Family, and the Law at the University of Virginia, concluded that as of 1999, on balance, few differences have been found in children's adjustment in maternal versus paternal custody homes.

Studies find that single-parent fathers and single-parent mothers have different strengths and weaknesses. Custody-retaining mothers are found to have more difficulties in allocating household tasks and with discipline, especially with their sons. Fathers with custody tend to have more difficulties with communication and with monitoring children's activities, school progress, friends, and health.

In case you're tempted to ask whether mothers should always have custody of *young* children, it may interest you to know that fathers who have custody of young children are found to demonstrate *similar* levels of warmth and nurturing, as well as a similar range of caregiving abilities as do their female counterparts. In his study of 1,000 single fathers, Geoffrey Greif of the University of Maryland found that fathers who seek custody of their children perceive themselves as more loving and nurturing than the average man.

SPLIT CUSTODY:
SHOULD SIBLINGS STAY TOGETHER?

The bond between siblings has been called the "longest bond," and there appears to be an almost universal assumption that siblings should remain together after divorce. In the Stanford Custody Project study of 1,100 families, parents almost always kept children together and their efforts to do so seemed to outweigh considerations for individual children's needs. In the study of appellate court decisions mentioned earlier, siblings were split up in only 3 percent of the 1995 cases reviewed, down significantly from the almost 10 percent found in 1960 cases. National polls suggest a widely held assumption among mental health professionals, as well, that siblings should remain together. One reason is the belief that siblings can pull together and support one another through the stress and trauma of divorce and its aftermath.

Does the research support this widely held belief? There has been rather limited research on the issue, but studies have found that warm and supportive relationships with siblings do help buffer children from the stress caused by parents' divorce. *However,* many children in divorcing families do not turn to siblings for support. In fact, when compared with siblings in intact families, siblings from separated or divorced families are found to be more disengaged from each other, less supportive of one another, and more likely to have hostile and rivalrous relationships with each other! This pattern is particularly evident in boys, whose behavior with siblings tends to be coercive and aggressive. The noticeable exception to this disturbing pattern appears to be adolescent girls, who tend to form more nurturing relationships with their younger sisters.

Why do sibling relationships frequently become hostile in separated or divorced families when conventional wisdom suggests that siblings would cling together for mutual support? In a combined research effort at Iowa State University and the University of North Carolina, Ronald Simons and his colleagues attempted to tease out the reasons. The primary culprit, according to their extensive study, appears to be the common tendency among divorcing parents to become less involved with their children and to respond to children's oppositional and demanding behavior, so common after separation, in a punitive and coercive manner (see Chapter 6). Siblings who had hostile and unsupportive relationships with one another were more likely to have parents who were less involved and more harsh with them. It appears that the children model their parents' uninvolved and coercive style of interacting with them! A different study, also conducted at the University of North Carolina, identified a somewhat different culprit, although quite similar. This study found that siblings' negative interactions could be predicted by their parents' negative interactions *with each other.* Once again, children are modeling their parents' behavior.

So what is the answer to the question "Should siblings stay to-gether?" Simons and his research team concluded that sibling interactions can play a *pivotal* role in children's well-being. When sibling relationships are warm and supportive, children benefit from remaining together. On the other hand, hostile sibling relationships appear to *exacerbate* children's adjustment problems. In other words, when sibling relationships are negative and hostile, siblings may fare better if separated than if kept together, concluded the research team.

These findings suggest that you should not automatically assume that children should move between the homes as a group. Consider the strength of their bonds and the nature of their relationships with one another. And consider each child's individual needs and relationships with each parent. There is more about this in the following chapter.

If you keep siblings together whose relationships are primarily hostile, start taking steps to foster healthier relationships between them, or their mutual hostility will be one more hurdle for them to overcome. To do this, work on getting the conflict with the other parent in control (see Chapter 19) and start following the positive parenting practices presented in Chapter 9 in your own home.

If you do separate siblings, try to have them spend a good deal of time together, such as every weekend, and perhaps a midweek evening, at one parent's home or the other, so they will still have the opportunity to develop bonds with one another.

The following chapter, "Parenting Plans: Blueprints for a Smooth Future," will guide you through arranging the best parenting arrangements for your family so that everyone's needs are met.

17

Parenting Plans:
Blueprints for a Smooth Future

Once you and your spouse separate, you enter unchartered territory in parenting your children. How will your children be parented in the future? What will each parent's role and responsibilities be? How will important decisions be made? When will children be with each of you?

Some parents find they can negotiate parenting roles and responsibilities as the need arises. Some find them to be an ongoing source of uncertainty. Others find them to be the arena in which ongoing conflict and power struggles are played out. Some resident parents find themselves overburdened, while some nonresident parents feel disenfranchised as parents.

Developing a parenting plan now will provide you with a blueprint for your future as co-parents. Your blueprint can be as detailed or as loose as you wish. The greater the detail, the greater the likelihood that everyone will have the same expectations and that co-parenting will follow a predictable and smooth course.

THE NUTS AND BOLTS OF A PARENTING PLAN

What follows are the nuts and bolts of a detailed parenting plan. It can be customized to meet your own needs. A word of caution: The more serious the parental conflict, the more detailed the parenting plan should be and the more strictly it should be followed until conflict subsides. Uncertainty and flexibility are breeding grounds for misunderstanding, more conflict, and power struggles. Some parents work out a parenting plan with the help of a mediator (see Chapter 2).

I. Decision Making

Will decision making about the children be shared, or will one parent have the authority to make major decisions? Following are issues that are likely to require decisions. Specify how *each* will be handled. Will each be shared? Will some be made only by Mom or Dad? Will some be made only by the parent the children are with at the time? If your intent is to maintain the status quo in specific areas (school, religious affiliation, child care provider), specify that. Also, decide how you will share information in each of these areas.

A. Education

Who will make decisions about the children's school of attendance, requests for specific teachers, placement in special programs, tutoring, summer school?

Mutually decide on the following as well:

- Will both parents attend parent-teacher conferences; if so, together or separately?
- Will both parents have access to all school records and be listed on school registration and emergency cards?
- Don't forget to decide how information will be shared. Will each parent be responsible for obtaining report cards and school information? Will one provide these to the other? Will each inform the other any time either becomes aware of an event or activity involving your child? Will all notices be left in children's backpacks until each parent has seen and signed them?

B. Religious Issues

Who will make decisions about religious affiliation and training? What about church of attendance? Specify if your joint intention is to retain your child's current religious affiliation. Would any other affiliation also be mutually acceptable?

C. Medical Issues

Who will make decisions about selection or changes of physicians and dentists? Nonemergency surgery? Nonroutine medical or dental treatment? Who is responsible for scheduling checkups? Specify that both parents are empowered to obtain emergency medical care and will call the other parent immediately.

D. Child Care Provider and Baby-Sitters

How will child care providers or day care be decided? Will each of you independently choose your own sitters you use occasionally?

E. Counseling

Who will determine if a child needs counseling? How will a counselor be selected? Will both parents attend the first session, provide input, and work with the counselor to meet your child's needs?

F. Recreational Activities (Sports, music lessons, etc.)

Which activities will children continue? How will new activities and summer camp be determined? Don't forget to specify how you will share information.

G. Teenage Issues

Who will make decisions about curfews, dating, obtaining a driver's license or job, quitting high school, or marrying underage?

H. Designation of Legal Custody

Many states draw the distinction between legal and physical custody. Legal custody is the *legal* power to make major decisions about the children. You may wish to check your state laws for the implications of joint versus sole legal custody. Review the pros and cons of joint and sole legal custody in Chapter 16.

II. The Parenting Schedule

A parenting schedule designates precisely when the children will be in each parent's care. It basically identifies which parent is the "on-duty" parent and which is the "off duty" parent at any given time. (See Chapter 18). There is help in planning a parenting schedule later in the chapter, and there are sample sharing schedules in Appendix C. Be sure to finish the chapter before attempting to plan out possible schedules. When thinking about sharing schedules, realize that the more specific you are, the less room there is for misunderstanding in the future. Include the following in your parenting schedule.

A. The Week-to-Week Schedule

What will the weekday schedule be? How about the weekend schedule? You may wish to specify the following: days and times the children will change homes; where the children will eat if the exchange is around mealtime; and who will oversee homework if there is an exchange on a midweek evening.

Will there be a different schedule during school vacation periods, such as summer, Christmas, and spring break? Will there be time away from both parents, such as an extended stay with grandparents or summer camp? Specify that you will share the children at additional times by mutual agreement.

B. The Holiday Schedule

How will you share the children on holidays? (The holiday schedule supersedes the normal week-to-week schedule.) Will holidays be alternated yearly or will the children be with each parent for part of each holiday? If you are sharing holidays, you may wish to specify the specific times the children will be with each parent on each holiday.

Common holidays parents specify are Thanksgiving, Chanukah, Christmas Eve/Day, New Year's Eve/Day, Easter, Passover, Mother's/Father's Day, Memorial Day, July 4th, Labor Day, Halloween, children's birthdays, parents' birthdays, Monday and Friday school holidays.

C. Changes in the Schedule

If the nonresident parent will be unavailable to care for the children during one of his or her scheduled times, how will it be handled? How much notice should be given the resident parent? If the resident parent is not available to fill in, will the nonresident parent be responsible for arranging and paying for child care? Will the missed time be traded for a different time?

If a child does not want to go with a parent during scheduled time for some reason, how will it be handled? Will the child speak directly to the parent and the decision be made between them?

D. First Option

If a parent will be leaving a child with a sitter at any time, will the other parent have the first option to care for the child instead? Many parents specify the need for a sitter will be at least so many waking hours or overnight. This avoids having to call the other parent if you simply have some errands to do or have a late date when the children are ready for bed.

E. Vacations

May each parent take the children on vacation? For how long? How much notice will be provided to the other parent? (Thirty days is common.) Specify that travel itineraries and emergency telephone numbers will be provided. How will the children and nonvacationing parent communicate? Is there any place (e.g. certain foreign countries) that will be off-limits for vacations?

F. Designation of Physical Custody

Now that you know how you will be sharing the children, decide how you will designate physical custody. Sole, joint, or split? Chapter 16 will help with this. Be aware that custody is a legal decision. You may wish to check your state laws for the implications of a custody designation.

III. Exchanges of the Children

Specify where children will be exchanged when switching from one home to the other. At each parent's residence? At school or child care? At a neutral exchange site? (See Chapter 19.)

Some parents feel a need to write in a *grace period*. How long is one parent required to wait if the other is late without a phone call? At what point is a phone call required if a parent will be late?

IV. Transportation

Will transportation be shared between the parents' homes? If so, how? Who will transport children to which activities and appointments? Can any person who is designated by a parent transport children? (Relatives, stepparents, significant others, parents' friends, babysitters?)

V. Communication

How will parents communicate about child-related issues? Phone calls as needed? Regularly scheduled "business" phone calls? Regularly-scheduled face-to-face meetings? Mail? Fax? E-mail? A communication journal exchanged with the children?

Will each of you be able to call the children at any reasonable hour, or will there be set days or times for calls? Will children have open access to call each parent?

VI. Financial

How will you share financial responsibilities for your children? If one parent will be sending a monthly support check to the other, what expenses is it intended to cover? Have you thought of child care expenses? What about children's activities, summer camp, lessons? What about teenagers' car insurance? Will there be cost-of-living increases?

You may wish to determine how you will handle these other financial considerations:

- Who will provide health insurance?
- How will co-pays and uncovered health care be covered?
- Will each of you carry life insurance so the children will be protected should you die? How will you designate the beneficiary? Check the legal implications of this one.
- Who will claim the children as dependents on income taxes? Will it be the same person every year?
- Will you consider private schools? If so, how will tuition and uniforms be handled?
- Will some provisions or financial commitments be made for children's college education?

VII. Moving

How will you handle it if the resident parent wishes to move with the children? This issue becomes very critical if the potential move involves a distance. At a minimum, specify the following:

- What is an acceptable distance for the children to move? (Many jurisdictions restrict acceptable moves to within the county.)
- How will you handle it if the resident parent wishes to move further away? (Many jurisdictions require either the written notarized agreement of the nonmoving parent or a court order.)
- How much notice will be required for a move beyond the acceptable distance? Within the acceptable distance?
- How might the parenting schedule change to allow the nonresident parent and children to maintain their relationship despite the move?

VIII. Ground Rules

Following are some ground rules you may wish to incorporate into your plan:

- Each parent will have autonomy in parenting and care of the children while they are with that parent.
- Children's Activities:
  a. Neither parent will schedule activities or appointments for the children during the other parent's scheduled parenting time without the other parent's prior agreement.
  b. Each parent will cooperate in the children's consistent attendance at their school, sports, and other extracurricular events.
  c. Both parents may attend all the children's activities.
  d. The children will obtain permission for their plans and activities from the parent they are scheduled to be with at the time.
- If either parent wishes to spend time with the children during the other's scheduled parenting time, the change in schedule will be negotiated with the other parent.
- Each parent will support the children's relationship with the other parent. Neither of us will make negative statements about the other parent in the presence or hearing of the children,

question the children about the other parent, or use the children to carry messages between us. Neither of us will expose the children to our disputes or to adult issues. Each parent will make every possible effort to ensure that other people comply with this agreement also.

- We will discuss marital, child-sharing, court-related, and financial matters only at a time when the children are not present or within hearing range.
- Neither parent will introduce a new significant other into the children's lives until___. Specify both time frame and conditions. (See Chapter 13.)

IX. Miscellaneous

The following areas are not always included in a parenting plan. However, reaching agreements on how they will be handled will curb the potential for future misunderstanding and make life smoother for children.

A. Shared Routines and Expectations for Children

Will you establish some common routines, rules, and expectations in your homes for the sake of consistency for your children? Some possibilities are bedtimes, standards for children's unacceptable behavior, discipline guidelines (what types used, who can discipline), whether very young children are allowed to sleep with a parent, maturity expectations for young children, allowances, curfews, unacceptable television programs and movies. Will each of you support the other in the event of a child's major infraction, such as a school referral, a failing grade, or drug or alcohol use?

B. Sickness

How will a sick child be cared for when both parents work? If a child is sick, will he or she remain in one home rather than follow the parenting schedule? How will you define "sick"?

C. Children's Belongings

What will travel with the children, and what will stay at each home? Will each parent have a set of clothes? For clothes that go back and forth, should they wait to be returned until laundered, or is it more important they travel immediately with the child? If a child leaves a needed item at the other home, which parent is responsible for transporting the item?

D. Extended Family

Is each parent responsible for maintaining ties to his or her family during that parent's scheduled time? Can extended family call the "in-law" parent if there is a special event during that parent's parenting time?

E. Shoring Up Parenting Skills

Will steps be taken to shore up either or both parents' parenting of the children? Examples include parenting classes, anger management classes, completion of a substance abuse program, refraining from use of alcohol while children are with the parent, initiating individual counseling to deal with personal or parenting issues. Are there any other protective issues for the children that need to be considered and dealt with?

X. Future Disputes

How will future disputes be handled if you cannot resolve them yourselves? Ideally, you will seek mediation (see Chapter 2) or co-parenting counseling (see Chapter 19) prior to resorting to court.

XI. Reevaluation of the Plan

Build in a time frame to reevaluate the plan to see how it is working. You may need to add clauses to deal with trouble spots. Certain events will require a reevaluation, such as a parent moving out of the area. Parenting schedules also need modifying to accommodate children's changing developmental needs. There is more on this later.

SELECTING A PARENTING SCHEDULE TAILORED TO YOUR FAMILY

Don't get caught in the trap of focusing on who has "custody" of the children. Custody is an unfortunate term, used with prisoners and things we own. Hopefully your children are neither! Instead, work out a *sharing* schedule that makes sense for you and your children. When will each child be with each of you?

There are no hard-and-fast formulas for a good sharing schedule for all children. You can find many examples of parenting schedules for school-age children in Appendix C, and shortly we will look at appropriate schedules for young children. As you read through the remainder of the chapter, have a large calendar handy so you can start visualizing different options for schedules. If you have a dry erase planner calendar, you can try out many schedules. Or you may wish to prepare your own blank calendar sheets and lay them out with different options on them. The idea is having visual aids. It might also help to have a calendar of the entire year so you have an overview of the year, including holidays and school breaks.

You will find a calendar essential to your life from now on. When you finally arrange a schedule with the other parent, keep one posted in each home so everyone will have a visual aid of when the children are with each parent. If you do not already do so, get in the habit of recording all your children's school events and activities on the calendar. There will no longer be another parent to remind you of them, and children may be in the other home when they occur.

Following are issues to consider in developing a parenting schedule appropriate for your family.

Respective Parenting Roles

Consider what your respective parenting roles have been. Have you shared parenting somewhat equally, or has one of you assumed the primary responsibility for children's day-to-day care and managing their lives. Try to provide children with some consistency so their lives will not change any more dramatically than necessary. Some experts propose an "approximation rule"—that is, the new parenting arrangements should approximate the parenting patterns during the marriage as much as possible.

Minimize Children's Losses

Consider each parent's ability to minimize each child's losses. For an older teen, staying in the family residence with its closeness to school, friends, and activities may be far more important than to be with one parent versus the other. For a young child, the loss of the family residence would pale in comparison to the loss of daily contact with the parent who provided most of his or her nurturing and care.

Be sensitive to children's relationships with each parent. Children with a special relationship with a parent should spend considerable time with that parent. Read about splitting siblings in Chapter 16.

In minimizing children's losses, also consider everyone's schedules. Try to maximize the time that children are with a parent rather than in child care.

One Primary Residence or Two?

If you recall from Chapter 16, whether a primary residence or dual residence is best depends upon the child, the parents, and the circumstances. Review the chapter to learn what might work best for your family. Recall that dual residence does not necessarily mean an *equal* child-sharing schedule. Usually spending one-third to one-half of the time in each home is considered dual residence.

Please realize that even if your children spend far less time than that in your home, you can still *create* the sense of their having a second home with you. You can find practical suggestions in Chapter 15.

Many parents elect to have a primary residence for the children during the school year, either because of the distance between them or the complications in coordinating schoolwork and school routines. However, they use school vacations to provide children the opportunity of having the full experience of being parented by the less-seen parent. Some parents divide school vacations equally in some manner, or the nonresident parent may have a greater share of school vacation periods. Some reverse the school time schedule during school breaks.

Aim for Balanced Time

Ideally, each parent will have some involvement with school and homework, with children's activities, and with children's free time.

School involvement can take any number of forms: participation in the child's classroom; a midweek evening contact of a few hours for dinner and homework; a midweek overnight with the parent taking the child to school the following day; a Monday morning return after weekends rather than Sunday evening; or one school week each month or during alternate months. Some parents split the school week, alternate school weeks, or alternate two week blocks of time. (Joint physical custody is discussed in Chapter 16.)

Each parent should also have some relaxing, off-school time, so children can experience the fun side of each parent. Alternate weekends are common. Some resident parents spend one weekend each month with the children, while the less-seen parent spends three.

What about Children's Input?

Do not ask children who they want to live with. Most children feel that choosing one parent is a rejection of the other. This is too heavy a burden on them. If older children have a strong preference, they are likely to make it known.

However, do consider your children's input about scheduling in general. The older the child, the more important it is to consider the child's input—particularly teens, who have busy lives. Recent studies report considerable resentment among young adult children of divorce who were never consulted during their teen years about moving between two homes or how their school vacations would be spent.

Transitions

Try to minimize the frequency of children having to switch homes. Frequent transitions between homes are hard on most children; each changeover requires them to shift gears and adjust anew. When children change homes frequently, they don't have time to settle in and regain their equilibrium.

Frequent transitions also break up the flow of parenting. When all their time together is spent in short spurts, parents and children have no opportunity to get into the rhythm of a relationship. Many parents who spend alternate weekends and a midweek overnight with their children prefer the overnight to be Thursday so it blends right into the weekend. The longer block of time allows more continuity.

Please read the section on special developmental needs for *young* children that follows.

To Overnight or Not to Overnight?

As soon as children are old enough, they should spend some overnights with their less-seen parent. Overnights provide special bonding time that daytime visits do not offer. Nonresident parents are also found to stay more involved in children's lives when they spend overnights together. Children's readiness for overnights is discussed below.

GUIDELINES FOR CHILDREN'S DEVELOPMENTAL NEEDS

Children of all ages need consistent and frequent contact with both their parents. However, children of different ages have different developmental needs, and for this reason, a parenting schedule that is appropriate for a six-year-old is inappropriate for either a one-year-old or an older teen. Various experts have offered guidelines based on our best knowledge of children's needs at different ages. I'll provide some guidelines so your children's developmental needs can be considered when planning a parenting schedule with the other parent. Again, it will help to visualize schedules on a calendar.

Infants

Parenting schedules for infants are the most difficult to arrange. Infants need a very stable environment, including stable caregivers and consistent routines and schedules. Long separations from their primary source of comfort and nurturing cause infants obvious anxiety. After all, how can they know if this person will ever return? For these reasons, experts agree that infants should have a stable home base and not be separated from a primary caretaker for long periods of time.

At the same time, babies should have *frequent* contact with the non-resident parent so they will get to know the parent well. Infants' memory is limited, so it is widely recommended that for optimum bonding, a non-resident parent spend a few hours with an infant every two or three days, engaging in lots of cuddling, rocking, talking, playing, and caring for the infant. It is this type of interaction on a frequent and regular basis and the parent's responsiveness to the baby's needs that create strong bonds.

What if a nonresident parent wishes *more* involvement with an infant? If an infant is in day care for long hours, it is difficult for both parents to get extensive quality time with their baby. If parents begin to divide up their infant's limited time too much, there is a danger that the baby will not develop a secure attachment to any one person, which is likely to be detrimental to later emotional and social development.

Forming a secure attachment *to at least one primary person* is critical because it provides a child with a sense of security and with a prototype for future emotionally intimate relationships.

If a baby does not have to deal with long hours in day care away from her primary source of comfort and nurturing, she can handle longer hours with a responsive and nurturing nonresident parent at that parent's home. At times, parents' work schedules complement one another, so both can be very involved in parenting during daytime hours, rather than putting the baby in child care. These parents should strive for consistency in schedules, routines, and handling the baby.

Throughout the first year, gradually increase the number of hours the baby spends with the nonresident parent. By the time your baby is approaching a year old, he or she will most likely benefit from full days with an involved and responsive nonresident parent. The familiar routines and schedule should be maintained during this time. Your child should see the nonresident parent at least two to three times distributed throughout each week since he or she should not be separated from that parent for more than a few days.

One-to-Three-Year-Olds

When *regular* overnights should begin is somewhat of a contested issue. More liberal guidelines suggest sometime between 12 and 18 months, *providing* the nonresident parent has been caring for the child consistently and frequently, is able to soothe the toddler, and the child is adaptable and very comfortable with the parent. You might start out with a 24-hour stay during alternate weeks. Longer stays on a regular basis can still be very stressful, even to an adaptable child. Toddlers' conception of time is poor, and they cannot grasp when they will return to their more familiar parent and home. Again, there should be contacts in between the overnights so the toddler is not separated from the nonresident parent for longer than a few days at a time. Some phone contact, too, will allow the child to hear the parent's voice.

During overnight stays, familiar routines and schedules should be followed, such as mealtimes, familiar foods, naptime, nightly routines, and bedtime. Watch for signs of stress—pronounced fears about separation, waking up crying through the night, listlessness or a lack of smiling, lowered frustration tolerance, reverting to previously outgrown behavior, or increased fussiness, aggressiveness, or tantrums. If your toddler shows signs of stress, don't push it. Return to a daytime schedule.

If your toddler is thriving on these overnights, *very gradually* work into a 24-hour period *each* week and then into a two-day/one-overnight stretch in alternate weeks. Again, maintain shorter contacts in between so the toddler is not away from the parent for more than a few days at a time.

How fast you can progress from one schedule to the next depends upon your toddler's adaptability and comfort level, how responsive the nonresident parent is to the toddler's needs, and how actively the non-resident parent is involved. Please read about flexibility in parenting schedules for additional considerations, such as when the nonresident parent has been very involved with an infant or toddler *prior* to separation.

Preschoolers

Once your child is thriving on the two-day/one-night stretch, more liberal guidelines suggest you try a 48-hour stretch of time during alternate weeks. Once again, there should be shorter contacts in between so the child is not away from a nonresident parent for more than several days. Phone contact will help too.

For preschoolers, the 48-hour stretches can progress to a 48-hour period each week if you are targeting a liberal sharing schedule. Once again, the criteria for increasing time are the child's comfort level, the parent's involvement, the bonds between the parent and child, and the special considerations discussed in "Flexibility in Parenting Schedules."

Preschoolers still have a poor concept of time and can't grasp the meaning of "next week" or "three days from now." It is helpful to show them on a calendar when they will see an absent parent again.

School-Age Children

Appendix C has many examples of parenting schedules used with school-age children. These are just examples and can be altered to meet your family's needs.

School-age children are ready to spend more extensive time with the less-seen parent. If liberal child-sharing is the goal, this is a good age to begin. Some parents liberally share children during school vacations. Some increase sharing during school time as well. (Please read about the pros and cons of joint physical custody in Chapter 16.) For younger school-age children, sharing weeks in some way is more appropriate than alternating weeks because it is still difficult for them to be away from a parent for an entire week.

As youngsters become older, their school life, peer group, and outside activities assume increasingly greater importance in their lives. These need to be accommodated in parenting schedules and supported by both parents.

Teens

Many teens prefer a primary home base because of the logistics of coordinating active social lives, long-term homework assignments, jobs, and all their "stuff." If given the choice, many would choose the home more convenient to their school, friends, and activities. As teens get older, many prefer shorter contacts with a nonresident parent. However, if parents live in close proximity and teens can get to their activities and jobs from either home, some are comfortable moving back and forth in some manner. Your teen should have some input into a schedule so it will work for him or her.

Some parents allow older teens to move flexibly between their homes. If you opt for this, make sure to build in some accountability so you always know where your teen is. Teens need supervision, and they need their parents to act as parents. Teens from divorced homes appear to be particularly vulnerable to making poor choices during their teen years when given too much freedom and poor supervision.

Flexibility in Parenting Schedules

The preceding are guidelines, not hard-and-fast rules. Here are some additional considerations:

- If a nonresident parent has been highly involved in a very young child's life before parents separated, the youngster is likely to benefit from spending more time with the parent than indicated in the preceding guidelines, so the relationship with the parent is not disrupted. Some experts recommend an ear-lier and more liberal schedule for overnights as well. However, parents *must* communicate frequently. Parents who are liber-ally sharing a very young child should maintain consistency in schedules and routines between their households, soothe their child in similar ways, respond to their child's needs similarly, keep their child out of any conflict, and both should be able to "read" their child well.

- In determining a more liberal schedule, be sure a young child is not continuously away from a primary parent more than *one day for every year of the child's age*. This is a common rule of thumb. A primary parent is the parent who has been most in-volved in the child's physical care, nurturing, and comforting.
- Consider your child's temperament when developing a sched-ule. An adaptable, easy-going child can move on to overnights and longer stays with the less-seen parent quicker than can a child who has a difficult temperament and adapts slowly to change.
- A young child who is close to older siblings is likely to be able to handle longer stays with the less-seen parent if siblings are along, too.
- Obviously, if parents live a great distance from one another, a parenting schedule in keeping with children's developmental needs is difficult if not impossible to arrange. Some guidelines for long-distance parenting can be found in Chapter 15.

The parenting schedule you first arrange will have to be modified over the years. If you are unable to work out changing schedules, a family mediator who has expertise in child development can help you. (Mediation is discussed in Chapter 2.) Some parents who don't wish to renegotiate agree on one parenting schedule until a child is two, an-other until he or she is three, another until school age, and so on.

While a thorough parenting plan is a *blueprint* for a smooth future, learning good co-parenting skills is the *structural foundation* for a smooth future. Making co-parenting work is the focus of the next chap-ter. It will take you step by step through building a workable, co-parenting relationship and guide you through seven basics of successful co-parenting.

18

Making Co-Parenting Work

Perfect Pals? Cooperative Colleagues? Angry Associates? or Fiery Foes? Which describes the co-parenting relationship that you have with your child's other parent? Which describes the co-parenting relationship that you would *like* to have? You may be wondering if this chapter is for you, especially if you are not in a joint physical custody arrangement. If both you and the other parent are involved with your child regularly at some level, the answer is yes. Children need *two parents* after divorce, not one parent and a "visitor." Ideally, your children will have two parents to *parent* them, which means that you need to make co-parenting a priority.

In a nineties study of 98 divorced couples one year and five years after divorce, Constance Ahrons of the University of Southern California identified four co-parenting styles. Her descriptive labels—Perfect Pals, Cooperative Colleagues, Angry Associates, and Fiery Foes—pretty well speak for themselves.

The Perfect Pals made up a small minority, 12 percent, one year after divorce, and an even smaller minority four years later. Perfect Pals described themselves as good friends. They trusted one another, asked one another's advice, were interested in each other's current lives, and participated in joint activities with their children. By five years after the divorce, one-third of the Perfect Pals had become Cooperative Colleagues and another third had deteriorated into Angry Associates. As you may suspect, the key factor in the deterioration of Perfect Pals into Angry Associates was usually new significant others.

Cooperative Colleagues constituted the largest group one year after the divorce—38 percent. This was a very diverse group. Cooperative

Colleagues were distinguished from other groups by their firm resolve to compartmentalize their anger and separate their parental responsibilities from their marital issues. Interestingly, as a group, they had the *same* level of anger as Angry Associates, but they were intent on placing their children's needs above their own personal issues. Because they were so determined, they were better able to manage their anger when interacting with one another. For example, they avoided controversial topics, constantly monitored themselves when interacting, met in public places, and used the mails for communication about issues that would likely provoke an argument. It was their considerable effort that enabled them to cooperate on issues related to the children. Five years after the divorce, close to 75 percent of this group remained Cooperative Colleagues; approximately one-quarter had slipped into relating as Angry Associates, while a few had become Perfect Pals.

Approximately 25 percent of the parents in Ahrons's study group functioned as Angry Associates one year after the divorce. Again, the main difference between Angry Associates and Cooperative Colleagues was not how angry they were but how they *managed* their conflict. In contrast to the proactive steps Cooperative Colleagues took to control themselves while dealing with one another, Angry Associates pushed one another's buttons, freely uttered digs and gibes to one another, and generally had tense, hostile, or openly conflicted interactions. They fiercely held onto their anger and allowed it to flow over into their parenting, thereby adversely affecting their children. By five years after the divorce, only one-third remained Angry Associates. One-third had progressed to relating as Cooperative Colleagues, and the other third deteriorated to relating as Fiery Foes.

Fiery Foes made up the final 25 percent of Ahrons's study group one year after the divorce. These were rageful, litigious parents, who were in and out of court repeatedly. They were entrenched in the past and stayed emotionally entangled with one another. They rarely talked, and when they did, a fight usually erupted. Five years after the divorce, approximately two-thirds remained Fiery Foes. What is encouraging is that approximately one-half of the remainder progressed to relating as Cooperative Colleagues.

A somewhat different picture of postdivorce relationships emerged from a study of 1,100 northern California families, also published in the nineties. Stanford University researchers reported that only 30 percent of divorced parents were able to cooperate several years after their separation and approximately 25 percent were embroiled in conflict. The remaining rather large group of parents avoided one another, rarely communicated, and basically parented independently—requiring their children to live in two separate worlds.

HOW TO BUILD A CO-PARENTING RELATIONSHIP

It will interest you that divorced parents who cooperate with one another as parents are better able to move on with their new lives and are happier in new relationships than are uncooperative parents. Parents who work together as parents are also found to be more satisfied with their parenting arrangements, and this is true whether they are custodial parents, noncustodial parents, or joint custody parents. As if these benefits of working together weren't enough, cooperative divorced parents are found to have better relationships with their children and to have better-adjusted children than do uncooperative parents. In fact, children whose parents cooperate with one another not only adjust better to the divorce but adjust better to their parents' remarriages as well! As you can see, *everyone* wins when parents learn to work together as parents.

This chapter shows you how to develop a *workable* co-parenting relationship and how to maintain it. With this chapter and the next (which guides you through the steps of managing and then ending conflict), you can avoid the sometimes lengthy trial-and-error process that many divorced parents go through in their often fruitless quest to co-parent their children constructively.

Just what is a *workable* co-parenting relationship? It is one in which parents keep unresolved spousal issues and conflict compartmentalized so they do not spill over into the business of parenting. Most parents who establish a workable co-parenting relationship do not have a personal relationship, and many don't even like one another. However, they have learned to separate their personal feelings for each other from their roles as parents. *They keep spousal issues separate from parenting issues.*

It may seem a tall order to you to separate spousal issues from parenting issues, particularly in the emotionally charged atmosphere of separation and divorce. Indeed, it will be very difficult to separate the two if you continue to relate to each other as you always have. It will be far easier if you *restructure* the relationship so that it becomes a *different kind of relationship*.

The best way to restructure the relationship is to break away from the old ways of interacting so that you can reconnect on a new basis—

as co-parents. For most divorced parents, breaking away from the old ways of interacting is a *must!* Remember, even one-third of the Perfect Pals deteriorated into Angry Associates several years after divorce. It is likely they would have benefited from developing a new kind of relationship early on that could have withstood the test of time and new significant others. Following are guidelines to help you restructure the marital relationship into a workable co-parenting relationship.

Establish Clear Boundaries

The first step in restructuring your old relationship is to define clear boundaries for the new one. With clear boundaries, you are less likely to fall back into the old ways of interacting. You are also less likely to be drawn into power struggles with one another. The more conflict there is, the clearer the boundaries need to be.

There are two primary steps you can take to establish clear boundaries: disengaging from one another and formalizing your new parenting roles.

Disengaging from One Another

This is a step never taken by Fiery Foes. If you remember, these intensely conflicted parents stayed enmeshed with one another. They neither disengaged nor created new boundaries.

The most effective way to disengage from the other parent is to eliminate your involvement in all areas except parenting. Following are specific guidelines that will help.

First, *respect one another's privacy.* Don't ask about personal matters, especially the other parent's social life, and don't offer personal information about yourself. At some point in the future, you may be able to discuss personal topics again, but most people do better if they refrain from doing so at least during the first year, reports Dr. Marla Beth Isaacs, director of the Philadelphia Families of Divorce Study.

Part of respecting one another's privacy is never entering each other's home unless invited, even if it used to be your home. If you still have a key, return it. If your children invite you in, check with the other parent before accepting their invitation. A surprising number of divorcing spouses freely enter one another's home and even help themselves to food in the refrigerator during exchanges of the children. This is out of bounds! If you are invited into the other parent's home, think of yourself as a *guest*, and don't do anything you wouldn't do as a guest.

Second, *do not rely on each other for any nonparenting tasks previously assumed during the marriage* (home-cooked meals, laundry, bill paying, car or house repairs, and so on). Although these may be a convenience, they come with a price: falling into the old relationship and blurring boundaries.

Third, *eliminate spontaneous and unnecessary communication with one another.* It is both tempting and common for a parent to make frequent and unnecessary calls to the other parent after separation. It is also common for a parent to stop at the former family residence unannounced, under the guise of visiting with the children or picking up a left possession. But such frequent and unstructured contact ties parents to their old relationship and clouds boundaries. Formalize how and when you will communicate. This formality will discourage unnecessary calls or unannounced visits. More on this shortly.

You can find additional guidelines for disengagement in Chapter 10, "Your Emotional Divorce."

Formalizing Future Parenting Roles and Responsibilities

The more clearly you formalize parenting roles and responsibilities, the better. Everyone's expectations will be the same, which means less opportunity for misunderstandings, power struggles, and future conflict.

The first step is to arrange a parenting schedule that specifies when the children will be with each of you. The more conflict there is, the more strictly parenting schedules should be adhered to. A predetermined parenting schedule eliminates the need for repeated communication to arrange future exchanges of the children. It allows both parents to organize their independent lives and schedules so neither is vulnerable to the last minute whims of the other. And it eliminates potential power plays over the children. Once parents begin working together, parenting schedules can become more flexible.

A clear parenting schedule is only the first step. Essentially, you and the other parent are entering new territory—establishing yourselves as independent parents—and you will need a road map. Issue upon issue will arise along the way that you will need to address. How will you make decisions about the children in the future? How will each of you keep informed about children's school progress and activities? How will you handle holidays, children's illnesses, medical checkups, and medical insurance? Will the two households have some rules in common? Can each of you take the children on vacation out of state? Suppose one of you wishes to move with the children?

The best way to establish clear parenting roles and responsibilities is to develop a thorough *parenting plan*. Chapter 17, "Parenting Plans: Blueprints for a Smooth Future," guides you through the process.

Use the Model of a Business Relationship

You and the other parent have a serious business to attend to: raising your children. Most parents find it very helpful to conceptualize their new relationship in terms of a business relationship. The business relationship model was first proposed two decades ago by Dr. Isolina Ricci, author of *Mom's House, Dad's House*. The model has withstood the test of time and has been used by countless divorced couples to build their new co-parenting relationship.

Anytime you interact with the other parent, assume a businesslike demeanor and try to create a businesslike atmosphere. Get into the habit of asking yourself, "Is this the way I would behave in a business relationship?" If the answer is, "Not likely," *don't do it*! If antagonistic parents behaved in a business relationship as they do with one another, their business would rapidly fail. Unfortunately, their children will fail, too!

Here are some guidelines you can follow:

- Make appointments to discuss issues. If you meet face-to-face, meet in a public place so there will be less temptation to raise your voices. Plan wisely. Don't meet when you're likely to be tired, and agree to limit your talk to under 45 minutes so you can keep on an even keel. If you talk by telephone, arrange a specific time so you will be in a businesslike frame of mind and your children will be out of the home or asleep. Plan ahead. As issues arise, jot them in a designated note pad so *everything* can be taken care of at designated meetings or during designated phone calls.
- Discuss only practical matters related to the children. Keep away from controversial topics (the marriage, spending habits, dating, gossip), and remember to avoid personal matters. Respect those boundaries! Preparing an agenda of the points that

you wish to discuss will help keep you on track and away from potentially volatile issues.

- Learn good communication and negotiating skills (see Chapter 12), and think before you speak. These will become your most powerful tools in attaining a positive outcome.
- Use cooling-off periods when conversations become heated. Don't make decisions in the heat of an argument; shelve volatile issues until you can both gain perspective.
- Be courteous and respectful. Refrain from sarcasm or digs, even if the other parent uses them.
- Demonstrate that you are trustworthy. When you say you'll do something, do it!
- Monitor your emotions.
- Put things in writing. When you believe that you are in agreement on an issue, put it in writing. Memos are convenient devices to confirm that your understanding is accurate. Get in the habit of using them.

Employ New Thinking, New Language

Your own thinking is a critical ingredient in restructuring the marital relationship into a co-parenting one. You need to redefine the relationship in your *own* mind, and since this is all new to you, you need to monitor your thinking. Keep your focus on the other parent's present role as a *parent*. The parenting role is very different from the spousal role. If you clearly compartmentalize the two, you are less likely to confuse them. On the other hand, if you allow yourself to focus on the other parent's past failures in the spousal role, you not only tie yourself to the old relationship, you muddy your perceptions with irrelevant data.

You also need to decide what to call the other parent from now on. End the negative labels (jerk, witch, bastard, gold digger). Also get away from the term "my ex"; it focuses on your failed marital relationship. What you need to focus on is the new co-parenting relationship. When you are not using your former spouse's name, try using "my children's mother/father" or "my co-parent." Get in the habit of using the new language not only in conversations with others but when you're *thinking* about the other parent, as well. You will be in a better frame of mind to constructively deal with "your children's other parent" than with "that jerk."

**RESTRUCTURING FROM A MARITAL
TO A CO-PARENTING RELATIONSHIP**

✓ Separate parenting issues from spousal issues.
✓ Create clear boundaries for the new relationship.
   • Disengage in *all* areas except parenting.
   • Formalize parenting roles and responsibilities.
✓ Use a business relationship as your model.
✓ Monitor your own thinking.
   • Redefine the relationship in your own mind.
   • Compartmentalize the present parenting role from the past spousal role.
   • Think and talk about the other parent as a co-parent or business partner; quit using negative labels or "my ex."

Chapter 10, "Your Emotional Divorce," can help you further in disentangling yourself from the marriage relationship and laying the past to rest.

SEVEN KEYS TO SOUND CO-PARENTING

For most parents, co-parenting is a long trial and error process through hilly terrain that often feels mountainous and sometimes insurmountable. In addition to restructuring your relationship, there are basic co-parenting ground rules you can follow to guide your way. You may wish to look into the availability in your community of classes that teach co-parenting skills, which are usually excellent resources. Whether you take a class or not, start putting into practice these seven fundamentals, and share them with your co-parent.

Respect the Other Parent's Autonomy as a Parent

Each of you is now a single parent in a one-parent home, and each of you has the right to parent in your own style, free of the other parent's control. Each of you also has the right to make the day-to-day decisions about the children while they are with you—such as appropriate playmates, nutrition, and your house rules. Because different things are important to each of you, you will likely have some different house rules. Karen knows that phone conversations are limited to 15 minutes at Mom's and that television is limited to an hour a day at Dad's. At Mom's, Danny knows he has to rinse his dishes immediately and put them in the dishwasher. At Dad's he knows he can't take food into the living room or put his feet on the furniture. Children do adapt to different house rules, just as they adapt to different rules at the grandparents', at school, and at friends' homes.

It would be beneficial for your children to have some consistency between your two homes in at least a few critical areas, such as consistent bedtimes, whether a very young child is allowed to sleep with a parent, standards of unacceptable behavior, and discipline. The younger the child, the more important is this consistency. For older children, experts differ widely in how much consistency is needed between homes. Obviously, the more consistent the homes, the less fragmented children's lives feel to them. However, if the quest for consistency becomes an arena in which conflict, power struggles, and attempts to control one another are played out, it will do children far more harm than good. If the separation has been recent, it will be easiest on everyone to simply stick to the routines, schedules, and expectations with which children are already familiar, providing they have been appropriate. Many parents decide on some basics to follow as part of their parenting plan (see Chapter 17). Even many highly conflicted parents can reach agreement on some basic consistencies between their homes by working them out with a co-parenting counselor (Chapter 19) or family mediator (Chapter 2).

The one exception to the autonomy principle is if a child is being placed in harm's way by the other parent. In this case, by all means intervene. For serious issues, such as sexual abuse, very abusive physical discipline, serious neglect, substance abuse with your child in the home, or domestic violence while your child is in the home, act immediately. Options include contacting your local child protective agency hotline to investigate and make recommendations to ensure your child's safety. In very serious situations, contact law enforcement directly. You may have to initiate emergency court action to protect your child while problems in the other home are being addressed.

For less serious issues, check your perceptions with an objective third party, such as a therapist or your child's doctor, to ensure that you are not overreacting. Perceptions of a former spouse's parenting are frequently flawed, and issues that some divorced parents are concerned about are rather minor when put in perspective. If, after you've sought an objective second opinion you believe a valid issue exists that requires intervention, speak to the other parent. See if you can arrive at a mutually agreeable solution to the problem. If the issue is emotional harm to your child, you might suggest that you initiate either family counseling or counseling for your child so a professional can help *both* of you better meet your child's needs during this stressful time. If the issue is the other parent's inexperience or poor parenting skills, suggest that each of you take a parenting class now that you will be parenting solo in your own homes. Even experienced parents can benefit from honing their parenting skills.

Use the On-Duty-Parent/Off-Duty-Parent Concept

Co-parenting will be smoother if you think of the parenting schedule as a designation of who is the *on-duty* parent and who is the *off-duty* parent at any specific time. During Dad's scheduled time, he is the on-duty parent, and he gets to make the day-to-day decisions during that time, and vice-versa. If you keep this model in mind, many problems that plague many divorced parents will not arise. Consider the following scenarios.

Scenario 1: Jennifer, who lives primarily with her father, is invited to a slumber party on the Saturday night of her mom's weekend. Jennifer asks Dad if she can go. What should Dad do? Dad needs to tell Jennifer to ask her mother. Since Mom is the on-duty parent on the weekend, Mom needs to make the decision. Mom may tell Jennifer that she has already made plans to take Jennifer away for a fun weekend, and it is too late to cancel them. Mom may agree to take Jennifer to the party and pick her up. If Mom lives too far to transport Jennifer, she may ask Dad if it's okay for Jennifer to stay with him for part of the weekend so Jennifer can go to the party.

Scenario 2: Dad's time with Philip is weekends. One Wednesday, Dad finds that he can leave work at 2 P.M., and he picks up Philip from child care to spend time with him. Since Philip is usually in child care until 6 P.M., and Dad plans on returning him by 5:30, Dad doesn't bother to inform Mom. However, Philip has a dental checkup that day. When Mom shows up at 4 P.M. to pick Philip up, he is gone, Mom is furious, and she calls her attorney. Had Dad followed the on-duty/off-duty principle, he would have realized that he had to check with Mom, as the on-duty parent on Wednesday, before taking Philip. A major confrontation would have been avoided. There can be only one parent in charge at a time!

Scenario 3: Angela wants to take ballet lessons, and Mom learns that the only time the dance studio offers ballet is on Wednesday evenings, which is Dad's evening with Angela. If you were Mom, would you sign Angela up for ballet? Mom needs to check with Dad to see if he is willing or able to take Angela to ballet. If not, she and Dad need to look for alternatives. Can Dad change his evening with Angela? Is there another dance studio? Can Mom take Angela and Dad pick her up and spend the rest of the evening with her?

Please realize that children should be able to participate in normal childhood activities and the on-duty parent should facilitate this during his or her parenting time. It's part of parenting!

Follow the Model of a Business Relationship

Plenty has been said about this earlier in this chapter. Take time to review it. Anytime you are interacting with the other parent, assume a businesslike demeanor and try to create a businesslike atmosphere. Remember to ask yourself, "Is this the way I would behave in a business relationship?" If the answer is no, then don't do it!

Acknowledge and Respect the Importance of the Other Parent's Relationship with the Children

Your children need a relationship with *both* parents, and this is their right. Divorce is bad enough for children, let alone losing a relationship with a parent. The other parent may have a different parenting style and a very different relationship with the children than you have. But don't do what some divorced parents do and trivialize the other parent's role in the children's lives because you perceive that you are the better parent. Recognize that each of you can contribute to your children's lives in *different* ways. Please read Chapter 7, "Critical Ingredients for Children's Adjustment."

If, after reading Chapter 7, you still have difficulty acknowledging the other parent's importance to the children, try doing two things. First, focus on the distinction between the other parent as a *spouse* and as a *parent*. These two roles are very different. Parents who confuse the two are often blind to the other parent's strengths *as a parent*.

Second, force yourself to think of at least three things about the other parent from which the children might benefit. Remember, this is the person *you* chose to be your children's parent. Why, if he or she has no redeeming qualities?

Even if the other parent had little involvement with the children during the marriage, this does not necessarily forecast the future. Many parents who left the parenting up to their spouses during the marriage become great parents after divorce, much to their children's delight.

Don't Make Assumptions: Give the Other Parent the Benefit of the Doubt!

Children from divorced homes are notorious for telling each parent something different. Sometimes, they tell each parent what they believe each wants to hear; it is a way for them to handle their conflicting loyalties and to please the two people they love most in the world. Sometimes it is a manipulation on children's parts to negotiate the best deal for themselves in each parent's home. "I can do it at Dad's. Why can't I do it here!" Some children stir up trouble because it is the only way they can get their parents to talk to one another. "They'll never get back together if they never even talk to each other!"

Parents who assume everything children tell them is gospel can create havoc in the co-parenting relationship. Many an irate parent has called the other parent in an attack mode because of an alleged irresponsibility that has no basis in reality. The outcome is an escalation in conflict and damage to future co-parenting efforts.

Don't jump to conclusions! Don't assume anything. Check with the other parent first, and seek out the information in a neutral tone of voice, not a belligerent one. "Carly's telling me she sleeps with you every night and is refusing to sleep in her own bed over here." "Ken tells me he and his friends are allowed to smoke and drink alcohol at your place." "Let me tell you what Carissa is saying over here."

A second area in which assumptions can be problematic is when former spouses automatically assume they know the other's point of view without asking. "After all," a parent says, "we were married for ten years. I should know him by now." People often change dramatically after divorce. Don't make assumptions without checking the facts first, either directly or by means of a memo to the other parent. Each of you should speak for yourself!

Finally, give your co-parent the benefit of the doubt until you can check things out. Events often have several interpretations but many divorced parents automatically assume the worst of their co-parent before they have the facts. What they fail to realize is that the conflict, anger, and leftover emotional baggage that go hand in hand with divorce often taint perceptions.

Communicate about Your Children

The key to *effective* co-parenting is communication. "Forget it," you say? "If we couldn't communicate when we were married, we certainly can't now!" Many divorced parents feel this way, yet many do learn how to communicate in a reasonable manner for their children's sake. Fortunately, the kind of communication needed between divorced co-parents is very different than the kind needed between spouses, and easier. Co-parenting calls for businesslike communication that is restricted to concrete and practical issues about the children, and Chapter 12 is devoted to easy-to-learn communication tools that will make all the difference.

Many children lead chaotic lives because their parents refuse to communicate with one another. Children are continually having to adjust to two separate worlds where there is little common ground. They are frequently disappointed because a parent is not at an award ceremony or a school performance because the parent did not learn about it in time. School projects are late because one parent didn't know the schedule. Illnesses are prolonged because a parent didn't find a medicine bottle in a suitcase and did not know to look for it. None of this is fair to your children! Furthermore, many children become master manipulators, telling each parent tales of what they can do at the other parent's home because they know parents will never check with one another. During the course of your children's growing-up years, problems will arise that can be more effectively dealt with if you and the other parent collaborate, but it will take communication!

The more equally the two of you share your children, the more important communication is, particularly during the school year. The more special needs or problems your child has, the more important communication is. The younger your children are, the more important communication is because young children thrive on consistency.

Although children whose parents do not communicate with one another are found to fare better than children who are faced with chronic parental conflict, they fare far poorer than children whose parents communicate and work together as parents. Parents who do not communicate also must settle for being in the dark about much of their children's lives, particularly when children are young and poor relayers of events.

If communication is a problem for you and the other parent, try the following:

- Use mail, e-mail, or fax machines.
- If your child is young, you can communicate in a journal and include it with your child's belongings that go to the other home. In the communication journal, each parent can record information that the other should know—for example, health issues (doctors' appointments, illnesses, medication, shots); changes in your child's schedule, routines, eating habits, or food preferences; whether the child napped or ate prior to the exchange; day care or preschool information; developmental milestones and the child's progress or problems.
- Create a form letter with headings so you just need to fill in the blanks—for example, upcoming events/appointments, medical information, school information, and so forth.
- Prearrange regular business phone calls with the other parent for the purpose of communicating about the children. Many parents agree that one will call the other on a specific evening after the children are in bed, whether monthly, biweekly, or weekly. Keep an agenda of issues that need to be addressed so you can keep focused on the business at hand and tie up all the loose ends at one time.
- Learn the communication skills discussed in Chapter 12, and *practice, practice, practice*!
- Keep all school notices in a sturdy folder in children's backpacks. Agree that each parent will routinely go through the folder, sign each notice after it is read, and return it to the folder for the other parent. Toss a notice only after both parents have seen and signed it.
- If both parents are involved with children's homework, send information about long-term homework assignments in children's backpacks. Include a checklist so each parent can sign off on what has been completed at the parent's home.
- Make a list of items a child takes to the other home that need to be returned, so the child and other parent can check them off. This will save a lot of follow-up calls and conflict. (It will help to have a designated place in the second home for your child to keep these items so they do not get lost.)

SEVEN KEYS TO SOUND CO-PARENTING

1. Respect the other parent's autonomy with the children.
2. Use the on-duty/off-duty parent concept.
3. Follow the model of a business relationship.
4. Acknowledge and respect the importance of the other parent's relationship with the children.
5. Don't *assume* anything; give the benefit of the doubt.
6. Communicate about the children using the communication tools in Chapter 12.
7. Make containing the conflict a top priority.

- Review the communication tips on pages 258 and 259.
- Initiate co-parenting counseling and participate in a session monthly, bimonthly, or quarterly so parenting decisions can be made and each of you can be updated on information about your children. Co-parenting counseling is discussed in the following chapter.
- If you feel that you *cannot* communicate with the other parent, it may be that you have not completed your emotional divorce. Go back to Chapter 10, and work on its principles.

Make Containing the Conflict a Top Priority

Conflict is the number one predictor of children's poor adjustment after divorce (see Chapter 8), and it is critical that you protect your children from it. If this sometimes feels like an impossible task, remind yourself that parents who relate as Cooperative Colleagues and those who relate as Angry Associates have the same level of anger. The difference is in Cooperative Colleagues' firm resolve to manage their anger and conflict so that it does not spill into their parenting and harm their children. Containing the conflict is so critical to both co-parenting and your children's well-being that the following chapter is dedicated to it. The chapter will guide you through steps to protect your children from the destructive conflict and then to end it.

19

Ending the Conflict: A Step-by-Step Approach

It is a puzzle to those who have not been through divorce, as well as to many who have, how people who once loved and cared so deeply about each other can come to hate and behave so callously toward one another after divorce.

Conflict can be expected after separation, as former partners grapple with their losses, resentments, unfulfilled expectations, thwarted needs, and inevitable anger—all while dealing with property, support, and custody negotiations. Many parents successfully contain or even end their conflict within a year of separation. However, studies indicate that approximately 25 percent of the divorced population remain embroiled in conflict year after year. Many of these conflicted former partners are still as angry and bitter years after the divorce as they were at separation, and their bitterness endures as a major issue in their lives. Those who are parents have chronic difficulty co-parenting their children. They distrust one another, are unable to discuss their children, and run the risk of a battle anytime they have contact. Many undermine one another. Many continue to bring each other back to court. For their children, feeling caught in the middle is the reality of their lives. These parents are usually referred to as "high-conflict parents."

What can you do to ensure that you do not become one of these high-conflict statistics? What can you do if you are already entrenched in emotional warfare? At what point should you worry about the conflict and try to do something about it?

The time to do something is *now*, whether you have just separated or whether you've been engaged in a vicious cycle of attack and counterattack for years. If you have not read Chapter 8, "Conflict! The Number One Predictor of Children's Poor Adjustment after Divorce," please do so. Parental conflict is exceedingly distressing to children of all ages—and when it becomes chronic, its harmful repercussions on children are likely to be both serious and long-term. Study after study in the United States and other countries, with children of all ages, have documented the devastating impact of chronic parental conflict on children. Children generally become emotionally troubled, expressing their distress in the form of any number of problems, including withdrawal, depression, poor self-esteem, poor grades, poor relationships with peers, impulsivity, aggressiveness, rebelliousness, and delinquency.

Conflict that lasts more than a year is generally considered to be harmful to children, and the more protracted and hostile it is, the more detrimental it usually is.

The quicker you take steps to contain and end the conflict, the less likely it is to get out of control. If it is already out of control, it is even more critical to take immediate steps so that your children are not harmed further. Do not wait for the other parent's cooperation. Start today—yourself! This chapter shows you how.

But first, understanding parents who are embroiled in emotional warfare will help you realize what you need to do and why. It will also help you determine whether you are already headed down this destructive path.

HIGH-CONFLICT PARENTS: COULD THIS BE YOU?

Researchers on both the east and west coasts have studied highly conflicted divorced parents to try to identify what distinguishes them from parents who are able to contain their conflict and work together for their children's sake, at least on a minimal level. Although no one profile emerges, researchers have noted many commonalities.

Highly contentious divorced couples continue to be emotionally tied to one another. The intensity of their emotion is a dead giveaway of just how much each is still hooked into the other. In fact, the intensity of their emotion is a far better barometer of their connectedness than whether their professed emotion is love or hate.

Many have never acknowledged either their losses or their sadness about the divorce. Instead, they mask their sadness with anger; as long as they can be angry at their former partner, they do not have to face the pain and loss that is inevitable with divorce (see Chapter 1). Typically, these highly conflicted divorced couples have very different accounts of what went wrong with the marriage, with each completely blaming the other and failing to accept any personal responsibility in the breakup. In a similar vein, many can only see their former spouse in a negative light, unable to recognize anything positive in the other or to construct a *balanced* view of the other. And very important for our purposes, they are unable to separate their former roles as *husband* and *wife* from their present roles as *father* and *mother*.

If you've read Chapter 10, "Your Emotional Divorce," you may recognize that the common thread here is these couples' failure to disengage and complete their emotional divorce. Their anger and conflict keep them chained to each other, preventing them from closing the doors on their marriages. Their anger and conflict also sap the energy they need to build new lives. For many, the conflict and repeated court filings are maneuvers of one or both to keep connected, albeit in a negative manner.

You may be thinking of divorced couples whom you know who have not completed the emotional divorce but are not entangled in conflict either. In a groundbreaking study conducted at San Francisco's Children's Hospital, researchers Janet Johnston and Linda Campbell found that what seems to distinguish these couples entrenched in prolonged conflict is that at least one partner, and sometimes both, has been *particularly* hurt by the other partner or is *particularly* psychologically fragile, when compared with the divorced population in general. Sometimes there has been a long history of hurt, perpetrated over the course of an antagonistic marriage. These former partners are likely to carry their long-term strife into their futures. For others, the intense hurt dates to the breakup of the marriage. Most usually, it is when the separation has been completely unexpected or traumatic, often involving a monumental betrayal (see Chapter 10). For others, one or both parties are psychologically fragile, perhaps due to past losses or adversity. These fragile parties do not have the resources to cope with the loss of the marriage and their pain. They convert their grief to rage and cannot let that rage go, because to do so would force them to face the new round of losses and rejection.

Highly conflicted couples demonstrate another distinguishing characteristic: Many have extended family or new significant others who, themselves, are so immersed in the conflict that they add fuel to the fire. For some, an attorney or therapist plays this role.

STEPS TO PROTECT CHILDREN FROM CONFLICT

In her studies of relationships between divorced parents, University of Southern California researcher Constance Ahrons identified four groups of parents, whom she labeled Perfect Pals, Cooperative Colleagues, Angry Associates, and Fiery Foes. The descriptive labels speak for themselves and are discussed more fully in Chapter 18. What is interesting is that the Cooperative Colleagues and Angry Associates had the *same level of anger*! The difference between the two was the Cooperative Colleagues' firm resolve to *manage* their anger so it did not contaminate their parenting and harm their children. Managing their anger took very deliberate effort. For example, when they had to discuss their children, they set appointments with one another and met in public places. They kept themselves in check and refrained from responding angrily, even when very tempted. For issues that usually provoked arguments, they used written communication. If possible, they completely avoided highly controversial issues.

Ending the strife may seem an impossible task to you right now if you are involved in an escalating cycle of emotional self-defense and retaliation. It takes time to break such a cycle. But as the Cooperative Colleagues demonstrated, there are ways to protect children from it, even when parents are still feeling intensely angry themselves. When children are not exposed to their parents' discord and do not feel caught in the middle, they are usually not harmed.

Following are effective means to shield your children from destructive conflict while you are working on ending it. As an added bonus, watch your own self-esteem soar as you develop your ability to maintain control and protect your children, too.

Communicate Away from Children

The most obvious way to protect children from conflict is *never* to have discussions with the other parent within their earshot. *All* discussions should be *scheduled* and should take place at times the children are not in hearing range. Some parents arrange discussions away from the home. If you are talking by telephone, do it in a room with a closed door after children are asleep. When the other parent calls the children at your home, remember that the phone call is for the children and hand the phone over to a child immediately. Don't take the chance of ruining the call for them by getting into a discussion that could end in an argument.

The Parenting Schedule

When parents are in conflict, sharing the children often becomes the focal point of their battles. The importance of having and strictly following a detailed parenting schedule cannot be emphasized enough! Such a schedule specifies when children will be with each parent and reduces the need for frequent communication, which often ends in confrontation. It markedly reduces the potential for future battles and power plays over children, such as one parent denying the other access to the children, a parent unilaterally canceling the other's time with the children, or a parent refusing to return a child. It also provides structure that enables children to go between their battling parents' homes in a somewhat orderly manner.

The greater the conflict, the more clearly the schedule should be specified, and the more strictly it should be followed. For parents who are in conflict, flexibility generally opens the door for new conflict. Chapter 17, "Parenting Plans: Blueprints for a Smooth Future," guides you in developing a detailed parenting plan. As your conflict subsides, the schedule can become more flexible.

You are likely to have a better chance of protecting children from conflict if you can settle parenting arrangements prior to involving yourselves with the legal system. Once the legal system is involved, conflict may *escalate*, and children sometimes become bargaining chips in support issues.

Transitions

Transitioning from one parent's home to the other can become a nightmare for children when parents are in serious conflict (see Chapter 8). It is during direct exchanges of the children that parents are most likely to have open battles because this is often the only time they see one another. Even if parents avoid open battles, children are very aware of their parents' tension, which usually begins building hours, and sometimes days, prior to an exchange and lasts for hours afterward.

Transitioning from one home to the other is also difficult for children because antagonistic parents, who do not communicate, frequently have very different household routines, schedules, rules, expectations, and discipline to which children are expected to immediately adapt. This is particularly distressing and confusing for young children.

Children show the effects of stress from transitions in any number of ways, including crying and clinging, having stomachaches and headaches, saying they do not want to go, and becoming withdrawn, sullen, or sassy.

Following are steps you can take to make transitions easier for your children and shield them from conflict's destructive fallout.

Minimize the Number of Transitions between Homes

There is wide agreement among experts who study and work with conflicted families that it is generally better for children to spend a longer block of time with a parent than to frequently move between the two warring homes. For example, if the children's schedule with the nonresident parent is alternate weekends and a Wednesday overnight, try replacing the Wednesday with a Thursday overnight, so that it blends with the weekend time in a single block. Other possibilities are replacing a midweek contact with either a longer weekend (Friday to Monday morning) or three weekends a month to minimize the number of transitions. The one exception is very young children whose developmental needs conflict with spending longer blocks of time (see Chapter 17).

Neutral Exchange Sites

Ideally, when parents are in emotional warfare, children should be exchanged without any parental contact whatever. For example, make the exchange at school, child care, or the home of a *neutral* relative or friend.

A neutral exchange site not only eliminates the tension and possibility of open conflict but also provides children with a buffer zone in which to regroup and prepare to shift gears to the other parent's home. Extending weekends from Friday after school or child care to Monday morning at child care is an option used by many parents to eliminate direct contact for weekend exchanges.

If you must exchange children directly and exchanges are very conflictual, you might try a *curbside* exchange: One parent remains in the car and beeps the horn, while the other remains in the residence. Each parent watches until the child is with the receiving parent, so the child's safety is ensured. This option is not feasible in some settings or with a young child who has no older siblings. Some parents can control themselves enough to walk a young child to the front door and hand the child over to the other parent. Both agree to no conversation other than a polite greeting.

A second option if you must exchange children directly is a public location with lots of people, which increases the likelihood of each parent maintaining self-control. Fast-food restaurants with play equipment are favorites of children. Other options are public libraries, where you *must* be quiet, and shopping malls. Aim for a comfortable place in which you can sit and relax in case one of you is late and the other must wait.

Easing Transitions for Children

The following suggestions will help to make transitions smoother for your children:

- *Send favorite items with your child,* particularly a young child. These will be comforting and help children bridge the gap between their two homes. Examples are a loved stuffed animal, a special toy, or some favorite clothing.
- *Develop set routines or rituals* with your children to prepare them for the transition to the other home. The ritual becomes a signal to children to gear up for the change in homes. You might start the ritual by helping them collect their things for their other home *early* so there will not be a rush, with an impatient parent waiting. Be upbeat. When their things are ready, engage in a quiet ritual activity with them that is calming and they will enjoy—reading a book, playing a quiet game, or sharing a favorite snack. You can develop these rituals whether you are the primary parent, a part-time parent, or a shared-custody parent.
- *Keep exchanges courteous and brief.* Try to manage a smile and a courteous hello for your children's sake, rather than the tense silent exchanges engaged in by many feuding parents. Don't prolong good-byes in front of the other parent; take care of them at home or in the car beforehand. And please don't grab children away from the other parent while they are saying good-bye. Exchanges are not the time to raise any issues that

might cause an argument or require extended discussion. If the other parent insists on doing so, don't get dragged into a confrontation. Cut the conversation off politely: "Thank you for sharing that. We'll discuss it later. I have to go now." Then remove yourself from the situation.

- *Don't take along a new significant other or family member who is involved in the conflict.* All too often this adds fuel to an already volatile situation, and children are exposed to a virtual free-for-all of name-calling, shouting, and shoving.

- *Recognize that each child copes with transitions in individual ways.* One child may become clingy. Another may be angry. A third may need to spend time alone. Give your children some space, and don't assume something is wrong in the other parent's home because of problems your children display when they arrive at your home. They are most likely responding to the transition.

- *Try to maintain some consistency in routines and expectations between the homes,* at least for young children. This may be uncomfortable for you, but it will ease your young child's distress.

Never Place Children in Loyalty Conflicts!

Children of battling parents usually feel *caught in the middle* and develop painful loyalty conflicts or loyalty binds. Although you may never have thought of such loyalty binds as a form of conflict, several studies have found them to be *more* damaging to children's well-being than open conflict. Loyalty conflicts make children feel as if they are being torn in two by the two people they love most in the world.

DON'T PLACE CHILDREN
IN PAINFUL LOYALTY CONFLICTS

✓ *Don't* pump a child for information about the other parent.
✓ *Don't* ask a child to be a message carrier or go-between.
✓ *Don't* ask a child to spy on the other parent.
✓ *Don't* pressure a child to take your side or to prefer you.
✓ *Don't* badmouth the other parent.
✓ *Do* give your child permission to love the other parent.

Parents put children in loyalty conflicts in many ways. The most common appear in the table on page 275 and were discussed extensively in Chapter 8. *Please* read about them and *avoid them, no matter how tempted you are*!

In addition to the *do*'s and *don't*s in the table, following are some less obvious ways to avoid placing your children in loyalty conflicts:

- *Don't* ask your children to keep secrets from the other parent. No matter what they do, they will feel that they are betraying one parent.
- *Don't* interpret their love for their other parent as a threat to you.
- *Don't* add fuel to the fire if your children are angry with their other parent. Let them talk about their feelings and empathize with them, but try to take a neutral stance. "You sound pretty disappointed Dad hasn't seen you in a while." Not: "It's terrible the way your father so seldom takes the time to see you." Encourage your children to talk to the other parent directly.
- *Don't* allow your child to take the role of a mediator, even if he or she volunteers.
- *Don't* talk about the other parent when your children are within hearing range, even if they appear to be preoccupied in an activity. Children have a sort of built-in radar that becomes activated at any mention of the other parent. They hear *every* word.
- *Don't* get drawn into a tit-for-tat game if the other parent is badmouthing you. Calmly explain that people often say things they don't mean when they are upset, but don't dwell on the issue. Focus instead on building a strong relationship with your children. This will be your best defense, and you will be the parent whom your children respect.
- *Don't* insist on your children calling you when they are with the other parent. Children often need to keep their two worlds separate when parents are in considerable conflict. You can let children know you always like hearing from them if they feel like calling, but do not pressure them to do so.
- *Do* keep your distance from the other parent at your child's events if a confrontation may erupt. It's not fair for your child to be humiliated or to have an event spoiled because of fear that conflict will erupt. If your child came to the event with you, give permission to your youngster to visit with the other parent, too.

Assume a Businesslike Demeanor with the Other Parent

Assuming a businesslike demeanor anytime you interact with the other parent will automatically help protect your children from conflict. People in a business relationship do not yell and scream at one another, make snide comments, insist on getting the last word, or involve customers (in your case your children) in their disputes! When you interact with the other parent, the key is to avoid doing or saying anything that you would not do or say in a business relationship. If it is the other parent who is behaving inappropriately, pretend you are the owner of a business and are dealing with a difficult customer whose business you need. Please review the previous chapter, which provides more detail on how to relate in a businesslike manner.

Provide Your Children with the Means to Cope

It is a boon for children whose parents are in conflict to learn some coping skills to deal with it. Most children whose parents are in considerable conflict benefit from counseling. The counselor's office is a child's safe haven where he or she can unload. This is hard for a child to do with either parent without feeling loyalty conflicts. Therapists teach children coping skills to deal with the tough situations they face. They also become a child's advocate and work with parents to better meet their child's needs. It is preferable for both parents to have contact with the therapist, so he or she has input from both and can work with both.

Many communities and schools now have group programs for children going through divorce that can be very beneficial to youngsters. Some deal with conflict and provide coping skills. Check with your children's school, local court, community agencies, or health maintenance organization.

You can teach your children some coping skills yourself. Let them know that they do not have to worry about adult problems and that it is their right to love both parents without feeling caught in the middle. Teach them to remind you—many times if necessary—that they do not want to be put in the middle, that they do not want to hear negative things about either parent, that it is not their job to carry messages between their parents, and that it upsets them to hear you and the other parent argue. Encourage them to speak with their other parent as well. Sometimes it only takes a child speaking up in this way to send a wake-up call to a parent, although some parents need repeated reminders.

STEPS TO PROTECT CHILDREN FROM SERIOUS CONFLICT

✓ Never have discussions within children's earshot.
✓ Develop a consistent parenting schedule and stick to it.
✓ Minimize the number of transitions between homes.
✓ Use neutral exchange sites.
  • School and child care.
  • Curbside exchanges.
  • Public locations.
✓ Take steps to make transitions easier for children.
  • Send favorite toys or clothing.
  • Develop rituals.
  • Keep exchanges courteous and brief.
  • Don't take along a new significant other or a family member involved in the conflict.
  • Allow children space to cope with transitions in their own way.
  • Try to maintain some consistency between homes, especially for young children.
✓ Never place children in loyalty conflicts.
✓ Assume a businesslike demeanor during parent interactions.
✓ Provide children with the means to cope.

STEPS TO END THE CONFLICT

The worst mistake you can make is to resign yourself to the notion that "things will never get any better. We will always be in this conflict." Unfortunately, this stance seems to be a hallmark of highly conflicted divorced parents. But in drawing this conclusion, parents create a self-fulfilling prophecy, and, thereby, seal their fate! If you assume that things will never change, you will never take steps to *make* them change. You will continue in the old destructive ways of relating. And yes—things will never change.

You can take some immediate steps to turn the tide on the conflict. Remember, the Cooperative Colleagues and Angry Associates in Constance Ahrons's study had the same level of anger. The Cooperative

Colleagues just managed it better. You can do the same. *Start NOW!* Progress is made in small steps, and it takes one of you to start.

Take Steps to Restructure the Marital Relationship

A critical early step toward ending destructive conflict is to break away from the old ways of interacting with one another. You do this by restructuring the marital relationship into a co-parenting relationship. The parental role is very different from the spousal role, and you need to separate current parenting issues from old spousal issues.

Restructuring the relationship consists primarily of disengaging from one another, creating new boundaries, interacting in a more formal and businesslike manner, and consciously redefining the relationship in your own mind. Chapter 18, "Making Co-Parenting Work," guides you through the restructuring process.

Once parents disengage and create new boundaries, *conflict usually starts to diminish*. It continues to decrease as you get further along in the restructuring process. Get started right away!

Take Responsibility for Your Own Behavior

Warring parents usually get caught up in one tit-for-tat battle after another. If you're caught up in these skirmishes, put an end to it! Start behaving as a Cooperative Colleague. Closely monitor yourself and keep focused on your children. Even though the other parent is still behaving as an Angry Associate, you can break the escalating cycle. Here are some specific steps you can take right away:

- Make a pact with yourself to start using a businesslike demeanor when interacting with the other parent and start implementing the business formalities discussed in the previous chapter.
- When you have an impulse to respond vengefully or in a tit-for-tat manner, sternly tell yourself, *STOP!* It may help, when interacting with the other parent, to pretend that a third person is present whose respect is very important to you, or that a tape recorder is running to record the interaction for posterity.
- Anytime you do have a confrontation with the other parent, learn from it. Ask yourself afterward what role you played and how you might have handled the situation differently.

- Avoid inflammatory or even controversial issues unless they concern your children's emotional or physical well-being.
- Avoid calling your attorney every time there is a problem. It only escalates conflict. Your attorney is there to make things better for you, not for your children or for the long-term co-parenting relationship. Be very selective in your confrontations, saving them for critical situations, such as if the other parent is placing your child in harm's way.
- Refrain from jumping to conclusions. You need to realize that when parents are in conflict, children commonly tell each parent what the parent wants to hear. Children want to please both. Sometimes they even grossly exaggerate things that take place at one parent's home so the other will feel like the better parent. *Do not* accept everything your child tells you as gospel, and don't start attacking the other parent because of something your child says. If the issue is a critical one and must be addressed, check out the facts first with the other parent to make sure they are correct.

Communication: It's All in How You Say It

Contentious divorced couples usually communicate in a manner that puts each of them on the defensive—thereby dooming the possibility of a constructive exchange before it even begins. Start using the 10 communication tools that will make a difference (see Chapter 12) when you communicate with the other parent. You are not only more likely to succeed in having a nonconfrontational exchange but also more likely to succeed in realizing some of your objectives.

Avoid Blame Games

Conflicted divorced parents typically get caught up in *blame games*. Anytime a problem arises, one or both points the finger at the other to assign blame for it. "If you had done . . . , this would not have happened." "He certainly doesn't learn behavior like that at *my* house!" "What do you expect when you have no rules or discipline over there?"

Playing blame games puts the focus on who is at fault. Parents get so caught up in round after round of attack and counterattack that they never get to the real issue at hand—how to deal with the problem.

The inevitable outcome of getting caught up in blame games is escalated conflict, a child feeling caught in the middle, and a problem that is no closer to being solved. Avoid trying to identify who is to blame, and focus your attention and energy on what can be done to deal with the problem.

Complete Your Emotional Divorce

If you are having difficulty taking steps to stop the conflict, you may need to do some basic work on yourself. If you recall, most highly conflicted divorced couples are still emotionally tied to one another and have not completed their *emotional* divorce. Remember, it is the *intensity* of your emotion toward the other parent that tells you how much you are still hooked into your former partner, not whether your emotion is love or hate.

Take a close look at yourself and the role you are playing in the conflict. If your first response is that you are blameless, take a closer look. Conflict is a two-way street. Read Chapter 10, and start working on its principles.

Make the First Move to Extend the Olive Branch

Someone has to make the first overt moves toward peace. Try sending the other parent a card or writing a short letter. Say that both of you need to end the conflict for your children's sake, that you are going to do your part, and that you hope he or she will join you in the effort.

If your separation was marked by betrayal and deception on your part, consider acknowledging the other parent's hurt and apologizing for the way the marriage ended. Don't expect a miraculous end to the conflict, but your acknowledgment may be the first step toward healing.

Be on the lookout for ways you can co-parent more cooperatively. If you haven't been diligent about sharing information about the children, start doing so in brief businesslike memos. Have your child call the other parent to share some exciting news about his or her day. Can you see that your child has a card or present for the other parent's birthday, Mother's/Father's Day, or your former in-laws' birthdays? Can you think of something the other parent is doing for the children that you can compliment? Can you agree, when asked, for the children to do something special with the other parent even though it is your scheduled time with them? Tell the other parent you are agreeing in a spirit of cooperation and reiterate that you really want to start working together as parents for the children's sake.

Don't expect your efforts to be reciprocated immediately, particularly if you have been in severe conflict. It may take time.

Start Following the Keys to Sound Co-Parenting

If both you and the other parent are involved with your children on some type of regular basis, you will be co-parenting them, regardless of what kind of custody you have. Children need two parents after divorce.

Chapter 18, "Making Co-Parenting Work," details seven keys to sound co-parenting, which are listed in the accompanying table. If you start following numbers one through five, you'll have some rules to abide by, and conflict will start to subside. Share the list with the other parent so you are both on the "same page." Learning good communication skills (see Chapter 12) will also go a long way in curtailing conflict and will make number six possible.

If you are in serious conflict, you might bristle at some of these co-parenting basics. Many parents who are in considerable conflict distrust one another, cannot separate spousal issues from parenting issues, focus exclusively on the other parent's shortcomings, and are blind to the other's strengths as a parent. Consequently, many antagonistic parents do not respect the other parent's relationship with the children, automatically jump to negative conclusions, and try to control the other parent's time with

---

SEVEN KEYS TO SOUND CO-PARENTING

1. Respect the other parent's autonomy with the children.
2. Use the on-duty/off-duty parent concept.
3. Follow the model of a business relationship.
4. Acknowledge and respect the importance of the other parent's relationship with the children.
5. Don't *assume* anything; give the benefit of the doubt.
6. Communicate about the children using the communication tools in Chapter 12.
7. Make containing the conflict a top priority.

the children. Moreover, because of their poor communication, they do not know, for a fact, what goes on in the other home. They rely on children's tales, which are often less than accurate!

Please review the co-parenting chapter (Chapter 18). You don't need to treat these co-parenting basics as an all-or-none package deal. If you find some very difficult, start working on one or two of the easier ones. As you put them into practice, co-parenting will become a little smoother, and tackling one or two more will seem less intimidating. You might find the self-change program in Appendix A helpful if you have difficulty with this. Co-parenting is not learned overnight. It takes time, conscious effort, and practice.

Tune Up Your Expectations

Even if you grant the other parent autonomy during his or her parenting time (key number one) you may still find yourself holding steadfastly to expectations about how the other parent should and should not behave. You may also find yourself frustrated and angry when your co-parent's behavior falls short of your expectations. If so, you need to do a tune-up on your expectations.

You cannot control the other parent. You cannot change the other parent. Your expectations are doing nothing but causing you resentment and frustration! Acknowledge the other parent's flaws, and make the best of the situation. Like it or not, this is the person whom you selected to be your child's parent, and nothing will change that. So stop obsessing on what you *can't* change or control and focus on what you *can* control: yourself—your own parenting, your own relationship with your children, and your expectations of the other parent. Start anticipating problems and *work around them*. It will take less energy than the conflict and frustration. You may also wish to review Chapter 5 and use some of the coping tools to diffuse self-defeating anger.

Take Steps to End the Family Wars

Conflict is sometimes fueled by extended family members and new significant others who have become overinvolved in the battle. If this is true for you, it's time you stop allowing your emotions to be fueled by others. Turn your focus to your children, and take control of the situation.

Share with your family or significant other the information you have learned about conflict's harmful repercussions for children (see Chapter 8). You might even ask them to read the chapter. Make a pact with them to be vigilant about protecting the children from further conflict and from any badmouthing of their other parent. They do not have to like the other parent, but they do have to accept that he or she is the children's parent and nothing will change that. It's time to lay the past to rest and move on for the children's sake.

EXTRAORDINARY STEPS FOR EXTRAORDINARY CONFLICT

If you've had one of those horrendous divorces and feel that your conflict either is or will be out of control, you will likely have to take more extraordinary steps to contain it, *in addition* to those already covered. Please don't allow yourself to join the ranks of parents who are so hooked on revenge and bitterness that they don't recognize their children's silent pleas for help.

Structure! Structure! Structure!

Above all else, highly conflicted parents need *structure,* in which rules are clearly spelled out and *nothing* is left to interpretation or misunderstanding. The more intense the conflict, the greater the need for structure, and the wider its net should be. When conflict is intense, flexibility breeds new conflict!

You can achieve the needed structure through a comprehensive and exceedingly detailed parenting plan. Follow the step-by-step guide in Chapter 17. Spell out every detail, and don't skip any of the components. Also try to anticipate situations that may cause unique problems for your family so you can hammer out solutions before they become volatile issues. Don't assume *anything.* Put everything in writing. Any loose end you leave is a potential fuse.

If you are in intense conflict, you are likely to need help in developing a detailed parenting plan. If your local court does not provide mediation, you can enlist the help of a private family mediator (see Chapter 2) or a co-parenting counselor (to be discussed shortly). If you are unable to work out all the details of a parenting plan, even with this help, you may have to allow the co-parenting counselor to call the shots for any disputed issues or ask the courts to do so. (Private mediators will not make the decisions for you.) Once you have a plan, agree there will be *no* deviations from it until you have the conflict under control.

Avoid All Direct Contact

When conflict is very intense, you are wise to avoid *all* direct contact, either face-to-face or by telephone, except when meeting with a mediator or co-parenting counselor.

First, *use only neutral exchange sites that require no contact.* Exchanges at school or child care usually work well when conflict is intense. If yours is an extreme case of conflict in which one or both of you have little control of yourselves and you have to exchange children directly, you might check to see if there are any *supervised exchanged sites* in your locality. These are professionally run facilities that allow one parent to drop off a child approximately 15 minutes before the other is to arrive. Unless it is publicly funded, there is a fee. A neutral family member or friend may be willing to do the same. Another option preferred by some parents is the police station. If this is the only way you feel safe or the only way that your conflict can be controlled, so be it. But consider the message you are sending your children if they must be exchanged at a police station.

Second, *put all communication in writing.* This not only eliminates the need for direct contact, it eliminates the verbal cues and body language that can easily push buttons. Faxes and e-mail now make communication convenient, and the equipment to send them is a good investment. If you have a young child, you might also try exchanging a communication journal with the youngster (see Chapter 18). If you have to rely on the U.S. mail, it will not be as convenient, but there are few issues that are so critical they must be communicated immediately. If you have a *neutral* friend or family member, you might ask if critical issues can be communicated through this person. In the case of a real emergency, however, such as an accident requiring emergency room treatment, pick up the phone and notify the other parent immediately.

Third, *don't rely on the other parent for information that you can obtain yourself.* Less conflict will ensue if each of you sets up your own relationship with teachers, coaches, doctors, and others involved in your child's life. Most people are willing to talk with you by telephone so you can keep apprised of your child's life and learn what you can do to help your youngster. Giving teachers self-addressed, stamped envelopes often facilitates having two sets of information sent out for one child.

Fourth, *keep a safe distance at your children's activities,* and if conflict is likely to erupt, divvy up which activities each of you will attend until the conflict can be contained. Eleven-year-old Mary Beth sobbed in my office as she relived her ruined elementary school graduation, during which her mother threw a cup of punch at her father with her horrified classmates looking on. Thirteen-year-old Jeb relayed his mortification when his father made a scene at his football game, screaming at his mother that she was a whore. Seven-year-old Tim refused to return to his soccer team after his father got into a physical confrontation with his mother's significant other at one of his games. Don't let this happen to your child. Children would rather have only one parent at an activity than be humiliated. A clear-cut way to divide activities is for each parent to attend only the activities that fall on the parent's scheduled days.

A WISE STEP: CO-PARENTING COUNSELING

Regardless of the level of your conflict and how long it has continued, you and the other parent are likely to benefit from co-parenting counseling. In co-parenting counseling, both parents meet together with a mental health professional who has special expertise in working with conflicted separated or divorced parents. During sessions, parents work on improving their communication and co-parenting skills, reducing their conflict, and resolving co-parenting issues.

When parents are in severe conflict, sessions are likely to focus on the minutiae of co-parenting rather than skill building. Co-parenting sessions provide a forum to develop some consistency between the homes and deal with problems when they arise, rather than letting them fester, taking them to court, or fighting in front of the children. As you gain more control of the conflict, you can move on to skill building. Sometimes it is very helpful for parents to be in individual counseling, as well, so they can complete their emotional divorces.

Sometimes highly conflicted parents never get beyond what is called *parallel parenting,* in which each parents the children independently with little or no communication with one another. When parents parallel parent, a co-parenting counseling session on a bimonthly or quarterly basis can be invaluable so children are not forced to have two completely disparate lives.

START REDUCING CONFLICT NOW!

✓ Beware of self-fulfilling prophecies.
✓ Behave as a "cooperative colleague."
✓ Take steps to restructure the marital relationship.
✓ Take responsibility for your own behavior.
✓ Use the 10 communication tools that will make the difference.
✓ Avoid blame games.
✓ Complete your own emotional divorce.
✓ Make the first move toward peace.
✓ Start following the seven keys to sound co-parenting.
✓ Do a tune-up of your expectations.
✓ Take steps to end the family wars.
✓ Take extraordinary measures for extraordinary conflict.
  • Create a detailed parenting plan that leaves nothing to interpretation.
  • Avoid *all* direct contact with the other parent.
  • Put *all* communication in writing.
  • Don't rely on the other parent for information.
✓ Initiate co-parenting counseling.

When parents have a co-parenting counselor on board, they have a resource to call anytime a problem arises so it can be nipped in the bud and quickly resolved. You can also enlist the help of a family mediator (see Chapter 2) to resolve problems before they escalate. Many issues that parents take to court could be more constructively and less expensively settled in co-parenting counseling or mediation. And how much better for children to see their parents working together as parents to resolve parenting issues rather than turning decisions for their lives over to a judge who doesn't know any of them!

20

How to Discipline Effectively and Still Be a "Good Guy"

Discipline plays a critical role in one-parent homes. It is a key ingredient that distinguishes well-functioning one-parent homes from poorly functioning ones. Compared with married parents, single parents (especially mothers) are generally found to be less effective disciplinarians. As a group, single parents are very permissive, for many seemingly valid reasons. Some believe their children already have been deprived enough due to the divorce and shouldn't be denied further. Some are afraid that children will prefer their other parent. Others find themselves too easily swayed by children's arguments because there is no other adult available to offer them support or an objective point of view. Some single parents are simply too exhausted from their workload to monitor their children carefully.

Many single parents seesaw back and forth between being permissive and temporarily coming down hard on their children when things get out of control. However, neither permissiveness nor restrictiveness is in children's best interest, nor is vacillating between the two.

Every parent can become a good disciplinarian with some knowledge and practice. This chapter provides the knowledge. Because discipline is a well-researched subject we have some good evidence about what is effective and what is not. The practice, of course, will be up to you, but it will be well worth your while. Effective discipline is likely to make your children more responsible and your home a more harmonious place to live—and it will not make you an ogre, either!

Before our discussion of effective discipline, you may find it helpful to learn why it is not in your children's best interest to be raised in *either* a very permissive home or a very restrictive one.

DIFFERENT PARENTING STYLES AND THEIR REPERCUSSIONS

For many years, researchers have studied three distinct parenting styles to determine whether they have any clear impact on children's development. The styles have been labeled *permissive, authoritarian,* and *authoritative,* although not every parent neatly falls under one of these labels. We now know that these parenting styles generally *do* influence children's development in important ways.

Permissive parents generally make few demands on children, impose few rules, and allow children to make their own decisions with little guidance. Children raised by permissive parents are often found to have a poor sense of social responsibility. In general, they are found to be impulsive, immature, and aggressive. The reason seems to be that the absence of parental controls makes it very difficult for these children and teens to develop their own self-control.

Authoritarian parents are the extreme opposite. In such households, the power and decision making is clearly in the parents' hands. Parents are very restrictive and controlling. They expect children to obey with no questions asked, and they punish disobedience sternly. Children raised in authoritarian homes generally have low self-esteem; this is not surprising if one considers the little respect they have received from their parents. As a group, these children also require a good deal of monitoring. Not only are they poorly self-motivated, but their internal standards of right and wrong are often poorly developed, for two reasons. First, punitive parents do not inspire children's loyalty to their values, and so their youngsters are less likely to accept those values as their own. And second, because their behavior is rigidly dictated with neither explanation nor opportunity to question, children have little opportunity to work out a value system that makes sense to them—a value system that can guide them when facing new situations requiring moral decisions. Compare this parenting style and its repercussions with an authorita*tive* style. In an authoritative parenting style, a parent—

- Is warm, nurturing, and respectful of children.
- Encourages open discussion and seeks children's input.

- Is responsive to children's needs and opinions.
- Provides clear expectations and guidelines.
- Follows through with consistent positive discipline.
- Is the one who is ultimately in charge in the family.

How do children raised in authoritative households develop? They tend to be socially responsive and altruistic (perhaps modeling their parents' responsiveness to them). Generally, they have high self-esteem and are assertive. (Remember, they have been treated with respect, and their needs and opinions have been considered important.) And they develop good self-control and strong *internal* standards of acceptable behavior. Why the latter? First, their parents provide them with clear guidelines to follow until they are able to develop their own self-control. Second, warm, nurturing, and respectful parents kindle children's loyalty to parental values, so children are more likely to internalize these values. Finally, the continuing give-and-take exchange between parent and child helps youngsters work out their own standards of right and wrong.

Learning good disciplinary practices will help you develop an authoritative parenting style.

THE PRINCIPLES OF POSITIVE PARENTING

The reason so many parents have a hard time with discipline is that many of their natural inclinations are counterproductive. The root of the problem may lie in a misunderstanding of what discipline means. Many parents incorrectly equate discipline with punishment. Discipline is not punishment. *Discipline is teaching* children responsibility, self-control, and how to behave appropriately. If you keep this in mind, discipline will take on a whole new meaning for you.

Because most parents incorrectly equate discipline with punishment, they typically ignore their children when they are good and punish them or yell at them when they are bad. Unfortunately, this is the *worst* thing a parent can do. Few people, especially children, like to be unnoticed and ignored. Ignored for too long, children will do something to get your attention. If the only time you notice them is when they do something bad or annoying, then that's what most children will do (become noisy, have a temper tantrum, throw something, run into the street, whine, start a fight, dress outrageously). Now they've gotten what they wanted. You stopped what you are doing and you're paying attention to them. You are rewarding the very behavior that you want to stop. Instead of stopping it, you are increasing the likelihood that it will occur again the next time they are not getting the attention they want! True, yelling or punishment is not the kind of attention children prefer, but at least they no longer feel like nonentities. They *can* have an impact on the world after all.

Reward Good Behavior

The first and foremost principle of effective discipline is this: Reward children's good behavior. This does not mean you should bribe them to be good. It means getting into the habit of noticing when your children are behaving as you would like them to, and then rewarding them with praise, attention, and affection. Give them lots of praise when they are following rules, being helpful, playing quietly, cooperating with one another, doing something nice for someone, and so on. (Younger children love hugs, too.) *The more you reward their good behavior in this way, the more likely they are to repeat that behavior over and over again.*

Because your children will come to associate their good behavior with your warmth and approval, they will start to feel good when they are behaving appropriately. Eventually, being good will become rewarding in and of itself. This is the beginning of self-discipline—quite a difference from children who behave only when someone is there to punish their misbehavior!

As good behavior becomes more natural for your children, you will need to praise them less frequently for it. This does not mean you should take your children for granted and pay no attention to them. Children always thrive on your love, attention, and appreciation and are likely to revert to some type of attention-getting behavior once again if ignored.

Ignore Annoying Misbehavior

What do you do about those annoying things your children do that drive you nuts—bickering, whining, temper tantrums? Forget yelling, and forget nagging. By now you have probably noticed that neither works. Neither do empty threats. How about a good swift swat, you wonder? If you have used this technique, ask *yourself* if it works. Your answer will probably be, "Well, it does for a while." Physical punishment usually turns out to be a poor teaching method. There will be more on this later.

Then what do you do? Believe it or not, the most effective way to stop the annoying things your children do (not the harmful or really obnoxious things) is to *ignore* them. The reason is that the behavior is usually designed to get attention. If you don't look, don't talk, don't even react, it will eventually stop. And the more you ignore it, the more likely it is to stop *permanently.*

The best strategy to stop misbehavior, therefore, is to *pay attention to children when they behave and to ignore them when they misbehave.* Consistency is important!

Time-Out

You are probably shaking your head and thinking of a list of things that your children do that would be ridiculous to ignore. What about dangerous or destructive behavior? What do you do when your children are being so obnoxious that you can't stand it?

The solution? When behavior is dangerous, destructive, or so obnoxious you can't ignore it, immediately send or remove your child to a place where he or she *can* be ignored. It is important to do this very calmly and without discussion, argument, or "another chance." (Remember that any form of attention will reward the undesirable behavior.) The more boring the place you send your child, the better. You don't want to reward him or her with television, toys, things to explore, or someone to talk to. This technique is called "time-out," and it is a very effective teaching tool. Examples of effective places for time-outs are a bathroom, a laundry room, a chair in a corner, or even a chair in a boring kitchen, as long as no one else is in the room. The youngster must stay for a designated amount of time (about one minute for each year of age is a rough guideline).

You say your children would never stay? Then they get nothing positive of any kind until they do. Again, no discussion or arguments. Just a short, calm, matter-of-fact statement: "I'm sorry but you can't watch TV (have dinner, play that game, go outside and play, and so on) until you've completed your time-out."

After the time-out, ask your child why it was necessary and what he or she could do differently the next time. Try time-outs with children ranging from preschool age to about 11. The technique is simple but effective.

Provide Clear Expectations and Limits

Children should not be expected to learn by trial and error what behavior is acceptable and what is unacceptable. Yet this is what many parents unwittingly expect their children to do. They will allow a child to engage in obnoxious behavior for so long, and then explode. The confused child wonders why it was okay the first 10 times but elicited an explosion on the 11th!

Telling children clearly when their behavior is unacceptable and *why* is an important facet of discipline. Equally important is providing them with alternatives that *are* acceptable. For example, a child who takes out his anger by kicking furniture needs to have some alternative ways to handle that anger. You might suggest he remove himself from the anger-provoking situation and engage in another activity until he calms down enough to talk about the problem. He might find some type of vigorous physical activity helpful, such as running, climbing, or throwing balls. Or he might find some calming activities helpful, such as listening to music, drawing, playing with clay, or taking a warm bath.

Your children will need clear limits from you until they have developed self-control and are mature enough to set their own. Being able to set appropriate limits for themselves will become more and more critical as they get older and have fewer people to monitor them. How do you help children get to the point of being able to set their own limits? Basically, follow the principles of an authoritative parenting style. Here are some specifics you can do.

First, remember that if you are warm, nurturing, and respectful of your children, they are more likely to internalize your values and make them their own.

Second, be sure they understand the *reasons* for your expectations and the limits you set. You can start this when they are very young. "If you throw sand, it can get in people's eyes and it will hurt." "When you treat people like that, it hurts their feelings." If you help children understand the underlying reasons for your expectations and limits, they will also be more willing to follow them.

Third, involve your children in a give-and-take discussion about limits and the rules you set, and allow them to help set some of them. The older that children are, the more important it is that they be involved. However, remember that your children need your guidance and experience and that you, as the parent, *always* have the final say in what limits are appropriate.

Use Rules for Really Important Things

You will want to have some *formal* rules for children to follow that are very explicit. Save formal rules for important things. You don't want to get bogged down in so many rules that children can't keep track of them. What formal rules you make will depend on your children, their ages, what is important to you, and what is currently an issue in your household. Safety, health, and the rights of others are prime areas for formal rules but are not the only ones. Following are examples of areas in which you may want to have clear rules: the way your children treat other people and property, "off-limits" activities when they are home alone, how far from home they can roam on their own, curfews, homework, and chores.

Consequences When Rules and Limits Are Broken

For rules and limits to be effective, there must be some consequences for breaking them. Children almost always test rules and limits and will conclude that they are unimportant if no consequences follow.

Sometimes children forget and just need a reminder. If a child is testing some limit, a warning glance from you may be all that is needed. If a child is about to throw something at a playmate, take it away from her and remind her that it is unacceptable to throw things, especially when it may hurt someone. If a child proceeds after a single warning, then it is time for consequences. There are some important things to remember about consequences.

Consequences Should Be Consistent

If children experience consequences one day and not the next, it will take far longer for rules and limits to become a routine part of their lives. Without consistency, they will always be testing your limits. Many parents threaten consequences over and over again ("If you do that one more time, I will . . ."). However, empty threats *do not work*. Give children *one* warning. If they continue, follow through with the consequences.

Consequences Should Be Realistic

Before you threaten consequences, be sure you are willing to carry them out. Then do so after one warning. If your children know you will not follow through, the threatened consequence will have no effect.

Consequences Should Be Fair

If consequences are too severe, they are likely to build resentment. A teen who is five minutes late for curfew should not be grounded for a week. Neither should consequences be too minimal. A teen who is an hour late for curfew (without having telephoned) is not likely to take curfew seriously if the only consequence is a comment about his tardiness. Some words of caution: Never deny a child time with his or her nonresident parent as a consequence for misbehavior. That relationship is critical and should not be interfered with.

Consequences Should Make Sense to Children

If at all possible, there should be a *logical* connection between the infraction and its consequence. When there is a logical connection, children learn that their behavior has consequences and that they must bear those consequences if they choose to engage in the behavior. If your son throws a dish and breaks it, he pays for it or does enough chores to work it off. If he roams too far from home, he's grounded the next day. If your daughter refuses to eat her dinner, she goes to bed hungry. If she doesn't do her chores, she can't go out until they are done. If she abuses a privilege, she loses that privilege for a short period. If a child does an injustice to a playmate, she must do something to make amends with the playmate. If your toddler leaves his fenced yard, he must come in the house. If your son deliberately breaks one of his toys, he does without it. If a teen misses curfew, she's grounded for a specified period. If consequences have no connection to the misbehavior, they lose much of their effectiveness as a teaching tool.

Suppose you can't think of a logical consequence? Try discussing consequences with your children and reach a joint decision. The older that children are, the more important it is to involve them in determining consequences when no logical ones are apparent. Discussing consequences with your children will increase the likelihood the consequences will make sense to them. If they make no sense, consequences lose their effectiveness as a teaching tool. Additionally, it is easy for children to perceive you as the "bad guy" who arbitrarily imposes punishment because you are in control. This kind of perception is more likely to lead to resentment than to learning.

ARE YOUR CONSEQUENCES EFFECTIVE?

✓ Do you use them *consistently*?
✓ Are they *realistic*?
✓ Are they *fair*?
✓ Are they *logical* or do they make sense to your children?
✓ Do you impose them *calmly* and *warmly*?
✓ Are they *timely*?

If consequences can be determined before they are needed, all the better. A child who knows the consequences beforehand and chooses to misbehave anyway has only him- or herself to blame. A family meeting is a good place to determine consequences, and brainstorming is a fun and effective way to do it. Family meetings and brainstorming are discussed in Chapter 14. Common consequences parents use include grounding (use only for a short period or it loses its effectiveness), extra chores, and withholding privileges such as being chauffeured, using the car, or watching television. With a brainstorming session, you may come up with far better ones.

Impose Consequences in a Calm and Warm Manner

The purpose of consequences is *not* to punish. It is to teach responsible behavior. If you impose consequences in a vindictive manner, your children are likely to see you as the villain who dispenses punishment because you are more powerful than they. Imposing consequences in a calm, warm manner reminds children that they were the ones who made the choices, and now they are the ones who must accept the consequences of those choices.

After you have followed through with the consequence, ask your child why the consequences occurred. You will then be sure your youngster understands the connection between the misbehavior and the consequence, and the incident is more likely to become a learning experience.

Consequences Should Be Timely

The sooner that children experience consequences for breaking a rule, the more likely they are to learn; the more removed the consequences are from an event, the less effective they are likely to be.

So What's Wrong with Spanking?

Spanking has been found to be the *least* effective form of discipline there is. It may stop unacceptable behavior at the time, *but only temporarily* or when someone is watching. Additionally, it has many negative side effects. Physical punishment often creates fear, anger, or resentment in children. It also has the potential to create aggressive children. Why? Think for a minute about the message you give children when you hit them: That it's okay to hit when you do not like something!

Generally, disciplinary methods that help children feel good about themselves are far more conducive to learning than methods that make them feel bad about themselves. Along the same lines, let me say emphatically to *never* use put-downs, name-calling or humiliation to discipline a child—or at any other time. Always distinguish between your child and his or her behavior. It's the behavior that is unacceptable, not the child.

What about Material Rewards?

Should you ever use material rewards, you wonder? Tangible rewards are a powerful tool at your disposal to teach children desirable behavior or change undesirable behavior. An effective way to use rewards is the program outlined in Appendix A, "How to Make Changes in Your Life and Stick to Them." Although designed for adults, the program can be adapted for children. In using the program, target a few problem behaviors that really upset you (no more than three at a time). Perhaps your children bicker constantly. Perhaps they leave their things all over the house, and you're tired of the mess. Frequent (at least daily) small rewards work best for children.

If you use the program in Appendix A with your children, you will never have to ask yourself the often-asked question, "Isn't using material rewards simply bribing children to be good?" If adults need tangible rewards to learn new behavior or change bad habits, how can we expect any more from children!

DISCIPLINE AND TEENS

Teenagers in many one-parent homes have an unusual amount of freedom. This is a serious mistake. Teens need supervision, and they need clearly defined rules and limits. In fact, teens who have experienced parental divorce often need supervision, rules, and limits even more than do teens in intact families. Why? Because a significant minority of teens express their distress about the divorce or their parents' continued conflict by experimenting with drugs, alcohol, and sex. Some act out their anger in destructive or antisocial behavior. These teens not only *need* firm boundaries and consequences for breaking them, many are *pleading* for them. Psychologist William Hodges once told the story of a teen client who confided to him that she wished she had been raised a Catholic. When asked why, she responded that the Catholic Church provided clear guidelines about how to behave. She went on to tell him that whenever she sought guidelines from her parents, they told her to do whatever she thought best. Clearly, she did not know what was "best"! Interviews with teens in one-parent homes often reveal that they interpret their parents' lack of rules as a lack of caring.

At the same time that they need clear rules, teens are blossoming into young adults and moving toward independence. They want to be their "own person" and do things their own way. Most important, they want to be treated with the respect they believe their emerging maturity should command. Though all children thrive on being treated with respect, it assumes monumental importance to a teen. When a parent does not grant that respect to his or her teen, their relationship can become very rocky indeed.

How do you achieve the balance between treating your teens with the respect they need and providing them with the rules and limits they need? An authoritative parenting style provides the right balance. With no other age group is this parenting style more necessary than it is with teens!

Sit down with your teen and *jointly* determine guidelines for acceptable and unacceptable behavior, through discussion and a sharing of ideas and concerns. Treat your teen with the same respect with which you would like to be treated, and respect your teen's personal rights as you want yours respected.

What kinds of rules and limits are appropriate for teens? They should have a curfew. They should be responsible for telling you where they are going, who they will be with, and what they will be doing. Of course, sexual experimentation, drug or alcohol use, and antisocial behavior are appropriate areas for clear guidelines. So are chores, homework, who can be in the home when a parent is not there, places a teen can go without checking first, and the language used when talking to parents (if abusive language is a problem). Within most of these areas,

---

THE PRINCIPLES OF POSITIVE PARENTING

✓ Discipline is teaching responsibility and self-control.
✓ Use an authoritative parenting style.
✓ Reward good behavior with praise, smiles, and hugs.
✓ Ignore annoying misbehavior.
✓ Use "time-out" for dangerous, destructive, or obnoxious behavior you can't ignore.
✓ Impose consequences when rules or limits are broken.
✓ Tangible rewards can be a powerful teaching tool to change undesirable behavior.
✓ With difficult teens, use the "no one loses" problem-solving method or contracting.
✓ The foundation of good discipline is a good relationship and mutual respect between parent and child.

---

there is room for parent and teen to negotiate and arrive at guidelines with which they can both live.

It is a good idea to try to get to know other parents of teens and talk to them for perspective. Without other adult input, a convincing teen can easily sway a single parent over to his or her viewpoint of what is acceptable. "Mom (Dad), this is the new millennium. *Everyone* does it! Get out of the last century!"

What can you do with a "problem" teen with whom life is one big confrontation and everything else you've tried has been ineffective? Two techniques are found to be particularly effective with teens (and can be used with mature, older children as well): One is a problem-solving technique and the other is contracting. Each has the flavor of the adult world about it and treats adolescents with the respect they need and thrive on. This may partially explain their effectiveness.

The "No One Loses" Problem-Solving Approach

This technique is one in which parent and teen use a problem-solving strategy to find a solution to their conflicts. If the solution has truly been jointly determined and both sides agree it is fair, teens usually feel a commitment to stick to the agreement. The atmosphere of the home usually becomes a lot less hostile as well. Here are the steps of the problem-solving strategy:

Step 1: Identify the conflict and define it in concrete terms. Each of you should tell the other what you think the problem is and how you feel about it. Set some ground rules: You will each listen to what the other says *with respect* and *without interrupting*. When it's your turn, try to avoid putting your teen on the defensive; it will only increase the chances of failure right from the start. The best way to do this is in the form of an *"I" message*. "I" messages allow you to set the tone for constructive problem solving. To use an "I" message, start with "I," state how you feel, and then state why: "I'm uncomfortable with you seeing Rod because of his drinking," *not,* "The problem is that you are seeing that no-good Rod." Stop for a minute and think about how your teen would react to each of those statements. Here's another example: "I feel very frustrated that you are not doing your chores," *not,* "The problem is that you are not doing a damn thing around here." Can you feel the difference? Or how about, "I'm very upset that we are fighting all the time," *not,* "The problem is that you cause one fight after another." Then listen openly and with respect as your teen tells you the problem from his or her perspective. Together, try to arrive at a joint definition of the problem in concrete terms that you can work on solving together.

Step 2: Brainstorm to generate a list of possible alternative solutions. In brainstorming, each of you comes up with as many solutions as you can, without regard to how practical they are. The rule is that during the brainstorming process no one evaluates or even reacts to any suggested idea. The purpose is to get your creative juices flowing. A ridiculous idea may set you off on a different train of thought that might yield a good idea. Write each idea down without comment.

Step 3: Go through the list and eliminate ideas that either one of you will not consider.

Step 4: Evaluate the remaining alternatives. Listen with respect to your teen's opinions. Try to offer reasons that alternatives are acceptable or unacceptable to you, such as, "I'm uncomfortable with this one because…"

Step 5: Try to reach some agreement on a solution. Because no single alternative may solve the problem, you may have to combine several, or you may have to renegotiate some to make them more acceptable to one or the other of you.

Step 6: Unless it is obvious, discuss precisely how you will carry out the agreed-upon solution. Both sides will have to make compromises.

Step 7: Make a commitment to keeping your end of the bargain, and ask your teen if he or she is willing to make a commitment, too. Decide on a consequence if one of you fails to follow the agreement.

THE "NO ONE LOSES" PROBLEM-SOLVING STRATEGY

1. Identify the problem in concrete terms.
2. Brainstorm to generate a list of possible solutions.
3. Eliminate solutions either of you won't consider.
4. Evaluate the remaining solutions.
5. Try to reach agreement on a solution.
   - Can some ideas be combined?
   - Can some ideas be modified?
6. Determine how to carry out the agreed-upon solution.
7. Make a commitment (each of you) to carry out your share, and jointly decide on a consequence if either fails to do so.
8. Evaluate the solution's effectiveness at a predetermined time. If it is not working, renegotiate and readjust.

Step 8: Decide on a time to discuss and evaluate how well the plan is working. Does it need readjustment or renegotiation?

Contracts

A contract is exactly what it sounds like: a written agreement between parent and teen in which each agrees to certain terms. Typically, the teen will agree to adhere to specific terms that a parent feels are important, and in return the teen will receive specific privileges. Contracts, of course, involve negotiation and compromise. They can be used in conjunction with the no-one-loses problem-solving strategy, although simple problems and simple contracts may not require as much negotiation. Contracts will always be more successful if they are created in an atmosphere of mutual respect.

Contracts should be written down and a copy kept by both parent and child or posted. The contract should be very specific so that each party knows *exactly* what is expected and whether the contract is being followed. A contract in which a teen agrees to follow "house rules" is too vague; the rules should be written down. Having everything in writing prevents misunderstandings later on down the road.

Signing a contract increases a teen's commitment to stick to the agreement. Once signed, its terms must be carried out by *both* parties. If your teen behaves in an objectionable manner not covered by the contract, you cannot renege on your part, although you can insist that the contract be renegotiated.

Consider the case of Maggie Jensen and her daughter, Valerie:

Maggie was uncomfortable with Valerie's boyfriend, Rod, because she had heard rumors that Rod was wild and drank. Maggie first forbade Valerie to see Rod, then learned that Valerie was seeing the boy behind her back. Furious, she grounded Valerie for a month. The next weeks were tense ones, with a virtual cold war between mother and daughter that made life miserable for both. One of Valerie's teachers told Maggie about contracts and the no-one-loses problem-solving strategy. Maggie and Valerie worked out agreements using the problem-solving strategy and formalized them in the contract that appears in the accompanying illustration.

A CONTRACT DEVELOPED
AND SIGNED BY A PARENT AND TEEN

I, Maggie Jensen, agree to the following:
   a. I will spend time with Rod and get to know him better.
   b. Valerie can see Rod a maximum of twice a week under the following conditions:
      (1) She can invite him to the house, providing I will be home. They can rent videos, listen to music, and have other friends over.
      (2) They can go to school activities together.
      (3) They may go out in a group, *if* I approve of both the friends and the activity.
   c. I will investigate the rumors I've heard about Rod to determine their accuracy.

Maggie Jensen

I, Valerie Jensen, in return for the above, agree to the following:
   a. I agree to see Rod only with Mom's knowledge and approval.
   b. I agree to see him only at our house, at school activities, or with a group of friends Mom approves of.
   c. I agree to see him a maximum of twice a week (and at school).

(Continued)

A CONTRACT DEVELOPED
AND SIGNED BY A PARENT AND TEEN
(continued)

  d. I agree to a curfew of 9 P.M. on Sunday through Thursday and 11 P.M. on Friday and Saturday. If I break this curfew without Mom's prior agreement, I will be grounded for the next seven days.
  e. I agree not to ride in Rod's car unless Mom learns the rumors are false. If there is no other driver, I will drive Mom's car.
  f. Rod agrees not to drink when he is with me.
  g. If I break the terms of a, b, c, e, or f of my contract, I will not be allowed to see Rod until I negotiate a new contract with Mom.

Valerie Jensen

YOUR RELATIONSHIP WITH YOUR CHILDREN: THE FOUNDATION OF EFFECTIVE DISCIPLINE

The discipline principle most frequently overlooked is the most important of all: a good relationship and mutual respect between parent and child. When a parent and child have a good relationship, a child is motivated to avoid behaving in ways that will displease that parent. When a child is the recipient of consequences imposed by a warm and nurturing parent who respects him or her, those consequences have a greater impact than they would have if they'd come from a cold and distant parent. The youngster is likely to respond with remorse and determination to try harder in the future. Moreover, children with warm and nurturing parents are more likely to be loyal to their parents' values and internalize them as their own. Keep this important but often-neglected principle in mind. Your efforts at discipline will be far more effective if your child is motivated to please you.

All relationships require effort to be successful, including relationships with children. With all that is going on in your life, this principle may be easy to forget unless you make a conscious effort to remember. Refer to Chapter 9 for steps you can take to shore up your relationships with your children and open the lines of communication.

If things have gotten so out of control with your children that nothing works, visit a family therapist. He or she can help get you back on the right track.

V

Stepfamilies

21

Stepfamily Myths versus Stepfamily Reality

Trueor false?

- Often, remarriage is just what is needed to help people get back on their feet after divorce.
- When we get married, we will be an instant family.
- When we get married, the children will be able to have a traditional family once again.
- Usually, well-adjusted people can adapt to stepfamily life after a brief adjustment period.

If you answered true to any of the preceding statements, you are not alone. Each represents a commonly believed myth. However, if you accept *any* of these myths as valid, you are setting yourself up for needless disappointment, discouragement, and mounting problems, just as so many others have. Each of these myths creates unrealistic expectations, and when reality falls short, most people believe there is something wrong with *them*. "Why do I feel this way instead of the way I *should*?" "Why aren't things working out as they *should*?" "Is my marriage on its way to failure?" "What's *wrong* with me?" Feeling inadequate, many try to hide their feelings and problems, even from their spouses. Others work harder to make the reality fit the myths, but in so doing frequently set in motion a new cycle of problems that can spiral out of control.

Remarriage and a stepfamily (sometimes called a blended or remarried family) *can* be a path to a fulfilling life. Studies report that the majority of remarriers have a high level of satisfaction with their marriages and are as likely as first-time-married men and women to be happy and optimistic about the future.

However, there is a catch. The divorce rate for remarriages is found to be 10 percent higher than that for first marriages, and more than 25 percent of remarriages never make it past their fifth year. This suggests that large numbers of unhappy couples are quickly weeded out of the remarried population, leaving a more select group to be interviewed by sporadically conducted national surveys.

The early years of your blended family's life will not resemble life on *The Brady Bunch* or that of other television families. However, knowing what is "normal" will buffer you from the feelings of anxiety, frustration, and guilt that so many couples feel during their stepfamily's fledgling years. And if you are aware of the common problems and reasons they occur, you can prevent many of them and minimize others. This chapter focuses on common stepfamily myths and compares them with stepfamily reality. The following chapters address the paths step-

---

STEPFAMILIES BY THE NUMBERS

✓ Seventy-five percent of divorced men and 66 percent of divorced women remarry.

✓ The divorce rate for remarriages is 10 percent higher than for first marriages.

✓ Remarriages with children in the home from a previous marriage have a 50 percent higher casualty rate than those without.

✓ More than 25 percent of remarriages end within the first five years. The rate is higher for families with children from a prior marriage.

✓ Among men and women who do not remarry, cohabitation rates are high.

✓ When stepfamilies are redefined to include cohabiting couples, the percentage of children living in stepfamilies increases by 30 percent.

Sources: Data from E.M. Hetherington, M. Bridges, and G.M. Insabella, "What Matters? What Does Not?" *American Psychologist* 53 (1998): 167–184, and L.L. Bumpass et al., "The Changing Character of Stepfamilies: Implications of Cohabitation and Nonmarital Childbearing," *Demography* 32 (1995): 425–436.

families so often take that lead to problems and recommended paths that lead to a smoothly functioning blended family.

Giving up the myths and replacing them with realistic expectations is a necessary first step toward creating a successful stepfamily, whether you have a full-time stepfamily, a part-time one with noncustodial children, or you are cohabiting with children in the home.

MYTH #1: REMARRIAGE IS OFTEN JUST WHAT IS NEEDED TO HELP PEOPLE GET BACK ON THEIR FEET AFTER DIVORCE

Although developing new relationships may help you let go of the past and get on with your life, *remarrying* before you are back on your feet is far more likely to create new problems than to solve existing ones. No one can invest the energy and commitment needed to make a remarriage work if he or she is stuck in the past or still emotionally wounded. The new marriage will begin with a serious handicap—being saddled with emotional baggage carried over from the previous relationship. The new marriage can be affected in any number of ways. To learn more about this, read Chapter 13, "New Romantic Relationships."

Before you consider remarriage, be sure you have completed your emotional divorce (see Chapter 10) and feel whole again (see Chapter 11). If you have already remarried without having finished your emotional divorce, it's not too late to work on it now, so you can completely close the door on your last marriage and get on with your life, unencumbered with the past.

MYTH #2: WHEN WE GET MARRIED WE WILL HAVE AN INSTANT FAMILY

The myth of the instant family is perhaps the most widely accepted stepfamily myth. However, a marriage ceremony cannot create an instant family. It merely marks the beginning of a long process from which a family may eventually evolve. Stepfamilies need to merge two disparate contingents, each with its own allegiances, its own lifestyle, its own perspective, its own ways of communicating, its own ways of doing things, even its own in-jokes. Noticeably lacking from this new "family" is any sense of belonging—of shared history or shared identity. Moreover, the bond uniting a biological parent and child predates and is frequently stronger than the bond uniting a newly remarried couple.

Early in stepfamily life, there are generally two distinct minifamilies; they may even distrust one another because their differences threaten each other's way of life. Or there may be one minifamily with its distinct identity and lifestyle and one "outsider" who is attempting to carve out a significant niche within that family's well-defined boundaries.

Blending these two disparate contingents into a single family with its own identity, lifestyle, traditions, allegiances, and shared trust is no easy matter; nor does it magically occur overnight. Until a family does blend, members of stepfamilies often complain, "This isn't a family. It's just a bunch of people living in the same house."

Hand in hand with the myth of the instant family is the myth of instant love. To most people, families and love go together. Couples commonly assume that stepparents will automatically love stepchildren and children will quickly come to love stepparents. When love doesn't magically blossom, many stepparents feel guilty because they do not feel as they "should." What's more, they feel hurt, frustrated, and rebuffed when their stepchildren are unresponsive to their overtures.

In reality, love and attachment between stepfamily members can neither be rushed nor taken for granted. Bonds of affection generally take one and a half to two years to develop in stepfamilies. And generally, bonds between a stepparent and stepchildren are never as strong as those between a biological parent and children. In some stepfamilies, affectional bonds *never* develop.

MYTH #3: WHEN WE GET MARRIED THE CHILDREN WILL BE ABLE TO HAVE A TRADITIONAL FAMILY

Most stepfamilies start out assuming their family and day-to-day living will closely resemble that of a traditional biological family. However, trying to force a stepfamily to fit the mold of a traditional family is bound to lead to trouble. A stepfamily can be a fine environment in which to raise children—neither necessarily inferior nor superior to a traditional family. However, a stepfamily is definitely *different* from a traditional family. One of the first steps in achieving a successful stepfamily is recognizing these major differences.

The first: A traditional family has a clear identity, whereas the identity and boundaries of a remarried family are very ambiguous. Who belongs to the family and who does not is often a matter of interpretation. This ambiguity was clearly evident in a large national study reported by University of Pennsylvania sociologist Frank Furstenberg and his associates that asked stepfamily members to list the members of their family. Thirty-one percent of the children did not list a stepparent with whom they lived as a family member, and 41 percent excluded stepsiblings with whom they lived. Though it is tempting to assume that it is only *children* who are confused about family membership, this was not the case. Fifteen percent of the parents failed to include *live-in* stepchildren as family members. Perhaps, then, the confusion is limited to newly formed stepfamilies? Wrong again. When the interviews of well-established stepfamilies were analyzed separately, the picture did not change! Confusion about who belongs to the family and who does not seems to persist over time for many stepfamilies. As you might imagine, stepfamily identity is even more clouded when stepchildren live with the family only part-time.

The second difference: In contrast to traditional family members, stepfamily members are often unclear about what roles they should play with one another. Is the stepparent a parent or a nonparent? Is good stepmothering the same as good mothering? Does a stepparent have authority over stepchildren? In most states stepparents have neither legal nor financial responsibilities for stepchildren. How much of a commitment should be made to a spouse's children? The situation becomes even more ambiguous when a stepparent and stepchild are very close in age. How should they behave with each other? What should their relationship be? What if there is a sexual attraction between them? And what if there is a sexual attraction between teenage stepsiblings? How are they to behave toward each other? One is not supposed to feel that way about a sibling, but are they really siblings?

A third difference: A traditional family operates pretty much autonomously, whereas most remarried families do not have this luxury. A stepfamily typically has to coordinate weekend schedules, vacations, holidays, and decisions about children with a parent living outside the home. It must accept that children's attitudes, values, and behavior will be significantly influenced by a former spouse, perhaps in ways that are incompatible with its own values. Stepfamily experts Emily and John Visher point out that children's status is akin to having dual citizenship. Many a stepfamily cannot even plan its own financial future because of uncertainty about child support coming in or unforeseen expenses incurred by the first family.

The complexity of stepfamily relationships is a fourth distinction that sets them apart from traditional families. It is not unusual for children in stepfamilies to have four parents, numerous stepsiblings and halfsiblings (some living with them full-time, some part-time), eight grandparents, and an array of aunts, uncles, and cousins who are related to each of their parents and stepparents. To make life even more complicated, stepfamilies are splintered, continually needing to juggle incompatible family contingents.

A fifth distinction of stepfamilies is that the bonds between parent and child predate bonds between the couple and are often stronger. Moreover, both adults and children bring with them preexisting expectations, often incompatible, about family life and how things are done, carried over from their former families.

Finally, a stepfamily is not likely to be as close or as cohesive as a traditional family because loyalties and emotional ties are split across households. Children in blended families need more psychological space than do other children so they can move between families without feeling torn by loyalty conflicts. Parents who have children living with former spouses are also likely to have split loyalties, preventing their complete emotional investment in their new families. In reality, except for the relationship between the couple itself, loose family relationships are more conducive to smooth stepfamily functioning than are close-knit relationships. Looser relationships are more compatible with the revolving door lifestyle stepfamilies must have, with children continually going to and coming from another family. The couple's relationship, however, must be very strong for smooth stepfamily functioning.

MYTH #4: WELL-ADJUSTED PEOPLE CAN ADAPT TO STEPFAMILY LIFE AFTER A BRIEF ADJUSTMENT PERIOD

Remarrying couples are usually optimistic when they plan their marriages, assuming things will fall into place quickly once everyone becomes a "family." But the reality is that just as there was an adjustment period after divorce, there is an inevitable adjustment period for life in a remarried family. Studies suggest two to seven years. Once you take a closer look at the fledgling stepfamily, you will understand why.

Children's Concerns and Adjustment Problems

A parent's remarriage is usually a time of crisis for children, particularly a resident parent's remarriage. Once again in their relatively short lifetimes, children's worlds are turned topsy-turvy, and they are powerless to influence events having a profound impact on their lives. Once again, the future is an enormous unknown. Once again, anxiety and questions become familiar companions: "What is it like to live with a stepparent?" "Will Mom (Dad) still have time for me?" "Will we still get to make breakfast together on Saturday morning?" "Where will I fit into this new family?" "Will I get lost in the shuffle?" "Will I have to share my room with stepsiblings?" "Will we have to move to their house?" "Will I have to leave my school and friends?" "What will it be like to have an older sister? *I'm* supposed to be the oldest!" "Will Mom (Dad) like the new kids better than me?" "Suppose they have a new baby? It will be *their* kid. Where will that leave me?"

Additional worries focus on the parent outside the home: "Will I still get to go to Dad's (Mom's) house as much?" "Will I still see Grandma and Grandpa?" "Will Dad (Mom) be angry if I like my stepparent?"

Besides anxiety, most children struggle with feelings of loss. Now the parent's attention, time, and love must be shared all the time. The more intense the parent-child relationship had been, the harder the change usually is for the child and the more the stepparent and stepsiblings are seen as unwelcome intruders. Children who have been confidants to their single parents or who have played other adult roles in the home are particularly hard hit. In fact, many feel betrayed, believing they have been replaced and insensitively asked to become children once again. For these youngsters, a parent's remarriage feels like a hostile takeover.

Children whose nonresident parent remarries and lives with stepchildren are also hard hit. Suddenly they must share their parent, whom they see only part-time, with children who see the parent daily. It seems so unfair! They yearn for a return to their one-on-one time together, a need to which many noncustody parents are insensitive, believing that "all the children should be treated the same."

Having to share a parent is not the only loss with which children must struggle. Many have never given up the fantasy of resuming their old lives, living again as a family with both their parents. A remarriage makes the futility of this ongoing fantasy glaringly obvious, and many youngsters feel as if the divorce is happening all over again. They must finally face the reality of losing the family and comfortable life they once had. Some stubbornly hang on to the cherished fantasy, hoping if they are indifferent enough or mean enough, this intruder will go away.

So, at the same time parents are thrilled with their forthcoming union, most youngsters feel sad, helpless, ambivalent, or angry. Data from one large nationally conducted study, analyzed by Princeton University sociologist Nazli Baydar, revealed that children developed more emotional problems after parental remarriage than they did after parental separation! Common problems surfacing were withdrawal, fighting, restlessness, unhappiness, poor concentration, and substance abuse. Fortunately, children's problems were generally not long-term ones.

Adjustment in Families with Two Sets of Children

When there are two sets of children, each contingent has its own well-established ways of doing things—from the very important, such as child rearing and how money is spent, to the mundane, such as manners and eating habits. One contingent is used to a scheduled life and advanced planning; the other prefers hanging loose and making last-minute plans. One group is used to eating together at the dinner table each evening; the other prefers eating in shifts in front of the television. One may prefer traditional and simple food; the other prefers foreign and gourmet meals. One is neat; the other is sloppy. One parent is a strict disciplinarian; the other is lax. One side buys only name brands in expensive department stores; the other has been raised with generic labels purchased in discount stores. One set of children is expected to do chores for their modest allowance; the other is used to a generous allowance, not linked with chores. One set of teens likes a quiet environment for studying; the other likes a constant parade of friends and loud rock music.

The rules of day-to-day living, once so automatic, now must be reviewed and renegotiated. The givens in life are no longer givens, and each person feels disoriented. Unlike in the first marriage, where only two people were negotiating the way things would be done, many people are now involved in the negotiations, some of whom are tenaciously clinging to the familiar because it represents security in an insecure new world. The usual result in the early stages of a stepfamily's life, perhaps after a brief "honeymoon" period, is stress, chaos, and confusion. There is a seemingly endless period in which nothing feels "right."

Adjustment in Families with One Set of Children

It might seem that stepfamily adjustment should be relatively easy when only one set of children is involved; however, that's usually not the case, particularly for the stepparent. Because single parents and their children have shared adversity together, many become close-knit groups, and new spouses often feel that breaking into these tightly knit circles is about as easy as breaking into a fortress. Things run smoothly as long as a stepparent adapts to the unwritten "rules" the family lives by and does not rock the boat, but this means feeling like a visitor in what is supposed to be his or her own home. Most such stepparents feel decidedly uncomfortable but are not quite sure what the problem is, reports Dr. Patricia Papernow, a Cambridge, Massachusetts, psychologist, who conducted a lengthy study of stepfamily development. Moreover, most of these stepparents have an additional handicap: Their new spouses see *no* problem. Everything seems perfectly normal and comfortable to them. So why is the stepparent having such difficulty?

A significant percentage of stepparents spend this period of time in a haze, reports Papernow. Most alternate between investing their energies in trying to join the family and withdrawing in frustration. They are continually on the outside looking in, feeling ignored and unappreciated, watching their spouses and stepchildren share in the warmth and love they would like to partake of themselves. Most often they feel isolated, lonely, and jealous. What is more disturbing, they think the problem is theirs and that something is wrong with *them*.

If the remarriage is going to work, such stepfamilies must also go through a blending process that takes time, patience, negotiation, and compromise. In these families, too, the process has its conflicts. Generally, the stepparent is the sole voice for change and the biological parent is torn between the conflicting needs of spouse and children.

I hope by now the common stepfamily myths are dispelled and you have a more realistic picture of what likely lies ahead. Don't be discouraged. There are steps you can take to smooth the transition and lay a solid foundation for your stepfamily's success. But equally important is knowing what to *avoid* doing. In the next chapter we'll look at the common paths stepfamilies take that so often lead to serious problems. Successful strategies for remarried families is the subject of the final chapter.

22

Losing Strategies:
Eight Common Paths to
Serious Stepfamily Problems

Starting out in a remarried family is not easy, and society offers no models or rules to guide families along the way. In their efforts to write their own rules, many remarried families rely on stepfamily myths as their guides (see Chapter 21). The myths not only cause disappointment and discouragement but lead many unsuspecting stepfamilies to invest their energies in misguided strategies. These losing strategies are the subject of this chapter. At best, they delay stepfamily adjustment. At worst, they lead to family breakup.

LOSING STRATEGY #1: TRYING TO REPLACE THE OUT-OF-HOME PARENT

In their endeavor to quickly create a perfect family, many remarried couples fail to see what is all too obvious to a child: A parent is a parent forever and cannot be replaced. There simply is no such thing as an ex-mother or an ex-father, even if a parent is only minimally involved in a child's life. Either overtly or covertly, a child usually remains loyal to a birth parent, and most children will resist an intruder who tries to encroach on what is perceived to be that parent's "rightful" place.

Some children respond by withdrawing. Some become torn by guilt and loyalty conflicts. Others become hostile and may openly rebel. The end result of attempting to replace an out-of-home parent is to delay or even prevent the bonding between stepparent and stepchild—a result diametrically opposed to that intended.

There are several ways stepparents try to take the place of the out-of-home parent. Sometimes couples insist that a child call the new stepparent "Mom" or "Dad," the same name used for the birth parent. Most children want to reserve a special status for a natural parent, and a name is symbolic of that special status. Youngsters need to be allowed to choose a name they are comfortable using for a stepparent.

Sometimes attempts to replace the out-of-home parent take the form of competition with that parent. It is quite natural for stepparents to feel competitive with their predecessors, but many new stepparents feel they must surpass the predecessor in every way to prove they are the better spouse and better parent. They set out to become supermoms and superdads, excelling in all areas. However, their efforts usually arouse steely resistance from children rather than gratitude. Children usually see the stepparent's behavior as a bid to take over, and they do not like to see their real parent on the losing end of a contest. The fallout from the competition is likely to be resentment of the stepparent and a fierce loyalty to the natural parent who is absent from the scene. Once again, the outcome is the opposite of that intended. How, then, should competitive feelings be handled? If you are a stepparent, realize that you have something unique to offer your stepchildren, as does their out-of-home parent. Allow yourself to shine in your areas and allow the biological parent to shine in his or her domain.

A third common way stepparents try to replace an out-of-home parent is by taking over some of the rituals that children shared with that parent, such as reading a bedtime story in a favorite chair, going for pizza after a soccer game, or making Saturday morning breakfast. Taking over these activities may seem harmless enough, and a stepparent may even be encouraged to do so by his or her new partner. However, unless youngsters specifically invite a stepparent to join in such a ritual, any attempt to do so is likely to be resented. To youngsters, these rituals represent the special relationship with their parent who is no longer in the home, and they are likely to be sacred. A stepparent needs to develop *new* rituals and a unique role with a stepchild, not move in on the absent parent's turf.

LOSING STRATEGY #2: CREATING A FALSE SENSE OF TOGETHERNESS

Spurred on by the myths of the instant family and quick stepfamily adjustment, many remarried couples try to force a sense of family togetherness that feels phony and contrived to their children, particularly older children. What these couples are doing is asking their youngsters to deny their own feelings and participate in what children often perceive to be a sham. Once again, the tactic has the opposite effect of that intended, reports Dr. Virginia Goldner of Albert Einstein College of Medicine. Rather than feeling like part of one big, happy family, youngsters feel alienated, angry, or ambivalent. Some withdraw; others openly rebel. Frequently, an unfortunate cycle is set in motion from which families have difficulty extricating themselves. The more that parents implicitly demand that children join their mythical happy family, the more children resist; the more that children resist, the more the parents become insecure and increase their demands. Instead of creating a family basking in togetherness, they create a family steeped in conflict, points out Goldner. The older the children, the more likely this scenario is. Feelings of togetherness may eventually evolve, but they *cannot* be forced.

LOSING STRATEGY #3: FORCED BLENDING

A somewhat related losing strategy is the failure to recognize that blending is a process and must evolve over time. In their eagerness to have an instant family, parents sometimes try to force the blending process. They decide how the family will operate and impose their decisions on children. Or sometimes it is a stepparent alone who forces blending by immediately setting out to change how the home and family will be run henceforth. The older the children, the more likely it is that forced blending or immediate radical change will lead to stepfamily problems.

Helen and Tony Catano each had three children. Tony thought Helen's kids were poorly disciplined and needed a firm hand. Helen thought Tony's children were undemonstrative and needed a mother's nurturing. Tony and Helen decided they would each assume traditional roles. Tony would be the family head, breadwinner, and disciplinarian. Helen would be a full-time mom for all six children. Tony, who was intent on immediately establishing ground rules for Helen's children, announced a lengthy list of "house rules" that all children would follow. Helen's children were livid. "Why should we have to follow *their* rules? It's not fair, Mom! Why can't they do things our way?" Helen's children resented Tony, his children, and Helen for betraying their way of life. Meanwhile, Helen made no points with Tony's children, either. She took over the shopping and cooking, stocking the house with unfamiliar foods and preparing meals her stepchildren picked at. Feeling the house needed "a woman's touch," she redecorated liberally, without seeking the family's input. Tony's children felt as if this intruder was taking over their lives. But worst of all, they agreed, were her maddening hugs, which she insisted they return.

The blending of a stepfamily is a process that *must* evolve over time, and if children are to become a part of the family, their opinions and needs must play a significant role in that blending process. Open and extended give-and-take communication is a must. At best, parents who force blending are likely to create a pseudofamily that doesn't feel like a family to anyone. At worst, they will create resentment and open rebellion.

LOSING STRATEGY #4: DRAMATICALLY CHANGING PARENT-CHILD RELATIONSHIPS

Children in newly remarried families have been through an inordinate amount of change and upheaval in their relatively short lives. A key ingredient that helps a child weather those disruptions is a good relationship with both parents. A good relationship with a parent functions as a cushion for a child that softens the impact of stress. It can be an enormous asset for a youngster as he or she is asked to make the adjustment to stepfamily life.

When parent-child relationships are dramatically changed in stepfamilies, it compounds children's already difficult task of dealing with their anxiety and coping with their losses. In fact, it usually forecasts problems for everyone. Children adjust poorly to the new family, the stepparent is resented, and family blending is delayed, or even prevented.

Two common scenarios lead to dramatically changed parent-child relationships. In the first, couples concentrate on forming a very tight couple bond immediately because they are so determined to make this marriage work. In so doing, however, many leave children on the outside looking in, resentful and bitterly missing the relationship they once had with their parent.

In the second, most common in families with stepmothers, the parenting role is turned over to the new stepparent immediately. When the shift is too sudden, children resent this intruder taking over activities they previously enjoyed with their single parent and sorely miss the old relationship they once had. How can a child like or appreciate a person who robs them of such an important relationship and their way of life? Usually, children respond with withdrawal, indifference, or hostility. A parent's demands for them to appreciate or accept their new stepparent only make a bad situation worse.

LOSING STRATEGY #5: ASSUMING AUTHORITY TOO QUICKLY

This is probably the most common cause of problems in stepfather families, but it can cause havoc in stepmother families, too. Discipline is usually a thorny issue in stepfamilies, particularly with stepfathers. Before marriage, most men try to be popular with children, but afterward they usually try to assume the traditional fatherly role of disciplinarian. Many mothers even encourage this.

To children, however, the stepparent is still a guest in the family, and they perceive any attempts to discipline them as out of line. "You're not my father, and you have no right to tell me what to do!" is a common cry. The older the children, the more serious the problems over authority and discipline are likely to become.

The situation worsens if the stepfather's style of disciplining is different from the mother's. In children's perceptions, he is not only out of line, but he is arbitrarily changing the standards they have lived by and believe are "right."

When mothers stand behind fathers, children often feel betrayed and are likely to be at odds with both stepparent and parent. But it is not uncommon for mothers, even those who initially invited their new husbands to become the family disciplinarian, to perceive their new partners as too strict and come to their children's defense. Many mothers essentially form a coalition with their youngsters that undermines the stepparent's position in the family—a poor way to start off a marriage. To keep the peace, mothers sometimes overtly agree with new disciplinary rules set by their new partner but subtly sabotage them. A mother may "agree" that youngsters should be in bed by eight but continually "forget" to enforce it. She may "agree" that a teen's curfew should be earlier but insist on accepting weak excuses when it is broken. When children perceive that their real parent does not agree with new rules (and they sense this easily), they ignore both the rules and their stepparent.

Few children willingly accept discipline from a stepparent until the stepparent and child have developed a relationship. Trying to assume authority too quickly only courts disaster. A long-term study conducted by University of Virginia psychologists found that when stepfathers moved into a disciplinary role before developing a relationship with children, they were generally rejected by the children. Moreover, a significant number of the children developed behavior problems, acting out their anger at home and at school. Sometimes this kind of family conflict continues for years in stepfamilies. Sometimes stepfathers, feeling frustrated and inadequate, retreat into passivity. Some marriages do not make it through the turmoil.

LOSING STRATEGY #6:
RESISTING FAMILY BLENDING

The stepfamily problems discussed so far have all had a common denominator. They all stem from remarried couples moving too quickly, denying their stepfamilies the time needed to adapt and blend. Because the couple pushes too hard, they unwittingly set into motion a cycle of problems that stand in the way of becoming an integrated family.

Some stepfamilies' problems stem from the opposite cause. From the beginning, they make no effort toward blending and, therefore, never move forward. Perhaps part of the problem stems from the couples' unpreparedness for marriage and part from a naive assumption that the new family should develop naturally, without work or conscious effort.

In most families that resist blending, the married partners have failed to develop a strong couple bond and have never shifted their primary commitment from their children to each other. With no united executive team at its head, the family is left to drift without leadership. Strong coalitions based on old family ties continue, and a new family identity never develops.

Stepfamilies that include two sets of children sometimes live together for years as two separate families in a boardinghouse atmosphere. When there is only one set of children, the typical scenario is for the stepparent to always play second fiddle to the children, who continue to occupy center stage in the home. Correctly perceiving their overriding importance, children are quite happy to permanently exclude the "intruder" from the family's inner circle. Even after many years of marriage, many a stepparent sadly comments, "Anytime there's an issue between them and me, I'm always the loser."

LOSING STRATEGY #7: TRYING TO SHUT OUT THE OUT-OF-HOME PARENT FROM CHILDREN'S LIVES

In their attempts to function like a traditional family and quickly adjust to stepfamily life, many couples believe that life would be so much simpler if only the former spouse were out of the picture. After all, they reason, it would solve so many day-to-day complications—having to coordinate weekend schedules, having to share children on holidays, having to deal with a former spouse.

However, families that try to freeze out a biological parent from their children's lives often trade day-to-day inconveniences for long-term problems. In effect, they are saying to children, "This is your family now, and we are all you need." In doing so, they create enormous loyalty conflicts for their youngsters. They ask children to deny their own feelings, their pasts, and their roots. And they ask them to relinquish a relationship that is important to their future well-being. Children need *both* parents (see Chapter 7).

A child who is in intense loyalty conflicts or who has lost access to a parent is a child in distress, and this distress is likely to take its toll on both the child and the stepfamily. Many children act out their distress in behavior problems at home and at school, which places additional stress on their stepfamilies. Many others respond to a stepfamily's demands for complete allegiance by holding back and refusing to join the stepfamily psychologically. Forced to make a choice between their birth parent and a stepparent, they feel they have no choice but to remain loyal to their real parent.

LOSING STRATEGY #8: DENYING PROBLEMS AND CONFLICTS

Stepfamilies sometimes feel so vulnerable from their first families' collapse that they try to bury problems and conflicts when they arise. The pervasive feeling in the family is "Let's not rock the boat." How-

---

IS YOUR STEPFAMILY FOLLOWING ONE OF THESE LOSING STRATEGIES?

✓ Is the stepparent trying to replace the out-of-home parent?
  • In name?
  • Through competition?
  • By taking over the absent parent's rituals with children?
✓ Are you and your spouse attempting to foist the feeling on everyone that you are just "one big, happy family?"
✓ Are you dictating how the new family will be run without considering children's input?
✓ Is the stepparent moving quickly to change things?
✓ Has your stepfamily resulted in a dramatic change in the relationships between children and their natural parent?
✓ Is the stepparent moving into an authority role before building a good relationship with the children?
✓ Have you failed to shift your primary commitment from your children to your spouse?
✓ Have you failed to form a strong couple bond?
✓ Are you trying to freeze out the out-of-home parent?
✓ Do you brush off problems rather than deal with them?

---

ever, problems and conflicts can never be resolved if never brought into the open and discussed. Problems simply compound and fester under the surface until one day the calm facade erupts. *Every* stepfamily has its problems and conflicts, and the family needs to discuss and work on them as a family, not deny them.

This chapter has mapped common paths stepfamilies take that frequently lead to serious family problems. It is helpful to know what *not* to do. The next chapter looks at what *to do*. It discusses eight strategies that generally lead to success in both full-time and part-time stepfamilies and how to put those strategies into practice.

23

Learning What Works: Successful Strategies for Stepfamilies

"**I**f only we had known that before!" say remarried couples who seek out professional help because their stepfamilies are in trouble. Don't misunderstand. There is no *single* "right" way for a stepfamily to shape itself. To some degree, each stepfamily must find its own solutions and write its own rules. But as you discovered in the last chapter, some paths stepfamilies commonly take generally lead to problems. Other paths, however, generally lead to success and satisfaction, and these are the focus of this chapter. They are organized into eight broad strategies with practical suggestions to help you implement them. These eight strategies are guidelines, not hard-and-fast rules that must be followed to the letter.

If you are just starting out in a remarried family, you can begin on the right foot. Are you already in a stepfamily and having a difficult time? Then begin some serious work right now, using these strategies as guidelines. Additional sources of help and support are discussed at the end of the chapter. In case you are wondering, this chapter is as much for cohabiting families as it is for remarried families.

STRATEGY #1: COMMUNICATE OPENLY

Make open communication a top priority, both before marriage and after. You and your partner (and sometimes your children) will find it helpful to discuss the following areas.

Expectations

Make a list of the most important expectations you have about your marriage and stepfamily, and have your partner make one, too. Include the role each of you would eventually like the stepparent to play in the family. Once you have read the three stepfamily chapters, evaluate how realistic your respective lists are and how compatible your expectations are. If they are not compatible, can they be negotiated and some compromises reached?

> When George and Mara compared expectations, they found some important inconsistencies. Mara assumed that George would share household responsibilities fifty-fifty and envisioned entertaining and dining out frequently, particularly on weekends, since they both had full-time jobs. Although George had not thought much about his household participation, he admitted that he preferred a more traditional male-female split of responsibilities. An even more important area that needed negotiation was the way their weekends would be spent. George had hoped to significantly increase his involvement with his three noncustodial children now that he could provide them a real second home. He envisioned weekends revolving around family activities with them.

Practical Problems

Following are some major issues that frequently cause dissent in stepfamilies. Be proactive. Don't wait for problems to arise. The quicker you discuss these issues and resolve them, the better.

- How will finances be handled?
- How will discipline be handled?
- How will you deal with ex-spouses and ex-in-laws?
- How will you handle problems and conflicts when they *do* arise?

Once problems do arise, don't bury them and hope they will disappear. Work together as a team to find compromises or solutions.

Feelings

If you and your spouse make a habit of sharing your feelings, you will be able to empathize with each other's unique perspective. Fear, guilt, jealousy, anger, and resentment are common feelings in remarried families. They are natural and to be expected, so don't be ashamed of them or hide them. If you cannot understand how your spouse can feel as he or she does, don't be judgmental. ("There's no reason to feel that way.") The feelings are very real to your partner, whether or not they seem logical to you. Empathize with those feelings! ("I didn't know you felt that way. It must be pretty hard.") Your support and empathy will help. Moreover, understanding each other's feelings will increase the likelihood that you will search for solutions as problems arise.

You might also want to talk about the compromises each of you must make. Sacrifices are easier to make when they are recognized and appreciated.

Children's Concerns

If children are to feel that this is really *their* family, they should be involved in solving family problems and making some family decisions. The principle of open communication extends to them. It is a good idea to have weekly family meetings.

Begin by finding out what children expect of the new family and what role they anticipate the stepparent will play. If everyone starts off with incompatible or unrealistic expectations, the likely result is both dissatisfaction and disappointment. One child may assume the family will continue as usual and a new stepmother will somehow "fit in" inconspicuously, whereas a younger child may assume the addition of the stepmother will automatically create the close-knit family she has always wanted. A teen may assume his new stepdad will continue to be his pal, whereas his stepdad may assume he will become the head of the family, setting and enforcing the rules. Your young son may be excited about finally having a dad like his friends do, but his new stepdad may not be ready to step into a fatherly role. Each of these situations is ripe for problems unless expectations are drawn out in the open, discussed, negotiated, and modified to become more realistic.

Get children's input about what is working in the family and what isn't. Make it a rule at family meetings that each person gets a turn to be heard, and create an atmosphere in which everyone's opinions and feelings are respected regardless of age.

If you teach children to use "I" statements when they express their feelings, other members in the family are less likely to feel attacked and become defensive. To use I statements, start a statement with an "I" and follow it with the way you feel. "I feel I don't get any privacy," not, "Everybody keeps barging in on me and won't leave me alone." Or, "I feel like I'm always on the short end around here," not, "*Her* kids always come first around here." Or, "I'm angry that I have more chores than Philip and Emily," not, "It's not fair. Philip and Emily don't do a thing around here, and I get stuck with all the work."

STRATEGY #2: SET REALISTIC FAMILY GOALS

Agreeing on some long-term family goals will help set you in a positive direction. With agreed-upon family goals, everyone will be working together as a team toward the same ends. You and your partner, as the "executive team" in the family, should first formulate some clear ideas about the direction you would like the family to take. Then get the whole family involved.

To get everyone thinking about long-term goals, try asking family members to fantasize about the kind of family they would like in the future, suggests therapist David Mills, who works with stepfamilies in Seattle. Realize that the goals you set will be tentative and may change as the family develops.

Janet and Mark Rothstein and their children originally agreed that she would take little responsibility for his two older sons, who were already quite independent, and that he would take little responsibility for her two young sons, who were very involved with their father. They all decided they would be satisfied if they learned to respect one another, live in harmony, and have some enjoyable times together. Several years later, when the older boys had both moved out of the house, Mark wondered if he could play a more active fatherly role with his stepchildren. Since both the children had come to feel positively toward him and he made it clear that he did not want to replace their real dad, the youngsters were willing. Janet, who would now have to give up some of her influence and time with her children because of Mark's potential new role in their lives, also agreed to work toward this new family goal. All agreed that this new approach may make them feel more like a family.

Your goals, of course, must be realistic, and you might have to offer children guidance here. Don't let yourselves fall into one of the traps created by stepfamily myths (see Chapter 21). For example, functioning like a traditional family should not be a goal, unless perhaps all children are very young and former spouses and their kin have long since disappeared from the picture of their own accord.

In setting your goals, please remember that it takes time to feel like an integrated family. At least during the first two years, and likely longer, expect stress and expect relationships and family life to feel awkward and contrived. If you expect to feel like a family during this time, you are likely to be frustrated and disappointed.

The more information you have, the more realistic your goals are likely to be. You should be aware of the following.

Children's Ages

Preschool children have the least difficulty adjusting, and some may even welcome a stepparent in their lives. When children are very young, stepfamily adjustment is easier and may be quicker.

The older that children are (up to late teens), the more resistant they usually are to the new family and the longer the family's adjustment is likely to take. Some estimates are up to five to seven years. The older that children are, the more critical it is that they be allowed a voice in how the new family will take form, advise nationally recognized stepfamily experts Emily and John Visher. The more their input is taken into consideration in family matters, the more likely they are to grow to feel that it is truly *their* family.

Teens have a particularly difficult time in a new stepfamily because their developmental needs collide with the needs of the new family. While remarried parents want all family members to make a commitment to the family, adolescents have strong developmental needs to loosen emotional family ties. Teens are also grappling with sexual issues, and most teens find the obvious sexual implications of the new marital relationship disturbing. Discipline from a stepparent is another thorny issue.

It is best to give teens some space rather than make strong demands for family participation. Without this leeway, there may be constant friction in your home. It is also likely that the biological parent will have to be the permanent disciplinarian with a teen. Parents, however, should lay the ground rules for teens to treat stepparents with respect. Teens should not be allowed to treat a stepmother as a convenient housekeeper or a stepfather as a meal ticket.

It may be reassuring to learn that many young people become closer to their stepfamilies after their stormy teen years are over. In fact, many become friends with a stepparent they disliked while growing up.

Boys versus Girls

Girls generally have more difficulty making the transition to a remarried family than do boys. In fact, sometimes boys thrive when a stepfather joins the family—especially younger boys. Girls, on the other hand, tend to have more stressful relationships with both stepmothers and stepfathers. Why this is so can only be speculated. Girls generally become close to their single moms, and it would be natural for them to perceive a new stepfather as a competitor and threat to their close mother-daughter bond. Girls are also more likely to feel threatened and displaced by stepmothers, since daughters are often elevated to the prestigious status of "woman of the house" in their single dads' homes.

Stepmothers versus Stepfathers

The role of a stepmother is more difficult than that of a stepfather, and stepmothers generally have a more stressful time in remarried families. Much of the problem seems to lie in the fact that women in our society generally shoulder the primary responsibility for the care and nurturing of children, as well as for the smooth functioning of the home. Because a woman is a stepmother does not seem to relieve her of these expectations. However, her pivotal position in the family increases her vulnerability for disharmony with her stepchildren.

Stepmothers are sensitive to the stereotype of the "wicked stepmother." Most also accept the myths of the instant family, instant love, and instant adjustment (see Chapter 21). Consequently, as a group, stepmothers are found to create unrealistically high expectations for themselves, which they cannot possibly achieve. It is not unusual for a new stepmother to fantasize about the happy, close-knit family she will instantly create, in which she becomes a supermom to appreciative stepchildren who immediately return her love. The harsh reality she encounters is a shock. It must be that she is doing something wrong, she assumes, so she tries harder. But the more she pushes, the more resistance she is likely to encounter from children who fear their acceptance of her will betray their real mother. Problems are exacerbated when biological mothers are possessive of children and feel threatened by their potential relationship with a stepmother—attitudes that appear to be more prevalent among biological mothers than among biological fathers.

Stepmothers are more successful when they move into new roles slowly, and they are generally happier when they have interests outside the family that provide them fulfillment and give their self-esteem a boost. Many stepmothers are firm advocates of stepparent support groups, which are now offered in many communities through family or community agencies and community colleges.

STRATEGY #3: BUILD A STRONG COUPLE RELATIONSHIP

There is wide agreement among stepfamily experts that the cornerstone of a successful stepfamily is a strong couple relationship. It is this relationship that holds the stepfamily together and prevents it from splitting into the original family groups.

In successful stepfamilies, couples generally assume the role of the "executive team" in the family. The couple discusses issues and decides on a direction they would like to take before airing the issues to the rest of the family. And if no mutually agreeable family decisions can be made, the executive team's combined judgment takes precedence.

When children see their parent and stepparent working together as a team to make the family successful, it is a signal to them that it is safe to make a commitment to this new family—that it is not likely to end in divorce, too. It is also a clear signal that they cannot divide and conquer the couple or make the stepparent leave by causing havoc in the marriage.

Many couples have trouble shifting their primary commitment from their children to each other because they feel it is a betrayal of their children. However, in the long run, youngsters benefit. The most obvious benefits are a stronger family and less likelihood that children will have to go through a second divorce. A secondary benefit for children is having a working model of a good marital relationship in which parents care about one another, work together, and jointly meet children's needs. This places children in good stead for their own future relationships.

Because of the constant presence of children in your lives, you and your spouse may have to be creative in arranging time alone to build your relationship. Try setting aside a time each day for yourselves. If you can't find privacy in your home, try taking walks. Meet for breakfast or lunch one day a week or arrange an evening out alone. Have frequent discussions about how your marriage and family life are going. Don't forget to plan some fun time, too.

A word of caution: In your efforts to work on your own relationship, don't go overboard and exclude your children from your lives. They very much need your support during the early years of your remarried family. It's one of the challenges of a stepfamily to strike a good balance between adults' needs and children's needs.

STRATEGY #4: MOVE SLOWLY; DO NOT PUSH

You may recall that many of the common problems stepfamilies develop stem from their trying to move too quickly, denying the new family the necessary time it needs to blend and adjust. Moving slowly is a *must*! Here are some important guidelines.

Limit Changes in Children's Lives

A stepfamily represents a major change for children who have already had more than their share of upset in their relatively short lives. Although children are adaptive and can usually adjust to some change quite well, the more changes heaped on them, the more difficulty they have coping. For this reason, keep children's lives and environments as consistent as you can.

Identify what things will need to change. Then prioritize them. Which things need to change immediately? What can wait for a short while? What can wait indefinitely? From your "immediate" list, choose a few to work on at a time. But introduce them slowly and proceed slowly, keeping other aspects of children's lives the same. As youngsters adjust to initial changes, you can introduce additional changes *gradually*.

The most critical area in which to limit change is parent-child relationships (unless relationships will be improved). Good relationships with parents provide children a buffer from stress, and there is a good deal of stress in the early years of a stepfamily. Moreover, for children, one of the most threatening aspects of a parent's remarriage is losing their relationship with their parent.

Assure your children of your continued love, and prove it by continuing to spend some time alone with each of them, doing some of the things you did together when you were single. If you are a stepparent without children of your own, allow your spouse and stepchildren the time they need together; that time is critical for the success of your family. Children also need to be assured that they can continue their relationship with the out-of-home parent without threat of displeasing you.

In trying to limit change, retain as many familiar routines, rules, and discipline policies as possible. Also think about the status and privileges each of your children had in your one-parent home, and try to find some way to preserve as many of these as you can. Be sensitive to children who lose their standing as oldest, youngest, or only child in the family. It is hard enough to lose their special positions without losing all the accompanying status and benefits too.

Limiting change may sound easy in theory, but what about a stepfamily that unites two sets of children from different homes, with different routines, rules, discipline, and privileges? It is quite a feat to keep life fairly consistent for each set and still be fair to everyone. Usually some routines from each family can be retained. But what about rules and discipline? Children generally object to differential treatment of stepsiblings.

It will take discussion, negotiation, and compromise to achieve some kind of balance in house rules and discipline policies. Have some preliminary discussions with your spouse. Then during family meetings, look for compromises and solutions on which everyone can agree. Don't work on too many things at one time or everyone will become confused. Zero in on a few areas (fewer than five) that everyone agrees are important to the smooth functioning of the family.

Even young children will benefit from feeling they have a say in some of these changes in their lives. With young children, point out the problems with having different rules for different children, and present them with a plan that is fair to each of them, asking whether they think the new plan will work. Their reactions might result in ideas you hadn't considered. Try to get a commitment from them to try the new plan; children are more willing to comply with changes they have agreed to than with changes that are forced on them. If they balk, suggest trying the plan for a week.

Limiting change in children's lives also creates problems for stepparents without children who enter a "ready-made" family. These stepparents usually feel like guests or boarders in what is supposed to be their own homes, and many have strong needs to change the status quo. If you are in this situation, try to identify one or two changes that would make a significant difference to you and work on changing these. However, your spouse should be the one to introduce the changes. As the changes become part of the family routine, you might try one or two more if they are really important to you. As you build your relationship with your stepchildren and become an insider in the family, you will be able to play a more significant role in how the family functions.

Slowly Build Your Relationship with Each of Your Stepchildren

Building a relationship with stepchildren cannot be rushed. *Any* relationship takes time to build, but stepparent-stepchild relationships take longer. A parent's remarriage usually creates loyalty conflicts for children, who worry their out-of-home parent may be upset if they accept their stepparent. Many must also finally relinquish old hopes of having their family back together again. This takes time.

Children need to keep their distance while they resolve their conflicts and losses. Many respond to a stepparent's early attempts at a relationship with indifference, passive resistance, or outright hostility. Even many stepparents who have had a friendly relationship with a child find that it falls apart once the marriage is official. Don't take negative behavior personally. Try to put yourself in your stepchildren's shoes and understand how they are feeling. Take a low-key approach, and *do not push.*

The following suggestions may be helpful to stepparents in building relationships with stepchildren:

- Let children know, right from the start, that you will not interfere with their relationship with their out-of-home parent. You merely hope that someday you will have a place in their lives, too.
- Be friendly and available, but let them take the lead. Give them the distance they need.
- Go very slowly with expressing affection, especially physical affection. Let it develop at its own pace. After a while, you might

give a child a brief, friendly touch, and watch for a reaction. The older the child, the more cautious you need to be.

- Look for ways to spend some one-on-one time with each of your stepchildren. Invite a child on an errand and stop for an ice cream. Help a child with homework, read a story, or play a favorite game. Ask a youngster to help you bake cookies, cook a special meal, or work on a fun project.

- Try to find some interest you have in common with each of your stepchildren and invite the child to spend time together enjoying it—sports, museums, music, cooking, crafts, movies, shopping.

- Aim to treat all the children in the family *fairly* so your stepchildren do not feel like second-class citizens. This does not mean you do exactly the same thing for each child; children have their own needs, likes, and dislikes. It also does not mean you must include all the children in everything you do. Children need one-on-one time with their own parent. This is particularly important for noncustodial children. It feels so unfair to them if they must share their parent throughout their limited time together with stepchildren who see the parent every day. Work at achieving a balance between individual time with children and family time.

- Work on accepting and respecting your stepchildren. Don't start out by trying to make them over or change the way they do things. They will only resent you and resist your efforts. If you are ever going to change anything about them, it will be *after* you have developed a relationship with them.

- Be positive! Find things to compliment them about, and pick up on any friendly overtures.

- When your stepchildren are around, try to behave *as if* they like you, advise Emily and John Visher, nationally recognized stepfamily experts. You will find that you behave differently and send out different messages. You may also find that they behave differently toward you. We sometimes create our own self-fulfilling prophecies.

- Open up the lines of communication by using the techniques in Chapter 9.

- Ask your spouse for help. Many parents keep the bonds with their children so tight that it is difficult for stepparents to form their own relationships with youngsters. Your spouse may have to stand back a bit.

STRATEGY #5: DEVELOP YOUR OWN UNIQUE ROLE WITH YOUR STEPCHILDREN; DO NOT TRY TO REPLACE THEIR OUT-OF-HOME PARENT

Most stepparents assume they will play a parenting role in their stepchildren's lives. But if they move into that role too quickly, they are usually rebuffed.

There are many roles stepparents can play other than a parenting one—that of an adult friend, a confidant, an adviser, a role model, a supportive person who offers encouragement, an aunt or uncle, an older sibling, a neutral third party who buffers conflict in the home. Whatever the role you play, it needs to evolve over time.

If you are a stepparent and trying to work out your role in the family, think about the role you would *like* to play, what you are willing to do, and what you are not willing to do. Explore possible roles with your partner, and talk with your stepchildren about the kinds of things they would like a stepparent to do and to avoid doing. See how they feel about your doing the kinds of things that you were hoping to do. Open discussion helps everyone feel they have at least *some* control over what is happening in their lives. Once everyone's feelings are understood, try out a role that seems comfortable for everyone, and see how it works. You may try several roles before finding your niche.

A University of Washington study of possible stepparent roles reported that the adult friend role was the most comfortable and effective from the perspective of both stepparent and their spouses. Many stepfamily experts agree that the role of an adult friend is likely to be the role most conducive to a smoothly functioning stepfamily.

Here are some things to remember about roles:

- Always be yourself and emphasize *your* strengths. Never try to compete with the out-of-home parent. If children make comparisons between you and their other parent, try not to become defensive. Simply state that each of you is different from the other.
- Keep in mind that you will not play a meaningful role in your stepchildren's lives until you have built a relationship with them.
- Your role may evolve differently with different stepchildren. With a young child, you may become another parent figure. For a 12-year-old, you may become a caring and supportive adult. To an older teen, you may become a confidant.

- If you are hoping to play a parenting role with your stepchildren, aim to be *another* parent rather than a replacement parent. Even if a parent has completely left the picture, he or she needs to be psychologically dead for a child before you are accepted as a replacement.

STRATEGY #6: LET THE BIOLOGICAL PARENT HANDLE DISCIPLINE WHILE THE STEPPARENT BONDS WITH STEPCHILDREN

How to handle discipline is a dilemma for every remarried family, and it is the most common source of serious stepfamily problems, particularly in stepfather families. The approach that usually works best is for the biological parent to continue to handle the discipline during the first year or longer while the stepparent works on building good relationships with the children. Until a stepparent is accepted as a member of the family, children perceive attempts at discipline as illegitimate and resent them.

When stepparents move too quickly to assume authority, there are a number of common outcomes, none of which are good. Many children reject their stepparents. Some act out their anger and develop behavior problems at school and at home. Many families become embroiled in prolonged conflict. Many others fail to blend. In these latter families, the stepparent is likely to withdraw from the family, feeling ineffectual and frustrated.

Here are some pointers for stepparents about discipline:

- Discuss discipline in depth with your spouse. If your family is to run smoothly, you need to agree on long-term disciplinary policies to work toward, and you need to support each other in this area. You should be working toward becoming a strong executive team that will work together and support each other. Otherwise, your children will adopt a divide-and-conquer strategy. Arriving at a mutually agreeable style of parenting may require *ongoing* frank communication and negotiation. Chapter 20, "How to Discipline Effectively and Still Be a 'Good Guy,'" will help. If you have very different parenting styles, it will help to take a parenting class together.
- If you think that any changes in discipline, standards, or house rules *must* be made right away, discuss them with your partner. Don't go overboard; focus on a few that are critical. At least

for the first year, have your partner introduce and enforce changes. Children are likely to respond more positively if they are brought into discussions about new rules and their input is considered. Sometimes, compromises can be reached that will make everyone happy. Jennifer discovered this principle after she created needless conflict.

When Jennifer joined the family, she thought her stepchildren's slovenliness would drive her crazy. Deciding she couldn't take it any longer, she laid down the law about picking up their things and cleaning their rooms. They balked at her new rules and ignored them, making her even angrier. When the problem was finally discussed calmly at a family meeting, some compromises were made fairly easily. The children agreed to keep their things out of the common living areas of the house, and Jennifer agreed their rooms were their domain, to be kept as they saw fit as long as the doors were kept closed.

- During the first year or longer, concentrate on developing some common ground with your stepchildren. Get to know one another, and build a warm relationship with each child individually. Refrain from lecturing, nagging, scolding, and punishing. Keep any attempts to control their behavior very positive—praise, appreciation, or incentives ("If we all work together to get the chores done, we'll have time to rent a movie.").
- During the first year, anytime you are with your stepchildren for long periods when your spouse is away from the home, he or she should specifically tell the children you are in charge and will enforce the rules and make decisions. Children should know what the rules are, what their parent expects of them, and the consequences if they do not follow rules or expectations. If these are clear ahead of time, it will be *their* decision whether to incur the consequences, and you will not become the heavy.
- Respect your stepchildren and expect respect in return.
- Set your own *personal* limits with them. Examples are setting a policy about their using your personal property or asking them to turn music down after a certain hour if it interferes with your sleep.
- At least for the first year, try to keep out of battles between your partner and your stepchildren, although occasionally siding with a child when you believe the child is right will help to build a child's trust in you as a fair person.
- As your relationship with your stepchildren develops, *slowly* move into a more active disciplinary role, working up to a role in which you are an equal partner with your spouse in setting

and enforcing rules. With a teen, your disciplinary role may be limited to actively supporting your spouse in his or her disciplinary actions. If discipline is not your spouse's strong suit, Chapter 20 will help. Teens *do* need clear rules and limits.

- When you do assume a disciplinary role, be sure to use an authoritative (not authoritarian) parenting style (see Chapter 20). Although an authoritative style is preferable for *any* parent, it is found to be especially effective for stepparents.
- Be aware that unless your partner supports you, you will make little headway in disciplining your stepchildren. If you find they continually ignore you or buck you on some issue, discuss the problem with your spouse. You may find that he or she does not agree with you, and the children have sensed this. If this is the case, you need to renegotiate the rules with your spouse, not demand compliance from your stepchildren.

If you tried to discipline too early and are already entrenched in conflict with your stepchildren, back off and allow their natural parent to handle *all* discipline while you remain completely neutral. You might also try this approach if your stepchildren have withdrawn or have developed behavioral problems at home or at school. Children often express their anger or distress in these less obvious ways. As the situation improves and you and your stepchild develop a better relationship, you can try to take a more active role once again, but do so *very gradually*. Some stepfamily counseling may be very helpful in getting your family back on track.

STRATEGY #7: BUILD A FAMILY IDENTITY

One of the most important tasks during the first years of a stepfamily's life is developing a sense of family identity. Much of it will emerge gradually as a result of the blending process.

Blending

As you work out the mechanics of living together in a mutually agreeable lifestyle, feelings of belonging will grow—*providing* there is a real blending of the two contingents rather than one swallowing up the other's identity.

As the executive team in the family, you and your spouse should first discuss possible ways of combining disparate lifestyles and identities.

Then seek children's input. Youngsters generally assume their family's ways of doing things are the "right" way and usually want to stick to those ways. Help them see there are no right or wrong ways, just *different* ways. Create an atmosphere in which differences are accepted, new ideas are tried, and ongoing negotiation and compromises are par for the course. Gradually, you will all begin to feel like members of the same team working toward a common future.

Many well-functioning stepfamilies report that weekly family meetings were an indispensable part of their lives while trying to blend their two contingents. During these meetings, they discussed problems, tried to find solutions, shared feelings, aired grievances, and congratulated one another for the progress made to date. Emily and John Visher suggest having two containers handy in your home in which family members can leave comments—one container for bothersome issues and the other for things that are appreciated and liked in the family.

Blending can be problematic if one contingent moves in with the other. Try to change the existing home so it reflects the new remarried family. Get the whole family involved in redecorating and using space differently. If stepsiblings must share a bedroom, can it be changed so the new room belongs to *both* children rather than having one child intrude on the other's territory? Allowing children to decide how to redecorate their own room is a good icebreaker for new roommates.

If you have trouble breaking down the walls between the two contingents in your stepfamily, a technique therapists often use is having each side of the family share its prestepfamily pasts with the other— memories of early childhoods, first families, one-parent homes, and the early months of the stepfamily. It is a great icebreaker, even for step siblings who appear to be hopelessly antagonistic toward one another. Twelve-year-old Jeanne opened up to 11-year-old Andrea after learning how Andrea felt about leaving her home, bedroom, school, and friends and moving into Jeanne's bedroom. Jeanne had been so busy resenting having to share her bedroom with Andrea that the two had primarily hostile exchanges before.

Family Traditions and Rituals

Family rituals and traditions bind a family together and give it a feeling of "we-ness" and legitimacy. Make a conscious effort to develop them for your family. Some can be taken from each contingent, and new ones can be created. To create new ones, try the following:

- Find things to do or places to go that the entire family enjoys—bicycling, camping, hiking, picnicking, going to the movies, visiting museums, playing softball, and so forth. Be sure to involve children in coming up with ideas. When you find a winner, make it a frequent family activity. It will soon come to symbolize the new family in each member's mind.
- Routinely do something together a few times each week—a weekly family meeting, a family breakfast, special family dinners, a time for everyone to do chores, renting a video, an evening of cards or board games, going out for pizza or ice cream. When you find something that works well, make it a weekly routine. Don't go overboard. Your children are likely to resist excessive attempts at family unity.
- Develop some new family traditions around birthdays, holidays, and your stepfamily's anniversary. Deciding how to spend holidays is difficult for many stepfamilies; each side understandably feels its way is best. Discuss both families' traditions and see if you can find some way to combine the two.
- Try brainstorming (see Chapter 14) to arrive at creative solutions for new traditions. If a family identity is going to take shape, both sides of the family should agree rather than one foisting its traditions on the other.

Building a Family History

Family identity also evolves from building a history together. Celebrate your stepfamily anniversary together and reminisce from time to time about the wedding, the early months, and events you've shared. Keep a scrapbook of the new family in a visible place, and occasionally spend time looking at it together. If you add new pictures to it while everyone "happens" to be present, it will seem less contrived to invite children to go through it.

STRATEGY #8: DO NOT TRY TO SHUT OUT THE OUT-OF-HOME PARENT OR FORCE LOYALTY

Contrary to the instincts of many remarried couples, stepfamilies usually work best when children are able to freely continue relationships with their out-of-home parent. Many remarried couples try to shut out the outside parent, either physically or psychologically, hoping to replace the parent with the stepparent. However, to a child, a stepparent is someone *in addition to* a natural parent, not a replacement. Children reserve a special slot in their lives for a natural parent and usually fight any attempt to fill that slot with someone else. At some point, a stepparent may earn a special place in a child's life, but it is usually a *new* slot that a child gradually creates.

The outcome of trying to shut out the out-of-home parent is frequently the opposite of that intended: Generally it is the stepparent who loses. Children are more likely to be comfortable in the stepfamily when they are not caught in loyalty conflicts and their relationship with their other parent is not at risk.

You will be better able to support your children's relationships with their out-of-home parent if you model your family after what stepfamily experts call a *linked* family, a term originally coined by Doris Jacobson of the University of California at Los Angeles. A linked family consists of two households—the resident parent's and the nonresident parent's, with children representing the link between the two.

Here are some pointers to help you develop a linked family for your children:

- Develop a strong couple relationship so contact with a former spouse does not cause jealousy and suspicion. Stepparents are found to be more at ease when their spouse maintains strictly businesslike interactions with an ex-spouse.
- Follow the co-parenting principles in Chapter 18 and share them with the out-of-home parent.
- If you and the other parent are in conflict, take action to end it. There are steps you can take on your own (see Chapter 19).
- When your children return from the other home, give them time and space to make the transition between homes. Don't try to compete with or undermine the other home, and don't pry into what is going on there.
- Although your children should be able to move freely back and forth between the homes, a former spouse should not be free to interject him- or herself into your lives. Maintain your family boundaries.
- Linked families work best if everyone's roles, responsibilities, and expectations are clear (see Chapter 17). Some linked families

EIGHT SUCCESSFUL STRATEGIES
FOR STEPFAMILIES

1. Communicate openly.
   - Have you discussed expectations, finances, discipline?
   - Do you discuss feelings, problems, and conflict?
   - Do you seek children's input and involve them in some decisions?
2. Set realistic family goals.
   - Don't be misguided by the four stepfamily myths.
   - Is everyone working on the same team for the same goals?
3. Build a strong couple relationship; be an executive team.
4. Move slowly; do not push.
   - Are you limiting the changes in children's lives?
   - Are you protecting parent-child relationships?
   - Are you allowing children space to resolve losses and conflicts and time to develop relationships at their own pace?
5. Develop your *own* unique role with stepchildren.
   - Are you allowing your role to evolve over time?
   - Never try to replace the out-of-home parent.
6. Let the biological parent handle the discipline while the stepparent bonds with the children.
7. Build a family identity.
   - Is *everyone* involved in blending the new family?
   - Are you developing new traditions?
   - Are you consciously building a family history?
8. Follow the model of a linked family and support children's relationships with the out-of-home parent.

work out their respective roles and responsibilities with the help of a family mediator (see Chapter 2).
- It is best for parents to communicate directly about their children. If you are a stepparent, back off. If parents have never been able to communicate directly, see if it is agreeable to everyone to have a stepparent act as the go-between. In some

linked families, the two stepparents make all the arrangements for children.

Although in years past, stepfamilies were left to forge their own way, there are now a multitude of resources to help you be successful. Support groups are available in many communities, and for many stepparents, they are a lifeline. If you cannot find one, consider starting your own by placing a notice in a local school, church, or community newspaper. There are plenty of stepfamilies around, and most would welcome some support and new ideas.

There are two well-known national organizations for stepfamilies, which are good sources of information and support: The Stepfamily Foundation (333 West End Ave., New York, NY 10023. Phone: 212-877-3244. E-mail: Stefamily@aol.com. Web site: www.stepfamily.org) and The Stepfamily Association of America (650 J Street, #205, Lincoln, NE 68503. Phone: 800-735-0329. E-Mail: stepfamfs@aol.com).

Stepfamily classes are now being offered in many communities and will provide you with both good information and contact with other stepfamilies. Check your local community agencies or educational extension programs.

Many stepfamilies initiate stepfamily counseling to work on relationship issues and sort through the complexities of stepfamily living. Be sure to use a counselor with specific expertise with stepfamilies. Other families use a family mediator to find creative solutions to practical problems and negotiate how they will implement those solutions. Many older children who object to the idea of counseling find the idea of mediation more pleasing. Mediation is discussed in Chapter 2.

If you've read all three stepfamily chapters, you have probably developed a detailed road map of what generally works and what generally does not work for remarried families. Remember, these are not hard-and-fast rules but guidelines. You may find other paths to success that work for *your* family. If you do find your family getting into trouble, however, take another look at these successful and losing strategies. See if you can identify the root of the problems so you can nip them in the bud and get back on track.

VI

Overview and Appendixes

24

Closing Remarks

Divorce is the death of a marriage. With it, you enter a new, changed world. For most, the fallout from divorce is a confusing mix of anxiety, sadness, grief, anger, euphoria, uncertainty, and feelings of failure—all present in amounts never thought possible. These emotions and feelings, so understandable, eventually need to be brought under control, sorted out, dealt with, and let go.

Broadly speaking, three phases make up this changed world: surviving change, adapting to change, and, finally, growth. You will encounter them again if you enter a new relationship and create a stepfamily. Loosely termed, the entire process is the achievement of new beginnings, and it has been the focus of much of this book.

As the old adage says, "It is a wise person who profits from the misfortunes of others." Fortunately, during the past two decades, divorce and family researchers have intensively studied and analyzed countless divorce and stepfamily experiences. From others' misfortunes, much has been learned. And much of it is encouraging, offering valuable help in finding shorter and smoother paths through divorce, rebuilding, parenting in a one-parent home, co-parenting, and creating a stepfamily.

First, however, some hard lessons of divorce must be faced. A disconcerting surprise for most people is that the aftermath of divorce is not short-lived. Most people expect to have a difficult time for a while, but when the difficult period extends month after month after month, a new stress, this one self-generated, appears: "Why is it *this* bad?" "What's wrong with *me*?"

For divorcing couples with children, stress and problems are compounded. Parents with custody must contend with distressed, bewildered children who are likely to respond to their families' ruptures with at least transient emotional or behavioral problems. Parents without custody must find a way to cope with being shut out of their children's day-to-day lives and to avert the real possibility of being demoted from a parent to a peripheral player in their children's futures.

And what of divorcing men and women who find a new love, remarry, and form a stepfamily? The unsuspecting majority believe an instant family, abounding in love and happiness, will soon be theirs, but research shows otherwise. Stepfamilies, too, face an extended transitional period of surviving, adapting, and growing before they can experience new beginnings as a full-fledged family.

The years surrounding divorce are likely to be the most challenging ones of your life, and there may be times when you wonder if you will emerge from them with some semblance of happiness and fulfillment. It may encourage you to learn that we human beings have an impressive ability to successfully overcome personal tragedy and serious setbacks of all sorts. If we can take self-reports at face value, studies find that the majority of people eventually manage to emerge with a level of satisfaction equal to, if not greater than, that which they had enjoyed prior to their personal misfortunes.

Within these pages are the maps for what lies ahead, whether you are divorcing, parenting in a one-parent home, or parenting in a stepfamily. Within these pages are also the coping skills you will need to survive change, to adapt to change, and, finally, to grow and thrive. With these, you need not forge ahead unguided. You can avoid many of the mistakes others make and the problems others encounter. An enormous amount of territory, information, and coping skills has been covered, and it defies summary in a single chapter. Yet there are key consistent threads running throughout this book that are important whether you are divorcing, learning how to parent solo, learning how to co-parent, or creating a stepfamily. In these final pages, I'd like to pull some of these threads together so you can keep them in mind in the coming years, regardless of what your future brings.

A critical theme throughout this book is the importance of completing your emotional divorce (see Chapter 10). Successful new beginnings can be yours, whether you wanted the divorce or it was forced on you, whether you remain single or remarry. However, unless you have completed your emotional divorce, you are likely to get stalled along the way. Your emotional divorce is the first necessary step and foundation for successful new beginnings. Don't minimize its importance, even if you are already remarrying; unresolved divorce issues can haunt your new marriage (see Chapter 13). Until you complete your emotional divorce, you cannot close the door completely on your ex-spouse. Your move into your future will be burdened with your past. Take a careful look at whether you have more work to do; it is never too late.

A second, yet related, theme throughout these chapters is the devastating repercussions of extended conflict for former spouses and children alike. For approximately 25 percent of divorced partners, conflict becomes a way of life. They hold on to their anger as if it were a badge of honor. But the anger and conflict entangles them in a web with their former spouse, the marriage, and the past. It creates havoc in their personal lives and saps the emotional energy needed to build successful new beginnings. If they are already in a new relationship, the new couple are treading on weak ground filled with sinkholes. When they have children, the repercussions of their conflict mushroom: Prolonged parental conflict is the number one predictor of children's poor adjustment. If you are one of these embittered, you may wonder if there is hope. The answer is yes. What you do not realize is that you have not completed your emotional divorce. It is the *intensity* of your emotion, not whether your emotion is love or hate, that is the real barometer of how much you are still hooked into your ex. You have the potential to create a future in which your former spouse will no longer trigger an emotional reaction within you. Your anger and resentment can be exchanged for indifference, or perhaps even concern. Complete your emotional divorce, so you can lay your anger to rest, close the door on your ex-spouse and your former marriage, and move on to new beginnings unencumbered. Chapters 5, 10, and 19 will guide your way.

A third theme is the importance of rebuilding. Many people assume that divorce adjustment involves only surviving the stormy emotions and upheavals. But unless you *consciously* move ahead to forge a new identity separate from that of your ex-spouse and a new life of your own design to replace your married one (see Chapter 11), you may emerge from divorce frozen in old patterns and fail to grow. If so, life after divorce may be less satisfying than married life was.

If you are a parent, there is another facet to successful new beginnings: to provide your children with the support, love, and good parenting they need now and in the future.

Parents seldom realize just how stressful divorce is for children. It turns children's worlds topsy-turvy, robbing youngsters of their families—their source of stability, security, and continuity. Divorce leaves children feeling vulnerable, overwhelmed with loss, and powerless to influence events that have a profound impact on their lives. Although we tend to think of divorce as a single event, it sets in motion a chain of events that can cast shadows over a large part of a youngster's childhood.

For children whose parents drift away from them, either physically or because of their preoccupation with their new lives or new loves, the pain of divorce and feelings of rejection linger throughout childhood and often into young adulthood. For children whose parents continue to battle each other, the pain of divorce is compounded by unrelenting feelings of being pulled apart by the two people loved most in the world. For children who are poorly parented after divorce, there is too much time with no guidance and too many opportunities for life to go awry. For children whose parents remarry, another long period of upheaval may be in the offing.

Yet children *can* emerge from divorce unscathed. They can bounce back and resume their childhoods with amazing resilience if parents can provide them with a few fundamentals, not only at the time of divorce but in the ensuing years (see Chapter 7). What children experience in the years *after* divorce can be more important than what they go through at the time. These same fundamentals are, therefore, important to children in one-parent homes and in stepfamilies, too.

First on the list is to put an end to your conflict with their other parent. At the very least, protect them from it. One of the most startling things researchers have learned is the devastating repercussions that prolonged parental conflict has for children (see Chapter 8); its scars follow children into adulthood. Chapter 19 is devoted to steps to contain the conflict and then to end it.

The flip side is the benefit to *everyone* of ex-spouses working together as parents. Everyone wins when they cooperate. Children adjust better to both the divorce and parents' new relationships. And ex-spouses are happier in their new lives and remarriages. Chapters 17 and 18 provide a map for you to co-parent your children successfully. These chapters are not only for parents who share joint physical custody of their children. They are for the larger majority of divorced families in which both parents are involved to some degree with their children after divorce. Children do better when they have *two parents who parent them,* rather than one parent and a "visitor" who functions more like an activities director. Never minimize the importance of the other parent.

This brings us to the second fundamental children need: good relationships with parents. Good relationships with loving and supportive parents provide a protective cushion for children that softens the negative impact of stress and sees them through the hard times in life—extending into young adulthood. Make your relationships with your children a high priority now and in the years ahead so your children will be afforded this protection. Just as important, support their relationships with their other parent. If you remarry, avoid the mistake that many stepfamily couples make—trying to freeze out the biological parent and substitute the stepparent. It causes problems not only for children but for stepfamilies, too (see Chapter 22).

A stable home and good parenting is a third fundamental children need. Although these are important to *all* children, they are particularly important to children who have experienced change and upheaval in their home lives through divorce or remarriage. Chapters 9 and 14 discussed the ingredients of a home life that enables children to adjust well to divorce and flourish in a one-parent home. The same ingredients are important to children in stepfamilies.

What is good parenting? The importance of using an authoritative parenting style (see Chapter 20) emerges repeatedly. Although this parenting style benefits *all* children, it is found to be particularly critical for children in divorcing families, one-parent families, and stepfamilies. And for those nonresident parents who fear they will have no impact on their children's development, research shows you can have a positive impact if you use an authoritative parenting style and behave as a parent instead of a pal.

Limiting additional stress in children's lives is a final fundamental for their good adjustment. Children can usually handle one major stress in their lives quite well, such as parental divorce or becoming part of a stepfamily. However, it is important that additional significant stress be minimized. The reason is that the negative effects of stress are not simply additive for children; they *multiply*. Each additional significant source of stress makes it increasingly more difficult for them to reconstruct their lives (see Chapter 7). Limiting stress is important to children in divorcing families, one-parent homes, and stepfamilies. How can you limit additional stress? Keep as much continuity in children's lives as possible, introducing changes *gradually* as they adapt to initial changes. Allow them their childhoods and adolescence; do not saddle them with adult problems and responsibilities, no matter how mature they seem. End the conflict with the other parent. Do not rob them of their needed good relationship with you or their other parent. Try to give them enough economic security so at least basic needs will be met without an emotional toll on the family. And find as many sources of social support for them as you can.

The years surrounding divorce, spent learning to parent solo, learning co-parenting skills, and creating a stepfamily, are challenging ones. Many people seek professional counseling during these years for both themselves and their children, and they are rarely disappointed. To many, a therapist or counselor is a lifeline.

Divorce thrusts you into a jungle of emotions and events. The emotions are deep, and the events are fast moving and not always easy to comprehend. It would be easy to let yourself become overwhelmed, confused, and bogged down with all the problems. Armed with the knowledge provided by thousands of people who have preceded you, the jungle will change its character from a dark, unknown, and threatening place to one with known but challenging obstacles. This book's goal, its purpose, has been to prepare you for the emotions and challenges you are likely to encounter now and in the future. With your new understanding, it is hoped that your venture will consist of a series of challenging obstacles and not a mass of paralyzing threats. Focusing on unknown threats leads to feelings of helplessness and the belief that mere surviving is the most you can hope for. Focusing on the challenges will encourage you to mobilize your resources so you can first adapt to and then grow in your new, changed world. With the knowledge and suggested coping tools contained in this book, you can discover a shorter and smoother road to new beginnings. With those new beginnings comes the promise of a *stronger* person entering into a *better* life.

Appendix A:
How to Make Changes in Your Life and Stick to Them

You may get excited about a number of the coping strategies discussed throughout this book. Filled with a new sense of optimism, you may vow to try some of them, and you may even use them for a time. But then you may find yourself back in your rut, saying to yourself, "I really should get back to those techniques. They worked while I used them." Or you may simply say to yourself initially, "They sound good. But I never stick to those things. So why try?"

How to get people to *start* and to *continue* using effective coping strategies was a dilemma psychologists faced for some time. Following is a five-step method that will help you make changes in your life and stick to them. It is not difficult, and it *is* effective.

Step 1. *Set a specific goal.* Be *realistic,* not grandiose. You don't want to set yourself up for failure and disappointment. There are three important keys to setting realistic goals:

- Make your goals *small.*
- Make your goals *short-term* (divide long-term goals into short-term segments).
- Be sure you can *realistically* fit your goals into your schedule.

As you achieve each small, short-term goal, set a new *realistic* goal.

Step 2. *Write a contract for yourself and sign it.* This may sound insignificant, but it is important. Signing a contract is an effective way of committing yourself to your goal. Your contract should include some positive reward for accomplishing your goal and perhaps some penalty for failing to accomplish it. (More about rewards and penalties later.) One Washington, D.C., man's contract looked like this:

> I will get up 20 minutes early each day this week and practice my deep relaxation technique. If I practice 20 minutes each day for five days out of the next seven, I will reward myself by going to see the new exhibit at the National Gallery. If I fail in my goal, I will contribute $15 to the Democratic Party (which I despise)!

Each time you fulfill a contract, write a new one. You may wish to extend the same goal for a similar period of time, or you may wish to increase your goal in some way. You may also wish to alter your rewards or penalties.

Step 3. *Record each day whether you met your goal.* Don't skip this step—it keeps you honest. It is a good reminder, and it will boost your commitment, too. Keep a daily record on a calendar. If you did not meet your goal, record how close you came.

Step 4. *Reward yourself for sticking to your contract.* The reward you choose should be something you will look forward to—buying a new book, allowing yourself a favorite activity you rarely take time to do, indulging yourself with a special meal or dessert. Make your reward appropriate to the amount of effort you put forth. Make it appealing enough to motivate you without going overboard. Save large or costly rewards for goals that take a major effort.

Rewards are far more motivating if they are *frequent* and if they come *soon after* you complete your task. Promising yourself a trip if you exercise three times a week for a year is unlikely to make an exerciser of you. Promising yourself a night out each week is likely to be far more effective. Or you may need a reward immediately after you exercise to get yourself started.

You may find that you are more motivated if you also include a penalty in your contract for not accomplishing your goal (washing windows, organizing a closet, or, as the man above did, donating to a cause you despise). Another effective technique is denying yourself television or some other favorite activity you normally do until you reach your goal for the day.

Besides material rewards and punishments, get into the habit of using positive *self-talk*. Pat yourself on the back and praise yourself for a job well done. If you did not reach your goal, praise yourself for your efforts and encourage yourself for the next time. ("I didn't meet my goal every day, but I did stick to it four days. I'll do better next week.")

Step 5. *Reevaluate.* If you accomplished your goal, set another one and sign another contract to keep yourself going. Can you increase your goal this time? Perhaps you are ready to either lengthen the time or the number of days you exercise. Are you ready to tackle two goals? Are you ready to write a contract for two weeks rather than one? Be sure to be realistic.

If you did not accomplish what you set out to do, reevaluate your contract. Are you certain your goal was realistic? What *would* motivate you to complete it this time? Might a different coping strategy work better for you?

Continue writing contracts in this way until the new behavior becomes a normal part of your life. If you find yourself reverting to old patterns, resume the contracts and rewards.

Appendix B:
Learning a Deep
Relaxation Technique

L earning a deep relaxation technique is not difficult, but it does require practice, as does learning any new skill. The following method was developed by Herbert Benson and is described in detail in his book *The Relaxation Response*. Here are the steps to Benson's relaxation method:

Step 1. Choose a quiet place and time when you will be free of distractions. A little creativity may make this easier than you think. One executive told his secretary he was in conference each day and was not to be disturbed for 20 minutes. One busy mother plopped her children in front of their favorite television program each day and retired to her bedroom for 20 minutes. She disconnected the phone and promised them an appealing snack if they stayed put. Other people get up 20 minutes earlier in the morning, use their coffee break at work, or utilize a daily train commute. Preferably you can find a time at least two hours after eating, since the digestive process can interfere with achieving deep relaxation, says Dr. Benson.

Step 2. Find a comfortable and relaxed position that will allow you to relax your muscles (but one in which you are not likely to fall asleep). Close your eyes.

Step 3. Tune into your muscles and try to relax them one by one. Start with your feet, and progress to your legs, torso, arms, shoulders, neck and throat, and finally to your facial muscles (around your mouth, jaw, nose, cheeks, temples, eyes, and forehead). Sometimes it helps to imagine the tension flowing from each muscle and leaving your body via your mouth, head, fingers, and toes. Do not worry if this is difficult for you to do; it will get easier with practice.

Step 4. Tune into your breathing. Breathe through your nose easily and naturally.

Step 5. Each time you exhale, silently say the word "one" to yourself. Focus on the word; it will help you to push away other thoughts from your mind.

Step 6. Assuming a *passive* attitude is very important, says Benson. A passive attitude simply means this: Don't try too hard; don't worry about how well you are doing; don't be upset if other thoughts pop into your mind. You cannot relax if you are worried. (When other thoughts do pop into your mind, and it will happen, just shift your focus to the word "one" and let the thoughts fade away slowly on their own.)

Step 7. Continue your breathing, saying the word "one." Relax your muscles for 20 minutes. Don't use a timer or alarm; it will startle you. But you can open your eyes to check the time.

Step 8. When you are finished, don't jump up. Continue to sit quietly for a minute or two, first with your eyes closed and then with them open.

It is important to practice relaxation consistently, preferably each day. Once you have learned the technique, you will be able to relax with little effort. Even better, you will be able to use a shortened method to relax before and during situations that are stressful, anxiety-arousing, or anger-provoking. Think of the tool you will have if you can relax, at will, during times of high tension!

This is how to successfully relax during these stressful times:

Step 1. Start tuning into signs of rising tension in your body, such as a lump in your throat, clenched teeth, your stomach churning, your hands fidgeting, or tension around your eyes or forehead. It is always easier to nip tension in the bud than to reduce it once it is full-blown.

Step 2. Once you notice your tension rising, take some deep, slow breaths and say the word "one" to yourself each time you exhale.

Step 3. Picture yourself in your favorite relaxing spot, and remember the feeling of relaxation you have achieved during practice sessions.

That is all there is to it, *once* you have mastered the technique. You can also use relaxation to help you unwind and sleep at night. However, don't use bedtime as your practice time. The physiological changes you achieve during relaxation are different from those that accompany sleep.

Appendix C:
Sample Parenting Plans

The following are examples of monthly parenting plans. A and B represent when the children are with Parent A and Parent B. A horizontal line through a day indicates the children spend several hours with Parent B, returning to Parent A one hour prior to bedtime. A diagonal line through a day indicates the children spend an overnight with the other parent. These are just examples and can be modified to meet your children's and family's individual needs. Please read Chapter 17 to learn about appropriate parenting schedules for children of different ages.

	M	T	W	Th	F	Sa	Su
Week 1	A	A	A / B	A	A	A / B	B
Week 2	A	A	A / B	A	A	A / B	B
Week 3	A	A	A / B	A	A	A / B	B
Week 4	A	A	A / B	A	A	A / B	B

Children share a 24-hour period each weekend with each parent (Friday 5 P.M. to Saturday 5 P.M. or Saturday 5 P.M. to Sunday 5 P.M.). They also see Parent B one afternoon/evening during the week.

	M	T	W	Th	F	Sa	Su
Week 1	A	A	A / B	A	A / B	B	B
Week 2	A	A	A / B	A	A	A	A
Week 3	A	A	A / B	A	A / B	B	B
Week 4	A	A	A / B	A	A	A	A

Children are with Parent B alternate weekends (Friday evening to Sunday evening) and each Wednesday afternoon/evening to one hour before bedtime.

	M	T	W	Th	F	Sa	Su
Week 1	A	A	A	A / B	B	B	B
Week 2	B / A	A	A	A / B	A	A	A
Week 3	A	A	A	A / B	B	B	B
Week 4	B / A	A	A	A / B	A	A	A

Children are with Parent B extended alternate weekends (Thursday afternoon/evening to Monday morning) and Thursday afternoon/evening during the intervening week.

	M	T	W	Th	F	Sa	Su
Week 1	A	A	A	A	A / B	B	B
Week 2	A	A	A	A	A / B	B	B
Week 3	A	A	A	A / B	B / A	A	A
Week 4	A	A	A	A	A / B	B	B

Children are with Parent B three weekends each month and for a midweek overnight during the off week.

	M	T	W	Th	F	Sa	Su
Week 1	A	A	B	B	A	A	A
Week 2	A	A	B	B	B	B	B
Week 3	A	A	B	B	A	A	A
Week 4	A	A	B	B	B	B	B

This is a 2-5-2 equal-child-sharing plan. Children are with Parent A every Monday and Tuesday, with Parent B every Wednesday and Thursday. They alternate weekends with each parent.

	M	T	W	Th	F	Sa	Su
Week 1	A	A	A/B	B	B	B/A	A
Week 2	A	A	A/B	B	B	B/A	A
Week 3	A	A	A/B	B	B	B/A	A
Week 4	A	A	A/B	B	B	B/A	A

Children split their week with each parent. They change homes Wednesday after school and Saturday evening.

	M	T	W	Th	F	Sa	Su
Week 1	A	A	A	A	A	A	A
Week 2	B	B	B	B	B	B	B
Week 3	A	A	A	A	A	A	A
Week 4	B	B	B	B	B	B	B

Children alternate weeks with each parent.

	M	T	W	Th	F	Sa	Su
Week 1	A	A	A	A	A	B	B
Week 2	A	A	A	A	A	A	A
Week 3	B	B	B	B	B	A	A
Week 4	B	B	B	B	B	B	B

Children spend alternate two-week blocks of time with each parent, but spend the intervening weekend with the other parent.

Appendix D:
Suggested Reading

FOR ADULTS

Ackerman, M. *Does Wednesday Mean Mom's House or Dad's? Parenting Together while Living Apart.* New York: John Wiley, 1997.

Ahrons, C. *The Good Divorce: Keeping Your Family Together When Your Marriage Comes Apart.* New York: Harper Collins, 1994.

Alberti, R. E., and M. I. Emmons. *Your Perfect Right: A Guide to Assertive Living,* 25th anniversary ed. Luis Obispo, Calif.: Impact, 1995.

Burns, D. D. *Feeling Good: The New Mood Therapy,* rev. ed. New York: Avon Books, 1999.

———. *The Feeling Good Workbook: Using the New Mood Therapy in Everyday Life,* rev. ed. New York: Penguin-Putnam, 1999.

———. *Intimate Connections.* New York: Signet, 1985.

Clarke-Stewart, A. *Daycare,* rev. ed. Cambridge, Mass.: Harvard University Press, 1993.

Cohen, M. G. *Long-Distance Parenting: A Guide for Divorced Parenting.* New York: New American Library, 1989.

Condrell, K., and L. Small. *Be a Great Divorced Dad.* New York: St. Martin's Press, 1998.

Davis, M., E. R. Eshelman, and M. McKay. *The Relaxation and Stress Reduction Workbook.* New York: MJF Books, 1995.

Einstein, E. *The Stepfamily: Living, Loving, and Learning.* New York: Macmillan, 1994.

Ellis, A. *How to Stubbornly Refuse to Make Yourself Miserable about Anything—Yes, Anything.* New York: Carol Publishing Group, 1990.

Ellis, A. *How to Control Anxiety Before It Controls You.* Secaucus, N.J.: Birch Lane Press, 1998.

———. *How to Keep People from Pushing Your Buttons.* Secaucus, N.J.: Birch Lane Press, 1998.

Ellis, A., and R. Tafrate. *How to Control Your Anger Before It Controls You.* New York: Carol Publishing Group, 1998.

Fisher, B. *Rebuilding: When Your Relationship Ends,* 2nd ed. San Luis Obispo, Calif.: Impact, 1992.

Kurcinka, M. S. *Kids, Parents, and Power Struggles.* New York: Harper Collins, 2000.

Leonard, R., and S. Elias. *Family and Divorce Law,* 4th ed. Berkeley, Calif.: Nolo Press, 1998.

Lewinsohn, P. M., et al. *Control Your Depression,* rev. ed. New York: Simon and Schuster, 1992.

Lofas, J. *Family Rules: Helping Stepfamilies and Single Parents Build Happy Homes.* New York: Kensington, 1998.

———. *Stepparenting: Everything You Need to Know to Make It Work.* New York: Kensington, 1985.

Lott, L., and R. Intner. *The Family That Works Together: Turning Family Chores from Drudgery to Fun.* Rocklin, Calif.: Prima, 1994.

Lyster, M. *Child Custody: Building Agreements That Work.* Berkeley, Calif.: Nolo Press, 1995.

Mattis, M. *Sex and the Single Parent.* New York: Henry Holt, 1986.

Neuman, M. G., with P. Romanowski. *Helping Your Kids Cope with Divorce the Sandcastles Way.* New York: Times Books, 1998.

Newman, G. *101 Ways to Be a Long-Distance Super Dad—Or Mom Too,* rev. ed. Mountain View, Calif.: Blossom Valley Press, 1999.

Ricci, I. *Mom's House, Dad's House.* New York: Simon and Schuster, 1997.

Scott, G. *Resolving Conflict with Others and within Yourself.* Oakland, Calif.: New Harbinger, 1990.

Ury, W. *Getting Past No: Negotiating Your Way from Confrontation to Cooperation,* rev. ed. New York: Bantam Books, 1993.

Visher, E., and J. Visher. *How to Win as a Stepfamily,* 2nd ed. Brunner/ Mazel, 1991.

Wanderer, Z., and T. Cabot. *Letting Go,* reissue. New York: Dell, 1987.

Watnik, W. *Child Custody Made Simple*. Claremont, Calif.: Single Parent Press, 1997.

Whitham, C. *Win the Whining War and Other Skirmishes: A Family Peace Plan*. Los Angeles: Perspective Publishing, 1991.

FOR CHILDREN

Banks, A. *When Your Parents Get a Divorce: A Kid's Journal*. New York: Puffin Books, 1990. (Ages 7–10)

Berman, C. *What Am I Doing in a Stepfamily?* Secaucus, N.J.: Lyle Stuart, 1982. (Ages 6–10)

Boeckman, C. *Surviving Your Parents' Divorce*. New York: Franklin Watts, 1980. (Teens)

Brown, L. K., and M. Brown. *Dinosaurs Divorce*. Boston: The Atlantic Monthly Press, 1986. (Ages 4–8)

Craven, L. *Stepfamilies: New Patterns of Harmony*. New York: Simon and Schuster, 1982. (Ages 11 and up)

Dolmetsch, P., and A. Shih, eds. *The Kids' Book about Single-Parent Families*. Garden City, N.Y.: Doubleday, 1985. (Ages 11–15)

Fassler, D., M. Lash, and S. B. Ives. *Changing Families: A Guide for Kids and Grown-Ups*. Burlington, Vt.: Waterfront Books, 1988. (Ages early elementary)

Getzoff, A., and C. McClenahan. *Stepkids: A Survival Guide for Teenagers in Stepfamilies*. New York: Walker, 1984.

Girard, L. *At Daddy's on Saturdays*. Morton Grove, Ill.: Albert Whitman, 1987. (Ages 4–8)

Johnston, J., et al. *Through the Children's Eyes: Healing Stories for Children of Divorce*. New York: Free Press, 1997.

Lansky, V. *It's Not Your Fault, Koko Bear*. Minnetonka, Minn.: Book Peddlers, 1998. (Ages 3–8)

Mayle, P. *Why Are We Getting a Divorce?* New York: Harmony Books, 1988. (Ages 4–8)

McGuire, P. *Putting It Together: Teenagers Talk about Family Breakups*. New York: Delacorte, 1987.

Nickman, S. L., *When Mom and Dad Divorce*. New York: Julian Messner, 1986. (Teens)

Rofes, E. E., ed. *The Kids' Book of Divorce: By, for, and about Kids*. Lexington, Mass.: Lexington Books, 1981. (Older children and teens)

Rogers, Fred. *Let's Talk about It: Divorce*. New York: Penguin Putnam Books for Young Readers, 1996. (Ages 3–6)

Stern, E. *Divorce Is Not the End of the World*. Berkeley, Calif.: Tricycle Press, 1997. (Ages 10 and up)

Thomas, S., and D. Rankin, *Divorced but Still My Parents*. Springboard Publications, 1998. (Ages 6–12)

Watson, J. W., R. E. Switzer, and J. C. Hirschberg. *Sometimes a Family Has to Split Up*. New York: Crown, 1988. (Ages 4–6)

Notes

Chapter 1

1. L. Halem, *Separated and Divorced Women* (Westport, Conn.: Greenwood Press, 1982), 166.
2. R. S. Weiss, *Marital Separation* (New York: Basic Books, 1975), 238.
3. S. Matthew, *Intimate Strangers* (Edinburgh: Mainstream, 1984), 32–33.

Chapter 2

1. R. Werland, "A Kinder, Gentler Divorce," *Chicago Tribune,* September 26, 1999.

Chapter 6

1. J. Krementz, *How It Feels When Parents Divorce.* (New York: Alfred A. Knopf, 1984), 25.
2. L. B. Francke, *Growing Up Divorced* (New York: Linden Press/Simon & Schuster, 1983), 16.
3. T. Arendell, *Mothers and Divorce: Legal, Economic, and Social Dilemmas* (Berkeley: University of California Press, 1986), 84.
4. D. Fassel, *Growing Up Divorced: A Road to Healing for Adult Children of Divorce* (New York: Pocket Books, 1991), 92–93.
5. J. H. Neal, "Children's Understanding of Their Parents' Divorces," in *Children and Divorce,* ed. L. Kurdek (San Francisco: Jossey-Bass, 1983), 7–8.

Chapter 8

1. Thanks to Drs. Janet Johnston and Vivienne Roseby, Center for the Family in Transition, Corte Madera, California.
2. Thanks to Julie Ross, keynote speaker at Family Court Services Southern Regional Training, Palm Springs, California, September 1997.

Chapter 9

1. Francke, *Growing Up Divorced*, 16.
2. R. Rosen (1977). "Children of Divorce: What They Feel about Access and Other Aspects of the Divorce Experience," *Journal of Clinical and Child Psychology* 6 (1977): 26.

Chapter 10

1. M. Hunt, *The Affair* (Cleveland: World Publications, 1969), 233–234.
2. K. Hallett, *A Guide for Single Parents* (Millbrae, Calif.: Celestial Arts, 1974), 8.
3. Judicial Counsel of California/Family Court Services Statewide Educational Institute, Newport Beach, Calif., March 25–27, 1999.
4. Halem, *Separated and Divorced Women*, 160.

Chapter 11

1. D. R. Kingma, *Coming Apart: Why Relationships End and How to Live through the Ending of Yours* (Berkeley, Calif.: Conari Press, 1987), 85.

Chapter 15

1. D. Dolmetsch, and A. Shih, *The Kids' Book about Single-Parent Families* (Garden City, N.Y.: Doubleday, 1985), 108–109.
2. J. Wallerstein, and S. Blakeslee, *Second Chances* (New York: Ticknor and Fields, 1989), 242.

Selected Sources

Ahrons, C. R. *The Good Divorce*. New York: Harper Collins, 1994.

Amato, P. R. More Than Money? Men's Contributions to Their Children's Lives. In *Men in Families: When Do They Get Involved? What Difference Does it Make?* ed. A. Booth and A. C. Crouter. Mahwah, N.J.: Lawrence Erlbaum Associates, 1998.

———. "Life-Span Adjustment of Children to Their Parent's Divorce." *The Future of Children 4* (1994):143–164.

Amato, P. R., and J. Gilbreth. "Nonresident Fathers and Children's Well-being: A Meta Analysis." *Journal of Marriage and the Family 61* (1999): 557–573.

Amato, P. R., and B. Keith, "Parental Divorce and the Well Being of Children: A Meta Analysis." *Psychological Bulletin 110* (1991): 26–46.

Baris, M. A., and C. B. Garrity. *Children of Divorce: A Developmental Approach to Residence and Visitation*. DeKalb, Ill.: Psytec, 1988.

Baris, M. and C. Garrity. Co-parenting Post-divorce: Helping Parents Negotiate and Maintain Low Conflict Separations. In *Clinical Handbook of Marriage and Couples Intervention*, ed. W. K. Halford and H. J. Markman 619–649. New York: Wiley, 1997.

Baydar, N. "Effects of Parental Separation and Reentry into Union on the Emotional Well-being of Children." *Journal of Marriage and the Family 50* (1988): 967–981.

Beck, A., et al. *Cognitive Therapy of Depression*. New York: Guilford Press, 1979.

Bianchi, S. M., et al. The Gender Gap in the Economic Well-being of Nonresident Fathers and Custodial Mothers. *Demography 36* (1999): 195–203.

Bricklin, B. *The Custody Evaluation Handbook: Research-Based Solutions and Applications.* New York: Brunner/Mazel, 1995.

Burns, D. D. *Feeling Good: The New Mood Therapy.* rev. ed. New York: Avon Books, 1999.

———. *The Feeling Good Workbook: Using the New Mood Therapy in Everyday Life,* rev. ed. New York: Penguin-Putnam, 1999.

Charlesworth, E. A., and R. G. Nathan. *Stress Management: A Comprehensive Guide to Wellness.* New York: Atheneum, 1984.

Clarke-Stewart, K. A., and C. Hayward. "Advantages of Father Custody and Contact for the Psychological Well Being of School-Age Children." *Journal of Applied Developmental Psychology 17* (1996): 239–270.

Cummings, E. M., and P. Davies. *Children and Marital Conflict.* New York: Guilford Press, 1994.

Depner, C. E. Revolution and Reassessment: Child Custody in Context. In *Redefining Families: Implications for Children's Development,* ed. A. E. Gottfried and Allen Gottfried 99–129. New York: Plenum Press, 1994.

Ellis, A. *How to Stubbornly Refuse to Make Yourself Miserable about Anything—Yes Anything.* New York: Carrol Publishing Group, 1990.

Emery, R. E. *Marriage, Divorce, and Children's Adjustment.* Thousand Oaks, Calif.: Sage, 1999.

———. *Renegotiating Family Relationships: Divorce, Child Custody, and Mediation.* New York: Guilford Press, 1994.

Emery, R. E., and R. Forehand. Parental Divorce and Children's Well-being: A Focus on Resilience. In *Stress, Risk, and Resilience in Children and Adolescents,* ed. R. J. Haggerty et al. New York: Cambridge University Press, 1994.

Fisher, B. *Rebuilding: When Your Relationship Ends,* 2nd ed. San Luis Obispo, Calif.: Impact, 1992.

Fisher, R. and W. Ury. *Getting to Yes,* 2nd ed. New York: Penguin, 1991.

Folberg, J., ed. *Joint Custody and Shared Parenting,* 2nd ed. New York: Guilford Press, 1991.

Furstenberg, F. F., Jr., and A. J. Cherlin. *Divided Families.* Cambridge, Mass.: Harvard University Press, 1991.

Garrity, C. B., and M. A. Baris. *Caught in the Middle: Protecting the Children of High-Conflict Divorce.* New York: Lexington Books, 1994.

Glenwick, D. S., and J. D. Mowrey. "When Parent Becomes Peer: Loss of Intergenerational Boundaries in Single Parent Families." *Family Relations 35* (1986): 57–63.

Goldner, V. Remarriage Family: Structure, System, Future. In *Re-Marriage Families,* ed. J. C. Hansen and L. Messinger. Rockville, Md.: Aspen System, 1982.

Grief, G. L. "Single Fathers with Custody Following Separation and Divorce." *Marriage and Family Review 20* (1995):213–231.

Heavey, C., J. Shenk, and A. Christensen. Marital Conflict and Divorce: A Developmental Family Psychology Perspective. In *Handbook of Developmental Family Psychology and Psychopathology,* ed. L. L'Abate. New York: Wiley, 1994.

Hetherington, E. M. "An Overview of the Virginia Longitudinal Study of Divorce and Remarriage with a Focus on Early Adolescence." *Journal of Family Psychology 7* (1993): 39–56.

Hetherington, E. M., M. Bridges, and G. M. Insabella. "What Matters? What Does Not? Five Perspectives on the Association Between Marital Transitions and Children's Adjustment." *American Psychologist 53* (1988): 167–184.

Hetherington, E. M. and J. Arasteh, eds. *Impact of Divorce, Single Parenting, and Stepparenting on Children.* Hillsdale, N.J.: Lawrence Erlbaum Associates, 1988.

Hetherington, E. M., and M. Stanley-Hagan. "The Adjustment of Children with Divorced Parents: A Risk and Resiliency Perspective." *Journal of Child Psychology and Psychiatry and Allied Disciplines 40* (1999): 129–140.

Hodges, W. R. *Interventions for Children of Divorce.* New York: Wiley, 1991.

Hunt, M., and B. Hunt. *The Divorce Experience.* New York: McGraw-Hill, 1977.

Jenkins, J. Sibling Relationships in Disharmonious Homes: Potential Difficulties and Protective Effects. In *Children's Sibling Relationships: Developmental and Clinical Issues,* ed. F. Boer and J. Dunn 125–138. Hillsdale, N.J.: Lawrence Erlbaum Associates, 1992.

Johnson, S. *First Person Singular: Living the Good Life Alone.* Philadelphia: Lippincott, 1977.

Johnston, J. R. "Research Update: Children's Adjustment in Sole Custody Compared to Joint Custody Families and Principles for Custody Decision Making." *Family and Conciliation Courts Review 33* (1995): 415–425.

———. *High Conflict and Violent Divorcing Parents in Family Court: Findings on Children's Adjustment and Proposed Guidelines for the Resolution of Custody and Visitation Disputes.* Final report to the statewide office of Family Court Services. San Francisco: Judicial Council of California, 1992.

Johnston, J. R., and L. G. Campbell. *Impasses of Divorce*. New York: Free Press, 1988.

Johnston, J. R., M. Kline, and J. M. Tschann. "Ongoing Postdivorce Conflict: Effects on Children of Joint Custody and Frequent Access." *American Journal of Orthopsychiatry 59* (1989): 576–592.

Johnston, J. R., and V. Roseby. *In the Name of the Child: A Developmental Approach to Understanding and Helping Children of Conflicted and Violent Divorce*. New York: Free Press, 1997.

Kalter, N. "Long-Term Effects of Divorce on Children." *American Journal of Orthopsychiatry 57* (1987): 587–600.

Kaslow, F. W., and L. L. Schwartz. *The Dynamics of Divorce: A Life Cycle Perspective*. New York: Brunner/Mazel, 1987.

Kelly, J. B. "The Best Interests of the Child: A Concept in Search of Meaning." *Family and Conciliation Courts Review 35* (1997): 377–387.

———. "A Decade of Divorce Mediation Research: Some Answers and Questions." *Family and Conciliation Courts Review 34* (1996): 373–385.

Kelly, J. B., and M. E. Lamb. "Using Child Development Research to Make Appropriate Custody and Access Decisions for Young Children." *Family and Conciliation Courts Review 38* (2000): 297–311.

Kitson, G. C., and L. A. Morgan. "The Multiple Consequences of Divorce: A Decade Review." *Journal of Marriage and the Family 52* (1990): 913–924.

Kressel, K. *The Process of Divorce*. New York: Basic Books, 1985.

Lamb, M. E., K. Sternberg, and R. A. Thompson. "The Effects of Divorce and Custody Arrangements on Children's Behavior, Development, and Adjustment." *Family and Conciliation Courts Review 35* (1997): 393–404.

Lampel, A. K. "Children's Alignment with Parents in Highly Conflicted Custody Cases." *Family and Conciliation Courts Review 34* (1996): 229–239.

Leonard, R., and S. Elias. *Family and Divorce Law*, 4th ed. Berkeley, Calif.: Nolo Press, 1998.

Lewinshon, P. M., et al. *Control Your Depression*, rev. New York: Simon and Schuster, 1992.

Maccoby, E. E., et al. "Postdivorce Roles of Mothers and Fathers in the Lives of Their Children." *Journal of Family Psychology 7* (1993): 24–38.

Maccoby, E. E., and R. H. Mnookin. *Dividing the Child: Social and Legal Dilemmas of Custody.* Cambridge, Mass.: Harvard University Press, 1992.

Mason, M. A., and A. Quirk. "Are Mothers Losing Custody? Read My Lips: Trends in Judicial Decision-Making in Custody Disputes—1920, 1960, 1990, and 1995." *Family Law Quarterly 31* (1997): 215–236.

Mattis, M. *Sex and the Single Parent.* New York: Henry Holt, 1986.

Mills, D. "A Model for Stepfamily Development." *Family Relations 33* (1984):365–372.

Morrison, D. R., and M. J. Coiro. Parental Conflict and Marital Disruption: Do Children Benefit When High-Conflict Marriages Are Dissolved? *Journal of Marriage and the Family 61* (1999): 626–637.

Mowatt, M. H. *Divorce Counseling: A Practical Guide.* Lexington, Mass.: Lexington Books, 1987.

Neely, R. *The Divorce Decision: The Legal and Human Consequences of Ending a Marriage.* New York: McGraw-Hill, 1984.

Nielsen, L. "Stepmothers: Why So Much Stress? A Review of the Research." *Journal of Divorce and Remarriage 30* (1999): 115–148.

Papernow, P. L. Stepparent Role Development: From Outsider to Intimate. In *Relative Strangers: Studies of Stepfamily Processes,* ed. W. R. Beer. Totowa, N.J.: Rowman and Littlefield, 1998.

Parke, R. D. *Fatherhood.* Cambridge, Mass.: Harvard University Press, 1996.

Parke, R. D., and P. N. Sterns. Fathers and Child Rearing. In *Children in Time and Place: Developmental and Historical Insights,* ed. G. H. Elder Jr. et al., 147–170. New York: Cambridge University Press, 1993.

Propst, L. R., et al. "Predictors of Coping in Divorced Single Mothers." *Journal of Divorce 9* (1986): 33–53.

Ricci, I. *Mom's House, Dad's House,* 2nd ed. New York: Simon and Schuster, 1997.

Ross, J. L. "Conversational Pitchbacks: Helping Couples Bat 1000 in the Game of Communications." *Journal of Family Psychotherapy 6* (1995): 83–86.

Saposnek, D. T. *Mediating Child Custody Disputes: A Strategic Approach,* rev. ed. San Francisco: Jossey-Bass, 1998.

Schwartz, L., and F. Kaslow. *Painful Partings: Divorce and Its Aftermath.* New York: Wiley, 1997.

Simons, R. L. *Understanding Differences Between Divorced and Intact Families: Stress, Interaction, and Child Outcome.* Thousand Oaks, Calif.: Sage, 1996.

Sorensen, E. D., and J. Goldman, "Custody Determinations and Child Development: A Review of Current Literature." *Journal of Divorce 13* (1990): 53–67.

Stewart, A., et al. *Separating Together: How Divorce Transforms Families.* New York: Guilford Press, 1997.

Tavris, C. *Anger: The Misunderstood Emotion,* rev. ed. New York: Touchstone Books, 1989.

Tompkins, R. Parenting Plans. A Concept Whose Time Has Come. *Family and Conciliation Courts Review 33* (1995): 286–297.

Visher, E. B., and J. S. Visher, *Old Loyalties and New Ties: Therapeutic Strategies with Stepfamilies.* New York: Brunner/Mazel, 1988.

———. "Stepparents: The Forgotten Family Members." *Family and Conciliation Courts Review 36* (1998): 444–451.

Walczak, Y. *Divorce: The Child's Point of View.* London: Harper and Row, 1984.

Wallerstein, J. S. Children of Divorce: A Society in Search of Policy. In *All Our Families: New Policies For a New Century,* ed. M. A. Mason, A. Skolnick, and S. Sugerman, 66–94. New York: Oxford University Press, 1998.

———. "The Long-Term Effects of Divorce on Children: A Review." *Journal of the Academy of Child and Adolescent Psychiatry 30* (1991): 349–360.

Wallerstein, J., and S. Blakeslee, *Second Chances: Men, Women and Children a Decade after Divorce.* New York: Ticknor and Fields, 1989.

Wallerstein, J., and J. Kelly. *Surviving the Breakup.* New York: Basic Books, 1980.

Wallerstein, J., and J. Lewis. "The Long-Term Impact of Divorce on Children. A First Report from a 25-year Study." *Family and Conciliation Courts Review 36* (1998): 368–383.

Wanderer, Z., and T. Cabot. *Letting Go.* New York: Dell, 1987.

Watnik, W. *Child Custody Made Simple.* Claremont, Calif.: Single Parent Press, 1997.

Weiss, R. S., *Marital Separation.* New York: Basic Books, 1975.

Wertlieb, D. Children Whose Parents Divorce: Life Trajectories and Turning Points. In *Stress and Adversity over the Life Course: Trajectories and Turning Points,* ed. I. H. Gotlib et al., 179–196. New York: Cambridge University Press, 1997.

Whiteside, M. F. "Custody for Children Age 5 and Younger." *Family and Conciliation Courts Review 36* (1998): 479–502.

———. "The Parental Alliance Following Divorce: An Overview." *Journal of Marital and Family Therapy 24* (1998): 3–24.

Index